Spring

GOD MUST NOT DIE! (OR MUST HE?): JUNG AND CHRISTIANITY

A JOURNAL OF ARCHETYPE AND CULTURE

Fall 2010

SPRING JOURNAL
New Orleans, Louisiana

CONTENTS

JUNG AND CHRISTIANITY:
A CRITIQUE BY GIEGERICH WITH RESPONSES

Guest Editor's Introduction
Greg Mogenson 1

God Must Not Die! C.G. Jung's Thesis of the One-Sidedness
of Christianity
Wolfgang Giegerich 11

"...until God's absence helps!"
David Miller 73

The Vicissitudes of Spirit in Jung's Psychology: A Response to
Giegerich's "God Must Not Die!"
Michael Whan 91

God, Man and Evil in Jung's Thought: Complementary Remarks
to Wolfgang Giegerich's Critique
Marco Heleno Barreto 107

Etwas geschah: Orphaned Event and its Adoptions
John Peck 143

The Ambiguity of Evil and the God of the Depths: A Response to
Giegerich's "God Must Not Die!"
John Haule 163

No As If, No Between: The Giegerich Inversion of Mind and Soul
Glen Slater 181

Jungian Analysis Post Mortem Dei
Greg Mogenson 207

ROMANYSHYN & GIEGERICH: POLES APART

REJOINDERS TO GIEGERICH'S CRITIQUE OF ROMANYSHYN'S "THE MELTING OF THE POLAR ICE"

Who is Wolfgang Giegerich?
Robert Romanyshyn 273

Robert Romanyshyn and Wolfgang Giegerich: Poles Apart
Susan Rowland 311

**Response to Wolfgang Giegerich's "The Psychologist as
Repentance Preacher and Revivalist: Robert Romanyshyn on the
Melting of the Polar Ice"**
Joel Weishaus 323

**Response to Wolfgang Giegerich's "The Psychologist as
Repentance Preacher and Revivalist: Robert Romanyshyn on the
Melting of the Polar Ice"**
David H. Rosen 325

INTERVIEW

**Neurobiology in the Consulting Room: An Interview with
Margaret Wilkinson**
Daniela Sieff 327

BOOK REVIEWS

Synchronicity: Nature and Psyche in an Interconnected Universe
by Joseph Cambray
F. David Peat 349

Analytical Psychology and German Classical Aesthetics: Goethe, Schiller, and Jung, Vol. 1, *The Development of the Personality* and Vol. 2, *The Constellation of the Self* by Paul Bishop
David Tacey 353

The Sungod's Journey through the Netherworld: Reading the Ancient Egyptian Amduat by Andreas Schweizer
Murray Stein 373

Possession: Jung's Comparative Anatomy of the Psyche by Craig E. Stephenson
Jean Kirsch 385

Perpetual Adolescence: Jungian Analyses of American Media, Literature, and Pop Culture, Sally Porterfield, Keith Polette, and Tita French Baumlin, editors
Blake Burleson 397

Tim Burton: The Monster and the Crowd: A Post-Jungian Perspective by Helena Bassil-Morozow
Terrie Waddell 401

SOURCES AND ABBREVIATIONS

The following abbreviations have been used for frequently cited sources:

CW: Carl G. Jung, *Collected Works*. 20 vols. Ed. Herbert Read, Michael Fordham,Gerhard Adler, and William McGuire. Trans. R. F. C. Hull (Princeton: Princeton University Press, 1957-1979). Cited by volume and, unless otherwise noted, by paragraph number.

GW: Carl G. Jung, *Gesammelte Werke* (Zürich and Stuttgart: Rascher, now Olten and Freiburg i:Br: Walter-Verlag, 1958 ff). Cited by volume and, unless otherwise noted, by paragraph number.

Letters: Carl G. Jung, *Letters*. 2vols. Ed. Gerhard Adler (Bollingen Series XCV: 2. Princeton: Princeton University Press, 1975). Cited by volume and page number.

MDR: C. G. Jung, *Memories, Dreams, Reflections*, Rev. ed. Ed. Aniela Jaffé. Trans. Richard and Clara Winston (New York: Vintage Books, 1965). Cited by page number.

RB: C. G. Jung, *The Red Book: Liber Novus*, S. Shamdasani, ed. (New York & London, W. W. Norton & Company, 2009). Cited by page number.

CEP: *The Collected English Papers of Wolfgang Giegerich*. 4 volumes (1-*The Neurosis of Psychology*, 2-*Technology and the Soul*, 3-*Soul-Violence*, 4-*The Soul Always Thinks*) (New Orleans: Spring Publications, 2005-2010).

GUEST EDITOR'S INTRODUCTION

GREG MOGENSON

It is Jung's (some might say, dubious) distinction to have developed a psychology "with God" at a time that he himself described as "a time of God's death and disappearance."[1] In this issue of our journal an essay by Wolfgang Giegerich that critically examines this important aspect of Jung's psychology project is examined in its turn by seven invited respondents. Conceived in the spirit of an immanent critique (all of our authors are long-time contributors to Jungian psychology), both Jung's treatment of Christianity and Giegerich's incisive questioning of this are discussed in a manner that dovetails with that recent trend within the broader discourses of philosophy and critical theory which goes by the name of the "theological turn." I refer here to the shift from the linguistic focus of postmodernism in general and deconstruction in particular to a focus upon that subject whose development by means of a succession of God-images, and culminating in the death of God experience of the 19th and 20th centuries, has been constitutive of modern consciousness. This is not to imply that Jung's understanding of the psychology that has come to bear his name was in step with this development. On the contrary, compared to this line of thought his "theological turn," if we may call it that, was a decidedly conservative one. Railing against what he regarded as the deleterious effect of the rationalistic spirit of his times upon the larger sense of man's soul that had traditionally been mediated by myth and religion, Jung championed the irrational psyche, that age-old storehouse of

animating images, as the enduring source of spiritual renewal for our
benighted modern age. "We should never identify ourselves with
reason," he warned (with the creeping scourge of intellectualism,
atheism, secularism, and political totalitarianism in mind), "for man
is not and never will be a creation of reason alone ...." Reiterating
this point, he then reached out beyond the horizon lines which he
believed reason to have too narrowly drawn: "The irrational," he
declared, "cannot be and must not be extirpated. The gods cannot and
must not die."[2]

The last line of this quote is very close to the wording of the title
that Giegerich has given to his essay in this volume, "God Must Not
Die!," while the earlier one in which we are cautioned against
identifying ourselves with reason alone is taken up in its subtitle, "C.G.
Jung's Thesis of the One-Sidedness of Christianity." It was Jung's
contention that the critical rationalism which had developed within
Christianity had gotten so carried away with itself that Western man
had landed himself in the predicament that his consciousness was
cut off from its life-source in the unconscious. Hoping to remedy
this situation, Jung trained his analyst's gaze upon Christianity.
Effete though it had become, it was Jung's position that a resurgent
version of its life-giving powers was immediately present in the
symptomatic suffering of neurotic patients even as what psychoanalysis
had conceptualized as "the libido" could be interpreted from above
(or more deeply from below) as the vitalizing reappearance of what
had formerly been symbolized as the wine of Dionysus and the
blood of Christ.

This, at any rate, was the vision of analysis that he proposed in an
early letter:

> ... we must give [psychoanalysis] time to infiltrate into people
> from many centers, to revivify among intellectuals a feeling for
> symbol and myth, ever so gently to transform Christ back into
> the soothsaying god of the vine, which he was, and in this way
> absorb those ecstatic instinctual forces of Christianity for the one
> purpose of making the cult and the myth what they once were—
> a drunken feast of joy where man regained the ethos and holiness
> of an animal. That was the beauty and purpose of classical religion,
> which from God knows what temporary biological needs has
> turned into a Misery Institute. Yet what infinite rapture and

wantonness lies dormant in our religion, waiting to be led back
to their true destination! A genuine and proper ... development
... must ... bring to fruition ... the agony and ecstasy over the
dying and resurgent god, the mythic power of the wine, the
awesome anthropophagy of the Last Supper—only this
...development can serve the vital forces of religion. (Jung to
Freud, Feb. 11, 1910)[3]

Steeped in mythology, Jung's conception of psychoanalysis was
modelled upon the pattern of its dying and resurgent gods. Just as the
resurrected Christ had appeared to the disciples after his death "... that
they might have life and have it more abundantly" (John 10: 10), so
analysis, in Jung's view, had reversed Nietzsche's verdict concerning the
death of God through the life-giving god-images from the unconscious
which it offered as its sacrament.

But did Jung get this right? Was the death of God in the modern
sense that Nietzsche had announced really nothing more than the latest
version of this age-old archetypal pattern? Or did it rather reflect an
altogether more decisive change in the life of consciousness: the passing
away or going under of the mythic mode of apperception *per se*, of the
religious mode of having a God as such—and this, moreover, not as
some pathological incursion of dissociated reason upon the soul, but
as the soul's own doing, its critical turning upon itself in a syzygial,
anima-negating/animus-sublating moment of itself?

In numerous papers written during the last few decades, and again
now in his essay for this volume, Giegerich's reading of what he calls
"the soul's logical life" has taken this tack. Basing himself upon Jung's
account of the death of symbols, Giegerich has reached the
conclusion—so very different from Jung's—that the death of God, or
as this has also been figured, the end of meaning, has had to do with
the integration of this great symbol into the *form* of consciousness itself
such that man comes fully and self-responsibly into his own *as* man.

The back-story here has to do with Jung's important insight
that the life of a symbol resides in its being an "expression for
something that cannot be characterized in any other or better way."
Likening this to a state of pregnancy, the great psychologist had
spoken in the same breath of its parturition and demise: "The symbol
is alive only so long as it is pregnant with meaning. But once its
meaning has been born out of it, once that expression is found which

formulates the thing sought, expected, or divined even better than the hitherto accepted symbol, then the symbol is *dead*, i.e., it possesses only an historical significance."[4]

Apropos of this development, Giegerich has read "the death of God" as the death of that greatest of all symbols. As for the "better formulation" or "better expression" that has been born from this symbol's death, this for Giegerich corresponds to psychology, which is also to say, to that determination of consciousness that is associated with and constitutive of psychology.

It is a matter of demythologization. Having arisen from the shift from *mythos* to *logos*, psychological consciousness no longer relates to itself in personified form as had formerly been the case with myth and religion. For the God(s) that consciousness, as religious consciousness, had had in front of itself or above itself as its contents have gone under into the universality of its self-acknowledging, self-relating form such that it now exists negatively, as Giegerich has put it, not as consciousness of some numinous being or thing, but as consciousness of consciousness, mindedness *per se*.

Now Jung, it is true, in keeping with his insight concerning the death of symbols, also regarded psychology to have arisen from a process of demythologization.[5] However, gravely concerned about the effect upon the soul of its having been turned out of its spiritual home in religion, he assigned psychology the task of continuing its religious life via the analysis of the unconscious. Though God had outwardly died (this seems to have been his view), he could still be accessed as the God-image within.

But is it really the psychologist's job to shore a symbol up against its ruin? In Giegerich's view, Jung's attempt to do just this with respect to God shows him to have not been willing to follow the soul's own process, at least not when in came to that rupture-point at which consciousness or the soul had turned against its having to have the form of God. This, of course, is a familiar resistance. In his poem, "The World is Too Much with Us," Wordsworth wistfully complains of the alienation that modernity has brought and then, in a line that anticipates Jung's effort to carry on what he called "the symbolic life," declares that he'd "rather be a pagan suckled in a creed outworn"[6] than give way to a modernity with which he feels so out of tune. But the modern world *is* with us! There is no denying that, or at least no credible one. Having emancipated itself from religion, "the spirit that bloweth where it listeth" (John 3:8) has now transformed itself into money, medial-technology, and cyberspace. Rather than deploring these uncanny phenomena of our modern situation (or seeking refuge from them, as Jung was wont to do, in the 16th century atmosphere of his Bollingen tower[7]), the challenge for the psychologist is simply to discern what they say about consciousness or show about the soul.

In numerous books and articles, Giegerich has taken up this challenge. Mindful of Jung's dictum that the doctor must be as much in the analysis as the patient, he has again and again brought analytical psychology before the bar of the phenomena that have concerned it in order to see whether its own constitution as psychology is truly up to or in accord with the interpretations it metes out. Now in his essay for this volume, it is not the aforementioned realities of our modern world—money, medial-technology, and cyberspace—that are subjected to this treatment,[8] but the interpretation of Christianity that Jung put forward in an effort to stave these off. Critical of Jung's efforts to therapeutically revivifying Christianity, Giegerich points out that the negation of God is inherent in Christianity itself. Long before Nietzsche had announced the death of God, the Christian soul had already (though, of course, only implicitly) emancipated itself from having to have a God through that central, form-changing mystery wherein its incarnate God empties himself of his divinity and dies on the cross as a man—or so Giegerich contends in the course of showing up what he regards as the errant positivity that Jungian psychology and popular Christianity both share.

These, of course, are contentious claims. In a veritable cascade of powerfully argued papers, and again now in his essay for this volume, Giegerich's Jungian critique of Jung has led him to a very different reading of what Christianity and psychology are about than the one that Jung promoted. The question arises: does this show, as some of his critics contend, that Giegerich is a contrarian who has gone off on a hobby-horse of his own? Or is it rather the case, as others maintain, that even where Jung's views are contradicted, Giegerich's contribution is to be seriously taken into account as a radical and contemporizing "return to Jung" inasmuch as its insights are the result of a deep fealty with and thoroughgoing application of essential impulses and interpretive gestures that are at the heart of Jung's own psychological vision?

To help us with this question responses from upwards of a dozen Jungian writers, many of whom have had a special interest in the topic of Jung and Christianity, were invited to contribute to this volume. Of course, not everyone that was asked to participate agreed to do so. This, as I was told, had mostly to do with being busy with other projects, the upcoming IAAP conference in Montreal being the most commonly mentioned reason for having to pass on the opportunity. In some cases, however, a particular colleague's decision not to participate seemed to have the quality of a response. There were a few, for example, who after reading Giegerich's essay expressed antipathy for the project. Giegerich, I was told in a somewhat reproving manner, is "a mere intellectual who has no understanding of the soul." Others expressed sentiments that were the reverse of this. Having not yet come fully to grips with the daunting challenge which Giegerich's writings pose, one of these said that he did not feel up to the task. Another who admitted to "a testy admiration" of Giegerich said she did not feel she should "punch above [her] weight-class"! So in the end, though I had solicited responses from far and wide, it was mostly long-time contributors to *Spring Journal* that accepted my invitation.

The first of these was David Miller. Giegerich had sent his paper to David and me just after it was written. While both of us were struck by its importance, it was David who brought it to Nancy Cater's attention, and she in turn who came up with the idea of building an issue of the journal around it. Writing from his background in religious studies, Miller's response contextualizes Giegerich's psychological perspective theologically by showing how it fits with and carries on from various ideas and movements from within early, medieval, modern, and postmodern theology.

Other complementary responses follow Miller's. Drawing upon Giegerich's discussion of the Christian God's emptying himself of his divinity even as he dies on the cross as a man, Michael Whan ventures a new interpretation of Jung's vision of the green gold Christ as signifying the Holy Spirit's self-iconoclastic release from the imaginal mode of thought to which Jung, regressing behind the *telos* of his own vision, clung. And in an essay that demonstrates an especially keen grasp of Jung's concern for man's spiritual predicament, Giegerich's psychological approach, and of the Christian ideas referred to by both, Marco Heleno Barreto acquaints us with the metaphysical anthropologist and Romantic *Naturphilosoph* in Jung who, forgetful of what Giegerich has called "the psychological difference," time and again transgressed the limits of a rigorously psychological approach. And then there is the essay by John Peck. After reminding us of the event/happening/pure occurrence character of Jung's psychology, Peck examines Giegerich's critique of Jung's formulation of this by reading it in relation to aphorisms of Pascal's having to do with thought as that "double inclusion" wherein the impactful surround of events and happenings are interiorized into themselves.

Less sympathetic with respect to Giegerich's critique of Jung are the contributions of our next two authors, John Haule and Glen Slater. Taking exception to Giegerich's having focussed so exclusively upon Jung's *Answer to Job*, Haule reminds us of Jung's early interest in spiritualism, of his work on synchronicity, and of his emphasis upon immediate experience of the God-within, while Slater, for his part, antagonistically inveighs against Giegerich's entire approach to Jung and to psychology as a treacherous "mind-trap" that should be avoided at all costs!*

The final essay is an essay of my own, "Jungian Analysis *Post Mortem Dei.*" Drawing upon the understanding of Giegerich's approach that I have gained in the course of many years of reading his texts on an almost daily basis, I have attempted in my response to both contextualize his essay for this volume within a larger appreciation of what he is aiming for in psychology and to provide a bridge from the consulting room into what I consider to be his enormous contribution to analytical psychology through the reflections I offer with respect to occasions when the analyst is asked by a patient that same question which was famously put to Jung: "Do you believe in God?"

----

* Of related interest as critical rejoinders to Giegerich are the articles contained in the "Romanyshyn & Giegerich: Poles Apart" section of this volume. Robert Romanyshyn, Susan Rowland, Joel Weilhaus, and David Rosen have written rebuttals to an earlier essay of Giegerich's, "The Psychologist as Repentance Preacher and Revivalist: Robert Romanyshyn on the Melting of the Polar Ice," published in the fall 2009 issue of *Spring*.

But before we turn to Giegerich's essay and to the rejoinders of his respondents, I would like to share what might be characterized as a scholarly fantasy regarding the *place* of this collegial exchange. This has to do with the 1910 letter to Freud that I cited above in which Jung enthusiastically writes of the vitalizing effect that psychoanalysis can have upon Christianity. When asked by one of his pupils to comment on this text some fifty years later, Jung answered with some chagrin,

> Best thanks for the quotation from that accursed correspondence. For me it is an unfortunately inexpungable reminder of the incredible folly that filled the days of my youth. The journey from cloud-cuckoo-land back to reality lasted a long time. In my case Pilgrim's Progress consisted in my having to climb down a thousand ladders until I could reach out my hand to the little clod of earth that I am.[9]

This is an important passage. Though it would be easy to argue that the Jungian movement has actually fulfilled Jung's youthful hopes for a psychoanalysis that would "serve the vital forces of religion" (we have only to think of the popular offerings of Jungian lay-societies world-wide and of the company that Jungian psychology keeps with New Age spirituality), Jung here distances and divests himself from his earlier views. But as Giegerich has pointed out, Jung's kenotic claim to have come down from the clouds is belied by his manner of expressing it.

> … the very formulation that Jung uses shows that he has not really come down. Because if one is really down, one cannot reach out one's hand to the little clod of earth that one is, inasmuch as being down means having *comprehended* that one is, and has always been, *just* oneself. As long as I want to reach out my hand to myself, I as the one who reaches his hand out still believe myself to be something else from, and above, the "clod of earth" which I graciously befriend. The idea that I would have to come down and humble myself *is* already presumption, arrogance. The noble attitude of humility is the way in which the simple recognition that in truth I am and have always been down here is kept at bay. There *is* nothing and nobody to whom I could lower myself, because the clod of earth is myself.[10]

Further to the imagery of Jung's which Giegerich here applies to itself in the course of criticizing Jung's claim to have fully come down from the grandiose ideas of his youth, I am put in mind of another image of Jung's from one of his late dreams. Recounted in *Memories, Dreams, Reflections*, this dream is the one in which his father is depicted as a distinguished scholar who is also the guardian of a crypt in which the sarcophagi of some famous personages are entombed.[11] Upon announcing to Jung that he will now lead him "into the highest presence," the figure of Jung's father immediately kneels down with his forehead to the floor. Following suit, Jung attempts to bow down in like manner. But again, just as Giegerich pointed out in his critique of the coming down from the clouds and reaching out to the clod of earth passage, Jung could not fully complete this action. "For some reason," he writes, "I could not bring my forehead quite down to the floor—there was perhaps a millimeter to spare."[12]

A millimeter to spare! It is just here, in the equivocating gap between forehead and floor, cloud and clod, that my editor's vision locates this collegial exchange. Distributed between thinkers of the same or similar schools, this millimeter might be thought to correspond to what Freud called "the narcissism of small differences." But this would be a superficial view. Jung's imagery, after all, is not "horizontal" and "extensive" in the manner of Freud, but "vertical" and "intensive." And in keeping with this the differences which the various discussants disclose have more to do with the soul-internal, psychological difference that runs through the discipline they share. When consciousness is conscious of itself, a restless tension, born of its awareness of being discrepant with itself, builds up. As if driven by a millimeter which it can never entirely close, thought goes under into new determinations of itself via the negation of its own base. And so it is in the present volume. Heir to the gap between Jung's forehead and the floor, Giegerich and his respondents try again those ladders between cloud-cuckoo-land and the clod of earth, driving Jungian thought into new determinations of itself in the process.

NOTES

1. C. G. Jung, *CW* 11 § 149.
2. Jung, *CW* 7 § 111.
3. C. G. Jung, *Letters, Vol. 1:* 1906-1950, ed. G. Adler and A. Jaffé, tr. R. F. C. Hull (Princeton, N. J.: Princeton University Press, 1975), p. 18.

4. Jung, *CW* 6§ 816. Cited by W. Giegerich, "The End of Meaning and the Birth of Man: An Essay about the State Reached in the History of Consciousness and an Analysis of C. G. Jung's Psychology Project." *The Journal of Jungian Theory and Practice* 6.1 (2004), p. 11.

5. We have only to think of his well-known statement, "Only an unparalleled impoverishment of symbolism could enable us to rediscover the gods as psychic factors, that is, as archetypes of the unconscious"(*CW* 9, i § 50).

6. William Wordsworth, "This World is Too Much with Us," lines 9-10.

7. For Giegerich's discussion of this problem see his "The End of Meaning and the Birth of Man," pp. 47-48.

8. For Giegerich's analysis of these topics see his *Technology and the Soul, Collected English Papers*, Vol. 2 (New Orleans, Spring Journal Books, 2007).

9. Jung, *Letters* 1, p. 18. fn. 8.

10. Giegerich, "The End of Meaning and the Birth of Man," p. 31.

11. C. G. Jung, *Memories, Dreams, Reflections*, ed. A. Jaffé, tr. Richard & Clara Winston (New York: Random House, 1961), pp. 217-220.

12. Jung, *Memories, Dreams, Reflections*, p. 219.

GOD MUST NOT DIE!
C. G. JUNG'S THESIS OF THE ONE-SIDEDNESS OF CHRISTIANITY

WOLFGANG GIEGERICH

"As far as the Christian nations are concerned," Jung tells us, "their Christianity has fallen asleep and has neglected to develop its myth further in the course of the centuries. ... People do not even realize that a myth is dead if it no longer lives and is not developed further any more" (*MDR* pp. 331f., transl. modif.). The last statement is a gross generalization. Genuine *myths* and similar folk tales are precisely characterized by their impressive conservatism; even in historically progressive Europe, fairy tales that probably date back to the Stone Age were kept alive in the traditions of the uneducated population way into the 18th century without having undergone *essential* changes. The Christian "myth" is of course not really a myth in the strict sense. It is a religious story, something that originated long after the radical shift from *mythos* to *logos* and

___

Wolfgang Giegerich, Ph.D., is a Jungian analyst who after many years in private practice in Stuttgart and later in Wörthsee, near Munich, now lives in Berlin. He has lectured and taught in many countries. His approximately two hundred publications in several languages include numerous books, among them *The Soul's Logical Life: Towards a Rigorous Notion of Psychology* (Peter Lang, 1998; 4th ed. 2007), and the four volumes of his Collected English Papers: *The Neurosis of Psychology, Technology and the Soul, Soul-Violence,* and *The Soul Always Thinks* (all published by Spring Journal Books).

philosophical reflection and has much of highly developed Greek thought as one of its fundamental ingredients. And, conversely, as the example of Islam (another religion that arose *after* that fundamental shift) shows, a religion, too, can stay vitally alive even if its doctrine has not been further developed for centuries. But in the case of Christianity we need to include the idea of its further development in its definition, although not in the same sense as here implied by Jung. In a letter Jung wrote something that is closer to what I have in mind. "The thought of evolution is Christian and—as I think—in a way a better truth to express the dynamic aspect of the Deity, although the eternal immovability also forms an important aspect of the Deity... The religious spirit of the West is characterized by a change of God's image in the course of ages" (*Letters 2*, p. 315, to Kotschnig, 30 June 1956). "What is remarkable about Christianity is that in its system of dogma it anticipates a process of change in the Deity, that is, a historical transformation on the 'other side'" (*MDR* p. 327, transl. modif.). This idea is closer, but still too theological, rather than solely phenomenological (Jung expresses an opinion about the nature of the *Deity*, capitalized!).

The Inner Motive Force of the Christian Ideas

What I am driving at is only a phenomenological observation. I do not speak about the deity, but simply about the logical character of the historical phenomenon of Christianity. My thesis is that Christianity did not begin as a finished doctrine. Its central message had much more the character of a seed or intuition that needed to be unfolded over the course of time. What it was really about could not be fully grasped right at the beginning. It needed centuries for it to come home to itself. Everything was already there at the beginning (there is for me precisely no need, as there is for Jung, of a further development of the myth through the *addition* of new doctrinal contents), but it was there only implicitly, enveloped, and it needed to germinate, incubate, be "alchemically distilled," in order at long last to become explicit and explicated and thus fully conscious and fully real. Christianity needed and wanted to be interiorized into itself (whereas what Jung had in mind, when he spoke of its further development, was obviously its *extrapolation beyond* itself).

This inherent dynamic nature, which is the logical or syntactical character of Christianity, at one point even comes out in the semantic message of Christianity itself, namely when Jesus says, "But the Comforter, which is the Holy Ghost, whom the Father will send in my name, he shall teach you all things, and bring all things to your remembrance, whatsoever I have said unto you" (John 14:26). The full realization of what is meant by the original teachings was considered as only becoming possible at some time in the future and needing a new teacher, and not one in the three-dimensional world, but in the spirit (*pneuma*). The Christian message required a *spiritual* understanding ("... not of the letter, but of the spirit: for the letter killeth, but the spirit giveth life" 2 Cor. 3:6). That we have and can read or hear the biblical text with its stories and its dogmatic statements is one thing. But then the real question arises, "Understandest thou what thou readest?" (Acts 8:30). That the teacher will only come in the future points to the fact that the achievement of a full understanding is not a matter of a few years of study or even the study of a lifetime, but a historical task, a task for centuries, if not millennia. Christianity has thus the character of an impulse or a project.

And the coming of the spirit should itself be spiritually understood: not as a mysterious apparition or sudden spectacular event, a literal arrival of a new teacher from outside, but rather as the slow coming alive of the inner spirit of the message from within itself. From the outset the Christian truth had everything it needed within itself. The Holy Ghost who *literally* was announced by it as being sent only at a later date was, for a spiritual understanding, already there from the beginning, and stirred and agitated from within. The spirit contained in Christianity's "letter" worked on its own releasement. All Christian truth needed was in the course of time to be unfolded, to slowly come home to consciousness.

COMPLEXITY

The inherent need of the Christian message itself to be driven beyond its immediate literal meaning to its deeper and more subtle pneumatic meaning through an interiorization of the ideas into themselves makes the Christian material on which to base our interpretation complex. There are always several levels of understanding for the same thing. But in addition to the complexity due to the implicit-explicit difference, there is another one which is due to the fact that after the decline of the Roman Empire, Christianity, which was a product of the deep and long-evolved Jewish religious and the highly sophisticated Greek philosophical thinking, was in the West taken over by intellectually and psychologically still primitive nations who had had no written culture and came from a pagan nature-based religious tradition. Their reception of the Christian message was naturally quite naive at first, restricted to the easily accessible biblical *stories* and rather literal. It mostly had to rely on Gospel harmonies, because coping with four different gospel versions (let alone with the theology of St. Paul and the Church Fathers) was already overtaxing.

It also stands to reason that the new religious contents and ideas were received by a consciousness that was still pretty much thinking and apperceiving the new message in pagan and concretistic, naturalistic terms. Also, some of the pagan traditions and rituals were even absorbed by the Church and merely "rechristened." But over the centuries, the Western mind was then slowly trained to acquire a higher-level, more philosophically *theological* understanding of its own Christianity (Scholasticism). The result of this complicated history is that we get versions of the same Christian ideas that belong to very different historical layers of understanding and different degrees of differentiation, as well as Christian phenomena that *de facto* are part of the actual historical tradition of Christianity, but in spirit are not truly Christian at all. And even one major present form of Christianity, Roman Catholicism, is *syntactically* (as far as its logical form is concerned) still a pagan religion merely with Christian contents (a Christian semantics). Its pagan spirit shows, for example, in the fact that it has priests, a sacrificial ritual, holy places and sacred objects and an only dimly disguised polytheistic cultic practice (with Saints and the Mother of God in addition to the Trinity), and that in general it appeals to the senses (splendid gowns and cathedrals, impressive public ceremonies, incense and holy water)—all of which is incompatible with the specific inner logic of the Christian idea. Christianity in its deepest essence is fundamentally beyond the naturalistic *worldliness* of sacred acts, things, persons and visible shows, because it finds itself *only* "in spirit and in truth" (John 4:23).

Because of this *embarras de richesses* to choose from, anybody can put together his own Christianity. When we now want to examine Jung's thesis of the fundamental one-sidedness of Christianity we need a criterion for what to consider as relevant. This criterion follows from what I discussed so far. We have to be guided by the inherent dynamic and inner momentum of the heart of the Christian message itself to let become explicit what had been implicit and to do justice to its need to come home to itself. The heart of the Christian message is what is absolutely new, special about, and vital to it in contrast to other religions or other ways of thinking. "The heart" is also the essential Christian impulse or thrust over against all the peripheral, marginal, sometimes serendipitous details found in the rich material that attached itself to this nucleus.

Our questions must be, does Jung and do we get stuck in the letter, the literal, the image, the narrative story, or was he and are we able to negate and push off from the letter so as to understand the teachings "in spirit and in truth"? Does the syntax of Jung's and of our thinking fully correspond to the semantics of the message, so that the semantic message is *released* into its truth? Does Jung and do we allow ourselves to be bound by the inner logic of the Christian teachings as having everything they need within themselves, or does he, do we approach them with external categories and expectations and bring in other stray elements from outside?

And, when coming from the other side, from the actual course of Western history, and looking at it with the question to what extent the workings of the Christian impulse can be discerned therein (or, the other way around, to what extent this history can be interpreted as the realization of the Christian impulse), does Jung and do we focus on the major transformations of *the general logical form of consciousness* or does he, do we cling to the semantic level, only having eyes for selected individual ideas, visions, dreams, images, opinions that, to be sure, actually happened to occur in history, but that are capriciously privileged by us as the psychologically significant ones?

THE CHARGE OF ONE-SIDEDNESS

Jung's views of Christianity are well known. "... the Christ-symbol lacks wholeness in the modern psychological sense, since it does not include the dark side of things but specifically excludes it in the form of a Luciferian opponent" (*CW* 9ii § 74). Christ "is one side of the self and the devil the other" (*Letters 2*, p. 133, to White, 24 Nov. 1953) "... one of the things they [the Gnostics] taught was that Christ 'cast off his shadow from himself.' ... we can easily recognize the cut-off counterpart in the figure of the Antichrist" (*CW* 9ii § 75). "Christ is without spot, but right at the beginning of his career there occurs the encounter with Satan, the Adversary, who represents the counterpole of that tremendous tension in the world of the psyche which Christ's advent signified" (*CW* 9ii § 78). "... the first thing Christ must do is to sever himself from his shadow and call him devil" (*Letters 2*, pp. 134f., to White, 24 Nov. 1953). Christ "has chosen the light and denied the darkness" (*Letters 2*, p. 473, to Kelsey, 12 Dec. 1958).

"In the Christian concept ... the archetype is hopelessly split into two irreconcilable halves, leading ultimately to a metaphysical dualism—the final separation of the kingdom of heaven from the fiery world of damnation" (*CW* 9ii § 74, transl. modif.). "The myth [= the Christian myth] must at long last go through with its monotheism and give up its (officially denied) dualism" (*MDR* p. 338, transl. modif.).

"We stand face to face with the terrible question of evil, and one is not even aware of it, let alone of how to answer it" (*MDR* p. 331, transl. modif.). "The old question posed by the Gnostics, 'Whence comes evil?' has been given no answer by the Christian world..." (*MDR* p. 332).

"I do not doubt that the alchemical figure of Mercurius is a medieval attempt at a compensation for the Christ figure" (*Letters 2*, p. 619, to A. Jung, 21 Dec. 1960, transl. modif.). "Alchemy was well aware of the great shadow which Christianity was obviously unable to get under control, and it therefore felt impelled to create a savior from the womb of the earth as an analogy and complement of God's son who came down from above" (*CW* 14 § 704, transl. modif.).

CHRIST'S INITIAL MEETING WITH THE TEMPTER

First I would like to take a closer look at Christ's encounter with the devil at the beginning of his career (Matth. 4:1ff.). Jesus had fasted in the desert for forty days and was hungry. In this situation the devil appears and tempts him, first by asking him to use his power as the Son of God to turn stones into bread, secondly by asking him to throw himself down from the pinnacle of the temple and allowing himself to be safely supported by angels, and finally by taking him to an extremely high mountain from which all the kingdoms of the world could be seen and offering them to him.

The first thing to be noticed is that obviously this devil is not Luciferian, satanic, absolutely evil. He does not represent the dark side. He does not want to seduce Christ to commit a crime, to gratify evil lusts (as, for example, sexual child molestation). Instead he merely represents the *natural*, concretistic perspective versus a non-literal one. The first temptation is ultimately about social welfare, providing enough to eat for everyone. The second temptation is about performing a spectacular miracle that would make him credible to the masses as someone to put their hopes on. And the last one is about becoming a political world leader, who would by no means have to be a cruel despot, but could just as well be a wise and just ruler, a benefactor of the world, maybe like Emperor Augustus bringing a long-lasting period of peace and the flowering of culture. These are the devil's offers. The issue here is not the choice between good and evil. It is by no means as Jung represents it: "Both sides appear here: the light side and the dark" (*Letters 1*, p. 268, to Zarine, 3 May 1939). In fact we see that as far as the semantic substance of the goals is concerned, the devil and Jesus are not at all apart. Both were thinking in the same direction. Jesus showed the same concern for people being fed and he would later teach his followers to pray, "Give us this day our daily bread," he performed numerous miracles, and he also conceived himself as the ruler of the world. The only difference is that Jesus gives to the goal shared by both a fundamentally other meaning: "My kingdom is NOT of *this* world" (John 18:36), "Blessed are they who have NOT seen, and yet have believed" (John 20:29), and "Man shall NOT live by *bread* alone, but by every word that proceedeth out of the mouth of God." What is at stake in the dispute between the devil and Jesus was beautifully highlighted by Dostoevsky in his parable, "The Grand Inquisitor."

There is no trace here of an "unspeakable conflict posited by duality" (*CW* 11 § 258) and, as a matter of fact, not a real *duality* either, not a thesis and an antithesis. Jesus and the devil are by no means divided by the strict opposition between good and evil, which is a horizontal opposition much like that between right and left. No, both aim for the good, namely "bread" and "kingdom." There is no dispute between them about the goal itself. Theirs is the vertical difference within one and the same semantic content or concept (e.g., "kingdom") between "of this world" and "*not* of this world." Jesus negates and *er-innert* (inwardizes) the notion of "kingdom" into itself. The crude moralistic opposition between two totally different desires or goals imagined by Jung thus gives way for us to the sophisticated difference between two different modes or styles of understanding of the same desire, between a naturalistic, external sense of "bread" or "kingdom" and an inner, logical sense, between the literal and the spiritual, between positivity here and logical negativity over there. Rather than rejecting "kingdom" altogether and opting for something totally different, Jesus pushes off from and sublates, sublimates, distills, evaporates the concept of "kingdom." What a kingdom that is not of this world is he cannot show. It does not exist as a positive fact. It is logically negative and exists only for (i.e., if there is) a soulful understanding. Much like the alchemists said, "*aurum nostrum non est aurum vulgi,*" Jesus says, "My kingdom is not of this world." He overcomes the worldly naturalism of the meaning of the words used and opens up a new dimension and inner depth of meaning of the same words that did not exist before. What *their* gold was, the alchemists, too, were unable to demonstrate because it exists only in and for the absolute-negative interiority of the mind or soul.

Jung does not see that what happens in the temptation scene is an act of logical negation and sublation. Instead, he says, "then, thanks to the function that results from every conflict, a symbol appears: it is the idea of the Kingdom of Heaven, a spiritual kingdom rather than a material one. Two things are united in this symbol, the spiritual attitude of Christ and the devilish desire for power. Thus the encounter of Christ with the devil is a classic example of the transcendent function" (*Letters 1*, p. 268, to Zarine, 3 May 1939). Maybe one can call the Kingdom of Heaven a symbol, although it lacks the sensory element so essential to symbols. But it certainly does not mysteriously "appear," and not appear from out of a conflict. No, it is produced by Jesus's consciously, deliberately pushing off from an initial superficial version of his idea of what he wants to a deeper one. If one wishes to think personalistically of a desire for power on his part (but why should that be a priori "devilish"? Do we not also need rulers in the world?), one could speak of his self-overcoming.

The mistake of thinking that the Kingdom of Heaven is a unification of two conflicting tendencies is that it overlooks the fact that "the spiritual attitude" must not be naturalistically presupposed as a personality trait that existed in Jesus from the beginning. It is not a question of a subjective attitude at all. A "spiritual attitude" could not exist because "spirit" in *this* sense had been unknown, it was not available; it was only the *result* of the revolutionary Christian move, a radically new creation. So what we witness here in this scene is the first-time conquest or birth of this new objective soul dimension, the dimension of spirit as logical negativity, through the process of negating the natural desire or the naturalistic understanding of the desire. Jesus, we might say, sees through the superficiality of the literal (political) kingdom. He gets a clearer, deeper self-understanding about his actual desire. He for the first time becomes aware that he is indeed striving for "kingdom," but also comes to realize that he would only fool himself if he gave in to this wish for "kingdom" in the external sense of literal, political power as offered by the devil, and that that sense of kingdom would not at all give him what his soul in truth needs. No *transcendent* function, no "symbol" as the resolution on a higher level of an insoluble conflict (and no conflict either). On the contrary, an absolute-negative *interiorization*. Instead of the clash of two opposite theses we find the logical movement from a preliminary thesis to a deeper, more sophisticated one.

Should we call the devil in this story Jesus's shadow? Maybe the possibility of misunderstanding his mission in the sense of positivity and acting it out is indeed a possible shadow aspect of what Jesus was striving for, but if so, then certainly not in Jung's sense of shadow here, as the "counterpole of that tremendous tension in the world of the psyche which Christ's advent signified."

The second point to be noted is that according to this story, Christ did by no means "sever himself from his shadow" at the beginning of his career. No cutting-off. If we accept for the moment Jung's view of the devil as his shadow, Jesus's behavior is an absolutely exemplary mode of how to deal with the shadow. He allows him to surface, he lets him state his case and show what he has to offer, he calmly and, I suppose, open-mindedly listens to him and even lets himself be guided by him to that high mountain. He lets "the shadow" become fully conscious and faces him directly. And rather than splitting the shadow off, suppressing him, fighting him, he merely *answers* him, openly contradicts him, says "no" to him. The encounter happens as a true dialogue, on the level of *speaking*. Both put their cards on the table and so *know* now where they stand with respect to each other.

Jesus's knowledge gained about "his shadow" (at least the one that appeared here) is neither repressed nor gets lost for Jesus in the times to come. Because inasmuch as his own goal is the determinate negation of what the devil offered him and is the result of Jesus's pushing off from it, he always carries with him what he pushed off from, the same way the alchemist who aims for "*his*" gold always stays aware of the gold in the ordinary literal sense. One might even surmise that the devil's spelling out his offers was indispensable for Jesus to clearly become aware of and define the totally other dimension of logical negativity ("spirit") that was to be his own specialty. Without getting the literal option clearly spelled out he could not have clearly pushed off to the figurative sense of kingdom that was his own goal. A negation presupposes the position. So the devil, rather than being his shadow in the usual sense of the word, was, as a literal devil's advocate, his maieutic psychopomp. He helped Jesus to find himself, to find into his own.

For a psychological understanding, this story is not really about two separate figures, the devil and Jesus, at all. Rather, what is actually one single process of self-reflection and self-clarification (acquiring a clearer, deeper understanding of himself and his project) in the loneliness of the wilderness is merely *narratively* played out as the interaction (or rather dialogue) between two figures. As psychologists we should not take literally this substantiating or personifying, which is only due to the needs of the narrative genre. But this means that the whole talk about Christ's shadow is misplaced as far as this story is concerned.

I said that a negation presupposes the position. However, in the sphere of the soul's logic the "position" is not an ontic fact, entity, or situation, nothing naturally existing and a presupposition not a literal *pre*-existing starting-point. Instead, the negation *posits within itself* the presupposition from which it "then" pushes off. This underlines our insight that the devil in this story must not be seen as an externally existing being, nor as a projection or split-off and denied part of the whole personality. He is precisely internal to the whole operation, namely as the soul's or mind's instrument for taking a radical step forward to a new status of itself.

It is amazing that Jung read the undialectical horizontal good-evil split and a "tremendous tension" between a thesis and an antithesis into this story and did not become aware of the very different vertical sublimation-inwardization process described in this story. Its topic or issue is very, very different from what Jung saw in it. Since Jung was a very intelligent and psychologically extraordinarily insightful man I can only assume that he could not see this because he was in the grip of an agenda of his own.

INCARNATION

With the topic of incarnation, we come to the very heart of the Christian doctrine and what distinguishes it from probably all other religions. Jung, too, considered it "the essence of the Christian message" (*MDR* p. 338). The theologically most significant passage is Phil. 2:5–8. There we are told that Jesus Christ,

> although he originally existed in the form of God,
> did not cling to his being-equal-to-God as his
> inalienable privilege,
> but emptied himself [of it] (*ekenôsen*, from which we
> get the key term *kenôsis*),
> took the form of a slave,
> having been born like a man
> and living like a man,
> he humbled himself
> and was obedient to the point of death,
> indeed, [a criminal's] death on a cross.

The *kenôsis* means that Christ relentlessly gave up his divinity. It is a voluntary renunciation, his own doing. The incarnation is one consistent downward movement from the height of divinity to the lowest possible form of human existence, that of a slave, and further to the most contemptible form of death. Christ went all the way to the utmost end. The passage makes it very clear that there is no reserve. Christ does not leave himself a way out. The descent is total.

His is not a *journey* from heaven down to earth, a change of location, nor merely a *metamorphosis* such as we know it from many mythological gods who appeared on earth in human or even animal shape. A metamorphosis is a form change. Those gods of mythology, when having taking on human shape, never ceased being gods. Their transformation concerned only their *physical* form, their bodily *appearance*, and was only temporary, reserved for a particular purpose. Christ, however, became man for good and in earnest. Instead of a journey or metamorphosis, his incarnation was therefore in addition to a loss of status or prestige ("he humbled himself") much more radically a *logical or ontological form change*, a change in his very essence, substance, or innermost nature, in his definition or identity, so that we could also think of it as an "alchemical" (mercurial) change, e.g., of a *putrefactio* and *mortificatio*. It was a *category* change (Christ switched from the category God to that of mortal man).

Our passage tells of one powerful dynamic, one vigorous movement of going under. The incarnation is not only about Christ's being *born* as man ("Christmas") in the sense of a one-time event, as it appears to the merely imagining mind. It is continued beyond his birth and goes through his life on earth as a whole right into his death. The incarnation is a complete going under and is only fulfilled with his crucifixion. And not even with this crucifixion as such alone, but only with its culminating in his absolute loss of God ("My God, my God, why hast thou forsaken me?"), which is not mentioned in our passage. Only with this experience or insight had the *kenôsis* become absolute. Only then was the last trace of divinity truly emptied out. As long as there was trust in God Father and the faith or hope that he, Jesus Christ, was God's son, his child, did he indirectly still possess his divinity, even if he did not possess it immediately in himself (who had in fact already become nothing but human), but in his other, God, and in his faith in Him. The complete *kenôsis* includes the death of God, the loss of "having" a God altogether. Without the loss of God it would only be a partial or token "emptying." And only if he has lost his God has he really, unreservedly, become human, nothing but human, and emptied his cup fully.

This radical dynamic movement of *kenôsis* is the thought and intuition that was the assignment given by early Christianity to all future generations to be thought through, to be slowly more and more comprehended and integrated into consciousness.

Christ's death on the Cross together with the absolute loss of God brought by it was, by the way, also the mode—and the only mode—how the dictum, "My kingdom is not of this world" could be in fact redeemed, made true and real. It is easy to talk big about a kingdom that is not of this world. But that it is more than an ideal representation in the mind, namely a reality, and what it actually means and involves, comes out only in Christ's *dying into* this kingdom of his, the imaginal sign of which is his crown of thorns. Before his death, it had been no more than an idea, an intuition.

Jung resists the logic of this movement. He is immune to the unambiguously vertical thrust of the *kenôsis* and immediately substitutes for it the horizontality of the good-evil opposition. "With the *incarnation* the picture changes completely, as it means that God becomes manifest in the form of Man who is conscious and therefore cannot avoid judgment. He simply has to call the one good and the other evil. It is a historical fact that the real devil only came into existence together with Christ. ... But becoming Man, he [God] becomes at the same time a definite being, which is this and not that" (*Letters 2*, p. 134, to White, 24 Nov. 1953). This passage is also a clear sign that Jung understood the incarnation as the one-time event of a God's taking on a human shape at the beginning of his life on earth, whereas what happens in his life as man was seen as wholly another story). And in the same spirit, Christ's crucifixion means for Jung his suspension *between* the opposites.

We see that Jung does not stay within the specific conception of the incarnation as offered by the biblical text. He brings to bear upon it an extraneous and irrelevant point of view. Jung approaches the incarnation with his own program. Good and evil are simply no topic and of no interest in the logic of *kenôsis*. They have no place in this thought. If you think practically, it is, to be sure, true that becoming Man means becoming a determinate being "which is this and not that" and which probably needs to "call the one good and the other evil." But why mention this? This is not at all the point made by the incarnation idea. Wrong categories. Of sole interest is the going-under movement and the dynamic of total self-depletion of the divine nature.

It is no doubt true that the idea of the devil as "the Adversary" appears in the New Testament, but it is a leftover from widespread conventions of contemporary Jewish thought (Qumran, *pseudepigrapha*, etc.) and precisely not on a level with the incarnation/*kenôsis* idea, so to speak not state-of-the-art. In interpreting, one always has to start with the *apex theoriae* and the heart of it, with where it is at its best, and judge all the individual more peripheral or incidental elements it also contains from there. They have to justify their existence within the doctrine up for discussion (and their existence in that particular *form*) in the light of its highest point and deepest principle. Noteworthy in our context is also that in contrast to those contemporary Jewish thought patterns the New Testament teaches that the might of Satan has been broken by Jesus, whereby this deprivation of Satan's power is subject to the "already / not yet" tension characteristic of Christian thinking. It is the tension between the logical and the positive-factual or empirical or between the implicit and the explicit.

It is also true that throughout the Middle Ages and even later the threat of the devil and the fear of eternal damnation in hell were (often extremely) powerful factors in the actual religious life and beliefs of Christians. Although these ideas and fears are part of the belief system of Christianity *as it historically existed* and developed, they are not elements of the authentically Christian message, Christianity as it is "in spirit and in truth." They had merely a *propaedeutic*, educational function: in a slow, centuries-long process they had to get collective consciousness psychically ready for the logical subtleties of the actual Christian idea. The terrible fear of damnation was no more than an instrument used by the soul to brutally, painfully dislodge and evict the mind from its *natural* state, its being bound by *imaginal* conceptions and expectations, to catapult the soul out of its *unio naturalis* and to thrust consciousness into the fundamentally post-natural constitution necessary for doing justice to the Christian idea (as it is expressed, e.g., in "My kingdom is NOT of this world," which is not an imaginal reality but a logical or intelligible one, one of absolute negativity). The damnation was eternal, that is, absolute, which shows that despite of its imaginal form it is actually an abstract thought, the thought of a total *determinate* negation (not a total annihilation!). The terrifying fear of eternal damnation was the *psychic* (emotional and still somehow imaginal) way how was made real what is actually a radical *(psycho-)logical* negation and sublation of the (to begin with pagan-mythological, imaginal) logical form of consciousness. As a total negation of all natural hope it had to once and for all block the way back to the imaginal mode of conception and initiate into the level of the Concept.

As psychologists we must not take at face value and for real what is purposely produced by the soul as a means to an end, to do something to itself. But Jung falls for the idea of the devil. And despite his long and thorough study of alchemy, he does not develop a mercurial understanding of the incarnation. He comes to the notion of incarnation with his dissociative moralistic mindset. And thus, despite his own methodological insight that the fantasy-image has everything it needs within itself and that we must not let anything from outside, that does not belong, get into it, he burdens the idea of the incarnation with what is external and detrimental to it.

The opposition of good and evil is also not a concern of Christ's preaching. On the contrary, he radically overcomes this harsh opposition. He himself stays with the "publicans and sinners"; against the Mosaic law, he saves the adulterous woman from being stoned; in his Sermon on the Mount he reduces to absurdity the idea of goodness, righteousness. In the same spirit, St. Paul teaches that "all have sinned, and come short of the glory of God" (Romans 3:23). If all have sinned, the "absolute opposition" (Jung) between good and evil is fundamentally relativized. Already *here* "the time or turning-point is reached where good and evil begin to relativize themselves, to doubt themselves, and the cry is raised for a morality 'beyond good and evil'" (*CW* 11 § 258), a time or turning-point that Jung wants to postpone to a late future past Nietzsche's 19th century. Clearly, it does not make sense to say that "The world of the Son is the world of moral discord" (*CW* 11 § 259), at least as long as one stays *within* the central thrust of the Christian message and does not, like Jung, bring in all kinds of external material or take as authoritative what *people* commonly made the Christian message to mean. *Christianitas nostra non est christianitas vulgi.* Christ precisely overcomes this discord, he frees, absolves people from this "unspeakable conflict posited by duality." "Son, be of good cheer; thy sins be forgiven thee" (Matth. 9:2). Christ has come to save the sinners, not the righteous. There will be more joy in heaven about one sinner who repents than about ninety-nine righteous ones. Man is *simul iustus et peccator* (Luther). We are also told the parable of the Prodigal Son who is unconditionally forgiven by his father. At the same time, we see that the shadow is also not denied or projected out into a separate figure, the Antichrist. Christ has no illusions about the *reality* of "evil," sin. In the authentic Christian stance—I mean of course in its objective logic, not necessarily in the actual practice and attitudes of those who call themselves Christians—the shadow has a priori been integrated: it is conscious and acknowledged.

There are above all five fundamental methodological lapses in Jung's approach to Christianity, that I will discuss under the following headings: (1) *Reductio in primam figuram*, (2) regression to naturalistic thinking, (3) theosophy, not psychology, (4) positivism, and (5) the disregard of the phenomenological evidence.

Reductio in primam figuram

Jung's insistence in practical psychotherapy on understanding psychic phenomena from within themselves instead of viewing them in terms of the past history that preceded them is well known. The fantasy image, he said, has everything it needs within itself, and in contrast to the Freudian method to understand neurosis from what happened in early childhood he made it very clear that for him, "The true cause for a neurosis lies in the Now, for the neurosis exists in the present. It is by no means a hangover from the past, a *caput mortuum*, but it is daily maintained, indeed even generated anew, as it were. And it is only in the today, not in our yesterdays, that a neurosis can be 'cured.' Because the neurotic conflict faces us today, any historical deviation is a detour, if not actually a wrong turning." (*CW* 10 § 363, transl. modif.). Instead of a causal-reductive and (in a narrower sense) analytical interpretation of psychic material, Jung opted for a final-prospective, constructive, or synthetic approach. What was the material heading for? That was generally his question.

What we find, however, in Jung's interpretation of Christianity is precisely a "historical deviation," his reading, e.g., the Christian incarnation in terms of the historical past, of what preceded it, of the "*caput mortuum*." He looks backwards. His question is: *Whence* evil? He comes to the Christian message with all the fixed ideas about the old angry Yahweh in his mind that he had developed in his (certainly interesting) study laid down in the earlier parts of his *Answer to Job*. He relies on the Old Testament and other pre-Christian texts (e.g., *Enoch*). He works extensively with the idea of prefiguration. What the idea of the Christian incarnation was aiming for, what it tries to achieve as its telos, is of course not totally disregarded by Jung, but he does not really give it a chance. He always keeps the old emotional powerful Father God in the background as the inescapable perspective. The New

Testament, sort of "the child" of the Old Testament, cannot really come of age and be seen as a "person" in its own right, much as in many 20th century novels about a father-son conflict. Jung does his best to hold his interpretation of the incarnation in the old rut. Christianity is reduced by Jung to one moment in a long historical *program*.

Because of his Old Testament bias, Christianity's having *overcome* the Old-Testament Jahweh and moved to Spirit and Love cannot be accepted as true by Jung. He meets this essential constituent of the Christian doctrine with a hermeneutic of suspicion. For him the Christian idea of God as Love is no more than, let us say, wishful thinking or a pious claim; as far as Christianity's truth is concerned, Jung precisely insists on "nothing but" the angry vindictive God: "The more desirable a real relationship of trust between man and God is, the more astonishing becomes Yahweh's vindictiveness and irreconcilability towards his creatures. From a God who is a loving father, who is actually Love itself, one would expect understanding and forgiveness. The fact that the supremely good God demands for the purchase of such an act of grace the price of a human sacrifice, and, what is worse, the killing of his own son, comes as an unexpected shock. "... One has to stop and think about it: the God of goodness is so unforgiving that he can only be appeased by a human sacrifice! This is an insufferable imposition, which in our days one can no longer swallow..." (*CW* 11 § 689, transl. modif.). The vindictive God is precisely *not* overcome. According to Jung's view, he even acts out his vindictiveness once more in the central event of Christianity, Christ's dying on the Cross.

This backwards interpretation of Jung's is also expressed in the very title of his work, *Answer to Job*, which is programmatic. The Christian truths are nothing in their own right. They do not have everything they need within themselves but refer fundamentally backwards outside themselves, to Yahweh's terrible injustice towards Job. Concerning the deepest point of the incarnation, Christ's "despairing cry from the Cross: 'My God, my God, why hast thou forsaken me?,'" Jung says, "Here is given the answer to Job..." (*CW* 11 § 647).[1]

There is no doubt a very old tradition of reading Old Testament stories or motifs as prefigurations of New Testament themes. But this hallowed prefiguration concept starts out from the Christian truth as its base and reads the old texts precisely in the light of the new Christian spirit. Jung's procedure, I submit, reverses this direction. For him the prefigurations that he sees are in a historical and more or less causal sense precedents that lay the determining conditions—the rut—for everything that comes later.

REGRESSION TO NATURALISTIC THINKING

Jung can only put through his own program concerning Christianity because he does not really go along with the Christian move and impulse and thus does not view it from within itself, from its inner logical dynamic, but holds on to a fundamentally pre-Christian and extra-Christian stance from which he approaches Christian ideas. It is true, Jung cites the *kenôsis*, but at the same time he resists the logical movement it performs. He does not *think* God's becoming Man, but merely pictorially imagines it.

He states, "... God wants to become man, but not quite" (*CW* 11 § 740). But part of the Christian message is that God *had become* man. This is part of the Christian "dream text." Psychologically a *fait accompli*. Jung taught us that, "What the dream, which is not manufactured by us, says is *just so*. Say it again as well as you can" (*Letters 2* p. 591, to Herbert Read 2 September 1960). When it comes to Christianity, Jung does not follow his own maxim. Instead of "saying it again," i.e., thinking it, letting it fully come home to himself, Jung evades the text and falls back on psychologistic speculative explanations of his own about the subjective intentions of a subject called God. Whether God "wants" to become man or not is not the topic at all. We are told that he did become man. That is the only point. Whereas the Christian thought of the incarnation demands of us to see it as absolutely relentless and total (and this also means to think it through to its utmost consequence), Jung does not allow it to go all the way. Yes, there is incarnation for him, but something reserves itself. God does not really get beyond his inner wishing to incarnate, for ultimately in Jesus Christ he stays God after all.

"If this God wishes to become man, then indeed an incredible *kenosis* (emptying) is required, in order to reduce His totality to the infinitesimal human scale. Even then it is hard to see why the human frame is not shattered by the incarnation. ... Above all he [Jesus] lacks the *macula peccati* (stain of original sin). For that reason, if for no other, he is at least a god-man or a demigod. The Christian God-image cannot become incarnate in empirical man without contradictions—quite apart from the fact that man with all his external characteristics seems little suited to representing a god" (*MDR* p. 337, transl. modif.). The incarnation, so we must gather, was not a full-fledged incarnation at all inasmuch as Jesus stayed a god-man or demigod. Therefore, in flagrant contradiction to the Phil. 2 passage, the *kenôsis* was for Jung only a token one; it did not *really* empty Christ of his divinity all the way. For Jung the incarnation is merely "the birth and tragic fate *of a God* in time" (*CW* 11 § 647, my emphasis). "Both mother and son are not real human beings at all, but gods" (*CW* 11 § 626, the whole sentence was italicized by Jung).

Jung reverses the meaning of the incarnation almost into the opposite. It precisely does no longer mean that the divinity is renounced, up to the utmost point of the loss of the trust in God Father. It now means the representation of *God* in human shape. This is how the incarnation is understood if one merely imagines it; the predicate brings only an external change to an immune subject: the very concept of God as a supreme being is not decomposed, but He stays God even when incarnated, which is sort of the reverse of our sending human beings in their spacesuits and space capsules into outer space where they also stay what they had been on earth. The incarnation does not really touch or reach God.

Only this can explain why Jung thinks that one would actually have to expect the human frame to be shattered by the incarnation. This worry is absolutely unfounded in the Christian idea of the incarnation, because there the *kenôsis* is total; there is nothing left that could be "shattering." But Jung clings to the notion and nature of God. He does not allow God to become man and to die as God. The divinity of God is to be rescued *against* the Christian decomposition of it in the *kenôsis*, which Jung reduces to mean a mere reduction of his all-encompassing totality to a more limited proportion: God squeezes himself into the tight human frame. For the Christian idea, by contrast, the *kenôsis* was not a question of *totality* (being the All) versus limited *finite nature*, but of the supreme *divine status* versus a *human, even slave status*. Not limitation of the all-encompassing extent of God to human proportions, but humbling and going under—logical decomposition—was the topic. If one *thinks* the sentence "God became man," the predicate dissolves the subject; the subject relentlessly dies into the process predicated of it.

The difference between merely imagining the incarnation and thinking it is like that between viewing things in terms of physics (my space travel example) versus in terms of chemistry/alchemy ("decomposition") or that between myth and logos. While the *kenôsis* idea describes a logical (or mercurial, alchemical) process, a process of a transformation of the inner constitution of the concept of God, Jung stays stuck in a naturalistic ("physical") thinking in terms of a substance or subject and its behavior, its (hi)story, the various changes (in the sense of external events) that happen to it. He speaks of the "life-process within the Deity" (*CW* 11 § 206), the process of the "divine self-realization" (*Letters 2*, p. 316, to Kotschnig, 20 June 1956). Jung sort-of writes the biography of God, the events in His life. It is a substantiating thinking, mythologizing and personifying, not one of psychological analysis or interpretation.

This becomes especially obvious in his evaluation of the crucifixion. When he wrote the sentence quoted, "... God wants to become man, but not quite," he continued, "The conflict in his nature is so great that the incarnation can only be bought by an expiatory self-sacrifice offered up to the wrath of God's dark side" (*CW* 11 § 740). The same view is expressed in stronger terms some pages earlier in the same work in a passage (partly) already quoted above: Christ himself "offers himself as an expiatory sacrifice that shall effect the reconciliation with God. The more desirable a real relationship of trust between man and God is, the more astonishing becomes Yahweh's vindictiveness and irreconcilability towards his creatures. From a God who is a loving father, who is actually Love itself, one would expect understanding and forgiveness. The fact that the supremely good God demands for the purchase of such an act of grace the price of a human sacrifice, and, what is worse, of the killing of his own son, comes as an unexpected shock. ... One has to stop and think about it: the God of goodness is so unforgiving that he can only be appeased by a human sacrifice! This is an insufferable imposition, which in our days one can no longer swallow..." (*CW* 11 § 689, transl. modif.). About Christ's helplessness at the Cross, when he "confessed that God had forsaken him," we hear in a letter to Victor White: "The Deus Pater would leave him to his fate as he always 'strafes' those whom he has filled before with this abundance by breaking his promise" (*Letters 2*, p. 134, 24 Nov. 1953). God is disloyal, in fact a betrayer.

Jung treats God and the Son personalistically as if they were people, separate, independent beings, who have their subjective passions and character faults and whose behavior needs to be explained in terms of them. Jung dwells on character traits and emotions: irascibility, vindictiveness, wrath, cruelty, irreconcilability, appeasement, expiation, and so it is not surprising that Jung also enters into this story with his own subjective emotions, *vide* his predicates "insufferable," "not to be swallowed," which is unprofessional. In Jung's hands, the act or event of redemption turns into a kind of Freudian family romance, a terrible, perhaps Kafka-like, human *drama* (if not soap opera) of an almighty, but vindictive, cruel father and an obedient son as his victim. "What kind of father is it who would rather his son were slaughtered than forgive his ill-advised creatures who have been corrupted by his precious Satan? What is supposed to be demonstrated by this gruesome and archaic sacrifice of the son? God's love, perhaps?" (*CW* 11 § 661). But this is the naive kindergarten version of the Christian idea, a simple story with a clear difference between a subject and a victim in an intimate family constellation perceived in categories of good and evil. Concerning the psychology brand to which Jung's thinking here belongs, we have to say that it is a personalistic object-relations psychology. All this is totally inadequate to do justice to what the incarnation and the crucifixion are actually about, if they are understood in their own terms, namely, as I indicated, "in spirit and in truth," or: if they are understood *psychologically*.

Here we see most clearly to what extent Jung falls short of the intellectual level on which the Christian message (at least in its highest form) is situated. In his writings about Christianity, we have a case of a true *abaissement du niveau mental*, but in a logical, not the usual psychic sense as a mere lowering of the *degree* of being conscious: Jung regresses to a much more primitive *level* of thinking, one that has precisely long been superseded by the degree of sophistication attained in Christian thinking (although not in the thinking of the popular believers). He is not up to the logical form of the Christian truths. It is preposterous to speak with respect to them of a "gruesome and archaic sacrifice of the son." Jung mythologizes, imagines in naturalistic terms. He himself cultivates an archaic thinking, whereas the Christian message ought to be understood in a highly advanced way, namely "in spirit and in truth" or "*in Mercurio*," as a so to speak alchemical process that is performed upon the 'substance' called God, and performed upon it not from without, but from within itself.

A truly psychological view would say that the Christian message with all its different moments (*kenôsis*, birth, crucifixion, etc.) has to be seen as one single soul truth, as the self-display of the inner dynamic logic of a particular soul situation at a particular historical locus. We must not construe the different figures that appear in the narrative form of the Christian message (here above all the Father and the Son) as independent and separately existing agents as if they were people in ordinary reality; they do not themselves *have* a psychology, but they are conversely—and only *together*—the imaginal portrayal of a specific psychology. They are especially not our patients to be psychoanalyzed by us for the purpose of revealing their true hidden motivations, their unconscious vindictiveness, resentments, doubts[2] and of speculating about what might have gone on in their minds. And in what passes between those figures in the narrative in which the Christian message articulates itself, we must (a) not see so many different events, but integral moments of the inner dynamic of this one soul truth, and we must (b) not view it as *empirical behavior* and personal *interaction* between those alleged separate people, but as the portrayal of the soul's *self-relation* and *self-unfolding*. We are psychologists, not behaviorists. The psychologist knows that we are dealing with images, symbols, and narratives that give pictorial expression to soul events or soul truths that in themselves are fundamentally irrepresentable (*unanschaulich*). This is generally true, even when interpreting ancient myths or archaic rituals, but doubly so when the theme is Christianity, whose specific purpose is to overcome the naturalistic level of understanding and to advance to *logos*, to the spirit ("in spirit and in truth"). The imaginal and narrative garb that a soul truth receives is, as I say with Jung, only a "thin veil" behind which—"behind the scenes"—"another picture looms up."[3]

Jung himself at one point insisted: "It is precisely of paramount importance that the idea of the Holy Ghost [*Geist*, Spirit] is *not a natural image* [*kein Naturbild*], but a recognition, an abstract concept ..." (*CW* 11 § 236, transl. modified, italics by Jung).[4] In other words, it is the free property of logos. Especially when turning to Christianity, but not only to it, this insight is the standard and measure for our interpretation behind which we must not fall. Why then in his discussion of the incarnation and crucifixion does Jung revert to the naturalistic level of a family romance?

In other contexts Jung knew: "In myths and fairytales, as in dreams, the soul speaks about itself, and the archetypes reveal themselves in their natural interplay, as 'formation, transformation / the eternal Mind's eternal recreation'" (*CW* 9i § 400, transl. modified). Exactly the same applies to the Christian story. "God Father" and "the Son" have no separate existence *outside* the Christian "dream," but are posited, invented, generated within and by this "dream thought" as its own productions, its own ("dream-internal") "dream" images. And these images represent moments of this ONE dream thought, moments into which the inner complexity of this one thought unfolds itself.

The thought that is narratively portrayed in a given dream or myth or fairytale and therefore also in the Christian message must be *thought by us*. A dream talks about *itself*, displays the one particular thought or soul truth that it is about. It spells out the inner logical movement or dynamic that is the essence of this soul truth. But Jung refused to *think* the Christian message. He did not approach it psychologically and he resisted the pull of its inner logic, its pull towards the death of God as a substance and his (God's) transformation into Spirit and Love. Instead, he stubbornly mythologized, i.e., took the story with its figures and happenings literally, personalistically, at face value, as if it were a *news report* about historical or empirical-factual acts of an existing God, acts occurring outside this narrative in reality (which they may do for the naive believer, but certainly not for a psychologist). Only because Jung construes Christ's death on the Cross *unthinkingly* as a terrible melodrama ("the God of goodness is so unforgiving that he can only be appeased by a human sacrifice!") does it for him become "an insufferable imposition," and under that condition naturally so. But the insufferable imposition is due to this melodramatic, personalistic construal and the childlike imagination of God as a being. For a consciousness used to motifs of dismemberment in myth, of pulverization, flaying, mortification in alchemy and ready to see the crucifixion *psychologically*, it is by no means anything insufferable.

We must not substantiate and literalize elements in a dream (or other soul story), that is, to set them up as existing outside the story.

Because this would be like giving the sounds or letters of a word an independent existence outside the word, instead of grasping, and exclusively concentrating on, *the meaning* conveyed by the word and letting the individual sounds go under in the very meaning produced, a meaning that could only emerge in the first place through *their* relentless *dying into* this meaning.

Theosophy, Not Psychology

The problem I found in Jung's discussion of the Christian message, his setting up "imaginal" figures from within a soul story as existing outside this story and thus literalizing them applies not only to individual episodes in the Christian story, but to his whole treatment of the Judaeo-Christian God image and thus to his whole discourse on religion in the Western tradition. His is not a psychological discourse, but a theosophic one. God is posited as existing outside *all* the different and separate stories from Old Testament times onwards. Jung reads all these stories as records of the development of *God* "in reality" from the creation onwards up to our time and beyond. The history of Biblical religious ideas or images is interpreted directly as a historical process of *God himself.* Jung's was "not the approach to 'Christianity' but to God himself and this seems to be the ultimate question" (*Letters 2*, p. 611, to Rolfe, 19 Nov 1960). Immediacy. The at first basically unconscious God, Jung suggests, slowly becomes more conscious and *he* later desires to become man, a desire which, for Jung, is not fulfilled once and for all with the birth and death of Christ, but—here Jung leaves history and extrapolates way into the future—requires "further incarnations" "in the empirical man" (*CW* 11 § 693) in the future. "God's Incarnation in Christ requires continuation and completion inasmuch as Christ, owing to his virgin birth and his sinlessness, was not an empirical human being at all" (*CW* 11 § 657 transl. modif.).

Both for a historian of religion and for a psychological point of view things would be different. The difference from the standpoint of the history of religion is twofold. First, all the different texts relevant to religion would be viewed as documents showing human conceptions, human views, what at certain times people imagined, namely that they imagined *that* there are in reality "gods" and *how* specifically they imagined them. Secondly, it would have to be seen how, in which sense, and to what extent the sequence of different religious documents in each case makes up one consistent historical development. Is, for example, a god in a later text truly identical with a same-named god in an earlier text? Each text would have to be understood in terms of its own time. In each new time, the notion god could possibly express something new and have a different function in the structure of consciousness as well as in the makeup of the society of the time. The difference could of course be the result of a further development of the same, but it could just as well be that a truly new function is merely called by an old name. It could be the opposite of what Freud called screen-memory: the name of the old phenomenon is retained, but what is now actually meant by it is something new.

For psychologists it would again be different. They would not view religious ideas as human fantasies, but as the self-expression, self-articulation of aspects of the soul. The different gods are garments in which the soul dresses itself (or aspects of itself) at certain concrete historical loci, and the sequence of god images in history would show the transformation of the soul, that is, of the *syntax* or *logical constitution* of consciousness. And to what extent new images or ideas have to be seen as a continuous further development or as a fresh start would remain to be seen in each case.

But for Jung it is really God himself who is the true subject of all history from the beginning to the present and into the future. He is for Jung the creator of the world; Jung speaks of his almightiness, omniscience, and his justice, but also of his unconsciousness, and it is, for Jung, *God's* wish or need to become man (not the soul's need to transform its own self-representation). This is also why Jung frequently capitalizes the personal and possessive pronouns referring to God (He, Him, His), which in German is only done in the particularly pious diction of believers. *God*, he thinks, needs to become conscious. Jung does not view all the changes in the image of God as a self-portrayal of the transformations of the logic of consciousness and God not as one garb of the soul itself. He always stays with "God" in "His" interaction with man.

Jung is of course *aware* of the fact that he is speaking from within the Christian *myth*. He insists time and again that he is by no means making metaphysical assertions. "I do not imagine that in my reflections on the meaning of man and his myth I have uttered a final truth..." (*MDR* p. 339). "The psyche cannot leap beyond itself. It cannot set up any absolute truths..." (*MDR* p. 350). He also explicitly declares that "the image and the statement are psychic processes which are different from their transcendental object; they do not posit it, they merely point to it" (*CW* 11 § 558). Even if the image and the statement may not posit the transcendental object, here: God, Jung obviously does. He asserts that outside the image and statement there is in fact a transcendental object that they point to. Which is a metaphysical hypostasis, a setting up of the object talked about as existing outside the soul's images or statements. For a psychologist this alleged difference between the image and the so-called transcendental object does precisely not exist,[5] because the image has everything it needs within itself. It does not point to anything outside of itself. It only points to itself.

Again Jung says: "When I do use such mythic language, it happens in the full awareness that 'mana,' 'daimon,' and 'God' are synonyms for the unconscious, inasmuch as we know just as much or just as little about the former as about the latter" (*MDR* p. 337, transl. modif.). But the first problem with this statement is that he does not merely make use of a *mythological manner of speaking* for rhetorical purposes, but rather himself mythologizes or theologizes. He insists on our having to dream the [Christian] myth onwards, on the further development of the myth (cf. *MDR* pp. 331–334), which amounts to his insistence on speaking about these matters as a *homo religiosus*, a theologian or better: theosophist,[6] and not as a psychologist. Instead of merely observing the actual development of "myth" and interpreting it, he spins his own yarn. He is here in the myth-*making* business and thus himself takes over the job of the soul as anima.[7] He knows better than Christianity itself what ought to happen with or in the Christian myth. "The myth must ultimately take montheism seriously and put aside its dualism..." (*MDR* p. 338): Jung argues myth-internally (or rather, since "myth" here means the Christian religion, religion-internally). "That [what "That" refers to is not relevant here] is the goal, or one goal, which fits man meaningfully into the scheme of creation, and at the same time confers meaning upon it. It is an explanatory myth which has slowly taken shape within me in the course of the decades" (*MDR* p. 338). Jung not only posits God and the Creator, but also the creation! To the extent that he does, he has left the precincts of the root metaphor of psychology, soul. By conferring meaning upon "the creation" and by coming up with an "*explanatory* myth,"[8] he established a quasi-religious belief system or ideology.

This is why he also vehemently rejects *demythologization*, which, after all, is inherent in the psychological approach to mythological phenomena. He says, for example, "How, then, can one possibly 'demythologize' the figure of Christ? A rationalistic attempt of that sort would soak all the mystery out of his personality, and what remained would no longer be the birth and tragic fate of a God in time, but, historically speaking, a badly authenticated religious teacher, a Jewish reformer..." (*CW* 11 § 647). This quote (together with the rest of the paragraph from which it is taken) is very revealing. In Jung's thinking there are (at least here) only these two abstract extremes: either mythologizing or becoming personalistic, reductive, banal. The third possibility—doing psychology, psychologizing—has no place in his thinking *when* it comes to the question of God and meaning.

The psychologist demythologizes because he does not take gods as gods. But he does not either reduce gods or mythic heros to no more than human ideas or, euhemeristically, to important but ordinary people who were later glorified and divinized. Rather, the psychologist sees them as products of the soul, as ways of the soul's speaking to itself about itself, as its displaying its highest values and the inner hidden logic of man's being-in-the-world *at concrete historical loci*. Of course they are not *gods* for the psychologist. For him, the soul merely gave one particular truth of itself the *form* of "god," because in the status in which the soul was when it felt the need to do so, it was part of the truth of this content that it had to be venerated and looked up to as infinitely superior. The logic of the soul at that time was such that the soul at its one pole (itself as the *really existing* consciousness) was not yet up to itself as its other pole, its own deepest, innermost truth, its logic. Consciousness could only be aware of the latter *as* projected out far away, high above itself, into heaven.

Mythologizing and demythologizing are characterized by reversed dialectics. With the former, you enter the myth and *ipso facto* take its figures and events at face value, adopting them as your own thinking or belief (at least for the duration of your mythologizing), so that you are completely within the myth, enwrapped by it. The dialectic of one's being inside it is that the figures and events become positivized for oneself, extrajected from the mythic or imaginal story as having an independent existence as real beings, rather than as mere fiction, forms given by the soul to its truths. Because of this, Jung's assurance and awareness that he is merely expressing himself in a mythic style of language does not undo the metaphysical hypostasis character of his statements in this area. The hypostatizing is inherent in the *objective* logical form of his myth-making. All the epistemological assurances to the effect that his statements are not metaphysical statements are external reflections and subjective declarations after the fact that do not reach the myth told and thus remain essentially helpless. We have to go by what is in fact said and done in Jung's statements, not by the ego's stuck-on external warnings about how they are not to be understood.

The psychologist with his demythologization, by contrast, does not adopt the standpoint of the mythic tale. Although it is true that he, too, needs to see a mythic image *from within*, this "from within" comes about through a totally different methodological move. Rather than interiorizing *himself* as human subject into the myth so that the latter becomes his own meaning-bestowing myth, the psychologist tries to absolute-negatively interiorize *the mythic image* itself into itself, into its concept, its truth, its soul. And the dialectic of this is that thereby, through this very inwardization, he succeeds in having the mythic tale vis-à-vis himself, distinguishing himself from it, seeing it from outside as an objective soul phenomenon, without adopting it as his own view.

That Jung did not really distinguish himself from the Judaeo-Christian God comes out most clearly in his style and his explicit profession about that style, namely that he was passionately wrestling with this God, his injustice and vindictiveness. "I cannot, therefore, write in a coolly objective manner, but must allow my emotional subjectivity to speak if I want to describe what I feel when I read certain books of the Bible, or when I remember the impressions I have received from the doctrines of our faith" (*CW* 11 § 559).[9] "How can a man hold aloof from this drama? He would then be a philosopher,[10] talking *about* God but not *with* him" (*Letters 2*, p. 34, to Erich Neumann, 5 Jan 1952). A favorite paradigm for Jung was "the story of Jacob who wrestled with the angel and came away with a dislocated hip..." (*MDR* p. 344).

So much about the first problem that is inherent in his awareness that with terms like mana, daimon, God he uses a mythic language.

The second problem lies in the idea "that 'mana,' 'daimon,' and 'God' are synonyms for the unconscious, inasmuch as we know just as much or just as little about the former as about the latter." Here Jung succumbs to a self-deception. The problem with the first three terms is not that we do not know anything about them. About the gods and the Christian God we know a lot, we have volumes of books on them. No, the problem is that this knowledge has no empirical referent. Daimon and God are noumena. Jung thinks that "the unconscious" is different because it is a "neutral and rational" term, "coined for scientific purposes, and is far better suited to dispassionate observation which makes no metaphysical claims than are the transcendental concepts..." (*MDR* p. 336). But "the unconscious" is just as transcendental a concept as the other ones. It is a metaphysical hypostasis, a noumenon, an *ens rationis*. It is precisely not a scientific concept, not an empirical concept. It does not refer to an empirical referent. By contrast, the "nature" that the natural sciences study is truly different. It has empirical referents: trees and animals, rocks, volcanos, cells, radiation, stars, etc. But "the unconscious" is just a word. It does not point to anything. It exists only in the *theories* or *fantasies* of certain psychologists. Its transcendental nature is only dimly disguised. It merely *sounds* scientific.

And if it were not a metaphysical concept, how could it be a synonym for "mana," "daimon," and "God"? The difference that does indeed exist between "mana," "daimon," and "God" and "the unconscious" boils down to that between honest positive names (the first three) and a name that within itself refrains from naming, pretending to say nothing and claim nothing. "The unconscious" is a name that semantically purposely leaves a blank, an empty slot, but nevertheless logically substantiates this empty slot just the same. "The unconscious" in Jung's parlance is a "theological" term. It has no place in a true psychology. The same applies to Jung's term "the self." It, too, is a metaphysical noumenon. Jung repeatedly stresses that the "symbols of the self cannot be distinguished empirically from a God-image" (*CW* 11 § 289, cf. §§ 231, 282, 757 and elsewhere). Of course not. Because the only empirically real thing are images or symbols, and "the self" and "God," to which they are *said* to refer, are empirically nonexistent metaphysical concepts which are *defined* as being mirror-images of each other. That, for example, the mandala symbol signifies "the wholeness of the psychic ground" may easily be conceded, if one views it psychologically (other equally valid traditional interpretations are: an image, statically, of the world in its wholeness, or an image of cyclical Time in its circular movement). But how Jung arrives from this comprehensible interpretation at the unrelated, ultimately *personalistic* ideas that *as such* it also expresses "the *wholeness of the self*" or, "in mythic terms, the divinity incarnate in man" (*MDR* p. 335) remains his secret. It is his ideology. Neither "self" nor "incarnation in man" are part of the "text" (phenomenological appearance) of the mandala symbol, nor is the notion of the deity.

There is, however, a real difference that Jung does not mention. It is the difference between a God that is part of a living religion, that is in fact worshiped by the people of a whole society because he expresses the deeper inner truth or logic of the mode of being-in-the-world at the historical locus in question, a God who makes a noticeable difference in the practical way how people live their lives and how social life is organized, on the one hand, and the already *psychologized* God—mere subjective inner experiences, God-*images*, as they might come up, e.g., in the dreams of modern people—on the other hand.

That Jung's interpretations are myth-making shows in the fact that (1) he writes about one figure that is only known from the myths and only exists in and by virtue of the myths, God himself, but he writes about him as if he existed outside the myths and (2) he presupposes that there is an *identity* and *continuity* of this God across all the separate mythic stories that originated at different historical times and are maybe expressive of very different concrete situations and different social climates. All the individual stories become interconnected moments of one single consistent story for him. Through this presupposition, Jung construes, as it were, a super-myth, a myth of his own about the slow maturation of God that extends from Creation to the psychological needs of our days. God is not only one and the same, he also remembers and learns from one episode to the next. Jung writes a *Bildungsroman* (novel of character development) about God.

It is one thing if one concludes from the changes in the God-image in different myths from successive periods that a certain development of *consciousness* in the history of the soul must have taken place. It is wholly another thing to suggest that across all of them the fate and development of God himself is displayed. Again it is one thing to say there is or was a tendency in the soul at a certain point in its history to bring its content "God" down from heaven by letting it become incarnate in man, and it is wholly another thing to say that God wants, or wanted, to incarnate in man. It is the difference between psychology and theosophy or myth-making.

* * *

I will now cite as examples a number of individual instances from Jung's descriptions that show his myth-making at work.

"... in omniscience there had existed from all eternity a knowledge of the human nature of God or of the divine nature of man. That is why, long before Genesis was written, we find corresponding testimonies in the ancient Egyptian records. These intimations and prefigurations of the Incarnation must strike one as either completely incomprehensible or superfluous, since all creation, which occurred *ex nihilo*, is God's and consists of nothing but God, with the result that man, like the rest of creation, is simply God become concrete" (*CW* 11 § 631, transl. modif.). Jung does not simply report what the myth says or draw conclusions from the mythic ideas. No, on his own he constructs a text-external background to it. He brings in from other sources God's omniscience, taking it as a fact, and finds corroborations for it in other myth-external *historical* facts (Egyptian records). Similarly, the following passage also shows that this mythic attribute, God's omniscience, as well as Satan are taken for real. Concerning the remarkable "unusual precautions which surround the making of Mary: immaculate conception, extirpation of the taint of sin, everlasting virginity" (all this is only part of a late 19th century new Church dogma), Jung comments: "The Mother of God is obviously being protected against Satan's tricks. From this we can conclude that Yahweh has consulted his own omniscience..." (*CW* 11 § 626).

The first incarnation that happened in Christ was according to Jung necessitated by what happened with Job: "Job stands morally higher than Yahweh. In this respect the creature has surpassed the creator. ... Job's superiority cannot be made away with. Hence a situation arises in which real reflection is needed. That is why Sophia steps in. She reinforces Yahweh's much needed self-reflection and thus makes possible Yahweh's decision to become man. ... he indirectly (acknowledges) that the man Job is morally superior to him and that therefore he has to catch up and become human himself" (*CW* 11 §

640, transl. modif.). This is not only Jung's addition, but also shows
how he takes Sophia for real, who also does not come from the "text"
of the myth, but belongs to Jung's own super-myth. The myth does
not say anything about Yahweh reflecting nor of Sophia stepping in.

According to Jung the moment when Christ at the Cross feels
forsaken by God is "the moment when God experiences what it means
to be a mortal man and drinks to the dregs what he made his faithful
servant Job suffer" (*CW* 11 § 647, transl. modif.). Similarly, the
"passion of Christ signifies God's suffering on account of the injustice
of the world and the darkness of man" (*CW* 11 § 233). Other than
in the "text" of the myth, it is God who is the real subject that suffers
in Christ's suffering through the loss of God. So the loss of God is
only a suffering, but not a true loss at all, inasmuch as it is God who
suffers. He stays.

"The new son, Christ, shall on the one hand be a chthonic man
like Adam, mortal and capable of suffering, but on the other hand he
shall not be, like Adam, a mere copy, but God himself..." (*CW* 11 §
628). Jung sees God as a real being that plans and needs to make several
attempts at realizing them until he arrives at a satisfactory result.

"We cannot and ought not to renounce making use of reason, nor
should we give up the hope that instinct will hasten to our aid, in which
case one God is supporting us against God, as already Job understood"
(*MDR* p. 341, transl. modif.). God is not a mythological idea, a form
of the soul's self-portrayal. God is a real being.

"For it is not that 'God' is a myth, but that myth is the revelation
of a divine life in man. It is not we who invent myth, rather it speaks
to us as a Word of God" (*MDR* p. 340). In this statement an essential
psychological insight is tainted with a theosophist dogma. The
theosophist bias lies in the fact that the *form* of "God," of "Word of
God," of "a divine life," and of "myth" is *absolutized* and *eternalized*.
For a truly psychological view, "God" and "myth" are particular ways
or forms that the soul uses at certain historical stages of its own
development to speak about itself.

Spirit and Love

Paradigmatic for Jung is the image of Christ at the Cross suspended
between the opposites. This is an image that parallels the situation of
individuating modern man whose individuation comes precisely about

by being not merely suspended between, but almost torn apart by the opposites in what Jung calls a *collision of duties.*[11] The same fundamentally undialectical structure of thought comes out when he speaks of thesis and antithesis and asserts that "between the two is generated a third factor as lysis..." (*MDR* p. 353, transl. modif.). It is a thinking about the opposites in terms of horizontality. I already pointed out that for the Christian thought of "the incarnation" the horizontal opposition of good and evil or of Christ and Satan is totally inappropriate. The Christian thought of "incarnation" is vertical, the dynamic move of a consistent going under all the way to the bitter end.

This applies even to the good-evil opposition. In John 1:29 we get the following image, "Behold the Lamb of God, which taketh away the sin of the world," which is probably modeled after Isaiah 53:4: "Surely he hath borne our griefs, and carried our sorrows: yet we did esteem him stricken, smitten of God, and afflicted," and has to be seen in the light of the fact that Christ dies the death of a criminal. Christ humbles himself, we heard before. He bowed down so low that he was beneath the evil of the world and could shoulder it. This is clearly a vertical relation. The lamb is of course the image of absolute innocence, sinlessness. But this sinlessness does not shirk away from evil, projecting it out so that it receives a separate existence as Satan or the Antichrist. No, it gets involved with it, burdens itself with it, bears it. And the (criminal's) death on the Cross is the mode in which this idea of bowing beneath evil and shouldering it is "practically" performed, that is, how it becomes a reality.

To do justice to what these images are driving at, we must keep away all naturalistic thinking, all imagining of the described events as the actions or sufferings of persons or figures. Nothing must be substantiated and imaginally literalized. The terribly naive conceptions of Jung's about a deal necessary to bring about a reconciliation between man and an angry God, about the vindictive Father God himself who demands an expiatory sacrifice, the killing of his son, in order to become placated, is totally out of place. A retrograde interpretation. *Psychologically* understood, these images portray a certain logic, the dialectical logic of how to relate to and overcome evil as well as the evils, the injustices and wrongs of the world: not by powerful conquest and subjugation, not by rejection and condemnation, but conversely

by, with resistanceless sufferance, allowing them to *be*, indeed, even
embracing them, and *ipso facto* unrelentingly exposing oneself to them,
letting them permeate oneself. Again, this must not be understood
naturalistically as precepts for practical behavior or political practice.
It is first of all a concept, an insight, a truth on a very deep and remote
soul level. It is a *logic* to be comprehended, not a maxim to be acted
out. It is the logic of Love.

The idea of a one-sidedness of the Christian message does not
make sense here at all. This new revolutionary logic does not have
any "sides" in the first place, it cannot take sides. Good and evil are
here in a vertical relation. And this logic is comprehensive, the logic
of integration and digestion in a quasi alchemical style, the logic of
absolute-negative inwardization. Jung's logic of a "mediation
between" the opposites, his image of being caught between hammer
and anvil is something completely different. It remains naturalistic,
an "ontological" thinking in terms of thing-like substances and
spatial relations. Since I just now mentioned the word "alchemical,"
I am again reminded of my earlier statement that Jung thinks the
incarnation in the style of "physics" and does not penetrate to the
(al)chemistry of the matter.

We see the same problem in his treatment of the topic of the
Trinity. In his hands it becomes, very externally and crudely, a
numeric problem, three figures, just as his solution is a numeric
one, the addition of the Fourth. Precisely the *logical* issue, the
contradictory nature of the Trinity, that originally fascinated him
so much as a boy in confirmation class ("Here was something that
challenged my interest: a oneness which was simultaneously a
threeness. This was a problem that fascinated me because of its inner
contradiction. I waited longingly for the moment when we would
reach this question" [*MDR* p. 52f.]) was in his later research on the
Trinity just as much ignored by him as this entire topic was, to the
boy Jung's profound disappointment, skipped by his father, the
minister and confirmation class teacher.

The Trinity is itself the imaginally expressed idea of a logical
movement away from mythic or natural image, substance, person
and the absolute-negative inwardization of God into his concept,
his truth (rather than an adding of more, a tripling). As such it is
at the same time the integration of what used to be mythically

imagined as God, a semantic content of consciousness, into the syntax of consciousness. Jung was aware that the "religious spirit of the West is characterized by a change of God's image in the course of the ages" (*Letters 2*, p. 315, to Kotschnig, 30 June 1956), that "As history draws nearer to the beginning of our era, the gods become more and more abstract and spiritualized" (*CW* 11 § 193), that with trinitarian thinking there is a "'change from father to son,' from unity to duality, from non-reflection to criticism" (*CW* 11 § 242), and that "the 'Son' represents a transition stage, an intermediate state... He is a transitory phenomenon" (*CW* 11 § 272). Jung even warns of the "danger of getting stuck in the transitional stage of the Son" (*CW* 11 § 276).

Yet despite all this and despite his thorough familiarity with alchemical thinking, with the processes of *distillatio, evaporatio, sublimatio*, he does not see the Trinity as one great dynamic, namely the dynamic of a logical distillation-evaporation process of the idea of God, of its going under into itself in the sense of its self-sublation into Spirit, which is of course tantamount to its coming home to consciousness, because by evaporating as a semantic content it enters the syntax of consciousness. The Trinity means, mythologically expressed, God's *dying*, <u>as</u> the Son (as the transitional form), on the Cross *into* his truth as Spirit and Love; his dying as a God of *this* world into a "God" who is NOT of this world[12] and *ipso facto* God *sensu strictori* no longer. The mythical or imaginal God, the God as a substantial being or person as he exists for and in *our* standard naturalistic thinking, is dissolved. From here we can see that Jung's demand that "The myth must ultimately take montheism seriously and put aside its dualism..." (*MDR* p. 338) bypasses the Christian truth, not only because the alleged moral opposition (God versus the devil) that Jung refers to with the word dualism is not a serious issue for Christianity, but much more radically because, seen from its telos, Christianity is the overcoming of *theism* as such.

Jung actually himself gets stuck in the transitional stage of the Son, of which he says it is the stage of moral conflict *par excellence*, which is not only why he is fixated on the Adversary as Christ's other and why he thinks that today "We stand face to face with the terrible question of evil" (*MDR* p. 331), but also has to insist that Christ lacks the stain of original sin which means that he had not really become man but was a demigod. This indicates that he imagines the incarnation naturalistically, positivistically, as if it were (or ought to be) an empirical fact. But it is, I think as a matter of course, a psychological event, an event *in the logic of the soul* or in the logic of the world. It is a change of the concept of God, not the literal process of a literal God. It is the emergence of a new insight, of a new way to think, a new status of consciousness unheard of before. This is why we have to insist that in Christ God became man without curtailment, notwithstanding his sinlessness.

This sinlessness, psychologically understood, is not the sign of a divine or semi-divine status since it is not empirical-factual sinlessness, the sinlessness of an empirical being. It is an ingredient in, and follows from, the *concept* and *logic* of Love; it is a logical aspect of Christ. Jung, by contrast, imagines it mythologically (naturalistically) as if it were a *natural inborn* characteristic of Christ (with today's concepts we could almost say "part of his genetics"), a leftover of Christ's divine origin, and proof of the *kenôsis* having been left incomplete. Similarly, he takes the virgin birth for granted. That is to say, Jung deserts the level of thought, logos, and *pneuma* reached by Christianity and regresses to the wholly incommensurate sphere of myth and naturalism. No, the *kenôsis* was complete (but complete only with his crucifixion and God-forsakenness), and the stainlessness of Christ does not come from his past (a "hangover from the past, a *caput mortuum*"), as something natural and an inheritance of his divine origin, but it is the fresh final result and *newly generated product* of what he achieved in his life.

It is, first and preliminarily, the product of his logical act of negation of the devil's splendid offers and his realizing that "My kingdom is NOT of this world." Christ's purity and his being free of darkness is logically generated by his pushing off from "this world," by his refusal to fall for the tempting idea of success in the world. Christ chose the path of logical negativity. And his sinlessness is, secondly and above all, the product, imaginally speaking, of his counter-natural obedience to the point of death "here in real life on the earth," his humbling himself and going under all the way, that is to say, his exemplifying the dialectical logic of Love (through which, as I pointed out, the said dictum, "My kingdom is NOT of this world" was first made *real*). Only by bowing under and bearing the sin of the world with resistanceless sufferance does he *become* the sinless Lamb of God. Not the other way around: an a priori sinless being shoulders the sin of the world. How can one, as a psychologist used to a final-prospective approach, think in such a simplistic fashion? "Do good to them that hate you" (Matth. 5:44). "For my strength is made perfect in weakness" (2 Cor. 12:9). *Contra spem sperare.* "If any man come to me, and hate not his father, and mother, and wife, and children, and brethren, and sisters, yea, and his own life also, he cannot be my disciple" (Luke 14:26). The *negation* of the natural way is so obvious in Christianity.

The generation of sinlessness through placing oneself under what is NOT of this world is to some extent structurally analogous to how for Kant a human being that is naturally subject to empirical causal conditions and constrictions can nevertheless become positively free by placing his will under intelligible, supersensory ethical law. Sinlessness is the result of Love (Love as logical negativity) and exists only within it, within its dialectical logic, as a logical moment of it, not as an empirical flawlessness. By the same token, Christ's virgin birth is not his literal (biological or biographical) beginning, but the result of his obedience to the point of death, because only through it does he *make* God's Spirit his true father.[13] The end is the beginning. Myths and soul tales follow a uroboric logic.

Does it make sense, when one has understood this, to say that Christ "has chosen the light and denied the darkness"? Or that Christ "is one side of the self and the devil the other"?

And is it reasonable to think that today "We stand face to face with the terrible question of evil," in fact, that evil is a real *question* for us, and a terrible one at that? There are for us terrible evils and terrible evil-doing, but this fact does not pose a psychologically essential question for us. The soul in modernity is psychologically hard-boiled. It has accepted that imperfection is part of the world. For the soul in modernity, there is not such a thing as the act of Creation by an exclusively good God. The world originated in a Big Bang and developed through Darwinian evolution (these are not only scientific theories, they express our psychology). There is therefore absolutely no reason for making a fuss about "Whence comes evil?" The soul no longer naively believes in or is interested in the Good anyway, and so it cannot be psychologically or "metaphysically" shocked by the existing evil any more, despite the fact that empirical man (as ego-personality) is still likely to be emotionally shocked when confronted with concrete empirical events of evil. Hannah Arendt was psychologically right when she spoke of the banality of evil. We do not think in terms of Evil, a numinous idea, but soberly of crimes, e.g., crimes against humanity. And today we explain human evil-doing rationally as coming from cruel parents or other bad social conditions in early childhood, from a lack of character education, from genetic causes, from political and economic misery, etc. Evil is human, all-too human and an attribute for us, not a substance (as Jung wanted it to be with his violent fight against the *privatio boni* idea). And the devil has simply gone up into thin air. He is only a memory image from the past.[14]

We also ought to remember that the radical good versus evil, light versus darkness antinomy is a historical phenomenon and not an anthropological constant. It is relative to a certain stage in the development of consciousness and seems to have come up in those cultures that changed from a "shame culture" to a "guilt culture" at some time during the first millennium B.C., especially (in a religious-metaphysical sense) in ancient Iran (Zarathustra), spreading from there to other cultures, but also (in an ethical sense) with the Greek turn from *mythos* to *logos* in pre-Socratic philosophy (around 400 B.C.). As already Nietzsche showed, there is a *genealogy* of morals, an original social distinction between "noble, aristocratic" versus "ill-born, worthless" or a practical distinction between "brave, good, capable" versus "bad, cowardly" slowly having become transformed into the absolute moral or religious opposition of good versus evil. As everything historical, the absolute good-evil distinction, just as it began in time, so it also has an end in time. Today it has had its time: because it has done the job it had in the history of the soul, namely to raise consciousness to a higher level of itself by producing an extremely pronounced sense of "I" and "person." For modern consciousness it *ipso facto* has become psychologically obsolete.

I spoke of the logic of Love. Christian Love is nothing "natural," not an emotion, a feeling, a liking, a preference. But Jung refuses to enter the logic of Christian Love and into the concept of Love *as* a logic. When it comes to the topic of Love, his thinking stays completely naturalistic and naive. We see this most clearly when he insists that we today "can no longer swallow" that "a God who is a loving father, who is actually Love itself," demands the sacrificial killing of his own son in order to be appeased. First of all, this is again the naive kindergarten idea of Love and of God, God as a kind, good-hearted, loving father. But it is not only childish, it is also absurd: Jung construes a *conflict* between Love and the crucifixion (this absolute conflict is what makes the Christian idea impossible to swallow for him).

For his external concretistic thinking there are four separate items. (1) There is a God as an existing being, of whom (2) it is said that he happens to be loving and a "God of goodness." (3) In open contradiction to his being Love, he demands, however, the crucifixion of his son, because (4) only then can he forgive man. But for Christianity there is only one single reality here, the logic of Love, and everything else is moments of the dynamic of this logic. Love and the crucifixion of the Son are identical. The dying on the Cross IS the absolute *kenôsis*, the going under, the resistanceless bowing down under evil, and this IS nothing else but a spelling out of what Love is. And it is *in itself* and *as such* absolute forgiveness or redemption. No purchase of a desired salvation by paying a price for it.

This Love is nothing harmless and nice. It is a logic not in the spirit of the kingly, majestic logos of the Platonic tradition. And the fact that it is a logic does not mean that it is something abstract, a merely mental idea, cut off from life. No, it is—provided that it *is*—the actual *kenôsis* and "dying on the Cross" in real life. It *is* only if and to the extent that it is an existing logic, the logic of actually lived life. But conversely, the fact that it is lived life does not make it empirical-factual behavior or experience. It *is* something logical, intelligible, a thought, but a *real* thought.

To show how God fits into this one dynamic we can refer back to insights gained in our discussion of the Trinity above. The first point to make is that we must not situate and keep God outside and prior to the incarnation, as the Father who wants his Son to undergo this process. No, in "the Son" God himself became man. For the second point I can turn to the culmination of the incarnation, Christ's despairing cry from the Cross: "My God, my God, why hast thou forsaken me?" The incarnation or *kenôsis* completes and fulfills itself in the irrevocable death of the ontologized, substantiated God, which, however, is *ipso facto* the birth of God *as* Spirit and Love. Just as Christ's untaintedness by original sin is the *result* and *product* of his relentless humbling himself, so is God not the originator of the incarnation behind the scenes, but its outcome and product. Christianity is a New Beginning.

Psychologically, it is a grave mistake to see its God as a continuation of the Old Testament Jahweh, as *"answer to Job."* "Old things are passed away; behold, all things are become new" (2 Cor. 5:17). The Christian God is a new God, a new creation. And he is the (holy) *ghost* of the old imagined God: the result of his death, of his absolute *kenôsis*; the product of the distillation and evaporation of God as a being or figure. That is to say: God as Spirit, logos, pneuma and as the logic of Love.

By the same token, Christ's resurrection is not the undoing of his absolutely emptying himself of his divine nature, not a return to the *status quo ante*. His resurrection is nothing but his going under into the logic of Love.[15] Kerényi showed that the ancient Greek concept of god, *theos*, was a predicate, not a subject (in Greek grammar the vocative, the case of address or invocation, did not exist for *theos*): originally nothing was predicated of *theos*, but *theos* was predicated of other things. Helena, in the tragedy by Euripides of the same name, exclaims for example: "Oh gods, for it is god when one recognizes the loved ones." The event of recognizing those one loves is god. Another example: *deus est mortali iuvare mortalem* ("it is god for man, if one helps another person"). Linguistically, according to the form of the word, the original content of the name Zeus seems to have referred to the event or phenomenon lighting up or shining out and only later did it take on the meaning of the originator of this lighting up.[16] In the same spirit we could say that the resurrection as well as the new Christian God are nothing else but the happening of the logic of Love.

"God *is* Spirit" (John 4:24) and "God *is* love; and he that dwelleth in love dwelleth in God, and God in him" (1 John 4:16). The subject goes under into the predicate. These sentences do not speak of a being who happens to have the nature or quality of being spirit and love. When these sentences are spoken and ended, heard completely and comprehended, then what is left is Spirit and Love.

THE *NEW* GOSPEL ACCORDING TO ST. JUNG

I admit, referring to Jung as "St. Jung" is a bit malicious. But all the authors of a gospel are automatically canonized, and Jung with his super-myth is not writing as a psychologist, but is the author of a new gospel, new not in the sense of just another one parallel to the four existing gospels, but of a radically revised version, a "corrected" and "improved" one. What is the *gód spel*, the "good tidings," the *euangelion*, the "Good News," brought by Jung?

The point of the "Good News" is to bring hope into a seemingly hopeless situation. It shows that there is a way out of being lost in "sinfulness" and alienation from God. It asserts that, completely unexpectedly, the way to heaven and redemption is open, after all. So we have to begin with the hopeless situation into which and against which Jung proclaims his new gospel.

The truth of modernity into which Jung was born, a truth personally keenly felt by him already at the early age of eleven years[17] and later in his mature years repeatedly expressed, was that God is dead and that "Our myth has become mute, and gives no answers" (*MDR* p. 332). "No, evidently we no longer have any myth" (*MDR* p. 171). Today "we stand empty-handed, bewildered, and perplexed [...]" (ibid.). "There are no longer any gods whom we could invoke [...]" (*CW* 18 § 598).

Nietzsche said, "Dead are all gods: now we want the overman to live."[18] Analogously, Jung said in the same situation—not in these very words, but in what he did—"there are no longer any gods; our myth is mute: now we want God to come alive in the future." Jung's project is one of rescuing the core of the old religion by kicking it upstairs into the future and kicking the old version of it down into the irreality of one-sidedness.

The message of Jung's gospel is that God is by no means dead. The myth has become mute only because we did not develop ("construct") it further. The incarnation in the historical Jesus Christ was not at all the real thing. The real thing, the real truth, lies in the future. It is still coming. "*God wanted to become man, and still wants to*" (*CW* 11 § 739). The real incarnation and the true revelation of God still lie ahead of us.

A future promise and a roping modern man in for a great task, the task of individuation *as* God's incarnation, is the best way to make the dead God appear to be alive again. Life means future. And the feeling of having a great task, agenda, or mission in the world gives *psychically* reality to this idea of a future, because it means active involvement, "*striving* towards wholeness."

There is a reciprocity, indeed, identity of empirical man's individuation and God's incarnation. It is one and the same process, seen from two sides. "Just as man was once revealed out of God, so, when the circle closes, God may be revealed out of man" (CW 11 § 267). "The human and the divine suffering set up a relationship of complementarity with compensating effects. ... The cause of the suffering is in both cases the same, namely 'incarnation,' which on the human level appears as 'individuation'" (CW 11 § 233). "The dogmatization of the *Assumptio Mariae* points to the hieros gamos in the pleroma, and this in turn implies ... the future birth of the divine child, who, in accordance with the divine trend towards incarnation, will choose as his birthplace empirical man. This metaphysical process is known to the psychology of the unconscious as the *individuation process*" (CW 11 § 755, transl. modif.). "The future indwelling of the Holy Ghost in man amounts to a continuing incarnation of God. Christ, as the begotten son of God and pre-existing mediator, is a first-born and a divine paradigm which will be followed by further incarnations of the Holy Ghost in the empirical man" (CW 11 § 693). "That is the meaning of divine service [*Gottesdienst*], of the service which man can render to God, that light may emerge from the darkness, that the Creator may become conscious of His creation, and man conscious of himself" (MDR p. 338).

This is Jung's Good News. It is, of course, a utopia. However, be that as it may: "That is the goal, or one goal, which fits man meaningfully into the scheme of creation, and at the same time confers meaning upon it. It is an explanatory myth which has slowly taken shape within me in the course of the decades" (MDR p. 338).

But in order to give a future to God and his incarnation and revelation in empirical man, after Christianity had taught for 2000 years that the incarnation and the true revelation of God had already happened in Jesus Christ, this existing Christian message has to be rendered ineffective and defunct. Christ's incarnation was not a real incarnation at all. "... Christ on the contrary lives in the Platonic realm of pure ideas whither only man's thought can reach, but not he himself in his totality" (CW 11 § 263). "In the Christian symbol the tree however is dead and man upon the Cross is going to die, i.e., the solution of the problem takes place after death. That is so as far as Christian truth goes" (Letters 2, p. 167, to Victor White, 10 Apr 1954).

Positivism

But in Jung's scheme the Good News must not come as a new religion, the incarnation must not be through the birth of a new Messiah, and Jung not be a prophet. No, it has to be a Good News in the spirit of scientific, empirical psychology. Jung wants to appear as no more than an observer and interpreter of the historical phenomenology of religious symbolism *and* the phenomenology of the modern inner experience of people. And the Spirit or Holy Ghost is for him not really spirit and teacher at all, not the event of a deeper understanding of the logic of Love and its becoming more real. No, "He is the spirit of physical and spiritual procreation who from now on shall make his abode in creaturely man" (*CW* 11 § 692). Physical and in creaturely (i.e., natural) man, man as animal! The statements about the development of the Trinity "can—and for scientific reasons, must—be reduced to man and his psychology, since they are mental products which cannot be presumed to have any metaphysical validity. They are, in the first place, projections of psychic processes, and nobody really knows what they are 'in themselves,' i.e., when they exist in an unconscious sphere inaccessible to man" (*CW* 11 § 268). "If such a process exists at all, then it must be something that can be experienced" (*CW* 11 § 447, transl. modif.). Following the Gnostics Jung thinks that Christ ought to be *real* "as a psychic centre in all too perilous proximity to a human ego," "as an inner, psychic fact," as "Christ within" (*CW* 11 § 446). Before I said that Jung's project is one of rescuing the core of the old religion by kicking it upstairs into the future and rendering the real Christian message defunct. Now I have to add that it is at the same time one of kicking the incarnation down into the positivity and literalism of a personalistic development and private experience in the empirical man as factual individual—as the individuation process.

Whereas psychology would locate the incarnation, if I may say so, *in Mercurio*, in the coldness and remoteness of the logic or syntax of the *soul*, and comprehend it as the appearance and continued deepening of a real dawning of the objective *insight* into the logic of Love in the culture of our Western world, Jung psychologistically and concretistically stuffs it into the *psyche* as the appearance, in *people's* private dreams or visions, of certain symbols (symbols of "the self").

Psychology is reduced to anthropology (a "psychology" of people, cf. Jung's "must be reduced to man"), and what is a soul *truth* is either reduced to an experience or to an image. What actually is a question of the syntactical form of consciousness or of the logic of man's being-in-the-world becomes something semantic. Jung operates with the binary opposition of "metaphysical validity" versus "can be experienced." But the Trinity, being a soul truth, is neither a metaphysical claim nor can it be experienced. The emergence of the idea of the Trinity is the manifestation of a transformation of consciousness, from the mythological and naturalistic Father stage to the fundamentally post-natural stage of Spirit and Love. The change from one stage or logical status of consciousness is something very real (nothing speculative, not an assertion of metaphysical entities), but it cannot be an experience, inasmuch as it is something syntactical and not something semantic, something psychological and not something psychic.

The correlate of experiences (even of so-called "numinous" experiences!) as well as of images is the modern ego. "Images" have their logical home in our modern world of television, advertising, slogans, labels, clichés, graphic arts, illustrations, pictures, and "experiences" belong to our modern world of entertainment, emotionality, excitement, thrillers, sensationalism. Whether images and experiences appear out there or inside people does not change their logical status. The *soul* has no stake in images, nor in private experiences. The soul is about truths, it exists in concrete universals, in logical *forms*.

Christianity's answer to Jung's Gnostic "Christ within, as an inner, psychic fact" is Matth. 18:20: "For where two or three have gathered together in My name, I am there in their midst." This does not mean that—naturalistically—Christ miraculously shows up among them. No epiphany, no literal appearance. Christ's *reality* is not the crude positivistic or naturalistic presence in literal experiences. It is a "subtle" reality, purely *logical*, intelligible: the logic of an interpersonal (communal) being-together *if* it is truly one *"in My name."*

With his concept of "the self" Jung tried to translocate the *objective-soul* character of the soul from its being all around us as the generality of a soul *truth* or as the general logical form of consciousness into each private individual and imprison it there, into "the empirical man," who, as Jung well knew, is synonymous with the ego ("the ego—that is, the empirical man" *MDR* p. 346, cf. "man—that is, his ego" *MDR* p. 337,

"the ego, i.e., the empirical, ordinary man as he has been up to now"
CW 11 § 233, transl. modif.).

Soul truths are logically negative. But they have everything they
need within themselves, including their realness. To the extent that
Jung operates with the disjunction or dissociation of two abstractions,
Christ living in "the Platonic realm of pure ideas whither only man's
thought can reach" here and "incarnation in creaturely man" there, he
shows that he has left the realm of soul, which—as truths or general
logical form—is neither, but comprises both.

Jung's psychologistic positivism goes hand in hand with a
metaphysical hypostatizing. Although he denies the possibility of
assigning "metaphysical validity" to the psychic processes that he has
in mind and says that they are no more than projections, he nevertheless
toys with the idea of an *Ansich* ("what they are 'in themselves'") and of
their existence independent of or outside human consciousness. This
is the same mystification as whether there is a difference between the
allegedly empirical images of the self and god-images and whether
behind the god-images in the soul there might or might not be an
existing God. Soul truths are neither positivistic nor metaphysical. They
neither need our emphatically exercising an artificial restraint
concerning their "validity" in the deliberate style of the empirical
scientist, nor any mystifying speculation concerning what they might
be "in themselves." They *are* what they are and suffice themselves. They
are existing concepts, existing logical form. They within themselves
encompass or permeate the mind just as well as the real.

THE DISREGARD OF THE HISTORICAL, PHENOMENOLOGICAL EVIDENCE

Jung's positivism is the result of his retrograde clinging to the logical
form of *myth* (substantiated figures, semantic contents) *at a time* that
had long left the form of myth behind and was well advanced on its
way into Spirit, i.e., syntax, logical form. He was already on the level
of logical form, so that by trying to rejuvenate myth what he came up
with was of course not myth in its authentic sense, but positivism,
semanticized modernity, modern so-called "myth," i.e., ideology.

I said, "Spirit, i.e., syntax, logical form." I take this opportunity
to expressly point out that "spirit" must by no means be understood
in terms of the popular idea of and widespread craving for so-called
"*spirituality*." The latter is a mystification and inflated abstraction. But

psychology has to stay down to earth and feel committed to concrete phenomena. It has to be able to account for what it is talking about. Much like the *Zeitgeist* is the inner form or soul of a real age, so our concept of spirit refers to the inner logical form of real phenomena. And just as the syntax of a given language can be analyzed, so the logical or syntactical form of real soul phenomena is (and must be) analyzable, demonstrable, communicable, not only an inner experience beyond speech. Spirituality is, as it were, one of our consumer goods; it is for people's subjective indulgence and gratification. Psychology has to be committed to the objective soul and its truths. Also, spirituality is the *remythologizing* understanding and *naturalistic* conception of the very thing that, as spirit, is precisely the overcoming of mythological image and naturalistic, substantiating thinking. Psychology must conceive of spirit "in spirit and in truth," rather than reifying it as "spirituality."

When one looks at "the case" that Jung presented for his utopia, one is struck by the fact that he spun his yarn mostly from very old material (Old Testament, New Testament, especially the Apocalypse, certain immediately pre-Christian Jewish texts, Gnostic texts, Church Fathers) plus one single isolated event from modernity, indeed from his own lifetime, the declaration of the Dogma of the *Assumptio Mariae* by Pope Pius XII in 1950. It is really a stray and rather obscure event, at the periphery of our real world, a piece of the Middle Ages belatedly emerging completely out of context in modernity and of no noticeable further consequence or impact, although Jung considered it "The only ray of light" (*MDR* p. 332) in our benighted days, which, however, only confirms how isolated it is.

This is a very thin phenomenological basis for a grand theory about soul history and what is historically needed today. Jung prided himself upon his empiricism. But except for a few passing references to Joachim of Flora, Meister Eckhart, Jakob Böhme, in other words, references merely to individual *semantic* phenomena, *the whole real development* of Western culture over the centuries, the rich phenomenology of the *real history of the soul* in the West, is ignored, that powerful history in which a consistent series of tremendous *form changes* concerning the syntactical constitution of consciousness took place. It is amazing that an empirical researcher passes the major mass of evidence by. What we think ought to have happened or ought to happen is psychologically neither here nor there. Psychologically relevant is only what in fact comes out in the "documents of the soul," the actual phenomenology of the real. Psychology has the task of studying the soul in the Real. It has to go by what actually happened in order to find out what the soul's *opus* is. Not archaic myth and not the texts of 2,000 years ago (which are only relevant for historical psychology), but the development that led to where we or rather where the soul is now have to be the basis for our conclusions.

Western culture underwent a historical development in which, as Jung correctly noted, among other things "The otherworldliness, the transcendence of the Christian myth was lost" (*MDR* p. 328). And this probably provides the answer why Jung did not deign this historical material worthy of his *psychological* attention. The soul, this was his bias, (a) simply had to be about transcendence, it had to be a soul *with* a God, and (b) only what had the form of mythic or archetypal image and of natural, personified figure, only what was substantiated—semantic—, could be considered as psychologically relevant. Jung was unable (or unwilling) to see that the mentioned consistent evolutionary progress in the direction of a *transformation* of consciousness—which is precisely what Western history is about and what is its absolutely unique achievement—is exactly that *real* "further development" of the Christian "myth," that *real* "further development" of the incarnation that he demanded (although of course as a very different one from his idea of it). It is the consistent deepening of the *kenôsis* and a movement from myth to logos, from substance to Spirit (logical form, syntax, function). God had become man. How could Jung expect him to still be transcendent and otherworldly? God himself had died on the Cross. "My God, my God, why hast thou forsaken me?"—was this to be no more than an isolated one-time cry by one particular individual, without any consequences and without any *truth*, that is, without *general* validity? Just a subjective experience, literal personal suffering? Of course not. The process of the integration and realization of the *kenôsis* was the Western soul's *opus magnum*.

"The further development of the myth should probably begin at the point where the Holy Ghost was poured out upon the apostles and made them into sons of God..." (*MDR* p. 333, transl. modif.). Jung sees that the point of this further development is the spirit. But he refuses to see that the historical *form change* hinted at by me *was* the work of the spirit and the only way how the workings of the spirit could manifest themselves. Jung wants to begin with the spirit alright, but he has no relation to spirit and therefore does not see the spirit where it has already long in fact realized itself. For him the spirit is not spirit at all, but simply another event belonging to *mythological* and *ritualistic* cultures: a status change of the *human persons*, namely their divinization ("that they were more than autochthonous *animalia* sprung from the earth, but as twice-born ones had their roots in the deity itself," *ibid.*, transl. modif.). This is something for which the Christian Holy Ghost is certainly not needed, since this was what in the initiations performed by the pre-Christian cultures of the mythological and ritualistic age had been perfectly achieved all along.

With Christianity the "Holy Ghost" *stage* of consciousness had been entered. This is something totally different from the task of turning people into sons of God. It is about a new syntax and as such beyond people's psychology and their inner experience and individuation process. In the Bible, the story of the outpouring of the Holy Ghost upon the apostles is not presented as turning the latter as individual persons into sons of God at all. It has nothing to do with their own inner process, their self-actualization. Rather, this outpouring leads to a *linguistic miracle*, the speaking "with other tongues," a speaking that is understood by all "in our own tongue, wherein we were born." Psychologically and symbolically understood this points to the fact that the spirit expresses itself in something general or universal, communal, in language, in logos, in something that is interpersonal (or transpersonal) and public (just as Christ's presence requires communality, the congregation, *ecclesia*: "For where two or three have gathered together in My name, I am there in their midst"). Not individuation, nothing private and personalistic. Rather, other *tongues*, new general *logical forms* of consciousness, *within which* individual persons may have their place.

Although with Christianity the "Holy Ghost" *stage* of consciousness had been entered, it nevertheless took about fourteen centuries until man's implicitly already being in this new stage was really caught up with and the new truth had been integrated into the very structure of consciousness, its syntax or logical form. The very further development of the "myth" that Jung demanded and projected into the future had already happened in real history. But because it had happened in the objective soul, in the general logic of man's being-in-the-world during the early modern period (starting early with Dante, Meister Eckhart, Nicholas of Cusa, the Renaissance and the Reformation and continuing up to Kant and Hegel) rather than in creaturely man as positive-factual individual and because it as a matter of course amounted to the loss of "the otherworldliness, the transcendence of the Christian myth" and to the death of God as a semantic content, as a mythic god, a being or figure, Jung had to reject, condemn, and ignore it. God as a mythic figure and the archaic phenomenon of man's "*filatio*—the sonship of God" (*MDR* p. 333) had to be preserved at all cost, or rather atavistically reinstituted, which at the same time amounted to the scotomization of the whole level of syntax or logical form and to psychological consciousness's being restricted to focusing on semantic phenomena. And so Jung came up with a compromise formation. The very thing responsible for the actual historical dissolution of the transcendence of God, namely the Holy Ghost, was rightly supposed to be the point of departure for the further development of the Christian myth, but, as Jung's "further *construction*," it was supposed to be a matter of the future, of future incarnations of God in empirical man as the latter's private individuation or self-actualization.

THE CAMPAIGN FOR THE REALITY OF EVIL

Summarizing the moves necessary for Jung's theosophy to come about we can say:

Both the Incarnation and the "further development" were long accomplished facts in the real history of the soul. This their reality character had to be denied, they had to be rendered ineffectual and negligible (1) through the one-sidedness thesis concerning the Christian message and (2) through the psychological-irrelevancy thesis concerning the actual development of Western culture. The latter was denounced as merely expressive of ego-consciousness and abstract rationality, whereas the soul was declared to be active only in niches, in subcultures like Gnosticism, alchemy, heretic movements, the modern Roman Catholic Church, and of course inside of man in the famous "the unconscious." What had already happened and become real in the past had (3) to be unhinged and projected into the future as a new program, whereby a *retrograde* move donned itself as its opposite, a *utopia*. What was and would have to have the form of a soul truth had (4) to be newly construed as a positive-factual event

and experience in empirical man; a concrete universal had to be reduced
to a private occurrence. And (5) the God who had already distilled
over and vaporized into Spirit and Love had to be repaganized,
remythologized, resubstantiated as a figure; this was tantamount to
the view that the core of the Christian message, the logic of Love or, as
Jung put it, the "gospel of love," was "one-sided" and needed to be
"supplemented ... with the gospel of fear" (CW 11 § 732). Jung's
message that God is not dead falls, inevitably has to fall, behind the
logic of Love and brings the "Good (?) News" that "*God can be loved
but must be feared*"[19] (*ibid.*, Jung's italics).

The lever to perform this feat was the idea of the reality of evil and
that *the* important psychological question that we are confronted with
today is evil. Evil is the cornerstone in Jung's theosophic edifice. The
topic of evil in Jung's thinking has its origin (efficient cause) not in
phenomenology, in an empirical observation that evil is a central soul
topic, which it clearly is not today (except for some fundamentalists
who speak for example of an "evil empire" or an "axis of evil"), but needs
to be understood in terms of its *causa finalis*, the functionality it has
for the edifice of Jung's thinking about religion and God. Evil was an
absolute necessity for his project of exposing Christianity as one-sided.

By declaring evil as *the* terrible question that modern man is faced
with and by passionately rejecting the *privatio boni* idea of evil, the
devil as a personified embodiment of evil could be resurrected and, far
beyond the question of the devil, the renewed pagan, mythological
mode of thinking in terms of personified figures could be solidified.
Of course, historically the devil had long been obsolete, even more than
God. But other than God, who has no practical anchor in real life for
modern man, evil behavior and tendencies, what we call the shadow,
are still a concrete experience and very real. With this experience of
the reality of evil acts or motivations Jung could catch the psyche of
modern man, touch him at his weakness, his unconscious guilty
conscience due to his subliminal awareness of his personal shadow
aspect and inferiority feelings. "Evil" emotionalizes. The absolute moral
opposition and the hopeless "collision of duties" bring man into a
terrible, but indispensable fix ("between hammer and anvil") and *ipso
facto* corner him, nail him down, forge him into a positivity.

On the one hand, this could be used to boost evil up to become a
quasi metaphysical substance, the devil as a reality. On the other hand,

this alchemical solidification and congealing of man in his positivity *is* the individuation in Jung's sense. Individuation means that the *psychological* is translated into something *psychic*, something literal (a process aiming at the ontic individual), that the soul is brought down and reduced from logical negativity to positivity. The soul (as the self) was not allowed to be only "underworldly" and to have its place only "*post mortem*" in "*'eternal'* life" "yonder." It had to be an immediacy here in this life as a psychic event.[20]

But this individuation as positivization was at the same time God's incarnation in empirical man, in creaturely man, man as literal individual. The one only happens *as* the other. God, too, had to become a positive experience, literal. It was not enough for him to be something in or for the soul, in faith and in a beyond. "I do not believe, I know." Jung obviously had fully understood that *for the soul* God was dead. In the logic of the soul God was obsolete. For this reason God could only be rescued or resurrected if he took his abode in empirical *man* (rather than in the soul), in other words, as something positive, as our *knowing* (no longer as faith, Love, and hope), as the immediate factual experience (*Urerfahrung*) of literal man. This is why psychology—actually psychologism (psychology anthropologized, personalistic)—was indispensable. "I cannot help believing that the real problem will be from now on until a dim future a psychological one."[21] God had to become incarnated (in Jung's new sense) *through* man's individuation (positivization), just as individuation could only occur through God's incarnation in the empirical man.

Jung could not want a new religion. It was clear to him that the time of religion, of Church, faith was over. Or rather, he could not want religion *in the logical form* of religion. He needed to preserve it in the form of "modern psychology," the "psychology of the unconscious." The place where it was to happen, the place where the real action was to be, was the empirical man's inner, his unconscious, "in all too perilous proximity to a human ego," "as an inner, psychic fact" (*CW* 11 § 446). The notion "God" had to be hid and stored away in "the unconscious" and given asylum in the absolute privacy of the inner experience of the literal individual, because it could no longer have a place in public "official" consciousness and in the *general* logic of modernity. Only in "the unconscious" and in the privacy of inner experience was God put out of reach of and immunized against consciousness and the critical mind, and had the notion God become absolutely unaccountable and unassailable, because it was merely subjective: "God is an immediate experience of a very primordial nature, one of the most natural products of our mental life, as the birds sing, as the wind whistles, like the thunder of the surf. ... You can just be glad to have such a conviction, like a man who is in a happy frame of mind, even if nobody else, not even himself, knows why, but certainly nobody could prove to him that he is unhappy or that his feeling happy is an illusion" (*Letters 2*, p. 253, to Snowdon, 7 May 1955). The incarnation had to become a positive fact in creaturely man. It was not allowed to be truly psychological: a mercurial reality, strictly intelligible, the logic of Love, and, above all, a *truth*. The singing of birds is not a moment of truth. It is only a natural event, and feeling happy is a subjective state.

Jung, as we have seen, operated with the abstract binary opposition between pure idea and positivity. For the soul's mercurial logic, which is neither merely intellectual nor a positivity, but nevertheless a reality, namely the reality of absolute negativity, there was no room in his thinking, at least his thinking about God.

"*The guilty man is eminently suitable and is therefore chosen* to become the birthplace for the continuing incarnation" (*CW* 11 § 746, transl. modif., Jung's italics). More than that: God is downright dependent on creaturely man and on the latter's superior awareness to become conscious of his, God's, own full reality, including his shadow. It is "evil," the "shadow," that gives—this is Jung's thesis—three-dimensional concreteness, earthly weight, and positivity to what otherwise would only be abstract thought, and forces God down into the empirical man.

Since the idea of God as an only good and loving Father had for the modern soul long degenerated into a sentimental cliché without the least power of conviction, merely an empty word, and had made "God" utterly boring, Jung's shocking ideas of the reality of evil and of the necessity of the "gospel of fear" had the function of making the topic God psychically exciting and lively once more. And Jung's harnessing the psychological mind for the task of "lodg(ing) the antinomy [between good and evil] in Deity itself" (*CW* 11 § 739) drew all attention to this great problem and so helped to divert the mind from the fact that this being, God, in whom the antinomy was to be lodged, was no longer real for it. If the devil or evil was a reality once more and if, furthermore, evil was to be internal to God, the faded idea of God received a seeming reality, too.

Only by integrating evil as substance (or as its personified and mythologized form, the devil) into the very nature of God as one of the latter's inherent aspects, could the God idea psychologically be reanimated and given again a seeming reality of its own, the God idea which by Jung's time had become a mere airy reminiscence of what former ages believed in.

Here we may want to remember that despite his frequent insistence on a *gnôsis theou*, God was apperceived by Jung primarily not at all as a truth and in terms of knowing, insight, revelation, but in terms of power: as an "opposing will" (*CW* 11 § 290), "a powerful *vis-à-vis* (*MDR* p. 335), a "numinosity and the overwhelming force of that numinosity" (*MDR* p. 336), as something "which sets us at odds with ourselves" (*Letters 2*, p. 28, to Schär, 16 Nov 1951). As what crosses our own human will it is obviously in itself already "the Adversary"! The prototypical construction of this God-concept seems to have happened during Jung's twelfth year, when the thought about the beautiful Basel cathedral being smashed by a huge excrement dropped by God came to the boy Jung, and he reacted with the questions, "Who wants to force me to think something I don't know and don't want to know? Where does this terrible will come from? ... *I* haven't done this or wanted this, it has come on me like a bad dream. ... This has happened to me without my doing" (*MDR* p. 37). As can be shown,[22] at least in this one instance the whole idea of the "terrible will" that forced him to think something that *he* does not want is an artifact of the boy Jung's making. This "overwhelming force" was by no means a spontaneous experience, a "phainomenon" (something that showed itself of its own accord). Rather, God as this "opposing will" was nothing else than the projection and hypostasis of his resistance, his refusal (i.e., *his own* opposing will) to think his own thought, a thought necessitated by his inner maturation process and aiming for his becoming undeceived about his cherished existence in childhood paradise and in childlike innocence. But if "God as terrible opposing will" was at this early time the result of Jung's own machinations, it is likely that these machinations were also the prefiguration for and *logical origin* of his mature ideas about God.[23] And then we see immediately why the integration of evil in the nature of God was indispensable for him. The reality of this God, born out of Jung's own powerful resistance, hinged upon God's "Adversary"-character.

Through his "incarnation," Jung had said, this God would come into "all too perilous proximity to [the] human ego." The ensuing peril was inflation (that the empirical man identified himself with God). Jung was only able to structurally, logically evade the danger of inflation by taking recourse to a dissociation. He had to split the identity of the I into the ego and the self. Contrary to the actual meaning of "self," which as reflexive pronoun refers back to the subject (the I), the self had to be a full-fledged other to the ego, a not-I. By the same token, consciousness had to be artificially split into two, consciousness itself and its other, "the unconscious." Although, for Jung, God incarnated in the empirical, creaturely, guilty man, he did not incarnate in him as conscious personality, but only in his unconscious and as the symbol of the self. By having shelved the incarnated God in the unconscious, Jung had, to be sure, to live with a fundamental dissociation, but in return gained the advantage of not having to make any metaphysical claims of his own or stand up as a religious teacher. All he did, so he at least thought, was to innocently describe facts, his empirical observations of the self or the God-images in the unconscious, "Christ within." He was only a scientist presenting his facts-based theory.

The dissociation is the telltale sign that Jung's project of individuation as God's incarnation in the empirical man does not work. As a content of "the unconscious," the self or the incarnated God is just as "only ideal" and just as out of reach for the ego as the Church God was for the traditional believer prior to the integration of the devil into God. The incarnation cannot be one in the empirical man, unless it were really to happen to the I, which, however, must not happen because it would be tantamount to inflation and psychosis. The dissociation cancels the "empirical-factual" aspect of the incarnation in Jung's sense. And it is how the soul's logical negativity appears when it becomes positivized (the *un*-conscious, the self as *not*-I).

We have seen that Jung's ideas about evil are not only, and maybe not predominantly, theoretical ideas or insights. What is at least as important is the psychological function they perform for Jung's psychology and for him personally. Jung's whole thinking about God, the incarnation, the Trinity, had the character of a utopian program. It was up in the air. The ideas of evil and the shadow had an anchor in the concrete personal experience of each individual. As such they had the psychological function to (psychically, for our human feeling) ground Jung's utopian views in empirical reality. This was Jung's deepest longing: to give *reality* and *conviction* to what he (unconsciously) felt was utopian or a mere ideology, a *counter-factual* agenda of his own (the rescue of God in modernity) against his already knowing better.[24]

This makes comprehensible the obsession with which Jung fought against the *privatio boni* idea about evil. It is very interesting to see how Jung tries with all his might to *rationalistically argue* against and disprove this idea as if it were nothing but an intellectual concoction, rather than a psychological idea. He needed to show that it was a *wrong* idea. But this is unpsychological, just as unpsychological as would be the insistence that, for example, the "virgin birth" is a wrong idea. Right and wrong are false categories for psychology. Jung himself warned of an "artificial sundering of true and false wisdom," of one's succumbing "to the saving delusion that *this* wisdom was good and *that* was bad" (*CW* 9i § 31, transl. modif.). "As psychologists we are not concerned with the question of truth, ..., but with living forces, living opinions which determine human behaviour. Whether these opinions are right or wrong is another matter altogether" (*Letters 2*, p. 417, to von der Heydt, 13 Feb 1958). When he expressed these views, he spoke as a psychologist. But when it comes to evil and to God, Jung ceases to be a psychologist, even if his intellectual argument against the *privatio boni* is that it is *psychologically* false, bad for the psyche. The *privatio boni* may be a metaphysical assertion, but is it not precisely as such also "a psychic fact which cannot be contested and needs no proof" (*CW* 11 § 554, adjusted)? It has first of all been a psychological phenomenon, the soul truth of many centuries of the history of the soul in the West. It is absolutely pointless to argue for or against a phenomenon. But precisely because it is first of all a phenomenon and only secondarily a rational philosophical justification of this phenomenon, Jung needed so passionately and obsessively to attack it and prove it wrong as if it were *only* an intellectual theory. He needed the deified "opposing will," or else his resistance against his own insight into the truth of modernity would lose its seeming justification. His program was, after all, a counter-factual one.

But that evil is a *privatio boni* makes perfect sense within the logic of Love. For this logic, evil is not a substance, not, for example, the body, particular desires, drives, or passions. It is not anything ontic, a natural "entity" like "the shadow." Nature is neither good nor evil. No, evil is something logical and, as such, negative (a *privatio*): namely one's NOT *negating* one's natural impulses and naturalistic imaginal perspectives, one's NOT placing oneself under supersensory ethical laws, one's NOT humbling oneself all the way and NOT (logically) bowing under the evil and evils in the world. It is the *omission*, or rather *refusal*, to overcome, time and again, one's "original sin"[25] by rising to the sphere of logos and the concept.

NOTES

1. Another question is whether there is any need for an *answer* to Job in the first place. Is the book of *Job* not itself the very answer to the question that according to Jung it raises, namely the question of the justice or injustice of God? It would seem to me that the very point of this book is to radically destroy the naive (Old Testament and Near Eastern) belief that ideas of morality and justice can be applied to God and that there could be a contractual relationship between man and God as if between equal partners or between feudal lord and vassal that would bind God in any way. Jung's thesis, however, is precisely that in contrast to Jesus Christ "Job ... was an ordinary human being, and therefore the wrong done to him, and through him to mankind, can according to divine justice, only be repaired by an incarnation of God in an empirical human being. This act of expiation is performed by the Paraclete; for, just as man must suffer from God, so God must suffer from man. Otherwise there can be no reconciliation between the two" (*CW* 11 § 657). What kind of consciousness is it that thinks about human misfortunes and terrible suffering as a "*wrong* done to him" (by God/Fate/Life) and as obviously requiring the repairing of an injustice? Do we have a vested right to be well-treated by life and to fairness? A category mistake. Behind it all is the innocent childlike belief in and demand for an ideal world and a good and just God. "We [modern man] have experienced things so unheard of and so staggering that the question of whether such things are in any way reconcilable with the idea of a good God has become burningly topical" (*CW* § 736): the

kindergarten idea of a good God! This consciousness was, to be sure, shocked to have to *semantically* admit that there is "unjust" suffering and terrible evil, but it is able to *logically* or *syntactically* defend its innocence by putting the cause for this suffering down to God's unconsciousness, his unconscious shadow, so that the *category* of God's justice remains unchallenged despite the forced acknowledgment of the *empirical* experience of what seems to contradict it. At the same time, consciousness can entertain the dream that there of course will have to be a full-fledged "reconciliation between the two." Jung's insistence that the gospel of love needs to be supplemented by a "gospel of fear" (*CW* 11 § 732) is a reflection of the innocence that still prevails in his consciousness. A psychologically mature consciousness knows that we live, so to speak, in the jungle, where a question like "Whence comes evil?" simply does not make any sense. But Jung insists on living in the innocence and "boundlessness of 'God's world.'"

2. As to "doubts" cf., e.g., "... Christ nevertheless seems to have had certain misgivings in this respect" (*CW* 11 § 691).

3. C. G. Jung, *The Visions Seminars*, From the Complete Notes of Mary Foote, Book One (Zürich: Spring Publications, 1976), Part One (Lectures October 30 – November 5, 1930), pp. 7f.

4. Cf. "... it is just the Trinity dogma, as it stands, that is the classical example of an artificial structure and an intellectual product..." (*Letters 2*, p. 423). But when Jung continues: "... It is by no means an original Christian experience...," we see that he operates with the binary opposition of "original experience" (which allegedly is not an intellectual product, but purely "natural") versus "artificial structures." He does not realize that even "original experiences" are as a matter of course intellectual products and "artificial," although more *implicitly* and *subliminally* so. The notion of "the unconscious" as pure nature is a mystification.

5. To be more exact and to avoid the impression of my making a metaphysical statement on my part, I should correct myself and say: for *methodological* reasons psychology has to *view* this difference as not existing. Psychological statements are only psychological if for them it does not exist. Psychology is the discipline of interiority: absolute interiority, that is to say, for it the difference between inside and outside is canceled. Everything that belongs has been absolute-negatively interiorized into the image or statement in question.

6. Whereas originally *theologos* simply meant "him who says the gods" and above all referred to the poets, nowadays theology is the name for the scholarly, rational unfolding and systematic explanation of Christian self-understanding (Christianity is the only religion that developed a theology in the strict sense). There is no room in it for what Jung means by "developing the myth further." But because this further development is Jung's concern, the term theosophist, "he who knows about God," seems more appropriate. However, we have to be clear about the fact that Jung does not claim to have *revelatory* knowledge of his own about God, like prophets do. Much like the theologians, he devoted himself to a careful interpretation of already given religious documents and ideas. But he drew forth from them a very different "myth" than the Christian self-understanding, a "myth" all of his own. It bases itself more or less exclusively on the Jewish and Christian corpus (except for the strong Gnostic slant), but makes something very different out of it. Because of this supcrimposed "overlay" character, his is an already reflected, one might almost say: meta-level, religion, the product of a modern intellect. This is an intellect which, as intellect and modern, nevertheless longs for a *religion* (although it calls it "myth"); it will not make do with a scientific worldview. What Jung did not see is that this religion is a compensation for long lost real religion and precisely *not* a further development of the Christian "myth" itself from within itself. Most revealing in this context is the term *Weiterbau* or *weiterbauen* that Jung sometimes uses for "further development" (e.g., several times in the German equivalent to *MDR* pp. 331-334). In contrast to a self-movement of the myth, *Weiterbau* means "further construction," an active doing. And so it is not surprising that Jung blames the ego: "The fault lies not in it [the myth] as it is set down in the Scriptures, but solely in us, who have not developed it further...," he says explicitly (*ibid.* p. 332). The *Weiterbau* of the myth is an ego obligation and ego work. Jung would of course protest (his explicit general theory is the opposite: "It is not we who invent myth, rather it speaks to us as a Word of God," *MDR* p. 340), but this is nevertheless what his own text here betrays.

7. Already the charge that Christianity is one-sided shows that Jung took on the role of arbiter over the soul's real development.

Who are WE to meddle in the soul's process with our value judgments? Do we not have to allow the soul to do its thing, whatever it may be? For a psychologist the real history of the soul is not one-sided or wrong; it simply is the way it is and needs to be described, interpreted and appreciated for what it is, but in any case as a full-fledged expression of soul. Only the soul itself would have the right to find situations produced by it one-sided and possibly in need of correction.

8. A contradiction in terms. *Genuine* myths are the soul's speaking about itself, its self-representation in a particular one of its many possible logical "moments," not attempts at explaining anything.

9. Cf. Jung's letter to Hans Schär, 16 November 1951, *Letters 2*, pp. 28f., where he discusses why he could not "avoid sarcasm and mockery" in writing *Answer to Job*. "Sarcasm is the means by which we hide our hurt feelings from ourselves, and from this you can see how very much the knowledge of God has wounded me..." From this statement one would have to conclude that the true author of *Answer to Job* was not C.G. Jung, the psychologist, but one of his unresolved complexes. In the preface to this book Jung writes that "Since I shall be dealing with numinous factors, my feeling is challenged quite as much as my intellect" (*CW* § 559). Why does he write a book about a topic when he is still personally gripped by its "numinosity"? Why did he not see it as his obligation as a psychologist to work off (to have long ago worked off for himself) this "numinous" affect and overcome his feeling "wounded" by it? Why has there not long been a scar, but is there still a wound? (The answer would probably have to be that "God must not die!" and that certain emotions [being gripped by something "numinous," a counter-will] and feeling wounded is Jung's form of a proof of the existence of God.)

10. I have to add here: or a psychologist.

11. *MDR* translates this violent expression meekly as "conflict of duties." Instead of "torn apart" Jung also uses the idea of being "caught between hammer and anvil" (*MDR* p. 345).

12. It is not transcendence that makes God be a God who is NOT of this world. To be transcendent is the most natural thing for a god. It is precisely part of our ordinary, this-worldly idea about God.

13. Soul and soul truths are *made*, not discovered as already existing facts, as if one could stumble upon them.

14. On the devil see Gustav Roskoff, *Geschichte des Teufels. Eine kulturhistorische Satanologie von den Anfängen bis ins 18. Jahrhundert* (Köln: Parkland, 2004, originally Leipzig 1869).

15. Similarly, "hell" is not naturalistically a place for burning people after death, and "damnation" not a future fate. "He that believeth on him is not condemned: but he that believeth not is condemned already, because he hath not believed in the name of the only begotten Son of God" (John 3:18). The damnation that Christianity speaks about is inherent in, and no more than one's not finding one's way into, the logic of Love.

16. Karl Kerényi, "*Theós*: 'Gott' auf Griechisch." In: *Idem, Antike Religion* (München: Albert Langen, 1971), pp. 207-217, here pp. 210–214.

17. See my "Psychology as Anti-Philosophy: C. G. Jung," in: *Spring 77* (Philosophy and Psychology), June 2007, pp. 11–51.

18. Friedrich Nietzsche, *Thus Spoke Zarathustra*, at the very end of Part One.

19. In other words, *love*: maybe, at times, optionally; but *fear*: indispensably, inevitably. From the point of view of the Christian truth God cannot be loved because God has transformed into Love itself so that he ceased to exist as a possible object of our love. The only way to still speak of God is in the style of what Kerényi taught us about the Greek word *theos*, as a predicate, not a subject. "It is god for man if one has in fact one's place in the logic of Love." And the moment you are in fear you are no longer (or not yet) up to the Christian truth, up to the logic of Love. For in this Love, fear cannot hold out.

20. Repeatedly Jung sees critically cases where a solution does not happen in this life. Cf. above his statement, "In the Christian symbol the tree however is dead and man upon the Cross is going to die, i.e., the solution of the problem takes place after death. That is so as far as Christian truth goes" (*Letters 2*, p. 167, to Victor White, 10 Apr 1954). Or concerning Goethe's *Faust*: "... the conclusion of *Faust* contains no conclusion" (*MDR* p. 318). "... Faust's final rejuvenation takes place only in the post-mortal state, i.e., is projected into the future" (*CW* 12 558). "It is an unconscious reality which in Faust's case was felt as being beyond his reach at the time, and for this reason it is separated from his real existence by death" (*Letters I*, p. 265 to Anonymous, 22 March 1939). A psychological view would not interpret the solution's

happening in a post-mortal state as a sign for its being projected into the future, but for its taking place *psychologically*, i.e., in the logic of the soul and "in spirit and in truth," rather than in the sphere of empirical *psychic* experience.

21. *Letters 2*, p. 498, 12 April 1959, to Werner Bruecher.

22. See my "Psychology as Anti-Philosophy: C. G. Jung," in: *Spring 77* (Philosophy and Psychology), June 2007, pp. 11–51.

23. This view is also corroborated by another event in Jung's life, his Uriah dream and the discussion of it in *MDR* pp. 217 ff. See my "Jung's Millimeter. Feigned Submission – Clandestine Defiance: Jung's Religious Psychology," unpublished.

24. Because evil was *the bridge* necessary for God to be able to come down and incarnate in "the guilty man" and because this incarnation means that each of us becomes a son of God (even if only "in the unconscious"), evil had, in the last analysis, also the function of rescuing for Jung personally the grandiosity of the psychological ("metaphysical") child-status, the *filiatio*. "Ye are gods"—precisely by "metaphysically" staying children.

25. "Original sin," in a psychological sense, means the discrepancy between man's implicitly having become human and thus having logically sublated his animal nature, on the one hand, and his explicitly staying a priori conditioned by his emotions and desires, on the other hand, emotions and desires which of course are the *human*, and thus post-natural, already fantasy-guided equivalent to the animal's animal nature, its instincts. "Natural" means something different depending on whether it refers to humans or to animals (or even to inanimate nature, for that matter). Our impulses are "natural" for us humans, mere events, but as impulses of *humans* they are *in themselves* beyond the merely natural. They are already, although of course only implicitly, ideas or concepts (in contrast to mere triggered "release mechanisms").

" ... UNTIL GOD'S ABSENCE HELPS!"

DAVID L. MILLER

Furchtlos bleibt, aber, so er es muss, der Mann
Einsam vor Gott, es schützet die Einfalt ihn,
Und keiner Waffen brauchts und keiner
Listen, so lange, bis Gottes Fehl hilft.

—Friedrich Hölderlin[1]

The epigraph, from which the title of this response to Wolfgang Giegerich's essay is taken, is from the last lines of Friedrich Hölderlin's poem, "Dichterberuf" ("The Poet's Vocation"). It is one of the poems in which Hölderlin affirms that the vocation of the poet is to name the gods,[2] but the author acknowledges that this may be impossible, because, as he puts it in other poems on the same theme,

David L. Miller, Ph.D., is the Watson-Ledden Professor of Religion, Emeritus, at Syracuse University, and a Core Faculty Person (retired) at Pacifica Graduate Institute. His teaching and writing are in the areas of Religion and Myth, Depth Psychology and Literary Theory. Dr. Miller has taught at the Jung Institute in Zurich, Switzerland, and in the clinical programs at Pacifica Graduate Institute in California, as well as having given seminars in Jung training programs in Los Angeles, Toronto, San Francisco, Chicago, New York City, Kansas City, Pittsburgh, and Kyoto. In 2002, Dr. Miller was elected to be an Affiliate Member of the Inter-Regional Society of Jungian Analysts, and in 2004 he was made an honorary member of the International Association of Analytical Psychology. He is the author of five books and more than one hundred articles and book chapters. For more information, see the website: http://dlmiller.mysite.syr.edu.

the times are "destitute" and "holy names are lacking."³ This announced
vocation is related to Giegerich's observation, with reference to Karl
Kerényi, that originally the Greek word *theologos* ("theologian") meant
the one who "says the gods" and that it referred to poets.⁴ According
to Hölderlin, in the contemporary world the task of naming the gods
is especially difficult, not only because the times are destitute and
holy names are lacking, but because in the past "all that is divine
has been exploited for gain," the "powers of heaven have been trifled
away," and generations have "ungratefully used up divinity for their
own pleasure." Meanwhile, God, according to Hölderlin, "does not
like what is savage," i.e., inappropriate naming, and so He has "covered
our eyes with holy darkness."⁵

Now, as the lines of the epigraph say, people stand alone (*Einsam*).
It would seem that the only help is in naïvete (*die Einfalt*), since ego's
tools of power (*Waffen*) and cleverness (*Listen*) are of no use. In fact the
real help in this situation will be when God dies (… *bis Gottes Fehl
hilft*) and people are thrust deeply back upon themselves. The poetic
thinking of Hölderlin seems at odds with itself: namely, that the absence
of God might be useful in the time of the darkness of God. Such
thinking may seem to some as strange, just as the argument by
Wolfgang Giegerich about Christianity and Jung's view of it in the essay
"God Must Not Die!" may seem strange to some. It is the apparent
strangeness of such arguments—Hölderlin's and Giegerich's—that I
want to address in my response.

Specifically, I would like in this essay to attempt to contextualize
the perspective of Giegerich's argument, not psychologically, but
theologically. I find Giegerich's psychological argument so compelling
and powerfully reasoned that I have no quarrel with it at all, neither
with his psychological reading of Christianity nor with his critique of
Jung. But what I find interesting to think further about is how
Giegerich's argument relates, not to the psychological tradition, but
to the theological tradition. I want to attempt to locate his
psychological reading of Christianity theologically. What I should like
to demonstrate is that the argument is not far out and weird, but
actually fitting to Christian theo*logic*, and I shall specifically look at
four of Giegerich's central points in connection with early, medieval,
modern, and postmodern *theo*logy.

1. "God himself ... died on the cross." Already early in his argument about Christianity and when speaking of the notion from Philippians of *kenôsis* ("emptying"), together with Jesus' utterance, citing a Psalm, "My God, my God, why hast Thou forsaken me?," Giegerich says that "Christ's death on the cross" implied "the absolute loss of God." Then late in the essay, when speaking about Jung's resistance to the historical and phenomenological loss of a transcendental sense of the Christian myth, precisely because of Jung's assumption of the identity of soul and transcendence, Giegerich counters, affirming this loss of a transcendental referent, that "God himself had died on the cross." This implies that what in these latter days has come to be associated with Friedrich Nietzsche—"the death of God"—is actually built into Christianity from the beginning. In a recent work the theologian Thomas J. J. Altizer has said basically the same thing. Altizer writes: "Why is it not possible to understand the death of God as occurring in the crucifixion itself?"[6] and, again he says, "Crucifixion is ultimately the crucifixion of God."[7] For Giegerich, this is a critical insight *psychologically* because it makes possible for *soul* to manifest in a "consistent deepening of the *kenôsis* and [in] a movement from myth to logos, from substance to Spirit. God had become man. How could Jung expect him [God] to still be transcendent and otherworldly.... The process of the integration and realization of the *kenôsis* was the Western soul's *opus magnum.*"

This may sound a bit strange to some *theologically*, but, as Altizer implies, it is a Christian theological idea that is very old, even if in ways that Altizer does not entirely approve. The idea has a name: *Patripassionism* (also "Sabellianism," "modalism," and "monarchianism").[8] The name "patripassionism" is made up of the words "*pater*" (= Father) + "*passio*" (= suffer), and expresses the notion that God suffered on the cross. This was a view that existed from the time of the early Church, and it was based on a Trinitarian theologic. The reasoning was that the Trinity, in order *not* to be construed as tritheism (three gods), had to be thought of as radically monotheistic. Modalists note that the only number associated with God in the Bible is one. So the so-called "persons" of the Trinity were not persons at all—which would be a pagan polytheistic and mythic perspective—but were modes (hence modalism or modal monarchism). The divine is one essence, appearing interchangeably as Father, Son, and Spirit in different periods of time. If the divine is a unity, the crucifixion is the death of God the Father as well as Jesus the Son.

There is Biblical support for this perspective. For example, according to the Scripture, Jesus says: "I and the Father are one" (John 10:30) and "anyone who has seen me has seen the Father" (John 14.9). And this view persists into the contemporary world in Oneness Pentecostalism and, according to some, Emanuel Swedenborg.[9]

The patripassionist perspective is often attributed to Sabellius, though little is known about this person, and the perspective is only known through the anti-heresiologists, especially Tertullian, who may well have misconstrued the teaching and reasoning because of his bias against it.[10] In fact, the evidence is that Sabellius' views were not a minority opinion, but were supported by large numbers of early Christians, However, in addition to Tertullian, Cyprian, Dionysius, Demetrius, and Hippolytus (who said that he knew Sabellius),Victorinus and others, Church theologians declared Sabellius' views to be heretical. The second general council at Constantinople in 533 declared his baptism to be invalid, but not before *patripassionism* had become a part of the complex tradition of Christian thinking. As Giegerich puts it: "God himself had died on the cross." From this it is a small, but crucial step, to the next insight.

2. "… Trinity means … God's dying as the Son on the Cross into his truth as Spirit …."[11] For Giegerich, to whose psychological thinking a Trinitarian logic is so important,[12] this reading of the Trinity points to dynamic process, "a logical distillation-evaporation process of the idea of God, of its going under into itself in the sense of its self-sublation into Spirit." This is important because, as Giegerich says, "the Christian message required a *spiritual* understanding," and "spiritual" here is *itself* to be understood, not in letter, but "in spirit." Giegerich makes a Johanine text central to his argument, the command to worship "in spirit and in truth" (John 4.23), a phrase he repeats in the present essay like a mantra over and over again. The reason for this is that psychologizing, if it be true to the name of the logic of soul, is also to be understood as having the logical status of being "in spirit." The referents of psychological discourse are transformed from being understood as natural (in the order of God's creation of all beings) or

as literally developmental or historical (like the Jesus of history or the Christ of the Church's dogma). As Giegerich puts it, "the mythical or imaginal God, the God as a substantial being or person as he exists for and in *our* standard naturalistic thinking, is dissolved." Additionally, one may observe, as Giegerich does, that

> the Trinity, being a soul truth, is neither a metaphysical claim nor can it be experienced. The emergence of the idea of the Trinity is the manifestation of a transformation of consciousness, from the mythological and naturalistic Father stage to the fundamentally post-natural stage of Spirit and Love. The change from one stage or logical status of consciousness is something very real (nothing speculative, not an assertion of metaphysical entities). But this change cannot be a human experience, inasmuch as it is something syntactical and not something semantic, something psychological and not something psychic.

"Spirit" and "love" do not refer to objects in the empirical world.

Once again, this viewpoint may sound a bit odd to some conventional Christian ears, i.e., it may sound odd that the theo*logic* of God the Father and Jesus the Son, who is taken to be the Christ, implies that these are superseded (or as Giegerich says, sublated). After all, popular Christianity has largely been binitarian, not Trinitarian, focusing on God and his nature and Jesus and his history, not knowing quite what to do with the Spirit, if not fearfully suppressing it altogether, except in some extreme forms of evangelical Christian ritual and some New Age spirituality.[13] But, in spite of this witting or unwitting omission in conventional Christianity, the emphasis upon the dynamic process of coming into Spirit is not unknown to the serious, and not pop, Christian *theo*logical tradition, even though this is hardly disclosed in orthodox Sunday School lessons. I am thinking, of course, of Joachim of Fiore, whom Giegerich mentions in passing (along with Meister Eckhart and Jacob Böhme, both of whom also focused on Spirit).

Joachim of Fiore lived in southern Italy at the end of the twelfth century.[14] After a trip to the Holy Land in his mid-twenties he became a hermit and applied himself to intense Biblical study. He was ordained a priest in 1168 or thereabouts. His views are contained mainly in three books: *Harmony of the Old and New Testaments, Exposition of the Book of Revelation,* and *Psaltry of Ten Strings.*

Joachim's version of the "eternal gospel" mentioned in Revelation 14.6 included a reading of the history of Christian ideas that involved a dynamic process. It began with an understanding of religion as the obedience of people to the laws of God (the Age of the Father), continued through the transition enacted when God became human (the Age of the Son), and culminated in a time of a new dispensation (the Age of the Spirit). The Age of the Spirit was to have begun in 1260 C.E. (see Revelation 11.3 and 12.6, both of which mention 1260 "days"). This new age was not to be manifested by the *parousia,* by the second coming of Christ, but by a new time of peace in which the "location" of religion would be "in spirit,'" making the hierarchy of the Church, the outer and external religious institution, unnecessary. The ages of God the Father and Christ the Son in the person of Jesus would have been superseded.

Whether in Joachimite theology or in Giegerich's psychology of Christian thinking, the reading of the logic of the Trinity as the dynamic process of the coming of religious understanding in(to) "spirit" implies a transformed location (*topos*) of religion. It no longer abides in an external and literal reference to transcendental objects. This transformation of understanding leads to a third thematic.

3. "The so-called transcendental object does precisely not exist." The whole sentence from which this phrase in Giegerich's essay is taken indicates that it is the difference between an image and its transcendental referent that does not exist, but the implication is that *psychologically,* unlike for Jung, the transcendental object does not exist. This surely puts Giegerich at odds with conventional Christianity, just as he observes that it puts him at odds with what is at least implicit in Jung. In footnote five of his essay, Giegerich explains that he does not intend this statement to be understood metaphysically or theologically. That is, he is not making an onto-theological statement about the being or non-being of objects that some persons may imagine or believe to be "transcendental." Rather, this is a perspectival or epistemological statement (Giegerich calls it "methodological"). Soul psychology, as opposed to ego-psychology, views a *difference* between an image and its referent as not existing because psychology is a science of interiority, absolute interiority, so that the difference between what ego conceives of as "outside" and as "inside" is bracketed. The images of, say, dreams,

fantasies, myths, and religious narratives have all they need within themselves. That is, they are their own self-referents. For Giegerich this is a depth psychological insight, but once again there appears to be a connection between his view and a modern theological development.[15]

Amos Wilder, in a book published in 1976, wrote about a movement in Christian theology of culture that he called "theopoetics." Wilder, a Harvard University Biblical scholar, said: "I believe that I had picked up the term 'theopoetic' and 'theopoiesis' from Stanley Hopper and his students, no doubt in one or another of the remarkable consultations on hermeneutics and language which he had organized at Drew and at Syracuse to which many of us are indebted."[16] Wilder is alluding to conferences at Drew University in 1962,[17] 1964, and 1966,[18] and a fourth conference at Syracuse University in 1970.[19] These consultations were located intellectually at the intersection of left-wing Bultmannian Biblical interpretation ("demythologizing"), the thought of the late period of Heidegger's existential phenomenology, and the Religion and Literature movement. The first conference focused on hermeneutics and Biblical interpretation. The second, a follow-up to the first, was more theological. In the third and fourth conferences, literary and philosophical perspectives were added.

Because of the centrality of Heidegger's perspective on language and poetry to these events, prior to the second consultation Stanley Hopper, Dean of the Graduate School of Drew University, and Karfried Froelich, a colleague of Hopper's, visited with Heidegger at his home in Germany and they invited him to be in attendance. He agreed. But as things turned out, because of illness Heidegger could not come to the United States. Instead, he sent a letter in which he urged three questions upon the deliberations: (1) what is the nature of the referent of theological utterance; (2) what is the nature of thinking that is objectifying; and (3) is a non-objectivizing thinking and speaking possible?[20]

The problematic of objectivizing discourse is theologically the problem of idolatry, i.e., making God or Being into *a* god or *a* being, a some*what* or a some*thing*.[21] The challenge of Heidegger's questions is to ask whether it is possible to think theologically without positing, at least by implication, a transcendental object and thereby committing idolatry. It may well be that all human speech reifies its subject in some manner simply by using nouns and verbs, i.e., by naming things and by referring to actions. But it does not follow—or so it was the experiment of these consultations to probe—that all language has to be read always as objectivizing. It may be possible to view language as performing an entirely different function: namely (to use Heideggerian language), to bring Being to appearance, to allow the unveiling of Truth (*a-letheia*), and to let that which *is* appear *as* that which it is.

The "as" is crucial. Already in *Being and Time*, Heidegger had argued that all language has an *as*-structure, i.e., that it is interpretation or construction (*poiesis* = "a making").[22] In the third Drew consultation, this led to the implication that theology is not actually a theo-*logy*, but is ineluctably theo-*poetic*, where poetry is interpreted as radical metaphor. Beda Allemann referred to such radical metaphor as "anti-metaphor" or "absolute metaphor,"[23] and Stanley Hopper, following Philip Wheelwright, called it "diaphor" as opposed to "epiphor."[24] That is, one is not viewing poetry as mere metaphor, simile without the word "like," which would be the expression of the likeness of like things, ignoring difference and fragmentation and multiplicity. Such a weak reading of the notion of metaphor would constitute a reinscription of objectivization and of the onto-metaphysical tradition in which Being is viewed as *a* being or God as *an* idol.

Hopper saw this move in the direction of a radical poetic (interpretive or hermeneutical) consciousness as "theopoetical," and he said, in his introduction to the third consultation: "What *theo-poiesis* does is to effect disclosure through the crucial nexus of events, thereby making the crux of knowing, both morally and aesthetically, radically decisive in time."[25] The attempt of a theopoetical perspective in religious discourse is to de-nominalize and de-objectivize theological referents in a manner consistent with the apophatic intentionality of what has been called negative theology.[26] The point is that theopoetical discourse does not have as its reference transcendental objects, because it does not have objects as referents at all. It is theopoetical perspective unfolding into self-expression. In Giegerich's terms, the logical status of its utterance is "in spirit." This implies one other phrase in Giegerich's essay.

4. "Christianity is the overcoming of theism as such." This phrase comes in Giegerich's essay at the end of the paragraph in which he is discussing the dynamic of the Trinity, i.e., "God's dying as the Son on

the Cross into his truth as Spirit." In fact, each of the three central points that I have so far highlighted—1. God himself dying on the cross; 2. Trinity means God's dying as the Son on the Cross into his truth as Spirit; and 3. The so-called transcendental object does not exist—implies clearly that Christianity is the overcoming of theism, i.e., it is a going-beyond a positive belief in a posited deity that reassures me and my people salvifically (both the belief and the deity function to save individual and collective "me," where the "me" is also a posited identity). Such a the*ism* would be the opposite of faith, since a theism works as a guarantee that does not need faith. It is something upon which "I" can be dependent, like a drug or opiate or illusion. Theism does not imply faith; it only needs belief.[27] It is an –ism. An –ism takes matters out of the realm of spirit and places them ontologically in reality, i.e., it objectivizes and concretizes spirit in matter. It is what earlier I called idolatry. It ignores the view of Christianity as God dying as the Son on the Cross so that Spirit, but not some transcendental object, lives. We live in it, not it in us.

Once again, Giegerich's reasoning has a corresponding context in a postmodern theological movement: namely, the movement referred to as the Death of God movement. I am thinking especially of the recent work of Thomas J. J. Altizer and Mark C. Taylor, but their perspective has roots almost fifty years ago in the so-called "death of God" movement of the 1960s.

This issue of the continuing importance of the "death of God" in religious studies and theology, after its earlier announcement in the 1960s, has recently emerged in reviews of three books by celebrated authors: *Living the Death of God: A Theological Memoir* by Thomas J. J. Altizer, *After the Death of God* by John D. Caputo and Gianni Vattimo, and *After God* by Mark C. Taylor.[28] In her review Lissa McCullough carefully distinguishes the perspectives on the "death of God" represented by these books' authors. For Caputo it is the "ongoing work of the critique of idols," i.e., the death of finite human views of the infinite divine. For Altizer the "death of God" is a real death, a final and irrevocable transformation of God. For Taylor the matter is dialectical and complex, neither a positing of something positive as it is for Caputo nor the positing of something unambiguously negative as it is for Altizer. For Vattimo it is Christendom that has failed (i.e., died) in its lack of charity and love.²⁹ These differences matter because they imply different functions for the word "after" in two of the books' titles, as Jeffrey Kosky has noted in his review. For example, for Vattimo, and presumably also for Altizer and Taylor, "after the death of God" means "living on in the wake of God," whereas for Caputo "after the death of God" means "we can put the death of God behind us and be nourished anew by the name of 'God.'"³⁰

These thinkers do have something in common, according to McCullough. They all may be viewed as "apologists for the vocation of straying toward an infinite nothing, or erring 'after God,' or waiting for the Messiah who never comes, or loving one's neighbor in the void as the only alternative to the bad faith of arbitrarily declared absolutes."³¹ But the significant difference is that Caputo, according to Kosky, thinks that "postmodernism is and should be done with the death of God."³² Whereas Altizer, on the other hand, according to McCullough, believes that "we live in an era when it is thinkable to discuss a 'religion' without rituals and beliefs, a 'faith' purged of religion, a 'theology' without God, and an atheism that is 'an expression of faith itself.'"³³

Like Giegerich, both Altizer and Taylor take clues for their (*theo*)logics from Hegel, not so much the Hegel of the metaphysics of spirit, but the Hegel of the logic, and especially the part of the dialectical logic that speaks of absolute negation, or the negation of the negation. The idea of the negative in the "negation of the negation" has to be subtly understood. In another essay, Giegerich insists that negative is not to be taken as negative evaluation (the opposite of positive evaluation) or as saying no (the opposite of affirming something). Rather, negative is over against "positive" in the sense of positing something, as suggesting that some-*thing* is existing. Giegerich gives an example from the field of law. The written laws of governments are positivities, he says. But

> the idea of justice, by contrast, is something different. Many actions and many court decisions may be fully in agreement with positive law, but we may nevertheless feel that justice has not been done. Justice is logically genitive, which does not mean bad or undesireable, but rather the opposite. Justice can*not* easily be spelled out; it is *not* tangible, visible. And in this sense it is 'negative.'³⁴

Justice—like love, soul, God, etc.—is not a *thing*, not a posited object. Further, absolute negation "is not the negation of the content, the semantics. It is the negation of the logical form of the content."[35] And the syntactical and logical negative that Giegerich is pointing to is "absolute negativity" because it "is 'absolved,' freed, from the binary opposite of something versus nothing." Justice is not something, but it is also not nothing. It is other than yes and other than no.[36] One can see from this why Giegerich would say that "true religion" is negative.[37] It is not a something (this would be idolatry or ideology); but it is not nothing (which would be a positing of a negative positivity). It is beyond theism and, of course, by the same logic it is beyond atheism. As Mark Taylor says about the work of Thomas J. J. Altizer: "Altizer's theological vision ... provides an eloquent testimony to the *impossibility* of theology in a postmodern world. Theology ends with the death of God."[38] And the end of the "-ology," like the end of the "-ism," ends a soteriological (salvationist) version of Christianity.[39]

For both Taylor and Altizer, the clue to a reinvigorated logic for religion is Hegel's dialectical logic, just as Hegelian logic is crucial to Giegerich's argument concerning depth psychology. Giegerich's version of Hegel's insight goes this way.

> The dialectical process does not begin with Two, but with One, with a *Position*. ... by committedly sticking to this one position ..., the mind discovers, or is forced to admit, that this position proves to be untenable.... This experience amounts to a *Negation* of the initial position. If before the position was A, the negation of the position results in non-A,... The negation, if tested, again proves to be untenable and is accordingly negated. So we get the *Negation of the Negation* (not- [non-A]). But the negation of the negation as such is *Absolute Negation* and as such the reinstitution of the original *Position* (=A). However it is now the Position on a fundamentally new level, because it is no longer the 'naïve' (immediate) position of the beginning, as a simple given, but *mediated* and tremendously enriched by the history of all the negations.... It has been greatly differentiated, is much more subtle, refined."[40]

This Hegelian notion of absolute negation that is at the same time not a negative some*thing* leads Thomas Altizer to conclude: "As always, our most powerful theology is a negative theology."[41] And it is not surprising that both Taylor and Altizer, like Giegerich in the present essay, focus on the dynamic of *kenôsis,* "self-emptying," as critical to their understandings, not unlike Meister Eckhart's prayer, "I pray to God that he may make me free of 'God.'"[42] *Kenôsis* is an emptying of ego's positivities (things posited).

* * *

I have been attempting to show that there is Christian theological contextualization for Giegerich's radically psychological reading of Christianity, a reading that means to correct Jung's holding on to transcendental objects in his Christian revisionism. There is ancient Patripassionism (God died on the cross), a medieval Joachimite Age of the Spirit (a radical Trinitarianism), a modern theopoetics (decrying objectivization), and a postmodern death of God theology (announcing the end of the*ism* and a religion that will save human beings). But now I need to add a caveat to my own attempt. The theological movements that I have identified are finally theology and not psychology. They may sound similar semantically to Giegerich's argument, but syntactically they hold back from a perspective "in spirit."

Patripassionism retains a mythic view of the divine figurations. Joachim seems to have been (ironically) literal about the spirit. Theopoetics has more recently become theopoetry, i.e., simply the use (and misuse) of metaphor and image in literature to assert the same belief contents, without a change of consciousness, of earlier dogmatic religion. And the death of God theology is (at least in the persons of Taylor and Altizer) unable to make the transformation to psychology, in fact there is a resistance and blindness concerning the radicalness in depth psychology, a continuing to mistake soul-psychology for ego-psychology and personal-psychology. So, these theological movements finally do not represent the same perspective as that of Giegerich's essay.

But then Giegerich's essay does not need shoring up or being authorized theologically. It is a psychological argument. It is finally different from the theologies that I have cited. It is its own thing. It represents one more installment in Giegerich's insistence on keeping depth psychology from back-sliding into ego-psychology.

In fact, one may argue that the four movements to which I have referred are marginal. I have already mentioned that Sabellius was declared to be heretical by significant Church Fathers and his baptism was declared invalid by the second council of Constantinople. Pope Alexander IV condemned Joachim's writings and he set up a commission that in 1263 at the Synod of Arles declared his theories heretical. Aquinas argued against Joachim in the *Summa Theologica* and the Fourth Lateran Council in 1215 also condemned his ideas. Needless to say, official Christianity was not keen on a view that makes the hierarchy and the mediatorial function of the Church unnecessary. Theopoetics has become theopoetry, as I have already mentioned above, i.e., it has become, against its original intent, simply the use (and misuse) of metaphor and image in literature to assert the same belief contents, without a change of consciousness, of earlier dogmatic religion.[43] The Death of God movement, though it received a lot of press in the 1960s, is hardly alive and well as an alternative interpretation of Christianity, and everyone knows the quirky and radically edgy reputation of death of God theologians like Altizer and Taylor. So, someone could question the *importance* of my reference to such marginal, if not heretical, movements in relation to Giegerich's argument.

My response to those who question the importance of marginal moments in Christendom is that however much some theologians would like to delegate these movements to the radical fringe, they are nonetheless in fact a part of Christianity and its thinking about itself. Further, it strikes me as interesting that the intuitions that Giegerich is arguing for seem to have been present already in parts of the Christian tradition. As Giegerich says: there seems to be a "slow coming alive of the inner spirit of the message [of Christianity] from within itself," as if there was "a spiritual [i.e., psychological] understanding already there from the beginning." Again, Giegerich says: "This radical dynamic movement of kenôsis is the thought and intuition that was the assignment given by early Christianity to all future generations to be thought through, to be slowly more and more comprehended and integrated into consciousness." In my attempt to confirm this, I have also tried to imply that it is as if Christianity wanted to be psychology all along! and still wants to be! Perhaps psychology, taken as a way of living and perceiving, can be experienced as the realization of the moment when—as the poet put it—at last God's absence helps.[44]

NOTES

1. *Hölderlin,* tr. Michael Hamburger (Baltimore: Penguin Books, 1961), p. 138. "But with fear a person remains such a long time, as he or she must, alone before God, being protected by simplicity, needing no weapons or craftiness, until God's absence helps." (My translation.)

2. See Stanley R. Hopper, "On The Naming of the Gods in Hölderlin and Rilke," ed. C. Michalson, *Christianity and the Existentialists* (New York: Charles Scribners' Sons, 1956), pp. 148-190. Cf. Wolfgang Giegerich, "Beisichsein im Anderen: Hölderlin," *Animus-Psychologie* (Frankfurt am Main: Peter Lang FmbH, 1994), pp. 170-74.

3. "Heimkunft" ("Homecoming"), *Hölderlin,* p. 134: "*es fehlen heilige Namen.*" "Brot und Wein" ("Bread and Wine"), *Hölderlin,* p. 111: " *... wozu Dichter in dürftiger Zeit?*" See also Martin Heidegger, "Wozu Dichter?" *Holzwege* (Frankfurt am Main: Vittorio Klostermann, 1972), pp. 248-95 (English: Martin Heidegger, *Poetry, Language, Thought,* tr. A Hofstadter [New York: Harper, 1971], pp. 89-142). On the Heideggerian description of "destitute times" as synonomous with the concept of "the death of God," see Simon Critchley, *Very Little ... Almost Nothing* (New York: Routledge Books, 2004), pp. 14, 115, 227.

4. See Giegerich's footnote #6.

5. "Dichterberuf," Hölderlin, p. 137.

6. Thomas J. J. Altizer, *Living the Death of God: A Memoir* (Albany: SUNY Press, 2006), p. 106.

7. *Living the Death of God,* p. 98.

8. I am grateful to Patricia Cox Miller for alerting me to this connection.

9. Basic information about "Patripassionism" can be found at http://en.wikipedia.org/wiki/Patripassionism, accessed August 15, 2009.

10. Basic information about "Sabellianism" can be found at http://en.wikipedia.org/wiki/Sabellianism, accessed August 15, 2009. See Tertullian, *Adversus Praxeas,* ch. 1.

11. Giegerich's actual sentence is the following: "The Trinity means, mythologically expressed, God's dying, as the Son (as the transitional form), on the Cross into his truth as Spirit and Love; his dying as a God of this world into a "God" who is NOT of this world and ipso

facto God *sensu strictori* no longer." See the present author's treatment of the saying of Jesus in John 16.6: "Truly, truly I say to you, it is to your advantage that I go away, because if I go away the Paraclete [i.e., Spirit] can come to you": "The Paraclete: Ghosts of Scripture," *Hells and Holy Ghosts* (New Orleans: Spring Journal Books, 2004), pp. 137-44; and, "Holy Ghost and the Grateful Dead," *Eranos 52-1983* (Frankfurt am Main: Insel Verlag, 1984), pp. 277-346, especially pp. 314-24.

12. See *Animus-Psychologie,* pp. 323-58.

13. The point that certain forms of practical and pop spirituality belong to the domain of ego and not to psychology in Giegerich's sense is confirmed by Huston Smith in an interview on NPR's "Morning Edition," on December 1, 2000. Lynn Neary did a special on "The Changing Face of American Religion," i.e., on how "spirituality" is replacing mainline religion. The point of most of the interviews was that it doesn't matter what you pick, all religions take you to the same place. But when it was Huston's turn, he was not so sure. He said: "Organized religion gives spirituality traction. Without it spirituality can become a self-centered pursuit. Spirituality is individual and subjective, and it can refer indiscriminately to experiences of elevation and joy, sort of the cream on the cream puff of life. Many people take a salad bar approach to spirituality, picking and choosing what's easy from different traditions often leaving the hard parts behind. The danger of the salad bar approach is that it worships Saint Ego, and it assumes that you know what you need."

14. Basic information about Joachim can be found at http://en/wikipedia.org/wiki/Joachim_of_Floris, accessed August 15, 2009.

15. Paul Kugler's mapping of the demise of "transcendental signifiers" seems on the face of it similar to Giegerich's claim that the transdendental object does not exist. Kugler observes, with Saussure, that "there is no fixed point outside particular systems of meaning relations, no transcendental referent ...." (*The Alchemy of Discourse* [Einsiedeln: Daimon Verlag, 2002], p. 105). In another essay, Kugler writes about the "twilight of our god-terms" (e.g., truth, reality, center, self, unconscious, soul, wholeness, unity, origin, wish, energy, etc.), and he says: "The more we attempt linguistically to account for the authority of these ultimates, the more the absoluteness in our god-terms begins to deliteralize, dissolve, and disappear. ... all systems of

interpretation gain their authority through a grounding in a god-term, a transcendental 'ultimate,' but this 'ultimate is no longer so absolute, so ultimate" (*Raids on the Unthinkable* [New Orleans: Spring Journal Books, 2005], pp. 36, 37). However, the diction of Kugler's statements sounds semantic rather than syntactic, implicating his discourse in ontological claims. This would mark a difference from Giegerich.

16. Amos Wilder, *Theopoetic: Theology and the Religious Imagination* (Philadelphia: Fortress Press, 1976), p. iv.

17. The proceedings of this consultation were published in James Robinson and John Cobb, eds., *The New Hermeneutic* (New York: Harper & Row, 1964).

18. The proceedings of this consultation were published in Stanley R. Hopper and David Miller, eds., *Interpretation: The Poetry of Meaning* (New York: Harcourt, Brace and World, 1967).

19. For a review of the first three of these consultations, see Stanley R. Hopper, "Introduction," in Hopper and Miller, eds., *Interpretation,* pp. ix–xxii. Much of what follows in the next paragraphs is indebted to Hopper's account. Cf. David Miller, "Theopoiesis," in Stanley R. Hopper, *Why Persimmons and Other Poems* (Atlanta: Scholars Press, 1987), pp. 1–12.

20. Hopper, "Introduction," in Hopper and Miller, eds., *Interpretation,* p. xiv. This letter, without attribution of its context, appears in Martin Heidegger, *The Piety of Thinking: Essays by Martin Heidegger*, tr. James G. Hart and John C. Maraldo (Bloomington: Indiana University Press, 1976).

21. See Henry Corbin, "Letter," in D. L. Miller, *The New Polytheism* (Dallas: Spring Publications, 1981), pp. 1-6.

22. Martin Heidegger, *Being and Time*, tr. J. Macquarie and E. Robinson (London: SCM Press, 1962), pp. 188-91.

23. Beda Allemann, "Metaphor and Anti-Metaphor," in Hopper and Miller, eds., *Interpretation*, pp. 103-24.

24. Stanley R. Hopper, *The Way of Transfiguration,* R. J. Keiser and T. Stoneburner, eds. (Louisville: Westminster/John Knox Press, 1992), pp. 166, 249, 288-90, 295, 298, 300. See also Philip Wheelwright, *Metaphor and Reality* (Bloomington: Indiana University Press, 1962), pp. 85, 88, 91.

25. Hopper, "Introduction," in Hopper and Miller, eds., *Interpretation,* p. xix. Compare Hopper's other writings on theopoetics,

especially those collected in Hopper, *Way of Transfiguration*, pp. viii, 1–4, 9, 12, 169, 298 and *passim*. For example: "Theo-logoi belong to the realm of mytho-poetic utterance and . . . theo-logos is not theologic but theopoesis" (p. 225).

26. See Chris Boesel and Catherine Keller, eds., *Apophatic Theologies: Negative Theology, Incarnation, and Relationality* (New York: Fordham University Press, 2009), pp. 137-46.

27. On the difference between "faith" (Greek *pistis*) and "belief" (Latin *credo*), see David L. Miller, *Gods and Games: Toward a Theology of Play* (New York: Harper Colophon Books, 1973), pp. 166-67.

28. The reviews alluded to are Lissa McCullough, "Death of God Reprise: Altizer, Taylor, Vattimo, Caputo, Vahanian," *Journal for Cultural and Religious Theory*, 9/3 (2008): 97-109 (www.jcrt.org); Jeffrey L. Kosky, "Review of *After the Death of God* by John D. Caputo and Gianni Vattimo, ed. by Jeffrey W. Robbins," *Journal of the American Academy of Religion*, 76/4 (2008): 1021-25; and, John D. Caputo, "Review of *After God* by Mark C. Taylor," *Journal of the American Academy of Religion*, 77/1 (2009): 162-5.

29. McCullough, "Death of God Reprise," p. 107.

30. Kosky, "Review," p. 1024.

31. McCullough, "Death of God Reprise," p. 108. As Altizer puts it, "As always, our most powerful theology is a negative theology" (Thomas J. J. Altizer, *Living the Death of God: A Theological Memoir* [Albany: SUNY Press, 2006], p. 125).

32. Kosky, "Review," p. 1022.

33. McCullough, "Death of God Reprise," p. 107. See Altizer, *Living the Death of God*, p. 93.

34. Wolfgang Giegerich, "Once More 'The Stone Which Is Not a Stone': Further Reflections on 'Not,'" C. Downing, ed., *Disturbances in the Field: Essays in Honor of David L. Miller* (New Orleans: Spring Journal Books, 2006), p. 128-29.

35. "Once More 'The Stone,'" p. 132.

36. "Once More 'The Stone,'" p. 131.

37. "Once More 'The Stone,'" pp. 129, 131.

38. Mark C. Taylor, "Introduction" to Altizer, *Living the Death of God*, p. xviii.

39. See David L. Miller, "Eschatizing the Soteriological: Worlding the Word" (a review of *Praise of the Secular* by Gabriel Vahanian), *Journal for Cultural and Religious Theory*, 10/1 (Winter 2009): 118-123.

40. Wolfgang Giegerich, David L. Miller, and Greg Mogenson, *Dialectics & Analytical Psychology: The El Capitan Seminar* (New Orleans: Spring Journal Books, 2005), pp. 5-6.

41. Altizer, *Living the Death of God*, p. 125.

42. For example, see Altizer, *Living the Death of God*, pp. 12, 109, 118, 135, 150, 164; and Taylor, *After God*, p. 202. The Eckhart prayer is in his sermon, "*Beati paupers spiritu, quoniam ipsorum est regnum caelorum*" [Blessed are the poor in spirit, for theirs is the kingdom of heaven], in E. Colledge and B. McGinn, trs., *Meister Eckhart: The Essential Sermons, Commentaries, Treatises and Defense* (New York: Paulist Press, 1981), p. 202, compare pp. 248-49.

43. See the website http://theopoetics.net/. And see Giegerich's warning about "metaphor" in "Once More: 'The Stone Which is Not a Stone': Further Reflections on 'Not,'" in C. Downing, ed., *Disturbances in the Field: Essays in Honor of David L. Miller* (New Orleans: Spring Journal Books, 2006), p. 137.

44. Compare my argument concerning Jesus' words in the Fourth Gospel, "It is to your advantage that I go away, for if I do not go away, the Counselor [Paraclete = Spirit] will not come to you" (John 16:7), David L. Miller, "The Paraclete: Ghosts of Scripture," *Hells and Holy Ghosts* (New Orleans: Spring Journal Books, 2004), pp. 133-44; "The Holy Ghost and the Grateful Dead," *Eranos 52-1983* (Frankfurt am Main: Insel Verlag, 1984), pp. 277-346, esp. pp. 314-24.

THE VICISSITUDES OF SPIRIT IN JUNG'S PSYCHOLOGY: A RESPONSE TO WOLFGANG GIEGERICH'S "GOD MUST NOT DIE! C. G. JUNG'S THESIS OF THE ONE-SIDEDNESS OF CHRISTIANITY"

MICHAEL WHAN

...The Holy Ghost is the deepest part of our own consciousness wherein we know ourselves for what we are...
> D. H. Lawrence, "God and the Holy Ghost"

One of the manifestations of Mercurius in the alchemical process of transformation is the lion now green and now red.
> C. G. Jung, "The Spirit Mercurius"

The process of the integration and realization of the kenôsis was the Western soul's opus magnum.
> W. Giegerich, "God Must Not Die!"

Michael Whan, M.A., is an analytical psychologist, a member of the Independent Group of Analytical Psychologists, the International Association of Analytical Psychology, a member emeritus of the Association of Independent Psychotherapists and the College of Psychoanalysts. He has published papers and poetry in *Spring, Chiron, Harvest, Journal for Existential Analysis*, the *European Journal of Counselling, Psychotherapy and Health*, and contributed chapters to four books. He has a private practice in London and St. Albans.

I n his illuminating and major critique of Jung's conception of the one-sided psychology of Christianity, Giegerich not only helps us to perceive the dialectical movement which unfolds in the Christian concept of the Trinity, but enables us to approach Jung's alchemical studies in a different light. I shall attempt briefly to explore an aspect of this critique in relation to the notion of *spirit*, drawing on Giegerich's own prior reflections on the nature of the alchemical Mercurius and the Holy Spirit, and also on passages in Jung which point in the same direction, even if the latter seemingly does not elaborate further in his thinking on these important notions.

One of Jung's own visionary experiences, I suggest, portrays in imaginal form the alchemy of the dissolution of the Christ figure in the corrosive force of the spirit, namely, the Holy Spirit seen with an Hermetic eye. Jung gives us the following account of this remarkable visionary event:

> In 1939 I gave a seminar on the *Spiritual Exercises* of Ignatius Loyola. At the same time I was occupied on the studies for *Psychology and Alchemy.* One night I awoke and saw, bathed in bright light at the foot of my bed, the figure of Christ on the Cross. It was not quite life-size, but extremely distinct; and I saw that his body was made of greenish gold. The vision was marvelously beautiful, and yet I was profoundly shaken by it.

Jung then provides his interpretation of his experience:

> The green gold is the living quality which the alchemists saw not only in man but also in inorganic nature. It is an expression of the life-spirit, the *anima mundi* or *filius macrocosmi*, the Anthropos who animates the whole cosmos. This spirit has poured himself into everything, even into inorganic matter; he is present in metal and stone. My vision was thus a union of the Christ-image with his analogue in matter, the *filius macrocosmi.* If I had not been so struck by the greenish gold, I would have been tempted to assume that something essential was missing from my 'Christian' view—in other words, that my traditional Christ-image was somehow inadequate and that I still had to catch up with part of the Christian development. The emphasis on the metal, however, showed me the undisguised alchemical conception of Christ as a union of spiritually alive and physically dead matter. (*MDR*, pp. 210-11)

Before going on to offer an interpretation of this vision in terms of Giegerich's critique, I want, first, to refer to a contribution by Murray Stein, "Jung's Green Christ: A Healing Symbol of Christianity,"[1] which broadly follows and, to a degree, extends Jung's own understanding of the symbolic meaning of this vision, though one that contrasts to the one I intend here. Then, second, I shall explore the collapse of alchemy in terms of Mercurius as an aerial spirit, drawing on James Hillman's 1981 Eranos Lecture: "The Imagination Of Air And The Collapse Of Alchemy."[2]

Stein's position is essentially that, like Jung, he conceives of the "alchemical conception of Christ as a union of spiritually alive and physically dead matter." For Stein, the "greenish-gold Christ ... is the traditional symbol of Christianity, but with a difference: He is an image of the *filius philosophorum* of the alchemists ... the son of the Mother, of matter, in contradistinction to the son of the Father, of spirit." Stein's analysis proceeds by way of the notion of external, undialectical opposites and the notion of Jung's "Transcendent Function." The *filius philosophorum* "represents the response of the unconscious to the conscious attitude of the Christian dominant ... which ... expresses itself in the structure of patriarchal values and thought-patterns." He is named as *Mercurius duplex*, which Stein describes as follows: "a highly problematical agent, the spirit of the earth and the unconscious, of instinctuality and impulse, of tricksterism and deception." Earlier in his essay, Stein eschews the psychoanalytic reduction of religious experience to the notion of "a transference God," yet contrary to this he then goes on to portray Mercurius in a classically psychoanalytical reductive way himself, as if regressing from the archetypal, imaginal form and decisively describing it in terms of an actual empirical person: as a kind of difficult adolescent, as "precisely one who will not be committed and tied down, crucified, nailed to the cross for the sake of anyone. He is, if anything *the spoiled child of the mother*, the second son, *the willful spirit of the rejected mother* who is not tamed or fettered to authority's structures" (italics mine). The vision of the green-gold Christ, he concludes, serves symbolically to heal "the split between spirit and nature ... the spirit of nature and the son of the heavenly father are brought together. Father and Mother are uniting and cooperating." This, for

Stein, is a "sign, or symbol, of nature's cooperation, finally, with the Judeo-Christian line of development."³

Nevertheless, there are difficulties with this interpretation of the green-gold Christ vision. For nature and matter are not one and the same. Stein does not unpack what he means by "nature," perhaps trusting to an idea of nature in terms of a naive empirical realism, a kind of "immediate" knowing, or better, perhaps sensing (knowledge as sense-certainty). Positing the alchemical spirit as nature fails to address the *alchemical meaning of nature*: for instance, Petrus Bonus, quoted by Jung, says, "alchemy stands above nature and is divine" (*CW* 12 § 462).⁴ Essentially, alchemy was rather an *opus contra naturam*, a "work against nature," that is, "nature" implicitly as a form of consciousness, as a way of being, mythic, naive, and spontaneous. The alchemical meaning of "nature" needs to be understood from the perspective of alchemy as "in the sense of a pivot or intermediary." Alchemy straddled between "the inherited ancient imaginal form of the contents of an innocent *anima*-bound consciousness" and "modern consciousness as a reflecting, self-conscious, and logos-bound consciousness;" which enabled the soul to pass from its mythologizing form "to its new, modern status of (psycho-) logic, the status of the Concept."⁵ Jung quotes Zosimos: "the nature that conquers the natures" (*CW* 12 § 472). And picking up on the term "matter," this is already an abstract notion, an alchemical distillation of a prior mythic known nature, worked on by an embryonic modern consciousness, the *artifex*, already the product of a metaphysically sophisticated mind and one preparing the emergence of the idea of "matter" as a scientific notion. To talk here of "cooperation" between spirit and nature is to conceal the notional rupture brought about through the alchemical "work against nature," to ignore the dialectical logic of the "Philosopher's Stone," namely, "the stone that is not a stone." Further, anthropomorphizing this "cooperation" in terms of "Father and Mother" turns regressively against the historical thrust of Christianity which, as Jung noted, is "the despiritualization of the world" (*CW* 11 § 140). "Nature" in the language of alchemy is already a working-through by way of the imaginal towards the release of the dialectical notion of the Mercurial spirit:

> "natura" did not refer to nature in our positivistic, materialistic
> sense, nature as mere fact and physical reality at large, because

such a sense did not yet exist. It developed only after the decline
of alchemy. All the substances used in alchemy were not seen as
merely chemical, positive-factual ones in our sense ... The prima
materia the alchemists worked with came as imaginally perceived
to begin with ... the goal of the opus was ... to free the imaginal
"material" from its imaginal coagulations and to release, through
many negating and refining operations, the spirit, the ambivalent,
self-contradictory Mercurius, i.e., the dialectical, logical life,
"imprisoned" in them ...[6]

What Stein and the "classical Jungian" standpoint he voices here does,
is to "unite" the "opposites" of a so-called patriarchal Christianity and
an earth-based, feminine or hermaphroditic alchemical *theoria* in a
"transcendent symbol." Yet, in doing so, this standpoint "fixes" both
Christianity and alchemy at a frozen point in time, blotting out their
truth as fundamentally cultural, *historical* moments of an unfolding
spirit, in which both have undergone a radical collapse and
transformation in order to release their germinal pneumatic, soulful
essence; and which, at their deepest level were already the *kenôtic*
working out of their one common ground: Mercurius as Holy Spirit.

To understand the dialectical movement of the Mercurial spirit,
we have to recognize the *collapse* of alchemy. As far as I know, Hillman
and Giegerich are the only ones in the "Jungian world" to have
addressed this important historical and therefore psychological
phenomenon. The breakdown of alchemy shows us the Mercurial spirit
working intentionally from within alchemy to decompose its modes
of imagining. Hillman, writing on the role of the aerial spirit or the
imagination of air in alchemy, states: "We can read the collapse of
alchemy and the transformation of chaos into the differentiation of gases
as the aerial soul's own intention—to be out, public, free, and to invest
itself in objects giving them a new intention."[7] Whilst Giegerich asserts
that the "collapse of alchemy was not due to outside historical factors.
It was the restless mercurial (logical) element within alchemy itself,
that slowly worked at alchemy's inner decomposition and self-
sublation."[8] Both authors give recognition to the self-negating,
dialectical movement of Mercurius.

Indeed, one can read the Grimm's tale of "The Spirit in the Bottle,"
with which Jung opens his essay "The Spirit Mercurius," as pointing
to the process of alchemy's dialectical decomposition in imaginal,

narrative form—namely, as the movement from alchemy to psychology (*CW* 13).[9] Surely, analytical psychology needs to attend to these vicissitudes of spirit, rather than return to the alchemical texts in a regressive and nostalgic way, as if the ruptures and decompositions of the workings of the Mercurial spirit had never happened. For Jung's psychology, as Jung himself observed, is the historical product of the Mercurial spirit's self-transformation, self-sublation; the dissolving of a number of the "figures" of consciousness in its working-through to itself *as* psychology (*MDR*, p. 228).

Jung cites a number of alchemical sources attesting to the restless *aerial* element of Mercurius in his chapter entitled, "Mercurius As Spirit And Soul." The various texts, he writes, "often use the terms *pneuma* and *spiritus* in the original concrete sense of 'air in motion'." He details the *Rosarium philosophorum*, in which Mercurius is termed *aerus* and *volans* (winged); or, elsewhere, as "*totus aereus et spiritualis*," meaning "nothing more than a gaseous state of aggregation." Ripley's *Scrowle* states that "Mercurius is changed into wind;" and Mercurius is also "the *lapis elevatus cum vento* (the stone uplifted by the wind)." And Penotus, a pupil of Paracelsus, calls Mercurius "'nothing other than the spirit of the world become body within the earth'" (*CW* 13 § 261). Alongside the designation of Mercurius as spirit, Jung points to its nature as soul, *anima*, for "*anima* appears to be connected with *spiritus*," sharing "the living quality of soul." Further, he quotes from a text describing Mercurius as the *anima mundi*, and, crucially, goes on to note that in several alchemical writings the authors relate their concept of the world soul to both that of the *Timaeus* of Plato and to the Holy Spirit itself. The duplex character of the "Mercurial life-soul" grants to human beings both the *anima rationalis* and "the *inflatio* or *inspiratio* of the Holy Spirit" (*CW* 13 § 263). For the alchemists, Mercurius was conceived not only imaginally-concretistically, but, in the refining of the alchemical, *philosophical mind*, metaphysically, and it is in this sense that the meaning of Mercurius as a dialectical notion, that is, as *thought*, is crucially implied through these many references. Referring to several descriptions, in which the Mercurial spirit is depicted as "ethereal ... and as having become rational or wise," Jung, finally, puts it decisively: "Mercurius is the Logos become world" (*CW* 13 § 265, 271).

Alongside his reflections on Mercurius, Jung also picks up on the *logos* essence of the Holy Spirit in terms of its *unnatural* and *reflective* character, in tune with the alchemical definitions of the Mercurius. Addressing the idea of the Father-Son aspect of the Trinity, he points out how the "third element" lifts (sublates) it "out of the natural order" (*CW* 11 § 197). He goes so far as to recognize the *negation* of the natural order in the notion of the Trinity's "third element." Speaking of the Trinity, Jung exclaims: "Why, in the name of all that's wonderful, wasn't it 'Father, Mother, and Son?' That would be much more 'reasonable' and 'natural' than 'Father, Son, and Holy Ghost.' To this we must answer: it is not just a question of a natural situation, but of a product of human reflection ..." And crucially, he perceives how through "reflection," [in this context, a gift of the Holy Spirit] "'life' and its 'soul' are abstracted from Nature and endowed with a separate existence"; for "reflection is a spiritual act that runs counter to the natural process ..." When Jung speaks of "thought" here, he means more than the "thinking function" of his typology, for reflection seizes the *whole man*, it is an "attitude," a "bending back," in which we take up a relation to something, "an act of *becoming conscious*" (*CW* 11 § 235, note 9). Clearly, the work of the Holy Ghost is a *contra naturam*: "the idea of the Holy ghost is not a natural image" (*CW* 11 § 236). Indeed, the Holy Ghost negates the impersonating element of the Trinity, its imaginal form of Father and Son: "unlike Father and Son ... 'Spirit' is not a personal designation but the qualitative definition of a substance of aeriform nature" (*CW* 11 § 276). In his recognition of the way the Trinity frees itself *internally* from a naturalistic form through the Holy Spirit's sublation of the Father-Son relation, Jung almost comes to a recognition of the Spirit as dialectical: "Its descent into a human body is sufficient in itself to make it become another, to set it in opposition to itself. Thenceforward there are two: the 'One' and the 'Other,' which results in a certain tension." Further, this "tension" can be understood as belonging to Christ's self-emptying, which culminates in his "admission of abandonment" (*CW* 11 § 204). Of course, here, Jung is thinking in terms of a "tension of opposites," but in the sense that the "tension works itself out" through Christ's suffered abandonment, as Giegerich indicates, the logic of abandonment—for the death of Christ is also the death of God, the Father—is the fulfilment of *kenôsis*, a complete and not a token abandonment. Finally, and similar to the working out of the Mercurial spirit in alchemy, the "noetic character" of the Trinity, which essentially means the sublating, denaturing, noetic character of its "third element," points to the freeing of "thought," an "independence of thought" that: "Historically, we can see ... striving at work above all in scholastic philosophy ... these preliminary exercises that made the scientific thinking" of modernity possible (*CW* 11 § 286).

This selfsame notion—of the "freeing" of alchemical thought, *through* and *from* the alchemical imagination, i.e., the noetic, dialectical character of the Mercurial spirit—can be seen, in certain aspects, in the movement of the "death of soul and its rebirth in a new form, from mythic body to chemical body ... this gaseous vapour of the anima that was the fascinating and elusive object pursued in the chemical revolution."[10] This was the shift out of the alchemical "retort" into the positive-factual retort of scientific *theoria* and experiment ("lab-oratory" as methodologically an empirical chamber, "hermetically" sealed to determine positive-factual, causal variables; in the same way, that Freud, in his theorizing of the transference neurosis, tried to mirror the classical laboratory of scientific method by supposedly screening out all "external" influences, save the notion of a "pure" transference; analyst as "blank screen"). In this movement of spirit into the "objects" of science, nevertheless, the thinking remains one of undialectical opposites or differences: "subject" and "object" as exclusive opposites; science being the attempt through experiment to exclude the "personal equation," except where this is itself the "object" of study.

Giegerich, in his paper on the setting free of Mercurius in "The Spirit in the Bottle" tale, has identified the dialectical sense of "setting free" as "closure," sealing Mercurius in the bottle—literalistically acted out in science through the hermetic seal of the experiment. The hermetic *vas*, he observes, has, "from the outset been absolute-negatively interiorized into itself so that it has the notion of outside totally inside and the very notion of exteriority is altogether gone ..."[11] Critiquing Jung's interpretation of the tale, he argues that:

> "closure" in this fairy tale and in alchemy and psychology is *a priori a hermetic, mercurial* closure that requires a dialectical understanding. It is not the simple self-identical fact which Jung took it for. The notion of closure *itself partakes* of the living mercurial spirit of alchemy enclosed by means of it. You cannot approach a story about the spirit Mercurius imprisoned in a hermetically sealed bottle with a positivistic sense of closure. With

a positivistic bottle, stopper and seal, the spirit Mercurius could not be contained in the first place. He would laugh at any such incommensurable attempt, or rather, he would not even exist for this mentality. Jung's mistake is that he comes to a hermetic notion with a positivistic conception of this notion. The logic of his style of thinking does not match the semantics that it is applied to ... closure has to be absolute so as to include and enclose *itself*, its own concept ... this closure that has relentlessly integrated every notion of "outside" or "around itself" into itself is *ipso facto* tantamount to the freeing of the imprisoned Mercurius.[12]

Granted that the shift to the empirical laboratory is an undialectical positive-factual one, still is it not an implicit expression of that devoted attention, that "waiting on" or "attending to," that psychology has appropriated as *therapeia,* which the alchemist also practiced in his imaginal observation and devotion to the detail of the substances and changes, the noticing, of the alchemical opus? In *Mysterium Coniunctionis,* Jung indicates the role of the Mercurial *telum passionis,* which belongs to the secret of the Conjunction, and which forms part of the alchemical *opus contra,* a philosophical eros, which longs to penetrate the mystery of the *prima materia* (*CW* 14 § 550). Could we not see the self-contradictory movement of Mercurius, the freeing/ closure, as a deepening or differentiating of the Mercurial passion, the philosophical eros, in a loving and knowing encounter with the world, that expresses itself, implicitly, through scientific *praxis*, with its single-minded attention to phenomena, like a lover attending to his mistress? What could be more mercurial than the thinking and language of "quantum physics," with its paradoxes and strange behaviors of light as self-contradictorily both "particle" and/or "wave," its "quarks," etc., the true subject of which is the dialectical relationship between consciousness (theory and method) and "nature"?

Despite Jung's often repeated protests that his psychology was an empirical one, eschewing metaphysical claims—"I am an empiricist ... and ... approach psychological matters from a scientific and not from a philosophical standpoint"—at other times he saw deeper into the nature of his project than that, recognizing his psychology as a psychology of soul, a work of interiorization, and what that entailed in terms of the constitution of psychology (*CW* 11 § 2). Indeed, he saw that psychology, in which the soul is both "subject" and "object," had methodologically to transcend itself as a "science." Rather, it was concerned in its making of itself *as psychology,* as the *logos* of the *soul,* with that soulful pulse, the interiority of science, rather than as asserting itself as a science as such. If Jung stated his case "empirically," arguing the role of the "unconscious" in positive-factual terms, he also sensed that Mercurial spirit, which could not be truly grasped in any empirical, or positive-factual way. Though Jung describes psychology as the unfolding of the "unconscious" as the actualization of "the unconscious urge to consciousness," can we not put this otherwise, as the Mercurial spirit's reaching through its self-estrangement for itself, psychology, the tradition of Jung's alchemical studies, as the Mercurial spirit's self-recognition, self-relation?[13] In other words, psychology is Mercurius' mediation of itself *for itself.* Instead of speaking of "the unconscious," can we not speak of the Mercurial spirit's failure to know itself completely; that it finds itself in and through the experience of losing itself? As *thought, dialectic,* it finds itself through symbol, image, through the experience of its own internal other, thus through an awareness of *not knowing itself fully* (what it does know about itself as *not knowing*), and hence, knows itself in terms of self-estrangement, through self-division, as the consciousness of itself as *other than itself.* Its self-knowing, in this sense, overcomes a one-sided knowing or consciousness, which would reflect itself as self-identical, since *self-estrangement* allows it to recognize itself by way of its self-contradiction, its internal other, thus, breaking-through one-sidedness.[14]

In his essay, "On the Nature of the Psyche," Jung states, in contradiction to his claims for his psychology as "empirical," that psychology stands apart, yet is central to the other sciences. He writes that psychology is:

> ... the coming to consciousness of the psychic process, but it is not, in the deeper sense, an explanation of this process, for no explanation of the psychic can be anything other than the living process of the psyche itself. Psychology is doomed to cancel itself out as a science and therein precisely it reaches its scientific goal. Every other science has so to speak an outside; not so psychology, whose object is the inside subject of all science. (*CW* 8 § 429)

This "living process" is the self-contradictory Mercurial spirit, the dialectic that *sublates* the characterization of psychology—the *logos* of the *soul*—as neither a natural nor a human science. Where the English translation employs the verb "to cancel," the original German has the expression "*aufheben*:" "*Sie muss sich als Wissenshaft selber aufheben.*" The term "to cancel" misses completely the dialectical notion of *aufheben*, a notion that Hegel uses to describe the supercessionary nature of dialectical thought, and which has been more usually translated in philosophical texts as "to sublate." Here Jung recognizes the subject of psychology as an absolute interiority, which has no outside external to it. Further on, in his essay, Jung, depicts this interiority as an "absolute subjectivity and universal truth" (CW 8 § 439). Clearly, in this statement, this "absolute subjectivity" cannot be confused with empirical subjectivity, but rather is the Mercurial dia-logic, the soul.

To return now to Jung's vision of the alchemical green-gold Christ, and to Jung's interpretation, which Stein follows. Their interpretation identifies the symbolic meaning of the vision as a union of opposites, as a coming together of spirit and nature. Yet, there are many comments and observations in Jung's own writings which indicate that this is a redundant interpretation, that he was, in some sense or other, onto a very different understanding concerning the meaning of the Mercurial spirit as an alchemical working of the Holy Spirit. Despite these scattered insights, Jung obscured them through insisting on the compensatory and complementary relation between the Christ figure and the alchemical Mercurius: "'Alchemy was well aware of the great shadow which Christianity was obviously unable to get under control, and it therefore felt impelled to create a saviour from the womb of the earth as an analogy and complement of God's son who came from above'" (*CW* 14 § 704, Giegerich's modified transl.). Thus with its goal of psychic "wholeness," psychology's task was their conjunction. As Giegerich has argued in his paper, "God Must Not Die!", the *kenôsis* of the incarnation, the self-emptying of divinity into man, renders this "union" unnecessary, since Christ's *kenôsis* already means a self-emptying into the world, of the Word made Flesh: "The *kenôsis* means that Christ relentlessly gave up his divinity … The incarnation is one consistent downward movement from the height of divinity to the lowest possible form of human existence …" It needs to be thought as a radical "*logical or ontological form change* … so that we could also think of it as an 'alchemical' (mercurial) change, e.g., of a *putrefactio* and *mortifactio* … Christ switched from the category God to that of mortal man." The *kenôtic* movement of Christianity, as Giegerich stresses, moves through the Christ figure to that of the Holy Spirit, noting Christ's own words in John 14:26: "… the Holy Ghost, whom the Father will send in my name, he shall teach you all things, and bring all things to your remembrance, whatsoever I have said unto you." The Holy Spirit needs to be understood as "the slow coming alive of the inner spirit of the message of Christianity from within itself." This centuries long historical process manifested its "subtle pneumatic meaning" by way of interiorization, and it was this work of interiorization that was implicit in the alchemical opus, figuring in the notion of the Mercurial spirit, and which then re-appeared in Jung's psychology.

Indeed, drawing on alchemical symbolism, Jung explores aspects of the meaning of *kenôsis* in the alchemical *coniunctio*. He points to the relation of the "'waxing and waning' of the bride (Luna, Ecclesia) that is based on the *kenôsis* of the bridegroom" (*CW* 14 § 28). Jung quotes St Ambrose, stating that the function of the *coniunctio* is the emptying of Luna to be filled by Christ, but also that, thereby, "she may fill the elements" (*CW* 14 § 29). This may suggest a transformation of lunar consciousness itself through a *kenôtic* movement as part of the opus itself, in turn re-figuring "the elements" (*CW* 14 § 30). Further, in a footnote, he recognizes the process of *mortificatio* at work in Christ's self-emptying within the Church itself, its historical fate, quoting Rahner:

> the earthly fate of the Church as the body of Christ is modelled on the earthly fate of Christ himself. That is to say the Church, in the course of her history, moves towards a death, as well in her individual members (here is the connecting-link with the doctrine of "mortification") as in her destiny as a whole, until the last Day when, after fulfilling her earthly task, she becomes "unnecessary" and "dies"…(*CW* 14 § 28, note 194)

These passages in Jung signify how the spiritual message of Christianity, far from needing to be reconciled with the chthonic elements of alchemy, continued its working-through within the alchemical opus. Again, Jung himself notes the connection, that alchemy was conceived of as "gift of the Holy Ghost or of the *Sapientia Dei*," though "still man's work" (*CW* 14 § 443). Conjecturing "that medieval alchemy, which evolved out of the Arabic tradition sometime in the thirteenth-century …, was in the last resort a continuation of the doctrine of the Holy Ghost," he added that this doctrine "never came to very much in the Church" (*CW* 14 § 444). Here, Jung cites, in a footnote, a comment made to him: "That the Church has not done everything it might have been expected to do in regard to the doctrine of the Holy Ghost was a remark made to me spontaneously by Dr. Temple, the late Archbishop of Canterbury" (*CW* 14 § 444, note 244). It is as if in all of this, there is an underlying recognition, which, for whatever reason, Jung does not fully take up, because, as Giegerich argues: "But Jung clings to the notion and nature of God. He does not allow God to become man and to die as God. The divinity of God is to be rescued *against* the Christian decomposition of it in the *kenôsis* ... If one *thinks* the sentence 'God becomes man,' the predicate dissolves the subject ..." So, in his reflection on the green-gold Christ vision, Jung says: "If I had not been so struck by the greenish-gold, I would have been tempted to assume that something essential was missing from my 'Christian' view—in other words, that my traditional Christ-image was somehow inadequate and that I still had to catch up with part of the Christian development" (*MDR*, pp. 210-211). Is this not Jung's own defensive *disavowal* of his own insights into alchemy as a work of the spirit, not so much complementing or compensating Christianity, but as a *continuation* of the meaning of the incarnation; the failure of his thinking "to catch up with part of the Christian development"?

Nevertheless, my reading of Jung's green-gold Christ vision interprets it as precisely and symbolically as being that "catching up" with "the Christian development." That is to say, the vision portrays imaginally the meaning of that process, but *unthought* or *implicitly thought*. There is a clue to this in *Psychology and Religion*, where, discussing a patient's mandala, Jung observes that the "centre is, however, empty. The seat of the deity is unoccupied." Instead, relates Jung, further on: "There is no deity in the mandala, nor is there any submission or reconciliation to a deity. The place of the deity seems to be taken by the wholeness of man" (*CW* 11 § 136, 139). Jung's own researches into mandala symbolism, at least in this instance, point towards a *kenôtic* meaning. As he puts it in the same essay: "Why did the gods of antiquity lose their prestige and their effect on the human soul? Because the Olympians had served their time and a new mystery began: God became man" (*CW* 11 § 137). The modern mandala

depicts the Christian *kenôsis*, in which the "God-image" is replaced
by that of the "wholeness of man," and which itself depends upon,
logically and ontologically, Christ's prior self-emptying of himself of
the divine to the point of utter self-abandonment (by God the Father
aspect of the Trinity) to mortal existence. If the self-emptying,
though, is to be thoroughly *kenôtic*, it would also be a further
negation of the negation, that is, a kind of emptying of the "divine
place," left empty. There is no "divine place" to be filled by some
other divinity or its symbol. The "content" has dissolved, corroded,
its container, the "empty vessel," the *vas hermeticum* has disintegrated,
which Jung here addresses:

> I am not, however, addressing myself to the happy possessors of
> faith, but to those many people for whom the light has gone
> out, the mystery has faded, and God is dead. For most of them
> there is no going back, and one does not know either whether
> going back is always the better way. To gain an understanding of
> religious matters, probably all that is left us today is the
> psychological approach. (*CW* 11 § 148)

It is the Mercurial spirit, which here is the corrosive element.[15] The
dialectical movement of the Trinity necessitates its unfolding *historically*
and alchemical putrefaction of those things that, in Jung's words, "had
served their time." Christ in undergoing the uttermost of his self-
emptying, subjecting himself to the extremity of mortal pain,
abandonment, and death, releases the Holy Spirit that comes *after* him:
a self-iconoclasm. There is a sense here of the spiritual genealogy of
the existential emptiness of modernity.

Jung's vision depicts this movement pictorially *in the greening of
the gold*. The Christ figure, in his mortal agony, made of the metal of
highest alchemical value, is undergoing a transformation denoted by
this greening process, a process represented by the colors of gold and
green—in the same way that the alchemical stages were themselves
imagined by the colors black, white, yellow, and red, and a process
that, as already suggested, was a "catching up" with the inner meaning
of the Christian development, which Jung sensed and then dismissed.
The color green is emblematic of both the Holy Ghost and Mercurius,
both of whom were identified anyway by the alchemists as one and
the same, as Jung states: "In the same way the Mercurius imprisoned
in matter was identified with the Holy Ghost"; and, quoting Johannes

Grasseus, "The gift of the Holy Ghost, that is the lead of the philosophers which they call the lead of the air ..." (*CW* 11 § 160, note 65). Indeed, Jung asserts that the alchemists preferred a religion of the Holy Ghost (*CW* 14 § 286, note 531). The Holy Ghost, Jung observes, was regarded as "the cause of the *viriditas* (greenness)"; "the cause of the 'greenness,' the *benedicta viriditas,*" and referring to Mylius, "' ... a kind of germination, which is the viridescence,'" and to Hildegard of Bingen's Hymn to the Holy Ghost, wherein "'the earth sweats out greenness'" (*CW* 11 § 119, note 10, § 151). And elsewhere, Jung affirms that: "Green is the colour of the Holy Ghost, of life, procreation and resurrection" (*CW* 14 § 395). This same greenness is linked to Mercurius, one manifestation of which is the "green lion" (*CW* 14 § 275), also connected to the *benedicta viriditas* (*CW* 11 § 151).

Green held a number of symbolic meanings for the alchemists. It was emblematic of the *prima materia*, the raw material, "unclean matter;" for the "green-gold is the fertile matter from which the gold may be grown."[16] It also indicates a state of immaturity or unripeness necessitating dissolution into the *prima materia*. This operation of dissolution is spoken of alchemically as the "green lion devouring metals." The alchemists are "referring to the way in which the mercurial blood is able to dissolve and reduce all metals into their prima materia or first matter." The *Rosarium philosophorum* shows a lion devouring the sun. The sun, Sol (in Jung's vision, the green-gold Christ), is being devoured or dissolved in the lion's mouth to obtain the "sperm" of the gold from which can be grown the seed of the philosophical gold. This dissolution represents the eclipsing of the sun, the darkness of the *nigredo* stage, to free the active element for the *coniunctio* of sun and moon.[17] Understood alchemically, the Mercurial spirit, analogous to the *de*naturing sublation or transformation of the Trinitarian Father-Son relation by the Holy Spirit, works to dissolve or devour the Christ figure. The Holy Spirit, identified by medieval alchemy with the spirit Mercurius, represents the "inner motive force" of Christianity, in Giegerich's words, a release of its "more subtle pneumatic meaning through an interiorization of its ideas into themselves ...," to find "itself *only* 'in spirit and in truth' (John: 4: 23)." The green-gold of Jung's vision, in this interpretation, signifies an alchemical *putrefactio* of the Christ. As Jung, too, though not followed through, appears inchoately to imply, when, discussing Joachim of Foire's "Third Age" of the Spirit, as denoting a "new attitude," a *"fructificatio,"* namely, "a new 'status' of the world" (*CW* 9, 11 § 139). Christ's loss of divine status through the *kenôsis* of becoming fully human enables the emergence of a new status, that of the spirit—in alchemy, the distillation of the spirit from "the stone," the work of interiorization, of the *logos*, that eventuates as psychology.

NOTES

1. Murray Stein, "Jung's Green Christ: A Healing Symbol for Christianity," *Jung's Challenge to Contemporary Religion,* ed. M. Stein and R. L. Moore (Wilmette: Chiron Publications, 1987).

2. James Hillman, "The Imagination of Air and the Collapse of Alchemy," *Eranos Jahrbuch* 50 (Frankfurt am Main: Insel Verlag, 1982).

3. Stein, pp. 10-11.

4. Also see, Yasuhiro Tanaka, "The Alchemical Images and Logic in Analytical Psychology," *Harvest: Journal for Jungian Studies,* 2001, vol. 47, No. 1, p. 19.

5. Wolfgang Giegerich, *The Soul's Logical Life: Towards a Rigorous Notion of Psychology* (Frankfurt am Main: Peter Lang, 1998), pp. 138-139.

6. Giegerich, *The Soul's Logical Life,* p. 139.

7. Hillman, "The Imagination of Air and the Collapse of Alchemy," p. 323.

8. Giegerich, *The Soul's Logical Life,* p. 141.

9. Cf., Wolfgang Giegerich, "Closure and Setting Free or The Bottled Spirit of Alchemy and Psychology," *Alchemy—Spring 74* (2006).

10. Hillman, "The Imagination of Air and the Collapse of Alchemy," p. 310.

11. Giegerich, "Closure and Setting Free," p. 56.

12. Giegerich, "Closure and Setting Free," pp. 57-59.

13. Cf. C. G. Jung, *CW* 8 § 429.

14. K. D. Magnus, *Hegel And The Symbolic Mediation Of Spirit* (New York: State University of New York Press, 2001), p. xiii.

15. Giegerich, *The Soul's Logical Life,* p. 148.

16. L. Abraham, *A Dictionary of Alchemical Imagery* (Cambridge: Cambridge University Press, 1998), p. 87.

17. Abraham, *A Dictionary of Alchemical Imagery,* pp. 93-94.

GOD, MAN, AND EVIL IN JUNG'S THOUGHT: COMPLEMENTARY REMARKS TO WOLFGANG GIEGERICH'S CRITIQUE

MARCO HELENO BARRETO

INTRODUCTION: CHRISTIANITY, MODERNITY AND ANALYTICAL PSYCHOLOGY

"I am concerned with the world as it is today, namely godless and spiritually disoriented. In history there is never a way back" (*Letters 2*, p. 346, to anonymous, February 1957). As can be easily confirmed through many statements spread throughout his works and letters, Jung nurtured no illusions about the spiritual predicament in which modern man is entangled. More than any other psychologist of his time, he knew that psychology was not a neutral and aseptic new scientific discipline emerging *ex nihilo* in a new historical setting, but was essentially linked to the fateful event of modernity. Consequently, he understood and consciously acknowledged that his psychological project was addressed to the modern mind.

On the other hand, Jung assumed explicitly the Christian standpoint, declaring that he was "entirely based upon Christian

Marco Heleno Barreto, Ph.D., is a Jungian psychotherapist working at Belo Horizonte, Brazil. He is also a teacher at Faculdade Jesuíta de Filosofia e Teologia (FAJE) and the author of *Símbolo e Sabedoria Prática. C.G. Jung e o Mal-estar da Modernidade* and *Imaginação Simbólica. Reflexões Introdutórias* (both by Edições Loyola, São Paulo, 2008).

concepts" (*Letters 2*, p. 524, to Hugh Burnett, 5 December 1959), but recognized that "for most people my Christian standpoint remains hidden, and because of the strangeness of my language and the incomprehensibility of my interests I am given a wide berth" (*Letters 2*, p. 226, to Pater Lucas Mensz, 22 February 1955). To understand the deep meaning of such statements, conjugating it with the quotation at the beginning of this article, we must remember that modern consciousness has Christian experience as one of its essential roots. The anthropocentric turn which is in its origin only can be fully understood if referred to the specific religious background in whose center is the radical notion of God becoming man—the dogma of incarnation. Considering the religious dimension of any culture, perhaps modernity's most original feature is its anthropological form of *atheism*. Modern atheism, to a large extent, emerges as an historical effect of Christianity: the theological themes of creation, incarnation, and sonship are the premises that, due to a peculiar unfolding and historical development, lead to the anthropocentrism of the modern logical form of consciousness, which is the specific and original foundation of both modernity and its correlate form of atheism.[1]

Besides that, Jung's concern with the godlessness and spiritual disorientation of modern man was justified psychotherapeutically inasmuch as from this predicament derives a particular form of psychological or spiritual *suffering*, the suffering brought about by the end of Meaning to a modern mind (or at least its "eclipse," borrowing the term used by Martin Buber in relation to the religious guarantee of Meaning: God). Jung considered the absence of meaning ("senselessness and aimlessness" of life) as "the general neurosis of our age" (cf. CW 16 § 83), and consequently addressed the suffering engendered by this (supposedly) neurotic position in his psychological project. Now, his stance concerning suffering in general (and the suffering of absence of meaning in particular) was decidedly modern (i.e., Western) and Christian-based. According to the report made by Walther Uhsadel of a conversation he had with Jung in 1938 (see *Letters 1*, p. 236, note 1, to V. Subrahamanya Iyer, 16 September 1937), Jung, pointing to a copy of the scene of the Crucifixion, said: " 'You see, this is the crux for us.' When [Uhsadel] asked him why, he replied: 'I've just got back from India, and it has struck me with renewed force. Man has to cope with the problem of suffering. The oriental wants to get rid of suffering by casting it off. Western man tries to suppress suffering with drugs. But suffering has to be overcome, and the only way to overcome it is to endure it. We learn that only from him.' And here he pointed to the Crucified."

To corroborate this personal report, and extend it to the cultural modern problem of absence of meaning, one needs only to read the reflection about the Western situation present in Jung's "On the Archetypes of Collective Unconscious" (in *CW* 9i, especially paragraphs 11 and 21-31). There we can see how Jung was deeply aware of the historical inscription of modern consciousness—and thus of modern psychology—in the unfolding of Christian experience, especially of its rooting in the protestant schism with its iconoclastic trend.[2] As a final result of this experience, uprootedness (*Entwurzelung*)—the subject's splitting off from his/her original tradition—reveals itself as coextensive with modernity, and thus is a central topic for psychology, inasmuch as from it derives the persistent malaise of modern subjectivity, entrapped in its self-engendered dereliction. Not only that: if psychology only makes sense within the logical framework of modern consciousness, being essentially modern itself, then its relations to the tradition from which it sprang forth are constitutive of its very identity, and historically this tradition is essentially determined by the Christian experience.

The same point is expressed from another angle when Jung claims for his psychology the historical heritage of Alchemy and of Gnosticism: as is well known, both are seen by him as cultural reactions to Christian consciousness and as compensations to its (alleged) one-sidedness, so that in the last analysis they are envisioned and *psychologically* rehabilitated from a Christian perspective. Moreover, the *psychological* nature of this rehabilitation is a clear sign that it is irrevocably *modern*: the original specific metaphysical framework of Gnosticism and Alchemy is transformed—dissolved and reconfigured—by the new anthropological-metaphysical foundation of modern consciousness, and this is the premise that opens up the possibility of a psychological assimilation of gnostic and alchemical symbolism. If "the efforts of modern psychology to investigate the unconscious seem like salutary reactions of the European psyche, as if it were seeking to re-establish the connection with its lost roots" (*CW*

18 § 1494), one should note that these roots are planted in Christian soil, and the loss of connection (*Entwurzelung*) is an effect of modern experience, "with the result that much of Europe today has become dechristianized or actually anti-Christian" (*ibid.*).

All this means that Christianity is not just one topic among others within the wide range of Jung's interests, but is structurally linked to his psychological project ("the incomprehensibility of my interests"). This is what is at stake, at bottom, in Wolfgang Giegerich's critique of Jung's understanding of the Christian message. It aims not only at the inadequate mythological assessment of Christianity by Jung, but to the very core of his (Jung's) project in its religious concern. As such, it is not only a problem of a methodological nature (eclecticism, breaking up the golden rule of sticking to the image and not letting in anything from outside, etc.), but mainly a thorough questioning of the project of rescuing religiosity in a modern frame of mind: in fact, Giegerich charges Jung of, while knowing "that the time of religion, of Church, faith was over" (p. 61), trying to preserve religion in the logical form of "modern psychology" (I would add: "within a Romantic framework"). So, at bottom, the discussion is about the understanding of modernity (as derived from Christian experience) and the *truth* of modern consciousness.

Having established the basis for a "rigorous notion of psychology," a basis which gets its inspiration in Jung himself, Giegerich—not only here, but in all his critiques of Jung's psychological project—submits Jung's thought to an alchemical distillation, exhibiting and rejecting the "impurities" that, according to that notion of psychology, distort its truly psychological status or hinders it from "coming home to itself." This distillation does not deal with a correction of accidental and localized mistakes on Jung's part. Giegerich aims at the logical consistency of Jung's psychology—meaning its truth, coherence, and purpose. In other words, it is the very structure of Jung's psychology which is submitted to a powerful critique.

As I have pointed out, Giegerich's text on Jung and Christianity criticizes Jung's psychology on two interconnected levels: 1) the (mis)understanding of Christianity and the Christian message, and 2) the project of preserving religion from its irrevocable dissolution in the general logic of modernity through smuggling the notion of "God" in to the transcendental concept of the "unconscious" (self-deceptively presented as a scientific and empirical concept), so that his psychology would be, in fact, a form of theosophy.

I have nothing to object to regarding the first level of the critique. I would only say that, though I completely agree with Giegerich in the statement that Jung does not reach the logic of Christian truth (*"christianitas nostra"*), one must recognize that he certainly reaches the *empirical- factual* Christian consciousness (*"christianitas vulgi"*), at least to a considerable extent. Therefore, if Jung's charge of one-sidedness is equivocated when we carefully examine the soul truth expressed in the Christian message, it hits the mark when we consider the many distortions and contradictions always present in empirically actualized Christian consciousness, and so it may help therapeutically this consciousness to recognize and express more clearly its deep logic, without having to change its formal foundation through importing heterogeneous elements to correct its empirical one-sidedness.

As to the second level of the critique, I think that Jung's position concerning religion in general is perfectly in tune with the general logic of modernity, inaugurated by the anthropocentric turn.[3] A careful and impartial examination of the religious trend present in his psychological project can show that, even if only imperfectly, religion is *sublated* in the modern logical framework of Analytical Psychology. As a matter of fact, Giegerich expressed exactly this in his *The Soul's Logical Life*, when thinking the dialectical relation of Jung's psychology to religion and science (and so to the two main roots of modern consciousness):

> Jung's work, we have seen, is neither that of the prophet or the founder of a religion, nor that of a scientist. What separates him from the prophet is the moment of negation or reflection that intercepted the immediate flow from the experience to the announcement. What Jung presented to the public had, as far as its logical form is concerned, gone through the Enlightenment, as it were. It had suffered the confrontation with the critical mind so offending to the immediacy of the naïve experience. Jung's work shares with science this Enlightenment moment. But whereas science naïvely absolutizes the Enlightenment stance and therefore has to ignore and reject the immediate experience from the unconscious and the idea of a "soul" altogether (as "irrational," "superstition," "metaphysical beliefs," etc.), Jung also negates the

scientific approach just as much as the prophetic stance. By also
negating the Enlightenment position, he is again free to take the
images from the so-called unconscious seriously on an entirely
new level, namely *logically serious* (not only empirically serious –
which many schools of "psychology" do), thereby becoming a
psychologist in the true sense, one whose entire thinking is rooted
in the Notion of the reality of the soul. It takes the images "and
in particular (their) form and content" *as* "*statement(s)*"[*CW* 9i,
§ 384] of the soul, which have their meaning, their "referent,"
their dignity *within* themselves. They do not point to something
else, are not results of external causation, in short, they are not
epiphenomena. They are *phainomena*. ... Jung's psychology is
both *sublated* religion and *sublated* science.[4]

We can see that Giegerich now apparently moves a step further
concerning the topic of the relation of Jung's psychology to religion:
if formerly he saw in it the sublation (*Aufhebung*) of religion (and
sublation means at the same time overcoming *and preserving on a
higher level*), now his charge is exactly that Jung needed to *preserve*
religion in the logical form of modern psychology, the psychology
of the unconscious, and that this is somehow illegitimate if we
consider the general logic of modernity. Consequently, Jung is seen
now in the stance of a new prophet—"Saint Jung," presenting a new
gospel in his psychology. In any case, in Jung's project we should see a
(disguised) regression, concerning the logical form of both Christian
and modern consciousness.

I was not fully convinced by the present charge, for it seems to me
that there is in fact a sublation of religion in Jung's work, and not a
simple regression or a mystification: this sublation is precisely the sign
of Jung's *modern* stance. Consequently, the problem that Giegerich now
exposes must be located in the "moment of negation or reflexion" that
intercepted the immediate flow from the grounding experience in Jung
to its theoretical formulation in his psychological discourse.

Trying to work out my relative divergence from Giegerich's
current position in this respect, it called to my attention that he
took Jung's use of the notion "God" as definitely having a meaning
radically different from the notion "Man," "Man" signifying simply
"ego," "empirical man." Consequently, and coherently, in reality
Jung's discourse on religion would amount to a form of *theosophy*, being

thus modern only inasmuch as theosophy is a *reaction* against the consequences of modernity.

But, what if we followed a complementary path, thinking the whole topic from the convergence of the notions of "God" and "Man" in Jung's concept of the Self, and examining the anthropological side of it? I submit that this way we can understand the "theosophical" dimension of Jung's discourse from an anthropological starting point and thus find, behind "the strangeness of [Jung's] language," the very dissolution of the notion "God" that characterizes the *general* logic of modernity, even if only as a not fully accomplished tendency. This would confirm the sublation of religion in Jung's thought, as formerly admitted by Giegerich. As a matter of fact, what prevents Jung from clearly reaching this position is his agnostic-skeptic epistemological stance which, however, is not consistently sustained in his thinking, due to decisive metaphysical compromises that can be indicated through a critical approach to his psychology. These compromises are twofold: anthropological and naturalistic. In the first case, if the tendency was fully developed, one would come to the Feuerbachian reduction of the classical *dictum*: "*Homo homini deus*"[5] (with the resulting consequence that "Anthropology is the secret of Theology"). In the second case, one would have a version of the pantheistic position expressed as "*Deus sive Natura*" (and again here a tangency with the second Feuerbach, with his changing the focus from the notion of "Man" to that of "Nature," could be appointed). I adopted this as my working hypothesis and try here to ground and develop it.

BENEATH THE "PSYCHOLOGICAL DIFFERENCE": JUNG AS A METAPHYSICAL
ANTHROPOLOGIST AND A ROMANTIC *NATURPHILOSOPH*

Returning to the previous quotation from *The Soul's Logical Life*, we should note that it is not absolutely true to state that in Jung the images do not point to something else.[6] They do: sometimes to the metaphysically posited "archetype in itself," sometimes—more poetically or philosophically—to the equally metaphysical "secret of all existence," as when Jung declares that his symbols, carved in stone at Bollingen, "try only to point in a certain direction, viz. to those dim horizons beyond which lies the secret of existence," being "partly even futile or dubious attempts at pronouncing the ineffable" and "a mere expression of and a reaction to the experience of an ineffable mystery." (*Letters 2*, p. 290, to Maud Oakes, 11 February 1956) In both cases, and in many other passages in his writings, Jung goes beyond the limits of a rigorously psychological position and talks as a metaphysician, *malgré lui*.

This probably explains why, eager to bring to light the pseudo-scientific status of the transcendental concept of "the unconscious," Giegerich nowadays raises against it the positivistic anti-metaphysical charge ("the unconscious" is just a word that does not point to anything, having no empirical referent—see "God Must Not Die," this volume, p. 39)[7]. But, again, Giegerich himself knows that Jung was not so naïve concerning the relation between his psychology and science:

> "The fact that psychology has to be the sublation of religion and science was also in Jung's conscious awareness. He expressly stated that psychology "is doomed to cancel itself out as a science and therein precisely it reaches its scientific goal."[*CW* 8 § 429] This idea suggests that psychology has to be a discipline that *within itself* 1) starts out within a fantasy of being a science, 2) pushes off from this initial self-definition as a science (negating it), and 3) thereby does not turn into the undialectical opposite of science (into superstition, subjective beliefs or the like), but rather fulfills on a higher plane what it expected to achieve with its initial self-interpretation in terms of a science. As sublated science, psychology is in some way logically above and beyond all sciences, rather than being one voice in the concert of all the sciences, as the conventional idea goes. All the sciences are, in a special sense, "sublated moments" within psychology, inasmuch as all scientific research stems from the soul activity of humans.[8]

True: not only all scientific research, but all *human* diversified forms of expression stem from the *soul* activity of *humans*. Due to this connection, Jung often moves unreflectively back and forth from "soul" to "man," and thus simply leaves the "psychological difference" aside. But in so doing he is not led logically (and reductively) back to a *scientific* anthropology, but penetrates inadvertently in the field of *philosophical* anthropology, which is an ontology of the human mode of *being*. What Giegerich in the last quotation ascribes to psychology can be compared to what is claimed by philosophical anthropology's discourse: all the particular sciences presuppose the human mode of *being*, as well as from a psychological standpoint they presuppose *soul activity* (according to Jung, we are irrevocably immersed in soul, i.e., soul is an insurmountable *mediation* in all human activities). If there is a plausible essential relation between "human mode of being" and "soul activity," then Jung's positions concerning religion can be adequately understood from a philosophical-anthropological perspective.

Also from the theological side this approach could be supported: one of the decisive and distinctive consequences of God's incarnation, according to Christian belief, is theologically formulated in the conscious and explicit acknowledgement that any statement about God implies something concerning Man, and vice-versa: any statement about Man implies something about God.[9] This wider Christian horizon strengthens my opinion that it would be valuable to complement Giegerich's critique of Jung's stance concerning the relations of psychology and religion by the approach of Jung's *anthropological* perspective on the *Self*—this core concept in any discussion of the religious trend in Analytical Psychology.

In the light of such an external reflection, the methodological lapses that Giegerich finds in Jung's approach to Christianity and to religion in general could be seen as rooted in this negligence of the "psychological difference," pointing to the anthropological-metaphysical and Romantic bias of his psychology, so that in Jung's discourse "anthropology would be the secret of theosophy," or at least its entrance door. To be sure, the correspondence between images of the Self and God-images is obviously and definitely stressed by Jung. But he equally stresses the definition of Self as "human totality," *Anthropos* or *totus homo*, and thus we should not forget that "the self that stands behind or within the great archetypal images is after all a human self, an expression of our humanity—not only a God-image or an abstraction of completion through conjunction," so that its rich and variegated phenomenology displays "the affliction of just being human, each human being living the experiment of human Being."[10]

The anthropological bias in Jung is so prominent, that, despite being the psychologist who has, according to Giegerich, a real Notion or Concept of "soul,"[11] he systematically overlooks the "psychological difference" (between "man" and "soul"), and thus his psychology frequently ceases to be strictly psychological (regarding its epistemological status) and becomes a mixture of metaphysical anthropology and psychology. To corroborate this assertion, we need only to briefly examine some typical and recurrent formulations concerning the Self. Jung frequently defines "Self" as "the total man, i.e., man as he really is, not as he appears to himself," and inscribes the whole psychic sphere in this *human* totality—"to this wholeness the unconscious psyche also belongs, which has its requirements and needs just as consciousness has." (*CW* 9i § 314)

Sometimes, it is true, Jung speaks of the Self as just a psychic reality, but even then he subordinates it to an anthropological metaphysical entity, as when he writes: "the Self is a psychic *image* of the transcendent, because indescribable and inapprehensible, wholeness of *man*" (*Letters 1*, p. 487, to Gebhard Frei, 13 January 1948, italics mine). Besides being clearly metaphysical, this is a self-contradictory statement: if this metaphysical wholeness is "indescribable and inapprehensible," the Self cannot be a *psychic image* of it, for such an image would precisely apprehend and permit the description of that which it supposedly is the image of. This is exactly the same problem of postulating an archetype of the Self *an sich* (unknowable in itself) as an objective-positive referent to the *symbols* of the Self (or the Self as an apprehensible psychic image):

> I am utterly unable to tell you what the Self is; if I could do so I would be God myself. How can I tell you about a thing which is not, about which I have no immediate experience, which I can only try to grasp by blurred images? I can express it only in a very indirect way. Yet there is something of the sort there, otherwise we would not be forced to seek an expression of it.[12]

In this passage we find a rare confession concerning the impossibility of the frequently asserted "immediate experience" as opposed to "faith" in Jung's understanding of religious experience. Due to his precarious Kantian-based empiricism, Jung is unable to think "the soul's logical negativity" as sufficient to explain the "blurred images" of which one has immediate experience, and thus he positivizes it metaphysically in concluding for the existence of "something of the sort there." Ironically, this is Jung's form of "faith": an epistemologically unwarranted belief, supporting his famous declaration concerning believing or not in "God"—"I do not need to believe. I know."

Time and again Jung slips in the same problem: "Ultimately we all get stuck somewhere, for we are all mortal and remain but a part of what we are as a whole. The wholeness we can reach is very relative" (*Letters 2*, May 11 1956, to Rudolf Jung, p. 297-298). Jung inadvertently posits metaphysically the absolute human wholeness (and its knowledge) in this passage: how could he know otherwise that we remain but a part of what we are as a whole? According to his good-humored remark quoted above, only God could be in such a position. A comparative or phenomenological method would not be sufficient to authorize such an absolute knowledge—unless you define this transcendent wholeness of man as the sum total of the many parts or cultural symbols of the Self, but in this case it would not be transcendent, indescribable or inapprehensible: it would be just an artificial abstraction comparatively constructed. (A legitimate way of asserting the limitlessness of this "transcendent wholeness," so that the concrete, particular, empirical, and historical symbols of the Self could be (improperly) called "parts" and "relative," would be to make a *transcendental reflection*—in the Kantian sense—after the phenomenological moment; but this would simply change the very status of that "transcendent wholeness": it would be no more than the strictly formal *condition of possibility* of any given particular symbol, and not a positive *Wirklichkeit* as Jung insists it is. Rigorously speaking, it would be merely *transcendental*, and not *transcendent*.)

The metaphysical status of the concept of Self has in such passages a clearly *anthropological* specification. And if we remember that another constant definition of "Self" is "the totality of psychic structure," or the psyche itself, we come to the equation: "(total) man" = "Self" = "soul" (and we should remember also that, by definition, "man" as "ego" is included in "*total* man"). On account of this, we could apply to Jung's psychology what Giegerich elsewhere has said about psychology in general: it "has *a priori* committed itself to the standpoint of the human being."[13] Consequently, it is also committed to the ego, which interprets and subsumes under itself "what actually is supposed to be non-ego."[14] One quotation should suffice to corroborate this trend in Jung: "The meaning of human development is to be found in the fulfillment of this life. It is rich enough in marvels. And not in detachment from this world. How can I fulfill the meaning of my life if the goal I set myself is the 'disappearance of individual consciousness'?

What am I without this individual consciousness of mine? *Even what I have called the 'Self' functions only by virtue of an ego which hears the voice of that greater being"* (*Letters 2*, p. 381, to Meggie Reichstein, 2 August 1957, italics mine).

This explains the unnegotiable primacy of *experience* in Jung, and vice-versa: ego and experience are structurally correlate notions. (To meditate on this not often recognized Cartesian—and thus modern/Western—feature in Jung, see *Letters 2*, p. 466-467, to James Kirsch, 10 December 1958, where Jung states, against the "uncritical and unpsychological statement" of the satori *experience* as an "imageless condition," that "if no ego is present nothing whatever can be perceived.")

Following thus my working hypothesis, grounded in the undisputable anthropological bias in Jung's thought, I prefer to take the possible "theosophical" implications of his statements concerning "God" and read them *firstly* from an anthropological perspective. But "Jung, the anthropologist-metaphysician" does not stay within the anthropological borders, and so his concept of "Self" often transcends the anthropological or psychic circumscription. "Self" is articulated with a decisive background notion in Jung's thought—the notion of "nature," and it is easy to see, tracking its many uses in his writings, that ultimately it is not employed as a scientific category but as a metaphysical one, and more specifically a clear-cut Romantic one. Therefore, in the last analysis, Jung's anthropological psychology becomes embedded in Romantic *Naturphilosophie*. This can be seen in the many passages in which the concept of Self is given its extra-human amplitude, and again Jung does not speak psychologically. For instance:

> In medicine, fantasies are *real things* with which the psychotherapist has to reckon very seriously indeed. He cannot therefore deprive of all justification those primitive phantasms whose content is so real that it is projected upon the external world. In the last analysis, the human body, too, is built of the stuff of the world, the very stuff wherein fantasies become visible; indeed, without it they could not be experienced at all. Without this stuff they would be like a sort of abstract crystalline lattice in a solution where the crystallization process had not yet started.
>
> The symbols of the Self arise in the depths of the body and they express its materiality every bit as much as the structure of the

perceiving consciousness. The symbol is thus a living body, *corpus et anima* ... The uniqueness of the psyche can never enter wholly into reality, it can only be realized approximately, though it still remains the absolute basis of all consciousness. The deeper 'layers' of the psyche lose their individual uniqueness as they retreat farther and farther into darkness. 'Lower down,' that is to say as they approach the autonomous functional systems, they become increasingly collective until they are universalized and extinguished in the body's materiality, i.e., in chemical substances. The body's carbon is simply carbon. Hence 'at bottom' the psyche is simply 'world'. In this sense I hold Kerényi to be absolutely right when he says that in the symbol the *world itself* is speaking. (*CW* 9i, §§ 290-291)

Carbon, chemical substances, materiality, autonomous functional systems are not *psychological* concepts, and are not being envisaged *psychologically* in this passage: they are taken at face value in order to convey the idea that a symbol can express an objective, valid kind of truth or knowledge about the positive world—precisely its symbolic truth. Moreover, it establishes the viewpoint of a common material constitution of psyche and the world, and this is not a rigorously psychological issue. Despite the scientific appearance of the terminology, what is concealed in this viewpoint is the *Romantic metaphysical* framework within which Jung thinks, which alone permits us to understand his notion of "nature."

It is exactly this framework that allows him to indulge carelessly in an ontological-theological speculation of unmistakable pantheistic flavor, enlarging the extra-human character of "Self," when he says that the "innermost self of every man and animal, of plants and crystals, is God, but infinitely diminished and approximated to his ultimate individual form. In approximating to man he is also 'personal', like an antique god, and hence 'in the likeness of a man' (as Yahweh appeared to Ezekiel)" (*Letters 2*, p. 120, to anonymous, 3 August 1953). As one may easily see, "God," "Nature," and "Self" are often mutually interchangeable coins in Jung's Romantic pantheistic discourse.

A step further and we meet another strongly metaphysical key-concept associated with "Self" in Jung: synchronicity. For the identity "at bottom" of psyche and world, by means of which the world speaks through psychological symbols, sanctions from another angle the hypothesis of acausal correspondence between human psyche and physical world, due to which meaning has an objective, trans-human referent:

> If I call this unknowable the 'Self', all that has happened is that the effects of the unknowable have been given an aggregate name, but its contents are not affected in any way. An indeterminably large part of my own being is included in it, but because this part is the unconscious I cannot indicate its limits or its extent. The Self is therefore a *borderline concept*, not by any means filled out with the known psychic processes. On the one hand it includes the phenomena of synchronicity, on the other its archetype is embedded in the brain structure and is physiologically verifiable: through electrical stimulation of a certain area of the brain-stem of an epileptic it is possible to produce mandala visions (*quadratura circuli*). From synchronistic phenomena we learn that a peculiar feature of the psychoid background is transgressivity in space and time. This brings us directly to the frontier of transcendence, beyond which human statements can only be mythological. (*Letters 2*, p. 258-259, to Walter Bernet, 13 June 1955)

One should stress that Jung uses here the notion of "borderline concept" in a way far different from Kant's way of thinking the thing in itself (*das Ding an sich*) as a merely *negative concept*: Jung applies it to the Self as a *positive* (though "unknowable," "invisible," "intangible") effective-reality, *Wirklichkeit*. This is a way of resuming a procedure of antique and medieval metaphysical thought: we can only imperfectly and indirectly know any substance (*ousia*[15]) through its correlate specific accidents, its distinct operations, or—in Jung's modern version— through its "effects." However, even when the concept of Self is given its maximum ontological-theological amplitude in Jung's theoretical speculations, he never *unambiguously* acknowledged its metaphysical status, refusing to admit that he was positing the correspondent transcendental object, *especially when he envisaged the Self as God-image*. On the other hand, *when by Self he meant human wholeness*, he insisted that there was something objective to which symbols of the Self pointed to. So, in the last analysis, my position here is that, while carefully trying to avoid the Scylla of a theosophical-metaphysical slip in positing God on the grounds of the psychic God-image, *as a psychologist* Jung was inadvertently and *explicitly* engulfed by the Charybdis of an anthropological-metaphysical slip,[16] positing the transcendent wholeness of Man on the grounds of the psychic image of *totus homo*, or rather defining this wholeness as the Self, "that greater being."

Consequently, when Jung declares that he cannot empirically distinguish "symbols of the Self" from "symbols of God," that means that he also cannot distinguish two transcendent supposed realities: the wholeness of man, which he tacitly posits, and God, which he agnostically avoids to posit. But Jung's agnosticism concerning the existence of God is at bottom helpless: from the moment that he posits the transcendent wholeness of man, then states that the Self (or its symbols) refers to (or is) this metaphysical entity, and then declares that he cannot empirically distinguish "symbols of the Self" from "symbols of God," his own anthropological metaphysical hypostasis leaves him only two alternatives: either "God" is "nothing but" the Self (and here we would have either an anthropological or a pantheistic form of atheism, *Homo homini deus* or *Deus sive Natura*), or "God" transcends *absolutely* the Self, being the model of which the Self is the image (and here we would have a theistic position). As I have indicated, Jung's thought is more akin to the Romantic form of pantheism as a larger circle within which is incrusted his particular metaphysical-anthropological comprehension of human being.

This same Romantic *naturphilosophisch* framework is active when Jung focuses the relation of individual and "nature," or of consciousness and "nature." The production of consciousness, human being's *telos* in life,[17] is seen as a paradoxical *opus contra naturam*:

> [T]he unconscious has a history, it is not always the same. At first it is an absolutely natural animal-like condition; it is a thing that denies itself, it is a yea and a nay, it is good and bad, light and dark, it is the eternal play of nature that builds up and pulls down. Nature kills every autumn whatever she has created during the year, and in the spring she creates everything all over again. But there is a peculiarly disturbing factor even in the natural unconscious, and that is the germ of the individual, the germ of the Self, like a spark of light, that causes consciousness to be. And when man begins to be conscious he aims at union with the spark of light; he is always doing something which doesn't agree with nature, more and more he disturbs nature, he tries to put nature into a straitjacket. Look at the straight lines through nature: for

> instance, railways, roads; and woods killed, fields ploughed, certain plants cultivated only in certain places. Nature would never produce such a sight. And what one sees on the surface of the earth, one sees in the soul of the conscious man: things which would never have been abstracted or concentrated together in certain places – all the signs of civilization, things done against nature. It is quite natural that the unconscious should not like that intrusion of consciousness, that it should have a tremendous resistance against it.[18]

Here Jung partakes the Romantic notion of nature as conflictive dynamism, and the conflict between human consciousness and the "natural" unconscious is a particular moment of a "natural history": "nature" produces "the germ of the Self," which is "a peculiarly disturbing factor" in search of consciousness. As is evident, here the anthropological dimension of the concept of Self finds its dynamic counterpart: individuation. And, in consonance with the Romantic conflictive sensibility, the problem of evil arises.

EVIL AND INDIVIDUATION: THE "SINFUL" LEVEL OF JUNG'S STANDPOINT
CONCERNING HUMAN CONSCIOUSNESS

On the practical level, Jung's perspective on individuation has two sides: on the one hand, individuation is the normative criterion that renders intelligible Jungian psychotherapeutic *praxis*, i.e., in the last analysis it orients the conduct in psychotherapy; as such, individuation is seen as the *good* aimed at by the psychological dynamism (being the immanent *telos* that puts it in motion), and consequently also by the psychotherapist in his/her concern with soul phenomena. On the other hand, individuation is seen by Jung as a kind of fateful sin committed against the original "natural" collective unconsciousness, and therefore it maintains an indissoluble relation with the emergence or production of individual consciousness, being even convertible with it: that's the reason why Jung attributes to individuation a "Luciferic quality," so that it must be seen as an *evil* disturbance of "absolute peace":

> For we may assume that the collective unconscious is in absolute peace until the individual appears. Therefore individuation is a sin; it is an assertion of one particle against the gods, and when that happens, even the world of gods is upset, then there is turmoil. ... The individual is the manifestation of the trouble,

and an individual consciousness appears from nowhere. You don't know where that thing came from, you just find it. You can call it the individual and assume that the individual is the instigator of all that trouble. ... I would not count the existence of the individual from the beginning of human consciousness. I would speak of the principle of individuation, which was obviously in the world long before the appearance of any kind of organic life. For instance, I would say a stone or the plant was an individuation. ... I should say that [i.e., a principle of restlessness] was linked up with individuation. That is not only my personal conviction, it is generally thought that individuation is of Luciferic quality.[19]

Taken in the general sense and applied to human species, the "principle of individuation" would correspond simply to humankind's departing from a merely natural status—or, in other terms, to the emergence of human consciousness. But, as is well known and may be seen in the above quotation, Jung does not restrict individuation to this generic event (the birth of humanity out of nature), but envisages it also in the relation between the individual and the "collective unconscious" — or the community or tradition to which he/she belongs. Individuation as the production of differentiated forms of consciousness is an historical event, and the generic "beginning of human consciousness" (or the "germ of the Self") is presupposed in all its different historical stages or logical forms.

When individuation is considered as the process of empirical coming up of individuality (and not as a process occurring only at the archetypal level of *Anthropos*), its alleged evil disturbance character must be enacted by the "sinful" individual who is seized by the individuating impulse of the soul, ascribed to the "germ of the Self." Indeed, individuality entails at least the *danger* of evil, if we bear in mind that the concrete definition of what is good is collectively and socially established, and with reference to this definition the good attitude is conforming oneself to the ethical canons of a given community, actualizing its *ethos*. However, inasmuch as this actualization concretely (as it happens empirically and historically in a given culture) always leaves an indeterminate set of possibilities excluded from its symbolic cultural profile, the coming up of unassimilated differences in the process of cultural as well as individual[20] self-actualization may sometimes be potentially contradictory to the already established ethical tradition, and so it cannot avoid the shadow of evil when seen from the standpoint of collective consciousness in its already acquired ethical configurations. The fear of change—and individuation by definition implies change —, correlative of the fear of time, is responsible for the conservatism of the traditionalist mind, and it is from the traditionalist standpoint that evil may be seen in individuation.

This means that, from an ethical-philosophical perspective, individuation necessarily entails the *possibility* of *ethical conflict*. If we reflect upon a key text from Jung concerning this issue— "The Spiritual Problem of Modern Man" (in *CW* 10)—, we can see that he thinks both individuation and ethical conflict as correlates of the modern condition. (Even though there is no occurrence of the term "individuation" in this text, it is evident that its notion is implied in Jung's reflection.) There, Jung thinks modern condition on a phenomenological level, not on a strictly historical one (as can be seen by his presenting Socrates and Jesus as examples of "modern men"). What defines this modern stance, according to Jung, is the full consciousness of the present, furthered by the ample fulfillment of the duties appointed by one's world (or *ethos*) and one's outgrowing the stages of consciousness belonging to the past, leading to an estrangement "from the mass of men who live entirely within the bounds of tradition" (§ 150), and consequently—because this "higher level of consciousness is like a burden of *guilt*" (§ 152, italics mine)— to the ethical obligation to "atone by creative ability for [one's] break with tradition," in order not to be "merely disloyal to the past" (§ 152). The ethical ambiguity involving individuation as a correlate of modern consciousness is undeniable in Jung's stating that

> Every good quality has its bad side, and nothing good can come into the world without at once producing a corresponding evil. This *painful* fact renders illusory the feeling of elation that so often goes with consciousness of the present – the feeling that we are the culmination of the whole history of mankind, the fulfillment and end-product of countless generations. At best it should be a proud admission of our poverty: we are also the disappointment of the hopes and expectations of the ages. (CW 10 § 153, italics mine)

Meditating on the impact and danger that "modern men" such as Socrates and Jesus represented to their respective traditions and communities, we may understand the capital punishment to which they were convicted not only as accidental historical facts, but especially as soul events. Only through death can a higher logical status of consciousness be attained. Of course I mean here *symbolic* (or *logical*) death, though this does not exclude that in certain fateful events, decisive to soul's *Opus Magnum* —as in the episodes of Socrates and Jesus—, literal death is enacted and constitutes a visible historical mark signaling the new directions taken in soul history: in time, the empirical persons practically disappear behind the guiding symbolic images. Be as it may, death comes along with individuation. In fact, though this point cannot be developed here, on a broader and immanent sense *individuation means death*—the death of one's dearest illusions, the death of ego perspective, the death of the blissful containment in the collective consciousness of a given community or, more generally, the logical death of an obsolete level of consciousness.

I think that this necessary relation, *on the practical level*, between individuation, guilt, suffering, and death—or, in other terms, between individuation and what, *from the human standpoint*, constitutes the realm of evil—provides the deep reason for Jung's obsessive (and frequently misguided) involvement with this thorny metaphysical issue. Envisaged from this standpoint, there is no way of bypassing the *experience* of evil: even if we concede that on the logical level evil is no topic for soul's *Opus Magnum* anymore, as Giegerich sustains, we must on the other hand emphasize that it has been, is, and probably will continue to be a problem for *man* as far as his empirical existence is concerned. This was certainly Jung's position: "I believe that misery is an intrinsic part of human life, without which we would never do anything" (*Letters 1*, p. 236, to V. Subrahamanya Iyer, 16 September 1937).

Evil belongs to the problematic of *human freedom*, and consequently to the field of *ethics*. The concept of individuation, taken on a subjective level, is intrinsically connected with the problem or reality of evil, and may help us understand that psychology, at least as Jung sees it, is essentially an ethical enterprise. Thinking of individuation in an anthropological horizon, and applying it to the relation of the individual to his/her *ethos*, Jung understood it as a *moral achievement*,[21] and stated that nothing could spare us from the torment of ethical decision. If we stay at the level of *opus parvum*, this ethical dimension is included in soul perspective precisely through the goal-oriented process ruling soul's logical life. For the fulfillment of this goal—its *telos*—is precisely the immanent good aimed at in the process itself, and conversely, some obstacles to this fulfillment may be interpreted through the category of evil, though not as *absolute* evil, for frequently we are faced with *self-engendered* obstacles, i.e., obstacles created by soul dynamism in order to make possible the achievement of its own ends, and thus they are moments of its immanent good. Dialectically envisioned, the impulse of individuation may be reinterpreted as the soul's self-movement, a movement that requires the self-negation of soul, and so relative evil—implied in the moment of negation—is necessary to the accomplishment of that movement. One could see here the secularized dialectical-psychological version of the age-old Christian theological question concerning the role of evil in God's salvation plan. The sublation of evil—accomplished, in Giegerich's terms, through the relentless (logical) bowing under the evil and evils in the world—is a necessary moment in soul-making, a moment through which is attained a higher logical level of consciousness.

In my opinion, Jung did not clearly reach a satisfactory intellectual formulation of the *dialectical* essence of the ethical conflict that accompanies individuation because, though he sensibly had an intuition about this, he predominantly thought the problem of evil in a non-dialectical way, ultimately determined by his theoretical and ontological oppositionalism. This prevented him from correctly understanding the doctrine of *privatio boni*: he admitted the relativity of moral judgments, but ascribed a positive referent to "good" and "evil" in the substantiality of "*real* pair of opposites." Now I would like to say a few more words about that.

In a way that maybe exhibits the protestant presuppositions of his "personal equation," Jung inscribes the problem of evil in a place *essential* to man, and in such a way that any unifying perspective seems from the outset doomed to failure or to unintelligibility. These religious presuppositions are homologous to the strong philosophical presupposition concerning the ontological status of the *opposites*:

> In themselves, spirit and matter are neutral, or rather, 'utriusque capax' – that is, capable of what man calls good or evil. Although as names they are exceedingly relative, *underlying them are very real opposites that are part of the energic structure of the physical and of the psychical world, and without them no existence of any kind could be established.* (*CW* 9i § 197, italics mine)

Jung takes *actual existence* as a privileged basis to which all his theorizing should be referred to. This position is prolonged in and mixes itself with what we could call a *metaphysics of the opposites*, of a clear Romantic style.[22] And frequently it is this already complex *interpretation* of reality that underlies his much claimed "*empiricism.*" Jung's perspective is extended to his interpretation of the human condition, and consequently of soul phenomena at large and individuation in particular. He states that

> our basic nature is not a oneness; it is, you could almost say, a multitude of the most contradictory instincts or impulses. The very basis of our nature is the pairs of opposites, and pairs of opposites are instinctive, they are just spontaneous facts. ... The idea of the pairs of opposites is simply a philosophic formulation of the fact that the instincts are divided against each other; there is absolutely no biological situation where those opposing instincts are not operating.[23]

Obviously Jung thought the overcoming of the tension of the opposites by means of the concept of Self:

> Wherever our need for knowledge may turn we stumble upon opposites, which ultimately determine the structure of existence. The centre is the indivisible monad of the Self, the unity and wholeness of the experiencing subject (*Letters 2*, March 13, 1958, to anonymous, p. 423-424).

But, by adopting at the same time an ultimate ontological oppositionalism and a too narrow notion of the "rationality" of the "conscious mind," he considers the union of opposites an irrational event:

> But out of this collision of the opposites the unconscious psyche always creates a third thing of an irrational nature, which the conscious mind neither expects nor understands. It presents itself in a form that is neither a straight 'yes' nor a straight 'no', and is consequently rejected by both. For the conscious mind knows

nothing beyond the opposites and, as a result, has no knowledge
of the thing that unites them. (*CW* 9i § 285)

Indeed, if you radically start with ontologized opposites, "which
ultimately determine the structure of existence," there is no way of
knowing the "thing that unites them," because there is no such thing,
and the union of opposites could only be a helpless *desideratum*, or an
unintelligible anomalous or fictitious happening, not an experience,
the experience of Self.[24] On the other hand, if you posit "the indivisible
monad of the Self, the unity and wholeness of the experiencing subject,"
as a "center" that is free from the collision of opposites or that can unite
them, you ought to establish its relation with the "structure of existence"
ultimately determined by opposites, and this only could be done by a
dialectical approach. But Jung, making no concessions to "idealism,"
rejecting any "speculative thought," could not have satisfactorily
harmonized in his thinking the oppositional "structure of existence"
with "the unity and wholeness of the experiencing subject." In the last
analysis, this harmony would forcefully have to be thought of as
irrational and mysterious.

Now, if we read Jung's position in the light of the Christian notion
of human being, we may see how, despite declaring himself "entirely
based upon Christian concepts," he could not reach their deep sense
or be *entirely* based on them. As his insistence on the reality of evil
confirms, Jung thought humanness preferentially in the light of the
soul truth expressed in the Adamic myth (which he interpreted in a
way that corroborated his own view), but placing human's essence
essentially under the aegis of original sin, and simply disregarding or
distorting the previous moment, which only can give original sin its
full meaning. For the perception of opposites (Gn 3, 5: "ye shall be as
gods, knowing good and evil") and the consequent laceration by them,
interpreted according to the rule of "sticking to the image," correspond
to the *new* level of consciousness attained through the moment of
original sin. *Previously* (in the logical sense, of course), that dilacerating
perception was absent, so that human consciousness should be thought
of as not differentiated from divine absolute consciousness transcendent
to the opposites. This is precisely the meaning of being *created sine
macula peccati*, and this is consciousness's original *position*, a position
which *is not touched by* the opposites. Only thus there is a real possibility
of consciousness, after the negation of its initial position and the

consequent being afflicted by the opposites, attaining the final *complexio oppositorum*. But Jung comes to the Adamic myth with an oppositionalist anthropological presupposition, which commands his one-sided interpretation of the biblical conception of man, and thus cannot concede any real sense to a *sine macula peccati* state of humanness or consciousness.

Without the complete logical framework displayed in the Adamic myth, which conditions the possibility of thinking the actual liberation from being "thorn-asunder" by the opposites and the rebirth or resurrection motif as corresponding to the Christian way of presenting such liberation, Jung could not understand the novelty present in the Christian conception of human being's relation to evil, neither the deep sense of Saint Paul's naming of Christ as *Adam secundus*: full incarnation is a way of fully actualizing humanity by resuming the Adamic stance – only by "becoming human" and completely bowing under evil can "God" redeem humankind's longing both for the simple identity of "being like gods" and for the "lost paradise" by negating it, and thus (logically) pave the way to its final divinization in the absolute negativity of resurrection. At least in this point, it seems that Jung reduces the Christian novelty back to the Adamic model, instead of seeing in it the sublation of the myth of original sin. But then, how could he truly know and state that the overcoming of suffering through its endurance could be learned from the Crucified? He couldn't, and, no wonder now, his comprehension was doomed to stay aporetically stuck in the Adamic "sinful" level, unable to understand its dialectical overcoming in the Christian experience, which thus should be considered one-sided.

So, in the Christian perspective, from the very beginning (see Gn 1, 26-28) man is fully human,[25] distinct from any other being in his image and likeness of God, and created *sine macula peccati* (which means that evil, though being *radical*—we could even say that it is *fateful* -, is not *ontological*). This is the anthropological correlate of the *privatio boni* doctrine, and only within this perspective can there be any sense in stating that "suffering has to be overcome, and the only way to overcome it is to endure it" and that "we learn that only from [Christ]." In other words: the one-sided charge raised by Jung shows that he cannot understand appropriately the Christian stance concerning evil, as is perfectly demonstrated in Giegerich's text.

Let me summarize the argument presented here: Jung's thinking postulates the ultimately oppositional structure of existence, and not its unity—he considers such a unitary view as metaphysical/transcendental, and rejects it as not empirically based.[26] This ontological oppositionalism leads him to state the *reality/substantiality of evil*, and to entangle himself in the equivocated polemics against the doctrine of *privatio boni*. Transposed to the structure of *human* existence, it forces Jung to equate human condition with the laceration of opposites, and the (hopeless) longing to overcome it. That's the reason why he cannot admit Jesus as being fully human: the absence of *macula peccati* would pull him out of the essentially oppositional human condition.

Therefore, from a complementary angle we can see why Jung addressed to Christian thought the charge of one-sidedness, why he was unable to understand and accept the doctrine of *privatio boni*, and finally why he could only think of the unifying of opposites as an irrational mysterious event, at bottom unintelligible. Jung thinks human being, or human consciousness, "the specific light of the human being,"[27] on a *radical "sinful"* level.

Appendix: A Meditation on Giegerich's "Saint Jung" Sarcasm

In a recent polemical paper Giegerich states that "it is the ethical obligation of any writer striving for insight to first free himself of any emotion so as to become able to study his subject *sine ira et studio*."[28] One of the most admirable features in his critical writings on psychology is precisely the capability of fulfilling this ethical obligation, and the commitment to it. That is why I was surprised by his indulging in sarcasm in the "*God must not die!*" text, with the expression "St. Jung." Sarcasm points to the presence of an emotion and the possible loss of psychological objectivity in the critique.

Meditating on this surprising irruption of an emotion in Giegerich's argument, I tried to understand its occurrence. Could the same point have been expressed without the sarcastic expression? Yes, absolutely: the simple omission of the "St." in the title of the section would not alter the exposition and would be sufficient to eliminate the explicit sarcasm and the need to admit that there was a bit of maliciousness in the expression. Was the sarcastic stance relevant to the argument? Not at all. On the contrary: adopting Giegerich's own position concerning Jung's confessed sarcasm in *Answer to Job*, it unnecessarily throws a shadow of doubt over a, for the rest, consistent position.

Giegerich's excuse for his maliciousness ("all the authors of a gospel are automatically canonized") is not convincing. At best it could be addressed not to the "author" Jung, but to the "faithful" part of the community of Jungians who actually canonize the author and his thought. The excuse cannot cast off the suspicion that there may be a personal "feeling-tone complex" at work behind or together with Giegerich's critique of Jung's positions. Intrigued by this surprising emotion displayed in the "Saint Jung" sarcasm, I decided to examine it in the light of the thought expressed in note 9 of Giegerich's article, and see what would come out of this. Granting Jung's statement that sarcasm "is the means by which we hide our hurt feelings from ourselves" (*Letters 2*, pp. 28f., to Hans Schär, 16 November 1951), I would say that, from the "Saint Jung" sarcasm and what plausibly is hidden and at the same time discloses itself through it, one would have to conclude that the true author of *God must not die!* was not only W. Giegerich, the psychologist, but also an unresolved complex. The psychologist thinks and writes from the perspective of the famous Nietzschean announcement "God *is* dead" — or, in Giegerich's terms, God has vaporized into Spirit and Love, a statement disclosing the logical truth of modern consciousness. But the sarcastic emotion strongly suggests the intrusion of an ego perspective in Giegerich's psychological reflection. The presence of a "feeling-tone complex" in the form of sarcasm could be interpreted as an involuntary confession of a residual *personal* problem concerning the obsolescence of "Saint Jung," who announces that God is not definitely dead, being reborn in the soul. Why would Jung's religious stance stir this supposed complex? The answer would probably be that "*Saint Jung* must die!," maybe as a condition to the *personal* complete assurance concerning the project of a fully developed critical psychology. Of course, by "Saint Jung" what is meant here is the religious appeal in Jung's psychology, one of its logical "impurities," considering the status of truly modern consciousness, and the attempt displayed in the sarcasm would be to "kill" any possible legitimacy of this religious trend by showing its ridiculous character as a caricature of true religion (or truly logically dead religion). And so the answer should be read also as "Saint Jung *must* die!," an imperative, addressed to the will, to an ego fighting an *opposing* point of view that, through the sarcasm itself, is posited as somehow *personally* still very alive, notwithstanding being logically obsolete.

The sarcasm cannot help projecting over the whole critique the uncomfortable tone of an aggressive apologetics, remembering the dispute between some of the Fathers of the Church and certain heretical or opposing views concerning Christian truth. From this perspective, the polemics deflagrated by Giegerich's critique of Jung's stance concerning Christianity and religion may be envisioned analogically as a contemporaneous and secularized version of the religious dispute between idolatry/heresy and "true faith," or between theism and atheism. The sarcasm would have analogically the function of reassuring the thesis that "the time of religion *is* over," despite (or in face of) the *factual* exponentially growing consumption of diversified religious commodities in our times, a clear sign not of the end of religion, but of its persistence in one of its traditional forms.[29] "Saint Jung's" presenting individuation as a form of religious experience would be a stubborn denial of the logical obsolescence of religion. The sarcasm, precisely in fighting this stubbornness, falls helplessly in the same emotional-subjective level, though on the other side. (Alternatively, the stubbornness could have been only pointed out as a feature of Jung's position. There was no *objective* need to ridicule it sarcastically.)

Giegerich, the psychologist, dialectically negates Jung (his own "presupposition") in order to achieve a more differentiated position. But the sarcasm concedes to "Saint Jung's" project the status of an "opposing will," a still not definitely dead ghost, perhaps a split off and projected part of the sarcastic ego that *must* be overcome at *any* costs. And such a task is an ego affair. If this is plausible, if through the sarcasm an ego perspective insinuated itself in the psychological reflection constructed by Giegerich, then we could turn to the problem of *evil* and see if it helps us in further understanding the sarcasm itself.

When discussing Jung's interpretation of Christ's initial meeting with the tempter, Giegerich offers a valuable alternative and dialectical vision. And we should stress that the evil attributed to the "preliminary thesis" (the tempter in its devilish aspect) must be seen in its potential for blocking the logical movement towards "the more sophisticated thesis" reached by Jesus: the absolute-negative interiorization, inasmuch as it represents the *telos* of that movement, is the *good* determining the movement itself. The evil-devilish aspect is in the possibility of impeding the movement of "coming home to itself," and thus staying stuck in positivity ("Maybe the possibility of misunderstanding his mission in the sense of positivity and acting it out is indeed a possible shadow aspect of what Jesus was striving for"—p. 19).

Bearing that in mind, and considering "Saint Jung" as an evil-devilish shadow aspect of what Giegerich is striving for, somehow still *personally* painful, menacing, or simply (but symptomatically) irritating, maybe the final paragraph of his paper could offer a possible justification for the sarcasm:

> evil is something logical and, as such, negative (a *privatio*): namely one's NOT *negating* one's natural impulses and naturalistic imaginal perspectives, one's NOT placing oneself under supersensory ethical laws, one's NOT humbling oneself all the way and NOT (logically) bowing under the evil and evils in the world. It is the *omission*, or rather *refusal*, to overcome, time and again, one's "original sin" by rising to the sphere of logos and the concept.

Applied initially in ontology, the doctrine of *privatio boni* means, in this first level, the statement that there is no evil *substance*. As in antique cosmology there was a hierarchy of perfection in Being in the order of the universe, *privatio boni* also means that beings located in an inferior position in the hierarchical scale lack some degree of perfection when compared to beings located in a superior position (and all beings lack the absolute perfection of *Summum Bonum*). For instance: a rock lacks the perfection of a tree (vegetative life), the tree lacks the perfection of an animal (sensible life), the animal lacks the perfection of a man (intellectual life). But *privatio boni* in this level does not mean that there is anything wrong, or that a given being *should be* more perfect than it actually is. On the contrary: this order as a whole was considered good in itself, so that the limited degree of perfection (or imperfection) was also good in itself. Besides that, any *action* or *attitude* against the good order was necessarily regarded as *evil*. And here a second level, intimately and indissolubly associated with the ontological level, discloses itself: the *moral-ethical* level, where evil is given the status of a *reality*, though not of a substance. Only a free and rational being could oppose the good order of the cosmos and its dynamism, and it *should not* do so. This is the point where the notion of *sin* (as well as the notion of *hybris*) comes to the foreground. And to this level belongs moral judgment.

When Giegerich closes his text mentioning *privatio boni* in this undeniable moral-ethical level, we come to the conclusion that the methodological lapses indicated in Jung's approach to Christianity (and to religion in general) are seen not only as an epistemological or logical issue: they are *sins*, logical sins that simultaneously and dialectically block the way of consciousness and push it towards *the stance correspondent to the rigorous notion of psychology*. But, because *at bottom* the project of a "rigorous notion of psychology" is also and essentially an *ethical* project, there is always the possibility of switching from the strictly psychological-dialectical approach to the *moral* perspective, and this is precisely what seems to have happened in the sarcastic joke. Consequently, Jung's sins *should* be overcome: one *should* negate one's natural impulses and naturalistic imaginal perspectives; one *should* place oneself under supersensory laws, humble oneself all the way and logically bow under the evil and evils of the world; one *should* rise to the sphere of logos and the concept. The sarcasm, *nolens volens*, entails a moral judgment about the methodological and epistemological shortcomings of Jung's project: all that prevented Jung from reaching an unambiguous "rigorously psychological position" is seen as *evil*, and the resulting "theosophical gospel" is sarcastically attacked. Some of the fundamental (or "original") "sins" of Jung's stance are spelled out by Giegerich and implicitly contrasted with the main features of his (Giegerich's) own position. The "sins" in Jung's stance are *privationes*—through them he failed to reach the psychological *summum bonum* of a truly dialectical psychology, in tune with the logical truth of modern consciousness. There is a hierarchical order implied in this psychological *privatio boni*, and one can also hear the enlightened call to "coming of age," the age of reason and maturity, in the footnote about the meaning of "original sin." (In this context, we should note that the Adamic sin—wishing to be more or different than one actually is—may be seen psychologically as an intrinsically and logically "childish" impulse, an impulse that

precisely has its function in pushing consciousness, through failure
—or negation of negation—, towards "maturity"—*felix culpa*!)

It is not that Jung's position is simply wrong or false. Like the devil's
stance in the temptation story interpreted dialectically, Jung's position
is needed so that through its negation its deepest truth comes to light
—and, in Giegerich's thinking, this truth is the truth of "the soul's
logical life." But this dialectical negation does not remain in the "icy-
cold remoteness of soul" or of reason. The "Saint Jung" sarcasm shows
that it is "hot" because, no doubt, evil "emotionalizes" (p. 60), even if
evil is conceived merely as a *privatio boni* perceptible in Jung's
methodological lapses and shortcomings. The sarcasm is of the same
nature and level of the emotion underlying the "*refusal* to overcome,
time and again, one's 'original sin'," only with an opposed signal. And
if the "ideas of evil and the shadow [have] an anchor in the concrete
personal experience of each individual" (p. 65), the sarcasm is a strong
evidence suggesting that Giegerich was not immune to emotions in
this critique, that he *passionately* fights for his project because—of
course—he is *personally* identified with it. But through the sarcasm
the "hot" personal value has priority over the "icy-cold" psychological
truth to which it adheres, and as a consequence Giegerich fights *against*
"Saint Jung" and his psychological sins. Therefore, the psychological
critique becomes indiscernible from an ethical-moral rectification.

My point here is not to oppose Giegerich's *theoretical* stance. The
historical as well as theoretical background of the critique is the dispute
over two different comprehensions of *modernity*: one Romantic, the other
Hegelian. Jung, with his craving for a "second naïveté" (in the sense
defined by Paul Ricoeur), "reluctantly" but unmistakably partakes the
Romantic stance, whereas Giegerich, striving to overcome any naïveté
whatsoever, and thus incarnating one of the most genuine and
unmistakable features of the spirit of Enlightenment, espouses the
position of Hegel, who, as is well known, departed from Romanticism
and made the overall critique of its project.

Personally I agree and endorse Giegerich's theoretical position, but
this doesn't matter at all. My intention is just to separate from this
theoretical stance the "Saint Jung" sarcasm with all its underlying moral
judgment, which seems to me to indicate only a personal affair.

And, finally, a moral judgment is not alien to the emotional basis
of humankind, as Aristotle already taught us in his ethical thinking,

even if one *should* try to make it emotionally impartial, especially when implied in a rational critique of a theory, for this is the condition to achieve the maximum intellectual honesty possible. I think that Giegerich exhibited an all-too-human *emotional* commitment vis-à-vis Jung's religious project when he indulged in the "Saint Jung" sarcasm. I have no problem with this, except that it not only surprised me for being unusual in his writings, but also suggested that his study of the subject was not completely done *sine ira et studio*.

NOTES

1. Bearing in mind that, at the time when it made its entrance in history, Christianity was charged with atheism, we could say that modern atheism can be envisaged as a specific form of Christian heresy, a heresy that could be understood theologically from the perspective of Trinitarian doctrine as resulting from the negation of the person of the Father, in its trans-human transcendence, and the consequent statement of the full immanent status of the person of the Son, now considered as being exclusively coincident with humanity itself. This would be a modern and atheist interpretation of the dogma of incarnation. In this paper I have not discussed Giegerich's interpretation of Christianity, but I would like to stress that it is objectionable, especially from a theological standpoint. On this topic, I recommend the debate between Slavoj •i•ek (who defends the Hegelian reading of Christianity) and John Milbank (who criticizes it on philosophical as well as theological grounds). See Slavoj •i•ek and John Milbank, *The Monstrosity of Christ: Paradox or Dialectic?*, Creston Davis, ed. (Cambridge: MIT Press, 2009).

2. I do not follow Giegerich in stating that Jung simply ignores "*the whole real development* of Western culture over the centuries, the rich phenomenology of the *real history of the soul* in the West" (p. "God Must Not Die", this volume, p. 56). This seems to me a bit exaggerated, for Jung correctly sees that modern consciousness derives partially from the effects of protestant experience, on the one hand, and from those of Scientific Revolution, on the other. These are truly major events in the real history of the soul in the West, in which one can grasp those "tremendous *form changes* concerning the syntactical constitution of

consciousness" (*ibid.*). The point is that Jung, being a Romantic thinker (though of a "reluctant Romanticism," as Paul Bishop has classified it), *resists* this development, and romantically tries to give it a solution through the cultural project of reawakening the symbolic sensibility of modern consciousness.

3. This logic—as expressed in the metaphysics of subjectivity—is structurally atheist inasmuch as the place of the absolute, formerly attributed to God, is occupied by the (human) transcendental subject. The category of transcendence, *understood in a radical sense* and essential to any form of theism, seemingly has no place within the logical level reached by modern consciousness, and it is precisely a consequence of this logical form to swallow up, so to speak, all transcendence within the limits of immanence. In the new form of consciousness thus created transcendence is replaced by mere and immanent self-transcendence. I should add that even the later criticism of the philosophy of subject does not overcome the broader anthroponomic and immanentistic logical horizon of the modern form of consciousness.

4. Wolfgang Giegerich, *The Soul's Logical Life: Towards a Rigorous Notion of Psychology,* 3rd edition (Frankfurt am Main: Peter Lang, 2001), p. 66-67.

5. "The absolute essence, the God of Man is Man's own essence." Ludwig Feuerbach, *Das Wesen des Christenthums* (Stuttgart: Frommann Verlag Günther Holzboog, 1960), p. 6.

6. Now Giegerich corrects the statement made in *The Soul's Logical Life* by recognizing that Jung "asserts that outside the image and statement there is in fact a transcendental object that they point to ... [w]hich is a metaphysical hypostasis, a setting up of the object talked about as existing outside the soul's images or statements," and that such hypostatizing "is inherent in the *objective* logical form of [Jung's] myth-making" ("God Must Not Die," this volume, p. 36 and 38). My position here is that this mythologizing rests on a metaphysical conception of *human wholeness or totality*, and thus its metaphysical hypostasis is in the first place an anthropological one.

7. Even granting that the substantiated "unconscious" is a transcendental concept, one cannot say that it is *just a word* (on account of being devoid of empirical referent) without making oneself a (positivistic) metaphysical statement, as liable to suspicion as the

transcendental concept it wants to impugn. (Giegerich is evidently quite aware of this kind of risk, as is shown in his careful explanation concerning the metaphysical difference between image and the transcendental object that it supposedly points to, in note 5 [see "God Must Not Die," this volume, p. 67). Furthermore, a rigorous scientific thinking cannot pretend to *disprove* any metaphysical statement: it must only leave it aside. And, as Kant had already recognized—and Jung after him—, after their expulsion from scientific discourse, metaphysical assertions may continue to have *at least* subjective-anthropological or psychological meaning.

8. Giegerich, *The Soul's Logical Life*, p. 67-68.

9. This position derives from the dogmatic discussions and definitions concerning the "communication of idioms" (or properties) in the Council of Ephesus (431 a.d.)

10. James Hillman, *The Myth of Analysis* (Evanston: Northwestern University Press, 1972), p. 191.

11. See Giegerich, *The Soul's Logical Life*, p. 41.

12. C. G. Jung, *Visions. Notes of the Seminar Given in 1930-1934*, Claire Douglas, ed. (Princeton: Princeton University Press, 1997), p. 748.

13. Wolfgang Giegerich, "The Present as Dimension of the Soul," in *The Neurosis of Psychology, Collected English Papers. Vol. 1* (New Orleans: Spring Journal Books, 2005), p. 111.

14. Giegerich, "The Present as Dimension of the Soul," *CEP*, vol. 1, p. 112.

15. It may be helpful to remember that in Aristotle, what came to be later known as "Metaphysics" has four specifications: ousiology (knowledge of substance), aitiology (knowledge of the four causes), ontology (knowledge of *ens qua ens*) and theology (knowledge of the divine). Jung's inference of the "transcendent wholeness of man" belongs in the first place to Aristotelian ousiology—though in a modern version, just like Descartes posited a substantial *Ego* from the cogitating activity.

16. I call it a "slip" only with respect to a pretended rigorous psychological approach. It does not mean that I dispute (metaphysically) the validity of any metaphysical assertion *as such*.

17. "The extraordinary emphasis [Stewart Edward] White lays on consciousness also agrees with our view that the dawning of

consciousness, indeed consciousness itself, is the all-important goal of human evolution" (*Letters 1*, p. 432, to Fritz Künkel, 10 July 1946).

18. Jung, *Visions. Notes of the Seminar Given in 1930-1934*, p. 1081-1082.

19. Jung, *Visions. Notes of the Seminar Given in 1930-1934*, p. 263-264.

20. Here I should note that the "individuality" that emerges in the process of individuation must be understood not in the sense of the mere empirical individuality, but as identical with the *ethical individuality*. Individuation, in Jung's sense, always implies the conscious confrontation with one's ethical tradition, its norms and values, and this confrontation presupposes the active and reflexive differentiation from the mere "spontaneous" adhesion to the moral canons of one's tradition, or from its opposite: the sheer un-reflected "individual" refusal of the normativity of one's *ethos*. Only in this sense we can understand Jung's statement that the "possession of individual peculiarities is neither a merit nor, in itself, a valuable gift of nature. It is 'just one of those things', and it becomes significant only to the degree that consciousness reflects upon it, evaluates it, and subjects it to ethical decision." (*CW* 10 § 896)

21. I have developed this ethical dimension of individuation in "A Dimensão Ética da Psicologia Analítica: Individuação como 'Realização Moral', " in *Psicologia Clínica*, Rio de Janeiro, vol. 21, n. 1, p. 91-105, 2009. Also available through the link http://www.scielo.br/scielo.php?script=sci_arttext&pid=S0103-56652009000100007&lng=pt&nrm=iso.

22. On oppositionalism in Jung, see James Hillman, *The Dream and the Underworld* (New York: Harper and Row, 1979), p. 74-85: "Jung is more a follower of the romantic use of opposites. He sees them as constitutive of things more than modes of arguing about things. ... oppositionalism is mainly a vision of reality, a universal law, and only secondarily an epistemological procedure of ordering." (p. 76)

23. Jung, *Visions. Notes of the Seminar Given in 1930-1934*, p. 1063.

24. On the definition of Self as experience itself or the process of dialectical union of opposites, see Wolfgang Giegerich, "Jung's *Thought* of the Self in the Light of Its Underlying Experience," in *The Neurosis of Psychology, Collected English Papers, Vol. 1*, p. 171-189.

25. Here, and as an example of another typical kind of distortion, I must point out that Giegerich's interpretation of the psychological sense of "original sin" (see note 25, p. 71) partially falls prey to the very same kind of mistake that he charges Jung's approach to Christian message: he brings in something alien to the image (though of a different kind from Jung's oppositionalism) when he too interprets "original sin" presupposing "man's implicitly *having become human and thus having logically sublated his animal nature*" (italics mine). For, if one sticks to the *biblical text* (distinguishing it from its interpretations in the Christian tradition—to which the expression "original sin" belongs—), it is clear that, *from the outset*, "man" is biblically presented as distinct from mere "animal nature," inasmuch as humankind, and only humankind, is created "in the image and likeness" of God, and only this explains why man can negate God—an animal, as Jung liked to say, is a very pious being, and cannot be otherwise. Biblically, man does not *become* human, he is created *essentially* human. Giegerich inadvertently translocates the biblical notion of "original sin" to a sort of "evolutionist" mindset which determines the psychological sense he finds in it. Besides that, one cannot understand where is the alleged discrepancy—between "having become human and thus having sublated his animal nature" and "staying a priori conditioned by ... emotions and desires which of course are the *human*, and thus post-natural, already fantasy-guided equivalent to the animal's animal nature, its instincts"—i.e., these "fantasy guided" equivalents would be precisely a first level of the (presupposed) sublation of "animal nature," and so there would be no discrepancy, *concerning human status*, between different levels or dimensions of the same humanity. Of course Giegerich knows very well that "'Natural' means something different depending on whether it refers to humans or to animals (or even to inanimate nature, for that matter). Our impulses are 'natural' for us humans, mere events, but as impulses of *humans* they are *in themselves* beyond the merely natural. They are already, although of course only implicitly, ideas or concepts (in contrast to mere triggered 'release mechanisms')." But then, perhaps the discrepancy—internal to a being who is already essentially human in its origin—is between the "hot" *human* sphere of emotions and desires and the "icy-cold" *human* sphere of logos and the concept, between the implicitness of logos in human impulses and its explicitness in human reflexive consciousness, and not

between the acquired human status and a residual conditioning by a prior animal nature. Be as it may, I would say that the psychological meaning of "original sin," staying only within the biblical text, is to indulge in the human desire of being more than human, striving "to be like gods" *in a certain specific way*, namely *positivizing* or *acting out* man's likeness to God (which, in a Hegelian perspective, would correspond to the full-fledged surrender to the bad infinity of desire). As the tempter's episode analyzed by Giegerich shows, Jesus sort of "corrects" or takes this immanent human tendency to its final *telos* by negating it—which, of course, does not mean a simple repression, but the dialectical and Christian way of "being like gods."

26. Nevertheless, the same set of circumstances that pressed his thought towards the axial doctrine of synchronicity also led him to the undeniably metaphysical speculation about *Unus Mundus*, in which the *ultimate* ontological status of opposites is challenged.

27. Jung, *Visions. Notes of the Seminar Given in 1930-1934*, p. 1194.

28. Wolfgang Giegerich, "The Psychologist as Repentance Preacher and Revivalist: Robert Romanyshyn on the Melting of the Polar Ice," *Symbolic Life–Spring 82* (2009), p. 195.

29. It must be remembered that religiosity by itself is not immune to the powerful strength of Market: the merchantilization of the sacred is not a new phenomenon, and Jesus' anger in the Temple is just one of the episodes that confirm the antiquity of this practice or trend, seemingly insurmountable in the history and practice of world religions and deeply connected with idolatry, another widespread and persistent universal form of religiosity.

ETWAS GESCHAH:
ORPHANED EVENT AND ITS ADOPTIONS

JOHN PECK

Something Happened —the title by novelist Joseph Heller

Others try to understand with their brains only, and want to *skip the purely practical stage [*also: *pure occurrence or happening**]. And when they have understood, they think they have done their full share of realization…. [The fourth and final stage, beyond feeling,] has a very pronounced symbolism in alchemy: this is the anticipation of the lapis…, "the stone that is no stone."…. This keystone rounds off the work into an experience of totality for the individual. *Such an experience* is completely foreign to our age, although no earlier age has ever needed it as much.[1]

—C. G. Jung

It is one of the self-delusions of our time to think that the spirits do not ride again, or that the 'wild hunt' gallops no more. We are removed only from *the place of such*

John Peck, Ph.D., is a member of the International Association for Analytical Psychology with a practice in Higganum, Connecticut. The translator of several books by Luigi Zoja and co-translator of the *Red Book* with Sonu Shamdasani and Mark Kyburz, his chief publications are *Collected Shorter Poems 1966-1996* (Northwestern University Press, 2003) and *Red Strawberry Leaf* (University of Chicago Press, 2005).

happenings, carried away by our madness. Those of us who are still there, or have found their way back again, will be smitten by *the same experience,* now as before.[2]

—C. G. Jung

[In Jung's foundational observations of the solar-phallus man's fantasy,] *psychology unexpectedly happens…*[as] a speaking for which the people concerned are merely the place and vessel…. Psychology, as we find it in Jung, is not a methodically applicable science, but *event, happening!*... The actual concept of archetype…is not a relation that he establishes through a method, but rather, *one that happens to him.*[3]

—Wolfgang Giegerich

What one has to fall back on is always *the structure of the experience itself,* and you find that only the people who have the experience have analyzed that…. We have a knowledge that these questions gradually become clarified in consciousness in the history of mankind; and that is history…. One of the imaginary obstacles (to give a time-problem again) is that one believes much has happened in history. *Not much has happened.*[4]

—Eric Voegelin

My guess is that Jung's ground-zero for psychology, "the place of such happenings," now offers what Plato's *metaxu* or in-between offered to Western thought as a whole. Yet what shall I make of that hunch in view of Wolfgang Giegerich's arrival now, through long and systematic effort, at his massive critique of Jung[5] for backsliding into concretization, hypostatization of the unconscious, and crucial self-contradiction? In homage to Giegerich's recent essays in this vein, first I want to try out a provisional template for that "place of such happenings," as a structure of consciousness which of course changes (*of course*: from the run of events), and later explore matters in the *kenôsis* doctrine and revisions in the theory of projection. By "structure of consciousness" I intend a draftsman's sketch; necessarily historical, it remains up for grabs (changing grasp or understanding). In early Christian speculation, a parallel kind of structure was already experienced as mobile and startling: in Book X of the *Confessions*, Augustine marvels, "But there is no place." I shall begin to trace psychic event or *reinen Geschehens*, in Jung's phrase, into its adoptions by meaning, especially as orphaned event: metaphysically stripped down, and akin to the alchemical stone of exile, *the Orphan* whose 16ᵗʰ-century voice the older Jung chiseled onto one face of his square stone at Bollingen.

As Giegerich has often said, the place of happening has long been sited *inside*, although already with Plato's revolutionary construction of consciousness, in his tale of the Cave, such interiorization gets equipped with part of the outside which it repudiates: namely, his 5ᵗʰ-century rupture from mythical and initiatic thinking. In Giegerich's masterful summary of the tale, Plato's design became the self-bootstrapping Stephenson engine of Western metaphysics, paradoxically effective because it ingested a large self-contradiction.[6] This analysis supports Giegerich's new critique of Jung, in whom he sees something of the same paradoxical involution, another inside equipped with an outside-taken-in, entailing self-contradiction. Aspects of the long-felt rupture with metaphysics which Jung addressed head-on went *back into* the structure of consciousness which he fashioned. Such, at any rate, is Giegerich's assessment, which allows him to read Jung's assurance to Frau Koenig-Fachsenfeld in the second epigraph above as contradicting Jung's understanding of where his work comes out. "Nothing really happened."[7]

In nailing such theses to Jung's door at Bollingen, Giegerich has taken a stand on bare ground. In tune with the bleakness of our modern condition, he strips himself of remnants so as to suffer, as a grown-up, its continuous impact. Among recent heralds for this onset were Bergson on the flux and James on "blooming and buzzing confusion." But Giegerich's phrasing of this spiritual nakedness, as he commends it to us, echoes both Luther and Bonhoeffer: "Here I stand, I cannot do otherwise,"[8] and the "coming of age" of humanity (*passim*). Catching up with Giegerich in "The End of Meaning" and "God Must Not Die" has been an encounter with Chanticleer; roused from my dogmatic slumbers, and with hexagram 21 of the archaic *I Ching* in mind, *Stripping* or *Falling Away*, I sketch a provisional container for psychic event that one can fold into his massive critique.

My starting point falls in the early Cartesian era, with physicist and mathematician Blaise Pascal, in aphorisms 347 and 348 of the *Pensées*. I was led to them by Bourdieu's *Pascalian Meditations*, which paraphrases no. 348 as a structure of *double inclusion* built around the logical power of reflection.

> From this paradoxical relationship of double inclusion flow all the paradoxes which Pascal assembled under the heading of wretchedness and greatness, and which ought to be meditated on by all those who remain trapped in the scholastic dilemma of determinism and freedom; determined (wretchedness), man can know his determinations (greatness) and work to overcome them. "Man knows that he is wretched, because he is so; but he is really great because he knows it." [no.416][9]

Both aphorisms set Man as *a thinking reed* against the sway of the universe, which can destroy him with a vapor. But Man knows that he dies, whereas (no. 347) "the universe knows nothing of this. All our dignity consists, then, in thought. By its means we must elevate ourselves, and not by space and time which we cannot fill. Let us try, then, to think well; this is the principle of morality."

Paradoxes do return on themselves like racquetballs. Condensing a tautly compact symbolism (precisely when the Cartesian subject/object split opened its broad Western franchise), no. 348 rethinks *Geschehens* by pivoting on a literally comprehensive pun:

> *Ce n'est point de l'espace que je dois chercher ma dignité, mais c'est du reglement de mon pensée. Je n'aurai pas avantage en possédant des terres: par l'espace, l'univers me comprend et m'engloutit comme un point; par la pensée, je le comprends."*[10]

> [Nowhere in space must I seek my dignity, but rather through the government of my thinking. Through space, the universe comprehends and swallows me as a point; by thinking, I comprehend it.]

Pascal's reflection swiftly builds a double-inclusive side-door into the distinction he draws. It folds unlimited scope, an engulfing grasp, into the mind's respondent conceptual grasp and reach. Its beauty is indeed this doubly factored power, in one direction physical, geometric, and inconscient while in the reverse direction dimensionless and awake.

This pair of aphorisms offers a way-station for the tracking of containment structures for consciousness. Pascal's compactness, though it emerges from a Christian back wall, strips things to equilibrium between long suffering, pushed to the limit, and being opened *into* our capacity for reflection *by* that suffering. Dignity in this symbol precisely fits dynamic equilibrium, or suits it: *fitting* in the sense of worth and merit, from Latin *dignus*, more than putting on a fine show, from *decere*. Behind Pascal's majestic pun on *comprendre* hovers the concluding claim in the prologue to John's gospel: what comes to life in the divine logos is light, *kai to phos te skotia phainei, / kai he skotia auto ou katelaben* (the Jerusalem Bible, and then Willis Barnstone: "and light shines in the darkness, and darkness could not overpower it... / / and the darkness could not apprehend it").[11] Several English versions, including the King James, translate *katelaben*, from *katalambanō*, as "comprehend" (in both senses, surrounding or grasping, and grasping or understanding it). Tyndale set the tone in 1524, with the Geneva Bible of 1560 following suit: "and the light shineth in ye darkenes, & the darkenes comprehended it not."[12] A mid 20th-century French Bible chooses the terms of hospitality, with its main verb locking in a key parallel a few lines later (where most English versions, Barnstone's included, also resort to hospitality): neither the darkness nor his own people hosts the incarnate paradox: *"et les ténèbres ne l'ont reçue.... et les siens ne l'ont reçue."*[13] Hospitality to the gods thematizes an earlier tribute by Giegerich to Jung's psychology[14] but also a sharp revision of that view in his recent "End of Meaning and the Birth of Man." The French physicist's starting point may prove to be useful.

Even this brief tour discloses the charged semantic cluster around *comprehendere* and *katalambanō*. At one pole gather compelling power, capture, and seizure, the grasp of conquest, imprisonment, and torture: compulsion and *force majeur*, all the way down to a *convincing* argument. Behind these terms stand definitive containments of spirits in bodies, of meanings in discourse and narrative, of perception in its field of *a prioris*, of instances under species and kinds, of submission to duty under bonds of obedience (including slavery), and the enclosure of life by fate.[15] At the other pole gather the dignity of search and inquiry, of philosophic search or *zetesis* (as opposed to detective and even judicial inquest through torture), embraces by compassion and benevolence, the rooting into one's ground, the pregnancy of conception in every sense (*Let it be done unto me, let it be thought in me*), and the conclusive effect of achieved totality, completion, *Ganzheit*.

In this field of opposed meanings, understanding shines as light from the impact of events—from eventualities, finalities. In little, this field loops consciousness into a Moebius strip: *the grasp of understanding rises as the reciprocal of grasping impact.* As the counter-reach through such impact, consciousness frames the response to what happens; like a retort wrapped around its *a priori* happening, it focuses that site (literally furnishing the hearth or hot point) where changes of state, alterations of form, occur.

The opposites shaping this field are power and surrender, or victimization and liberation with consequent adoption. Arising from torque, aiming to turn itself inside-out within the mental world of physics, this opposition calls to my mind the Gnostic alchemist Zosimos in Jung's citations from Late Antiquity. The self-flaying in his own *krater* by the priest in Zosimos's vision brings the Redeemer, modeled on Christian *kenôsis*, down into matter as such.[16] *Kenôsis* had a second future, and it was alchemy.[17] As for the Redeemer or *Kurios ton pneumatōn*, however, the oppositions in this semantic field light up in Donne's devotional sonnet "Batter my heart, three-person'd God," where conquering siege and willing submission to invited rape fuse in the nuclear compressions of *kenôsis*—still a live wire for a 17th -century mind avid for the new science.

A bit more on Pascal's structure. The reciprocals in its field *make* luminous meaning by *taking in* the impact of necessity. Such meaning, though reflective, has tragic dignity, whose background Giegerich treats as embedded, initiatic meaning, with special force in his 1985 reading of Kafka's "In the Penal Colony" in "The Alchemy of History."[18] By design Kafka has such meaning register faintly, holding up the mirror of irony to us as his story's archaic, initiatic culture collapses.[19] While such irony comes easily to our belated standpoint, the act of diagnosing it left Kafka dissatisfied with his own narrative: in one alternative ending, the traveler, like some schizoid anthropologist, oscillates in terror between his enlightened disgust and acting like a down-on-all-fours yapping dog. In contrast, Pascal's phase in psychic history still afforded him classical meditative firmness. To him,

Donne's overheated paradoxes, let alone our late-terminal phase of paranoiac feeling—diffuse in Kafka, conscious in Pynchon—would have been unimaginable.

Pascal's spare means for his thinking reed wear a Stoic Ciceronian rather than Christian cast. Not that the Christian breakout through encirclement by fate does not lurk nearby. But it stays offstage to the double inclusion of Pascal's lean spatial determinations, the fate-measuring reach of his mental spear—in accord with Simone Weil's abidingly Pythagorean way of receiving both classical and then quantum physics alongside Isaiah's *deus absconditus* and Christ. Pascal's double inclusion, or reciprocal comprehension, does not yet blunt the impact of events with the breakout made by Johaninne and Pauline Christianity through the iron ring of necessity (bondage to fate, existential slavery) which Giegerich has laid out lucidly in his "Deliverance from the Stream of Evens: Okeanos and the Circulation of the Blood."[20] Therefore Pascal's double inclusion does set up a way-station en route to Jung's contradictions. Giegerich's rethinking of Jung's Bollingen—as a stout container in "Hospitality toward the Gods in an Ungodly Age: Philemon-Faust-Jung"[21] but a flawed one in "The End of Meaning"—give evidence of how patiently one must come at these contradictions.

The logic of divine incarnation or *kenôsis* Jung paraphrased in its full duality—dangerous inflation versus affiliation and adoption—in his great monographs of 1942/1948 on "The Psychological Approach to the Dogma of the Trinity" and of 1941/1954 on "Transfiguration Symbolism in the Mass." Both the agony and the elevation interfuse or counterpoise, as the prototypical disclosure of *double inclusion* as a lived structure prior to what fell in on Pascal: the drama of the Redeemer symbolizes "the events in the conscious life—as well as in the life that transcends consciousness—of a man who has been transformed by his higher destiny."[22] In view, however, of Giegerich's sustained recent attack on Jung's stances, inflation imports a back-story into some of Jung's applications of that diagnosis. Let me turn to one Pauline text and go on to one of Jung's from the mid-1930s, which Giegerich also takes up, and then finally turn to the theory of projection. Paul's text, from late in his hectic life, intriguingly works by way of another variety of the structure in Pascal's meditation.

Which is to say: early *kenôsis* thinking, still fluid and provisional in the first century, unfolds a double inclusion in which *two kinds* of divine Anthropos contrastingly enact affiliations with creative power. Primal human potential grabs at maximum expansion, only to be met across mythic history by radical downward contraction, the Son going under the human yoke.

Item: the *kenôsis* hymn quoted by Paul in Philippians 2:6-11 begins by contrasting Adam with Jesus, who compensates for Adam's theft (*rapinam*) of glory by emptying or depleting himself as slave and human being (*ekenôsen / exinanivit in formam servi accipiens*). This early hymn remarkably offsets naïve grandiosity with self-wounding in the Son, or sacrificial love in the pleroma. As Adam's presumption moves sweepingly to include creative power, so also that very power, wounding itself in a radical sacrifice of potency, submits to the iron grip of fate and death. Already, therefore, to borrow Giegerich's language, the logic of Love and its growing reality[23] frame events, moving to neutralize all-too-human lift-offs into the blue. This text from Paul's imprisonment in Rome therefore makes such illicit grasping the event to which Jesus' emptying and exaltation respond. These balanced inclusions of great and small enact a *symbolon*—project it, in Jung's way of reading symbolic function—which remodels a Greek antecedent in Pindar, from *Pythian 3* (the fifth epode, to be sung while at a stand):

> I will be small among the small,
> great among the great.
> >   The spirit embracing me
> from moment to moment I will cultivate,
> as I can and as I ought.[24]

How confidently this decorum breathes its ability to navigate the shoals of *kleos* or renown which it contemplates in the same passage! The early hymn quoted by Paul steeply descends a watershed well past Pindar's sixth to fifth centuries, which could not have imagined the irreversible *kenôsis* event. The same drama works behind Pascal's metaphysically bare meditation on space, whose existential yo-yo yarns out and back in, at first sickeningly but then composedly. Its stripped character echoes the vertiginous poise in J. V. Cunningham's "On the Calculus:"

> From almost naught to almost all I flee,
> And *almost* has almost confounded me,
> Zero my limit, and infinity.[25]

The asymptotic stretch in both Pascal and Cunningham's double inclusions, the one anticipating Einstein's cosmology and the other addressing it, more closely approximates Giegerich's stance than does Jung's paragraph on spiritual destitution from his essay of 1934 on the nature of archetypes. Giegerich cites this passage and its context;[26] I would choose it for its evocation of the *Kehre* or inward turn undergone during the *Red Book* years, reflected on after the fact:

> Just as in Christianity the vow of worldly poverty turned the mind away from the riches of this earth, so too spiritual poverty seeks to renounce the false riches of the spirit, in order to withdraw not only from the sorry remnants of a great past, which today means the protestant "churches," but also from all those alluring aromas from afar, in order to turn inward on oneself, where in the cold light of consciousness the bleakness of the world stretches out to the stars.[27]

The three paragraphs after this one subtly reinstate the spiritual environment of Pisces, spirit as water darkly containing its contents rather than spreading them out as Aquarian catches. Giegerich's assessment of the subtly retrograde movement in these several paragraphs is fully warranted. Yet taken alone, how emphatically this paragraph zooms down, then in, and then, once fully in, out again, suffering *kenôsis* to its zero degree, where the vast night of times is swallowed by metaphysically stripped reflection in tune with Pascal's reciprocal comprehension.

One way of taking Giegerich's challenge to Jung is to notice, then, that if certain key turns in Jung's testimony are stopped before running their full career, the structures of contradiction which they disclose in Giegerich's survey are kept from showing up. Held thus at poise, these turns also meet Giegerich's criteria for having come of age. They also recast my sketched-in Pauline and Pascalian double-dip authentically, but in the physicist's wake with a twist not apparent at first. That is, if one accepts Giegerich's argument—in which Jung holds back from arriving at a *new* form for the mythical-religious event and its impact, sprung from those barrens of immensity—then the zero-degree of *kenôsis* in this paragraph compelled Jung to produce a peculiar updating of Pascal's double inclusion. In Giegerich's summary, the next few paragraphs Kronos-like swallow mythic contents of the psyche in low-gathering waters, providing metaphysical barrenness with a fertile sister, in whose depth swims the primordial event, the Real Thing, which went for lost in the stripped-down paragraph of inward turn or *Kehre*. Thus double inclusion there, having just come of age, reverts immediately to a form of inclusion or in-ness, as Giegerich calls it, which forestalls a new form of containment—new in being something more than empty. While what gets thus included moves autonomously and freely, it is *comprehended*—enclosed, grasped—quite apart from the hospitality that Jung's Philemon gave to the gods. My simple template of double inclusion from Pascal only throws Giegerich's argument into sharper relief.

Yet the inward turn or *Kehre* itself symbolizes an arena for event, the cosmos now inside as maximal receptacle, strong in precisely those elemental ways which symbol as powerful thrust—*symbolein*—pushes defunct attachments aside and grounds new ones.[28] That strength, Giegerich implies however, also retains old musters that have been smuggled in. While I cannot assess every turn in his brief on Jung's immense achievement, Giegerich's theses on containment, swallowing, and old form stand up to scrutiny and merit more probing.

Giegerich's earlier essays include one on projection, the fundamental psychic event to which I turn in closing. The in-fall of metaphysical projections, and the natural attrition of symbols, themselves come in for review inevitably in our stripped day although with more than one outcome. After an Eranos conference paper in 1951 that derived from his work with Pauli on synchronicity, Jung told Gilles Quispel,

> "Es geht um die Erfahrung der Fülle des Seins;" it is the experience of the fullness, the pleroma, of Being that matters. And he said to me on another occasion that now the concept of projection should be revised completely [revamping the line from Lucretius through Feuerbach to Freud].[29]

Erich Neumann promptly turned an about-face at Eranos in 1952, proposing the Self field outside the psyche as cognate with extraneous cognition.[30] He was persuaded that synchronistic events compelled one to question primitive identity states as being necessarily illusory or projected. That is, because such events precipitated field awareness across psychic/material transitions, they defy conventional assignments of their location, the place of happening, to either exteriorization or interiorization. Thus right containment, *comprehension* in every sense, goes up for grabs. What had been neatly contained for focused mind turns, in a new variety of double inclusion, into a blurred, emotionally charged happening. The old framework shifts to a unitary field enclosure—swallowing focus and ratio in rupture, down an event crevasse—while feeling correspondingly engulfs the new field. Not "thinking well" at first, but feeling the raw impact, the pure happening, supplies the task that effects the reciprocal. Yet rupture and feeling enlarge experience, rendering containment dynamic and fluid, anything but a done deal.

What strikes me as decisive about this experience of expansive double inclusion is its obliteration of customary assignments of the psyche and meaning to inwardness. At least in the translation of Neumann's paper, "extraneous" for cognition points the way to that rupture, for the English word comes straight from Latin *extraneus*—external, and even, in Late Latin, irrelevant, therefore out of place, the strange factor, irrational—a veritable outrider's post for the psyche, on a buckboard seat atop the stagecoach.

The Western antecedent for this majestic extraneousness comes with emanation theory in Plotinus, which locates soul, regardless of embodied participation, dialectically outside the body, both as its force of coherence and its envelope.[31] Metaphysics in this vein pre-paves the road for a number of things. The loop cycle of going forth or emanation /indwelling /homecoming or return—which Proclus graphed as the educative triad, the mold for anthropology's initiation spiral—erases nothing of the source, "self-gathered" while other souls go forth having "deserted towards the abyss; a main phase in them is drawn downward and pulls them with it" [En. IV.3.6]. In view of the lively synchronicity events along the contemporary horizon of notice, or indeed of emergence theory, Plotinian ensoulment and eventual psychic exteriority, and extraneous, strange-indeed homecoming, scan as precocious readings of a syntax for psychological event. Commentators on Plotinus agree that soul in his scheme, as the heir to Plato's philosophic draw and search, *helkein* and *zetesis*, works as the regulative power of *turning back* to seek out one's *order*. It is the bootstrapper of

Kehrung or turn, pivoting from ensoulment to go *back outside and home.*
Yes, archetypal images guide descent and inclination, semaphoring to
this great traffic, but as for where it is,

> soul is no more contained than containing. Neither is it in body
> as in some vessel…. Nor can it be in the body as in some
> substratum…. Soul is no part of body…. If it were manifest in
> full force to the very outermost surface, we would no longer
> speak of soul as in body; we would say the minor was within
> the major, the contained within the container, the fleeting
> within the perdurable.[32]

Without being up on Wolfgang Pauli's physics, Ezra Pound in his later
Cantos none the less maintained the beat: "A soul, said Plotinus, the
body inside it. / 'By hilaritas,' said Gemmisto, 'by hilaritas: gods'; /
and by speed in communication."[33]

If Plotinian projections now sail down from the ceiling, they arrive
where quantum physics meets complex psychology. In von Franz's
words, *kenôsis* into the historically real figure of Christ "put a stop to
the development of the old hermeneutics" and enfleshed the entire
Gnostic pleroma in a myth that met Classical and Sophistic rationality
by stepping out as history.[34] If myth as history now ruptures along
the seams of strange events and attractors, then the prize within event,
the hap within happening, will seem newly orphaned, not by
dispossession alone but also by foster displacement, foiled expectation,
and synchronistic perturbation. The all-over-ness of occurrence, drifting
in smoke only apparently from memory—*impersonally abyssal* memory,
the kind that opened beneath once-orphaned Wordsworth as he recalled
a deceptively gentle crossing of the Alps ten years earlier—may pose as
rupture and anticlimax at the same blooming time. Wordsworth's term
was Imagination, "lifting up itself / Before the eye and progress of my
song / Like an unfathered vapor" which left him "Halted without a
struggle to break through."[35] Personal occasion with its little cowcatcher
myth on a sublimely paneled history splinters and freaks away; soul
smokes up, enwrapping them all.

Giegerich bets the house on syntactic openness, on verbs rather
than nouns, and so on progressive *kenôsis* or incarnation "as a matter of
course" (the run of happening) but also "without curtailment."
Incarnation is "a psychological event, an event *in the logic of the soul* or

in the logic of the world. It is a change of the concept of God, not the literal process..., the emergence... of a new way to think, a new status of consciousness unheard of before."[36] *Kenôsis* has a future once more, prefigured in Wordsworth's whiteout and in Keats's negative capability, rather than projection as Jung originally used it. One may condense much of Giegerich's critique into an argument along the following lines: that traditional projection theory, though it clears the path to the discernment of progressive incarnation, in Jung does not check his reversal of actual psychological history, which delays as a future potential *kenôsis* what has already incarnated and evolved. That devastating charge is certainly worth pursuing. It occurs to me to turn again to peak episodes in the prior evolution and begin anew; for instance, what of the wounding in Biblical encounters in which both parties suffer? Edinger cannily calls them instances of mutual *kenosis*;[37] but does such back-casting of the dynamic onto Hebraic foundations play into Giegerich's critique or not? Among early Christian experiences, how does the same question suit the intensely compact and dynamic symbolization from Late antiquity embodied in the chant by the Gnostic Christ of spirit in the Acts of John, a text cited several times by Jung? In the terms I cobble together here, it made *kenôsis*-unto-death a paradigm of double inclusion: in it the dance master makes those who join him leap in a syntax that teaches *suffering as access to the power not to suffer,* a prototype reciprocal to Pascal's on suffering and dignity. John's third verse startlingly rehearses the lancing of Christ's bodily counterpart out on the Hill of the Skull, a terminal sluicing of blood and water from that body of *kenôsis in extremis*: "I will be pierced, and I will pierce."[38]

Whatever new form might bring comparable luminosity to experience, probably it will pierce such experience as Kafka's "In der Strafkolonie" did early in the last century. Regardless, however, one may still say that projection remains the cornerstone of change, for it grounds the field of psychological event. More than cleverness aligns the kenomatic and pleromatic cycle of emptying and filling with the out-throws and homecomings of projected meaning. A devout modern materialist like Paul Valéry must be at least as spiritually keen as the alchemist Gerhard Dorn, or more so, since the life in matter which he refuses to project as spirit fully bears the dynamic charge of the elder dispensation. His dignity corresponds to Giegerich's stance of stripped maturity. But it also matches a maximal kenotic tension without benefit of doctrine, and accordingly also matches the vitality of any substantial projection that has been called home.

What this harmony compels one to question is any too-ready sorting out of these vocabularies, which collide inevitably in the crowded skies of modern speculation. The *place* of event and the *destination* of eventuality haunt novelists, psychologists, theorists of emergence, and philosophers of history alike because—to revert to Pascal and Bourdieu's double inclusion—both site and sense still quiver in the isotonic pulse of *animi iactus liber* against *mundi iactus necessarius*, of mind's free projection against the world's fated thrust.

Psychology true to its name therefore will make projection quiver as well. Giegerich's case for Jung's backslidings stands qualified by revisions of projection theory made at Jung's prompting, if not from Neumann then from C. A. Meier, whose pages on the cosmogonic circle of eros in the Renaissance Neoplatonist Leone Ebreo (Jehudah Abarbanel, 1460-1530) read our two isotonic pulses into Leone's great circle of eros. In Meier's handling, Leone's Sophianic dialogues on objective, divine love, although that power loops in from the divine realm and returns to it, goes to work practically. In this metaphysic Meier locates the *what* of objective psychological knowledge, the capacity to reconfigure projections within marriage relations into the syntax of love. Leone's cosmogonic dynamism Meier thus links to Proclus and Plotinus, its vector streaming down through chaotic incarnation and back. In Leone rather than Ficino, Pico, or Bruno,[39] Meier salutes erotic descent (in our terms here, kenotic) into the human muck of archetypal shadow as "no longer… a simple projection but…a genuine symbol formation."[40]

Meier's rereading of Leone Ebreo, prompted by the synchronicity hypothesis, amounts to an adoption of orphaned event. The symbolism Meier proposes complements iron necessity in archaic Okeanos or the stream of events, supplying two comprehending strengths or *festen Formen*[41]: an affiliative stream of events that takes shadow depths into circulation, thus into learning how to love well, and then a way of hearing anew Nietzsche's death-of-God chapter 19 in *Also Sprach Zarathustra* on compassion, which contemptuously laments the hell that God knows in pitying man. An erotic-noetic turn, an *epistrophē*, in Leone maps the practice of eating shadow to serve love.

Another eminent critic of Jung, the philosopher of history Eric Voegelin, saluted exactly this turn or *conversio* in the Renaissance Neoplatonic writers, particularly Ficino, as a slender bridge into modernity (first to Jean Bodin and then Henri Bergson) across which noetic symbolism worked securely, with Ficino's *fruitio dei* "not like being emptied but rather like being filled..., a being-carried in by love."[42] To my mind, Giegerich's manifestos on the logic of Love in "The End of Meaning," and on encompassing noetic forms in "God Must Not Die!," sound a note like Ficino or Leone Ebreo's. They may even offer hospitality to Simone Weil's tough-minded mysticism of love, a paradoxical *least force* evoked by our brutal age. Bearing in mind Giegerich's view of *kenôsis*, I see more clearly that Weil's rounding-off, minus its phsyics, had long since been achieved by Paul, whose letter to the Ephesians 3:18-19 was indeed dear to Weil for its traces of Pythagorean spatial mysticism: "May you have the strength to grasp the breadth and the length, the height and the depth, so that, knowing the love of Christ, which is beyond knowledge, you may be filled with the utter fullness of God [*plerothete eis pan to pleroma tou theou*]." Again we have the same tone, more so than the tones of either Gnostic psychic inflation or Paul's metastatic distortion as diagnosed by Voegelin in *The Ecumenic Age*. While there is no space here to study Giegerich's late-Hegelian thinking in contrast to Voegelin's point of departure in Schelling's philosophy of the myth, particularly on the motif of swallowing,[43] one may still say that Giegerich's apologia for soul truths evokes, non-metaphysically and psychologically, the major symbolism of experience in Plotinus and Leone Ebreo. In his own words, Giegerich's truths "are neither positivistic nor metaphysical.... They *are* what they are and suffice themselves. They are existing concepts, existing logical form." And then the Plotinian note: "They within themselves encompass or permeate the mind just as well as the real."[44] Though such harmony could not have been predicted, it welcomes both Giegerich and Meier's Leone, whose stream of cosmogonic eros circulates in counterpart to Giegerich's own study of the ancient and necessitous stream of events. This harmony suggests to me that however much the windows in Jung's house need to be flung wide by vigorous hands, the entrant air brings news of orphaned event that still finds adoption in keeping with the builder's motives.

158 JOHN PECK

NOTES

1. C. G. Jung, "The Psychology of the Transference," 1946, *CW* 16 § 489, 492 (tr. mod.) [* *Andere drängen nach dem denkerischen Begreifen* **und wollen das Stadium des reinen Geschehens ungeduldig überspringen.** –n.b. *reinen Geschehens*, the phase of pure occurrence or happening. See text in *Praxis der Psychotherapie, GW* 16 2. Auflage (Olten, Walter Verlag, 2006), § 489.]

2. C. G. Jung, *Letters* 2, p. 612, to Olga von Koenig-Fachsenfeld, 30 Nov. 1960. German text cited by Giegerich in "The End of Meaning and the Birth of Man: An Essay about the State Reached in the History of Consciousness and an Analysis of C.G. Jung's Psychology Project"(hereafter EMBM), *Journal of Jungian Theory and Practice* (6.1, 2004), p. 42. The German phrase: "Wir sind nur von **den Ort solchen Geschehens** entrückt oder verrückt."

3. Wolfgang Giegerich, "The Provenance of Jung's Findings" (1984), *The Neurosis of Psychology, CEP,* vol. 1, pp. 134-5.

4. Eric Voegelin, "Conversations with Eric Voegelin at the Thomas More Institute for Adult Education in Montreal" [1967], *The Drama of Humanity and Other Miscellaneous Papers*, 1939-1985 (*Collected Works of Eric Voegelin*, vol. 33, Columbia, U. of Missouri Press, 2004), pp. 295-304.

5. Wolfgang Giegerich, "God Must Not Die! C.G. Jung's Thesis of the One-Sidedness of Christianity," see this volume, pages 11-71. Hereafter GMND.

6. Wolfgang Giegerich,"The Occidental Soul's Self-Immurement in Plato's Cave," 1994 in *Technology and the Soul, CEP*, vol. 2.

7. Giegerich, EMBM, p. 42: "'Those of us who are still there…will be smitten by the same experience, now as before….' Nothing really happened. 'Our consciousness only imagines that it has lost its gods, in reality they are still there.' The phrase, 'Those of us who are still there' points of course to the (secondary restitution of) unbornness, the attempted denial of the emergence of consciousness after the fact of the insight into the emergence."

8. Giegerich, EMBM, p. 32.

9. Pierre Bourdieu, *Pascalian Meditations*, tr. Richard Nice (Stanford: Stanford U.P., 1997 [Paris: Seuil, 1997]), pp. 130-131.

10. Pascal: *Pensées* (Genève: Éditions Pierre Cailler, 1947), p.189.

11. *The New Covenant, Commonly Called the New Testament*, tr. Willis Barnstone (vol.1: *The Four Gospels and Apocalypse, Newly Translated from the Greek and Informed by Semitic Sources*) (New York: Riverhead / Penguin Putnam, 2002), p. 305.

12. *The Geneva Bible: A Facsimile of the 1560 Edition*, intro. Lloyd Berry (Madison: U. of Wisconsin Press, 1969), facs. p.42.

13. *La Sainte Bible*, tr. Louis Segond (Genève / Paris: La Maison de la Bible, new ed. with parallels, 1947), NT p.84.

14. Wolfgang Giegerich, "Hospitality toward the Gods in an Ungodly Age: Philemon – Faust – Jung," in *The Neurosis of Psychology*, *CEP*, vol. 1, pp. 197-218.

15. *Katelaben* from *katalambanō*: to seize or lay hold of (L. *occupare* and *copeiso*); to overpower or conquer; and to seize mentally, grasp conceptually, apprehend or comprehend. *Katalambanō* also indicates misfortune or wretchedness catching or overtaking one; being taken by surprise; and meeting with the compulsion of fate (fate happening to one). It also comprises decisive checking, repression, and arrest or imprisonment; making final or terminating; binding by oath or covenant, and forcing one's will on another, including the exercise of judicial torture (see DuBois below).

Comprehendere: to lay hold of, to surround on all sides; to seize or apprehend, to grasp or comprise; to attack, arrest, or capture; to detect or discover; to mark the range of a spear, knife, or scalpel; to contain or include, as the elements in a species or the items in a series; thus also to number or enumerate; to perceive; to understand; to comprise in discourse or narrative; to place under obligation, bind by oath; to embrace with kindness; to definitively enclose, as elements in a category or as the spirit in an effigy; to take root; to become pregnant. For the classical Greek ligature between legal findings of truth and the routine torture of slaves owned by contesting parties, see Page DuBois, *Torture and Truth* (Routledge, 1991). The slave has no interest in putting up a false front to protect rights or property that he does not possess.

16. See both Ch. 12 in *Aion* (1951), "Background to the Psychology of Christian Alchemical Symbolism," *CW* 9ii § 283, and Ch. 2, "The Psychic Nature of the Alchemical Work," in *Psychology and Alchemy* (1944), *CW* 12 §§ 406-413. The second passage moves from Nietzsche's embodied Anthropos figure to that of Zosimos.

17. Compare to Jung in "Transformation Symbolism in the Mass" (1941/1954): "The alchemists had already paved the way [for psychological purification and realization] by putting their *opus operatum* at least on a level with the ecclesiastical mystery, and even attributing to it a cosmic significance since, by its means, the divine world-soul could be liberated from imprisonment in matter." *CW* 11 § 448.

18. Wolfgang Giegerich, "The Alchemy of History," in *Soul-Violence, CEP*, vol. 3, pp. 382-414.

19. Stanley Corngold's reading of the story, a near-rival of Giegerich's in some respects, perceives only the irony. See "Allotria and Excreta in "In the Penal Colony," Ch. 4 of *Lambent Traces: Franz Kafka* (Princeton: Princeton UP, 2004).

20. In Giegerich's, *The Neurosis of Psychology, CEP*, vol. 1, pp. 233-256.

21. In Giegerich's, *The Neurosis of Psychology, CEP*, vol. 1, 1984, pp. 197-218.

22. Jung, *CW* 11 § 233.

23. Giegerich, GMND, pp. 44-50.

24. *Pindar's Victory Songs*, tr. Frank Nisetich (Baltimore: The Johns Hopkins U.P., 1980), p. 173.

25. No. 27 of "Epigrams: A Journal," in *The Exclusions of a Rhyme* (Denver: Alan Swallow, 1960), p. 79.

26. Giegerich, EMBM, pp.34-36, which take up Jung's §§ 30-34.

27. C. G. Jung, "Archetypes of the Collective Unconscious," 1934; rev. 1954, *CW* 9i § 29 (trans. mod.). Giegerich amplifies the critical phrase in this passage (*um bei sich einzukehren*) in keeping with his recommended stance in EMBM, p. 30: "in order to unreservedly enter one's own life 'as it really is'." Jung's paragraph follows the Liverpool-Citadel-Magnolia painting of the *Red Book* by around six years, and his *Systema munditotius* mandala by as much as 16 years.

28. *Symbolbildung* or symbol formation in Jung is nearly fortress-like in its establishment of capacity for *imago* coherence and draw: the emergent structure in *Psychological Types* (1921), Ch. V, is a tower-stronghold, which like any effectual symbol "must be by its very nature unassailable" (§ 401). In the Litany of Loreto, Maria "appears as a vessel of devotion, a source of wisdom and renewal." The authorized translation here, however, eliminates the phrase *als*

feste Form, which might be rendered as "an impregnable form." See the German text, *Gesammelte Werke* vol. 6 § 429 (Olten: Walter-Verlag, 1971), p.239: "*als Gefäss der Andacht, als feste Form, als Quelle der Weisheit und der erneuerung.*"

29. Gilles Quispel, "Gnosis and Psychology," *Harvest* 32 (1986), p. 91.

30. Erich Neumann, "The Psyche and the Transformation of the Reality Planes: A Metapsychological Essay" (1952), in *The Place of Creation: Six Essays*, tr. Hildegarde Nagel, Eugene Rolfe, Jan van Heurck, & Krishna Winston (Princeton: Bollingen / Princeton UP 1989), p. 12.

31. "Soul will stand as circle-centre to every object (remote on the circumference)" [*Ennead* IV.2], and "the Soul of the universe is, none the less, outside the body of the universe" [*Ennead* IV.3] although of course it also enters in, undergoing "ensoulment," the Platonic general-issue *kenôsis* with return ticket [*En.* IV.3.9].

32. *En.* IV.3.20. In the preceding note, so here: *Plotinus: The Enneads*, tr. Stephen MacKenna (Burdett NY: Paul Brunton Foundation / Larson Publications, 1992), pp. 296-317.

33. Canto 98 in *The Cantos of Ezra Pound* (New York: New Directions, 1970), p. 690, cf. p. 685.

34. Marie-Louise von Franz, *Projection and Re-Collection in Jungian Psychology: Reflections of the Soul*, tr. William Kennedy (La Salle: Open Court, 1989 [1978]), p. 41.

35. William Wordsworth, *The Prelude 1799, 1805, 1850*, eds. Jonathan Wordsworth, M. H. Abrams, & Stephen Gill (New York: Norton, 1979 [the 1805 text]), p. 216.

36. Giegerich, GMND, p. 46.

37. Edward Edinger, *The Bible and the Psyche: Individuation Symbolism in the Old Testament* (Toronto, Inner City, 1986), p. 142.

38. *The Apocryphal New Testament*, tr. & ed. J. K. Elliot (Oxford: Oxford UP, 1933), p. 318.

39. For a survey of all these writers, see John Charles Nelson, *Renaissance Theory of Love: The Context of Giordano Bruno's Eroici furori* (New York: Columbia UP, 1958).

40. C. A. Meier, *Personality: The Individuation Process in the Light of C. G. Jung's Psychology*, tr. David Roscoe (Einsiedeln: Daimon Verlag, 1995 [1977]), p. 170.

41. Recall note 23 above on Jung's *Symbolbildung*.

42. Eric Voegelin, *Anamnesis*, tr. & ed. Gerhart Niemeyer (Notre Dame: U. of Notre Dame Press, 1978 [1966]), pp. 195-196.

43. Whereas Giegerich's critique emerges from a thorough grounding in Hegel, Voegelin, an anti-Hegelian, developed his philosophy of history from grounds in Schelling. The outline for the philosophy of mythology in Schelling's late *Philosophy of Revelation* has been translated by Jerry Day in the appendix to his *Voegelin, Schelling, and the Philosophy of Historical Existence* (Columbia, U of Missouri Press, 2003), pp. 277-279. At a crucial phase in this outline, decisive obstruction to the emergence of oncoming dominants in the divine process writes the main plot. In this particular phase, a third epoch of combat begins with Cronos the swallower striving to stifle the onset of mythic regency by Phoenician Herakles. Neither the conventional reception of Schelling, nor of Hegel, presents us with this mapping of myth as nuclear history.

44. Giegerich, GMND, p. 55.

THE AMBIGUITY OF EVIL AND THE GOD OF THE DEPTHS: A RESPONSE TO WOLFGANG GIEGERICH

JOHN HAULE

An examination of Jung's views on the one-sidedness of Christianity and whether he harbored a hope for the future of that religion must surely begin with a judicious choice of texts. That Wolfgang Giegerich has based his study primarily on *Answer to Job* is most puzzling, for Jung warns his readers in no uncertain terms about the peculiar nature of his rant in that work. In the "Prefatory Note" to *Answer to Job*, Jung says that it describes "a personal experience, carried by subjective emotions," deliberately chosen "to avoid the impression that I had an idea of announcing an 'eternal truth.'" Five pages later, in wishing his reader "good luck" ("*Lectori Benevolo*"), he makes his intentions even more clear: "I cannot, therefore, write in a coolly objective manner, but must allow my emotional subjectivity to speak if I want to describe what I feel

John Ryan Haule has a Ph.D. in religious studies from Temple University and a diploma from the C. G. Jung Institute-Zurich. He has been on the faculty of the C. G. Jung Institute-Boston for the past 30 years. His published books include *Divine Madness* (1990), *The Love Cure* (1996), *Perils of the Soul* (1999), *The Ecstasies of St. Francis* (2004), and *Jung in the 21ˢᵗ Century* (in two volumes): *1. Evolution & Archetype*; *2. Synchronicity & Science* (Routledge, 2010).

when I read certain books of the Bible, or when I remember the impressions I have received from the doctrines of our faith" (*CW* 11 § 559).

I am very familiar with all the doctrinal formulations Jung cites, having been educated in a Catholic elementary school and a Jesuit high school and university before entering the Society of Jesus myself, where I spent the better part of the 1960's. It is therefore clear to me that what Jung is reacting to is what the Churches call "salvation history," an official gloss on the canonical scriptures, running from Adam through Noah, Abraham, Moses, Jesus, and Paul, all the way to the author of Revelation (or "the Apocalypse," as we called it). Central to this account is the tragedy of the original sin committed by our first parents, an act that excluded them and all their descendants from "eternal life," and set the stage for the incarnation of God's Only Begotten Son to redeem us all through his death on the cross. In this public teaching story, there can be no question about it: If he wanted to repair the damage done to us in the Garden of Eden, the Father God either had no choice about the brutal sacrifice of his Son or else he concocted the plan with relish.

In contrast to this grisly tale, I surely prefer Giegerich's graceful and compelling account of *kenôsis*. But it does fly in the face of Christian orthodoxy, according to which Christ was simultaneously "wholly God and wholly man." Interpreted in the light of this doctrine of "hypostatic union," therefore, Paul's image of Christ's "emptying" (*kenôsis*) has to have had a moral and psychological intention rather than a metaphysical one. That is, when Jesus did not "cling to his divinity," he carried out an heroic act of self-sacrifice by allowing his humanity freely to suffer humiliation and death, rather than hiding behind the potential "shield" of his divinity. He deliberately, if reluctantly, went along with the brutal plan. I doubt many Christians have ever been able to find the logic in this filiocidal drama: how *we* have been saved and "the gates of heaven reopened" by the death God arranged for his Son.

As I read *Answer to Job*, I find Jung ranting against this public account, fashioned by the Church to instruct and intimidate its members. He voices views as heretical as Giegerich's ("God wants to become man but not quite"). But Jung's motive is to point out the theological contradictions in the Church's teaching story. It is clear to me that he maintains his focus on that instructional gloss; for this reason, when he takes up the image of God and how it changes over the centuries of scriptural documents, it is always a God who is "out there," a transcendent metaphysical entity, for the reality of that sort of God is central to every exoteric reading of salvation history. It appears that Giegerich would not completely disagree with me, for he, too, refers to "popular believers": "Jung regresses to a much more primitive *level* of thinking, one that has precisely long been superseded by the degree of sophistication attained in Christian thinking (although not in the thinking of the popular believers)." (this volume, p. 31) Giegerich makes a similar observation regarding the devil and hell: "[T]he threat of the devil and the fear of eternal damnation in hell . . . are not elements of the authentic Christian message . . . had merely a *propaedeutic* educational function." (this volume, p. 24) In contrast with Giegerich, I do not see "Jung fall[ing] for the idea of the devil" (this volume, p. 25) any more than that Jung posits, as his own position, the metaphysical reality of a transcendent God.

Jung's intention in *Answer to Job* is rather to criticize the God of popular belief that is supported by the salvation history gloss, which is why he insists that it is the *God-image* that he is talking about. Whether it may have been "unprofessional" of Jung, as Giegerich claims, (this volume, p. 31) to have ignored the academic fields of exegesis and the history of religions, I would refer to Jung's confession of his subjective emotions and his claim to be responding as a "layman." Furthermore, it is worth mentioning that Jack Miles, a former Jesuit priest, educated in all the best Roman Catholic institutions and holding a Ph.D. in Near Eastern languages from Harvard, has written a very similar account of the God of salvation history in two volumes: *God: A Biography* and *Christ: A Crisis in the Life of God.*[1] Miles' story hinges, as does Jung's, on the Book of Job, and for pretty much the same reason, although his conclusions are rather different. He appears not to have been influenced by Jung—who is mentioned only once, at the end of Chapter One of the first volume—where Miles quotes Jung's famous declaration about God's existence: "I don't believe. I know." Miles goes on: "Can God become known? I leave that question unanswered. What I claim is only that God's life as found on the pages of the Bible can be told. This book aims to be the telling."[2]

Thus Jung's project in *Answer to Job* is surely defensible, but his emotional reactive style makes it a problematic text to analyze; and the fact that he is railing against Church doctrine leaves his own views on the nature of Christ and of evil hard to tease out. In my opinion there are better texts in the full Jungian opus for carrying out a project like Giegerich's.

I would begin by recognizing that Jung was born in 1875, when the western world felt itself battered by the progress of science and wondered if its theological foundations had been fatally eroded. The spiritualism craze, beginning around 1880 and continuing into the twentieth century and allied with psychological research into "somnambulism" (hypnosis, hysteria, automatic writing, etc.), which lent it respectability, gave our late Victorian grandparents real hope. It seemed that the spirits of the dead could be called upon to answer the questions of the living and thereby prove that the human soul survived bodily death. Jung was passionate about these things and lectured his college fraternity brothers in the Zofingia Society on the necessity of using their scientific education to enter the "border zones of exact science" and subject the phenomena of séances and ESP to rigorous examination.[3] This theme remained central in Jung's concerns for the rest of his life. The theory of synchronicity, which he published in 1952,[4] the same year as *Answer to Job*, was his personal response to the need for entering those "border zones." References to the idea of synchronicity begin as early as 1928 in his *Dream Analysis* seminar[5] and again in 1930 in his Memorial Address for Richard Wilhelm.[6] Between 1932 and 1958, Jung carried on a dialogue about synchronicity with one of the founders of quantum mechanics, Wolfgang Pauli.[7] The third chapter of "Synchronicity: An Acausal Connecting Principle" (CW 8 § 916-968) must not be overlooked as a late statement on what was certainly one of the central concerns of Jung's life: our relation with that God whom Jung said he "knew" and did not merely "believe."

The other work I would mine for evidence of Jung's attitude about Christ and evil would be a document that admittedly was not available to Dr. Giegerich in June, 2009, namely the recently published *Red Book*, which we have long understood in a general sense to be the foundation of all of Jung's work from at least 1920 onward. Now it is finally in the public domain.

I agree with Giegerich that issues concerning the one-sidedness of Christ and the importance of evil are tightly bound up with the central doctrine of Analytical Psychology: that is "individuation," the life-long dialogue between ego and self that characterizes human psychology. Giegerich and I may disagree, however, on the nature of that dialogue; for we certainly part company on the nature of "self" in Jung's thought. Giegerich calls it "a metaphysical noumenon": "The 'unconscious' in Jung's parlance is a 'theological' term. It has no place in a true psychology. The same applies to Jung's term 'self.' It, too, is a metaphysical noumenon. Jung repeatedly stresses that the 'symbols of the self cannot be distinguished empirically from a God-image.'" (this volume, p. 39) In putting it this way, Giegerich clearly makes "God" a transcendent object that may be "imaged" in the psyche. In contrast, I would point out how frequently Jung claims that whatever is the most powerful factor in the psyche is God. This is not a metaphysical God, but the God of experience. Jung places it firmly "within" the psyche and makes God immanent. But more importantly, I strongly object to Giegerich's claim that "self" is a "theosophical" construction, "a metaphysical noumenon." For me, "self" is a Darwinian notion, and I believe that my view does justice to all aspects of Jung's thought.

There are several places in the *Collected Works* where Jung insists that the human psyche must be understood in evolutionary perspective. In *CW* 8, I would draw attention to a passage in "The Structure of the Psyche" (1927) where Jung calls the collective unconscious, "common to all men, and perhaps even to all animals" (§ 321). "Theoretically it should be possible to 'peel' the collective unconscious, layer by layer, until we come to the psychology of a worm and even of an amoeba" (§ 322).

Now, if an amoeba has a primitive psyche, it must consist in the life process of that simple animal, the fact that in every instant the amoeba marshals into unity all of its organelles, all the sensing proteins in its cell walls, all the molecules floating in its cytoplasm. In every instant the amoeba acts as a whole, responds to its internal and external conditions in such a way as to make its next instant as favorable as possible. There is no organ or organelle, no protein, and certainly not the DNA in its nucleus directing this behavior. In this sense the amoeba's psyche, which is identical with its self, is "everywhere and nowhere"—or as Jung might prefer to put it, its center is everywhere and circumference nowhere.

The fact that an amoeba has no "ego" (so far as we know) means that it does not "individuate." For an amoeba, there is no tension between conscious planning and the organic requirements of the whole. As soon as an animal *has* an ego, however, that tension begins; and whether we know it or not, the reflective and planning processes of our human ego struggle against the holistic process of our entire organism. In its most basic sense, then, every human being—regardless of his degree of awareness—lives an individuation process. Some of us, through analysis or by some other means, become conscious of this dialogue; and when we attend to it, we find that we do not invent our ideas, we find them given to us; we do not direct our breathing, we are "breathed." I put it this way, because the everyday experiences of life take on a mystical significance when we attend to them carefully; and when the agent of these autonomous events comes to our attention, we may sometimes be inclined to call her "God." She sends us dreams and symptoms; and if we are sufficiently conscious, we fold them into our conscious dialogue with self.

Thus, even if Jung speaks as a theosophist as Giegerich claims, the doctrine of the self is not "theological" at all, but descriptive of our biological wholeness. In the end, our highly complex primate self operates to promote life, health, satisfaction, and comfort in every next instant in the same way that the much simpler psyche of an amoeba functions. In the human case, when a self like this thwarts our ego-based intentions, we may call it "shadow" and try to resist. We may be inclined to call such impulses "evil," for there is much in our animal nature that we do not know and probably do not want to know. The self is hardly a *Summum Bonum* in the scholastic sense of the term, but it is each animal's *summum bonum* insofar as it strives to preserve and enhance the life and balance of its being. To a human ego, the organic process of our animal self may appear divine and demonic by turns. It is still the God of experience, the strongest force in our psyche, now felt by the ego as a *coincidentia oppositorum*. In this way, individuation may be validly construed as a life of dialogue with God. Hence, a Jungian reading of John 17:21, where Jesus says: "May they be one; as you, Father, are in me, and I in you, so also may they be one in us . . ." (RSV).

The individuation dialogue is the theme of the *Red Book*, which begins with Jung's realization that he has lost his soul through the great ambition, success, and accomplishment he enjoys at age thirty-eight. He has served "the spirit of this time" (the *Zeitgeist*, collective consciousness, the requirements of an academic public world) and searches for his soul through "the spirit of the depths." In episodes of active imagination, this dialogue between persona and anima or self is portrayed in a variety of characters and scenes. The theme of Christ and evil lurks everywhere, but there is one sequence of events, entitled "Divine Folly," that takes place over five nights of calendar time (January 14-19, 1914) but fewer of dreamtime (*RB*: 292-305).

In the active imagination, Jung finds himself in a library that is heavy with a troubling scholarly atmosphere of ambition, conceit and vanity, where he astounds himself and the old librarian by asking for *The Imitation of Christ* by Thomas à Kempis. The librarian recommends Nietzsche's *Zarathustra* because it promotes superiority in its readers, but Jung insists he needs inferiority. In "layer two" of the text, where Jung reflects on the events of the active imagination, he says his thinking told him to live the divine and he wanted to "emulate Christ by living my life, while observing his precepts." But he knows he can only accomplish this by thoroughly becoming himself, as Christ became himself. In view of later statements in the *Collected Works* that God is whatever we find to be the strongest force in our psyche, it would seem that, in Jung's view, Christ's dialogue with his heavenly Father was precisely his individuation journey. And it is this task of emulating Christ that Jung wants to follow in his *Red Book* exercises.

The active imagination continues the next calendar night, where Jung finds himself in the library's kitchen—which he later calls "the realm of feeling"—with a fat cook who has her own copy of Thomas à Kempis. Jung opens to: "The righteous base their intentions more on the mercy of God, which in whatever they undertake they trust more than their own wisdom." Jung declares, "This is the intuitive method," (*RB*: 294) by which he apparently means that the "mercy of God" is met through the use of active imagination, which in turn offsets the arrogance of relying on the presumed wisdom of the ego. At this moment a great clamor arises as souls of the Anabaptist dead rush through, babbling and in panic. One tells Jung that though they "died in faith," they left something undone. Jung says they failed to live their animal. There can be no more simple image of living one's animal than that of the amoeba we have just considered. The *Red Book* context implies that living his animal is what Jung is trying to do with his active imagination exercises: to get out of the ego, with its simplistic conceptualizations and idealizations that serve the spirit of this time; to consult, instead, the spirit of the depths.

Immediately, the police burst in with the librarian and a fat professor of psychiatry who asks Jung if he has been hearing voices, to which Jung replies, "You bet!" He is then hurried off to an asylum and given a bed between one bearing an apparent dead man and another with a man whose brain is shrinking. Jung reflects: Here in the realm of divine madness, the "mercy of God which I had never relied on, for good practical reasons, is the highest law of action." (*RB*: 295) Here, one may no longer pursue goals. There can be no doubt that "the realm of divine madness" and "the mercy of God" are precisely where the spirit of the depths is found, a place where Anabaptist goals and academic ambition do not belong.

Jung's reflections in "level two" make it clear that the Anabaptist dead represent a caricature of goal-seeking. They represent "all the shapes we have assumed in the past" as well as "the thronging dead of human history." (*RB*: 296) It would seem that he means that our personal past and our collective past have together built a "spirit of this time" that goes unquestioned and influences us unconsciously and inexorably. Among such solid seeming realities is surely the notion of an all-good Christ whom, when we slavishly try to imitate, isolates us from our depths, the realm we reject as evil and the domain of our shadow. What we thereby exclude from our lives accompanies us as our evil spirit. "Break the Christ in yourself so that you may arrive at yourself and at your animal . . . Christ brought salvation through adeptness and ineptitude will save you." (*RB*: 296)

The next night, Jung's soul approaches him and urges him to accept his madness—"a special form of the spirit": "What you call knowledge is an attempt to impose something comprehensible on life." The professor then declares Jung mad and the man from the next bed rises from his death-like torpor and tells Jung the professor is the devil who is preventing him from marrying the Mother of God. Jung realizes we create truth by living it: "The work of men is steady, but it swims upon chaos." (*RB*: 299)

When we separate good and evil and try to live only the good, we fail to accept our roots that are deep in hell; and without nourishment from the depths, our tree will wither.

On the last night of the sequence, his soul tells him all barriers between the opposites must come down. The fat cook wakes him from the dream that began with the invasion of the Anabaptist dead, and Jung has a vision of the Good Friday Service from Wagner's *Parsifal* in which Jung is playing the role of the Pure Fool—in the drama, this is Parsifal, the only one who can heal the wounded Grail King. Jung/Parsifal changes into civilian clothes and walks off the stage. He reflects, "level two," that one's lowest is in a death-like sleep (the psychotic "fool" from the next bed) and needs warmth and life "which contains good and evil inseparably and indistinguishably." He concludes that, having shot down his enemy (presumably the hero Siegfried in an earlier episode of active imagination), he has made friends with a greater one. "Nothing should separate me from him, the dark one. If I want to leave him, he follows me like my shadow . . . He'll turn into fear if I deny him . . . I must prepare a sacrificial meal for him." (*RB*: 305)

From this one extended episode in the *Red Book*, we can gather that three distinct meanings of evil are swimming on or below the surface of the chaos of the depths. First and easiest to discern is the conceptual distinction between good and evil that characterizes "the spirit of this time," which, given Jung's remarks on the Anabaptist dead, we may confidently take to be more than what happens to be "politically correct" this season and more far reaching than the Ten Commandments. The spirit of this time is fully expressed in the *consensus gentium* ("the thronging dead of human history") whose moral weight profoundly influences what we call good and evil. This is the meaning of evil, reduced to a ghost of its psychic vitality in the doctrine of *privatio boni*, that Jung rails against in *Answer to Job*.

Next there is that indistinct realm far down in the depths where we may be frightened, horrified or appalled by what we encounter but nevertheless remain unable to find a line that divides good from evil. Here is the place where we "live our animal," a potentially more authentic realm but also far less conscious. Jung refers to this sort of moral instinct in the articles on conscience and good and evil that we find in *CW* 10, *Civilization in Transition*,[8] written six and seven years after *Answer to Job* and "Synchronicity." "[O]ur moral reactions exemplify the original behavior of the psyche, while moral laws are a late concomitant of moral behavior, congealed into precepts" (*CW* 10 § 838). "The reality of good and evil consists in things and situations that happen to you, that are too big for you, where you are always as if facing death. Anything that comes upon you with this intensity I experience as numinous, no matter whether I call it divine or devilish or just 'fate'" (*CW* 10 § 871). Here, clearly, is the root of all good and evil discussions and encountered only when we live our animal.

Finally, a third meaning of evil resides more or less implicitly in all these formulations. It is expressed in moral language perhaps most explicitly in what Erich Neumann called the "New Ethic."[9] Here, whatever serves psychic unity is good and whatever limits or prevents wholeness, whatever interferes with the natural functioning of our amoebic self, is the ultimate evil in Analytical Psychology. Because the very nature of individuation involves a tension between ego and self, employment of the transcendent function is, therefore, the ultimate virtue; and whatever thwarts it is evil. One of the most common impediments to the wholeness of "living our animal," is our egoic tendency to depend upon rigid conceptual distinctions between good and evil, as we find them "congealed" in the moral precepts of the spirit of this time. We move forward with integrity when we learn to hold the tension between opposites like good and evil and await the transcendent function. The rigidity of the Church's teaching story in giving us what borders on a Manichaean dichotomy between an all-good Christ and an all-evil Satan is the object of Jung's wrath in *Answer to Job*.

Giegerich's issue of whether Jung posits a metaphysical God somewhere outside of us would seem from the foregoing to be answerable in the negative. But we can be even more certain that Jung favors an immanent God if we consider another encounter with divinity that Jung had a week earlier than *The Imitation of Christ* sequence in the *Red Book*. On January 8 and 9, 1914 Jung, in active imagination, finds himself heading east, with some thought of learning wisdom from the Land of the Dawn. (*RB*: 277-83) Suddenly he is face-to-face with an armed giant, perhaps twenty feet tall, with a pair of bull horns on his helmet and carrying a huge bull-slaying axe. He is Izdubar, and Jung bows before him as to a powerful god. Izdubar is walking west to find the setting sun and asks Jung if he knows where it can be found. In giving him a scientific answer about the nature of the sun and its relationship to the earth, Jung inadvertently poisons Izdubar who falls to the ground and apparently lies at death's door. "Logos poisons us all," Jung discovers. Concerned and wanting to save the giant god, Jung paces the whole night long trying to decide how it may be done. Finally, he convinces Izdubar that, although he is surely real, he is nevertheless a fantasy and without weight. Eventually, Jung is able to roll up the god and stuff him into an eggshell that he slips into his pocket. His burden immensely lightened, Jung turns back westward in search of a place where the god might be healed. He reflects, "level two": "Thus my God found salvation and precisely by what people fear brings the Gods to their end," i.e., accepting that gods are "nothing but" images and fantasies. "The God outside us increases the weight of everything heavy, while the God within us lightens everything heavy. . . . If you are clever, take the God with you, then you will know where he is." (RB: 283)

Here again is the foundation of Jung's antipathy for the transcendent God taught by the Churches: an impossible ideal whose pure goodness cannot be imitated except at the price of dividing us from ourselves. The God who speaks to us from within with the holistic voice of the self does not sever us from our animal. Here, too, is a strong hint of what Jung imagines for the future of religion—if not for the future of Christianity. Stop the projecting and objectification that freezes God into immutability and alienates him from the ever-changing process of our daily lives and the progressive series of "this times" that describes human history. The spirit of this time preserves the ideas we have constructed concerning our gods, keeping them like ancient insects frozen in lumps of amber, while in other domains of life it contrives a clockwork universe that ticks on robotically without relevance to anything divine or indeed soulful. Terror inspired by this situation lies behind the spiritualism craze of a century ago. The inner division it fosters in all of us, too, burst out in the senseless brutality of World War I, which raged on just over the border while Jung worked on his Red Book.

There is no doubt that reports from the war induced a horror and depression in Jung, whose Red Book project began shortly after he had those hour-long visions of northern Europe covered in a sea of blood. The war that began with the murder of Archduke Franz Ferdinand was personal for Jung, even though he was relieved to discover that those bloody images were not a symptom of latent schizophrenia in himself. "My heart glowered in rage against the high and beloved, against my

prince and hero, just as the nameless one of the people, driven by greed
for murder, lunged at his dear prince. Because I carried the murder in
me, I foresaw it" (*RB*: 241). That war and that foreseeing had to have
heightened the urgency and violent imagery of Jung's encounter with
his depths. Outwardly the war was argued on both sides in the good-
versus-evil language of the spirit of the day. The depths taught Jung
that such dichotomizing is contrary to nature, contrary to reality. That
is why the all-good Christ image could not be Jung's savior—indeed,
why it could be no one's.

Spiritualism, hauntings by the souls of dead Anabaptists, one's
murderous brother living within one, foreknowledge of dreadful events:
all of these things have a cosmic and acausal dimension and lead us to
that other unusual statement Jung made in 1952, which also has at
bottom to do with our relationship to God, namely the doctrine of
synchronicity.[10] Careful reading of Jung's essay, particularly in
connection with the *Pauli/Jung Letters*, shows without a doubt that Jung
was proposing synchronicity as a cosmic principle that has to be added
to the universal principles physics already uses if we are to have a
complete and accurate picture of the world we live in. To that end,
Jung presented a "quaternity" of physical principles. Clearly, he was
thinking along the lines of Kant, who said that our knowing apparatus
automatically and unconsciously supplies all sensory input with the
context of space, time, and causality to make it comprehensible. Jung
took space, time, and causality as a triad of physical principles to which
he added a fourth, synchronicity, so that the acausal, atemporal and

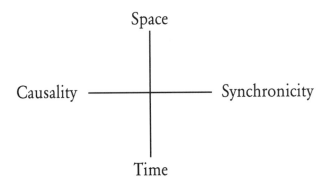

Fig. 1 First Synchronicity Quaternity (*CW* 8 § 961)

non-local nature of extra-sensory events could be included in our picture of the universe. Pauli rejected it, saying that no physicist would separate space and time.

Jung submitted another, a compromise with Pauli's ideas, that I think no one was happy with. But I have an alternate proposal that I think does full justice to Jung's intentions. First, let us note that all instances of ESP involve "action at a distance," and that every "action at a distance" problem in physics has been solved by proposing a field theory. Thus Faraday's magnetic field made magnetism comprehensible to the west some 600 years behind the Chinese. Faraday had been inspired by Leibniz's theory of Universal Harmony, which was influenced by his study of Chinese philosophy. Faraday's solution, in turn, inspired Einstein, who finally resolved the perplexity of gravity's apparent "action at a distance"—which Newton had imagined as "eros" between the planets and stars—in proposing space-time as a gravity field, bent by heavy masses. Quantum mechanics

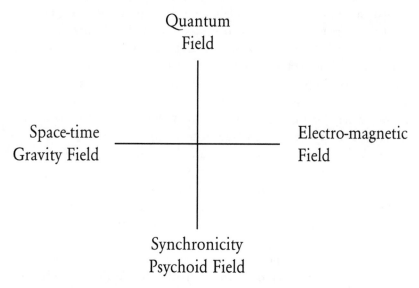

Fig. 2 The Four Universal Fields

describes the chaotic sea of subatomic particles as a collection of fields out of which the particles pop into existence and back out again on extremely short time scales. To complete this with Jung's idea of synchronicity, we would have a quaternity that looks like Figure 2.

In describing synchronicity as the "psychoid principle," Jung implicitly refers to his notion of the amoeba's psyche. The amoeba surely does not have a psyche in the sense that humans have, but its behavior is surely psyche-like, i.e., "psychoid." According to the psychoid principle, everything in the universe is related "meaningfully," very much like the molecules that comprise an amoeba. Both the human body and the amoeba may therefore be described as "nested hierarchies," that is all the parts belong to the whole, and every whole belongs to a larger whole. Thus the human psyche is the largest nest that includes the brain, liver, heart, etc., each of which has its own psychoid organization (or nest) that has an influence upon the whole psyche, while in the end being subordinate to it.

Just as we found the psyche of an amoeba to be everywhere and nowhere, so it is for the human organism. This means that like the fields governing quantum mechanics, the psychoid fields governing the growth and functioning of animals and plants are characterized by non-locality and acausality. For instance, according to Bell's Theorem, a pair of "entangled" electrons behave as though they are in communication, even when the distance between them makes any sort of physical transmission impossible. They seem magically in tune with one another even though they are not in the same locality. There is no known cause for this behavior. It is non-causal and non-local. So it is with ESP, which takes place not in a quantum field, but in a psychoid field that is equally non-causal and non-local. The qualities of non-locality and acausality describe the vertical axis in Figure 2. Meanwhile the more familiar horizontal axis describes the causal, local realm of masses and electromagnetic waves and particles operating in space-time and having causal influence on one another when they enter the same general locality.

Jung knows this scheme is foreign to us in the modern west, so he devoted Chapter Three of "Synchronicity: An Acausal Connecting Principle" to presenting alternate metaphysical schemes to describe the universe. His favorite example is the metaphysics of the *I Ching*, which holds that every event that occurs in a particular moment bears the same character as every other. Leibniz's principle of Universal Harmony, inspired by Chinese metaphysics is explicitly a view of the universe as a nested hierarchy—indeed a hierarchy of "windowless monads," "windowless" because they lack sensory connection with one another, rendering their harmonious behavior "acausal," or in Jung's terminology, "synchronistic." Jung also cites the views of several medieval alchemists, who accepted a microcosm/macrocosm view that resembles today's "Holographic Paradigm." All of these models represent the universe as a nested hierarchy, meaning that at bottom the universe may be conceived on the model of an amoeba; and the psyche of this largest of all amoebas would be what the alchemists called the *Anima Mundi*, the world soul. God is the world soul, and we are in touch with her through our own soul. She does not live on the heights, but in the depths. She is the deep meaning of everything that is going on, and she is not immutable. In *Memories* Jung alludes to this when he says, "the relationship between the eternal in man and earthly man in time was illustrated by two dreams" he had. In one of them he saw that we humans are projections from UFOs, and in the other he saw the yogi whose meditative dream he himself was (*MDR*: 323). Those dreams answered "the decisive question," namely whether we are "related to something infinite or not?" (*MDR*: 325).

The *Anima mundi* does not stand over against the world as the Christian teaching story claims about God. Rather, she "pervades" everything, as the Upanishads say of *brahman*. She changes in every instant, just as the psyches of the amoeba and of our own organism. If she is conscious in the higher sense that we humans are, she is conscious that way through *our* awareness. She has no plan for the universe, beyond its next instant.

> If the Creator were conscious of Himself, He would not need conscious creatures; nor is it probable that the extremely indirect methods of creation, which squander millions of years upon the development of countless species and creatures, are the outcome of purposeful intention . . . one cannot help suspecting the element of *meaning* to be concealed somewhere within all the monstrous biological turmoil . . .

> [T]he road [to meaningful consciousness] was ultimately found on the level of warm-blooded vertebrates possessed of a differentiated brain—found as if by chance, unintended and unforeseen, and yet somehow sensed, felt and groped for out of some dark urge (*MDR*: 339).

This view is very similar, also, to the twentieth century "process metaphysics" of A. N. Whitehead.[11] For him, God, like the *Anima Mundi*, is the "mental pole" of the universe in the same sense that the psyche of an amoeba may be described as the "mental pole" of the physical processes that constitute the amoeba's life. A God so conceived does not "transcend" the cosmos but is an integral part of its process. And because each of us is nested in the cosmic hierarchy, we are in psychoid "touch" at all times with cosmic wholeness. This is the source of what Jung calls the "absolute knowledge" of the unconscious. It is why some distant but emotionally significant events may become known to us in our dreams, visions and intuitions (ESP). The worldview implied in the doctrine of synchronicity, therefore, is deeply mystical and potentially religious. We are always in some sort of contact with the *Anima Mundi*.

> . . . we are hopelessly cooped up in an exclusively psychic world. Nevertheless, we have good reason to suppose that behind this veil there exists the uncomprehended absolute object which affects and influences us—and to suppose it even, or particularly, in the case of psychic phenomena about which no verifiable statements can be made (*MDR*: 352).

God does speak to us for the most part wordlessly through our self—though our psyche has the capability of translating such communications into word and image—and we speak to God through our every choice and activity. Human life is potentially a constant dialogue with God. Jesus may therefore be seen as the prototype of a human who had become conscious of his divine interchange. But if Jung saw this psychoid vision of the cosmos as "the future of religion," I doubt that explicitly including Christian metaphors in the picture was important to him. *Answer to Job* may seduce us into thinking that, in Jung's view, the future of religion must reside in some form of Christianity. But there are other more judicious choices to be made in the vast collection of Jung's writings, and I believe that the *Red Book* and "Synchronicity" come closer to the heart of Jung's intentions.

NOTES

1. Jack Miles, *God: A Biography* (New York: Vintage, 1995); *Christ: A Crisis in the Life of God* (New York: Knopf, 2001).

2. Miles, *God: A Biography*, p. 24.

3. Carl G. Jung, *The Zofingia Lectures.* trans. J. van Heurck (Princeton, NJ: Princeton/Bollingen, 1983), pp. 5-19.

4. Carl G. Jung and Wolfgang Pauli, *Natürerklärung und Psyche* (Zurich: Rascher Verlag, 1952).

5. Carl G. Jung, *Dream Analysis: Notes of the Seminar Given in 1928-30,* ed. W. McGuire (Princeton, NJ: Princeton/Bollingen, 1984), p. 44.

6. Robert Aziz, *C. G. Jung's Psychology of Religion and Synchronicity* (Albany, NY: SUNY, 1990), p. 1.

7. Carl A. Meier (ed.), *Atom and Archetype: The Pauli/Jung Letters, 1932-1958* (Princeton, NJ: Princeton University Press, 2001).

8. Carl G. Jung, "A Psychological View of Conscience" (1958) *CW* 10 § 825-57; and "Good and Evil in Analytical Psychology" (1959) *CW* 10 § 858-86.

9. Erich Neumann, *Depth Psychology and a New Ethic*, trans. E. Rolfe (New York: G. P. Putnam's Sons, 1969).

10. This argument about the nature of synchronicity is a highly simplified version of the thesis I developed in my *Synchronicity & Science* (London: Routledge, 2010).

11. Alfred N. Whitehead, *Process and Reality: An Essay in Cosmology* (1929) (New York: Free Press, 1969).

No "As If," No Between: The Giegerich Inversion of Mind and Soul

GLEN SLATER

You are all in air now. Your reasons are unreasonable.
Euripides, The Bacchae.[1]

The dead came back from Jerusalem, where they found not what they sought.
C. G. Jung, Septem Sermones ad Mortuos[2]

L et's consider the scope of the matter at hand: Jung's insight into the one-sided nature of Christianity drove his creative vision from inception, making it an intrinsic part of his entire opus and a major bridge between his psychology and the spiritual condition of modern life. His comprehension of the cultural-historical significance of the individuation process is rooted in this insight. His study of alchemy and Gnosticism, emphasis on archetypal femininity, as well

Glen Slater has been teaching depth psychology for the past fifteen years, specializing in Jungian and archetypal studies. He currently teaches at Pacifica Graduate Institute in Santa Barbara and at Antioch University in Seattle. He edited and introduced volume three of James Hillman's *Uniform Edition* of writings, edited *Varieties of Mythic Experience* (with Dennis Patrick Slattery), and has written a number of articles for *Spring Journal* and its collected essay publications.

as his turn to Eastern religion and comparative mythology are prompted by the same concern. His most prominent writings from the final years—particularly *Answer to Job* and *Mysterium Coniunctionis*—are direct outgrowths of this read on the Christian problem. His description of a personal myth in *Memories, Dreams, Reflections*, the initiatory dialogues now evident in *The Red Book*, his first dream of a chthonic, pagan divinity, and his vision of a divine bowel movement destroying Basel cathedral all converge on the theme of Christian one-sidedness. Jung came of age with Nietzsche's announcement of God's death, and he entered the field of psychology searching for religious insight befitting the spirit of the times. He would eventually suggest that the *very existence* of depth psychology resulted from the decline of traditional symbols and rituals—a decline that had a great deal to do with Christianity's one-sided, maladapted state. Essentially, Jung's confrontation with the spiritual excesses and shadow-making apparatus of Christianity is the cornerstone of his whole psychology.

There is no need to reiterate the work done by Jungians to amplify this point of view and expound its implications. Nonetheless, it should be noted that Wolfgang Giegerich takes his cue not only from Jung's work but also in no small way from that of James Hillman, where the notion of one-sided Christianity and the long shadow it casts holds even more sway. From Hillman's perspective Jung failed to see just *how* one-sided Christian monotheism and its impact on psychic life has been, making Jungians ever prone to monotheistic perspectives and ensuing dualisms. Hillman's turn to the Greeks, to the pagan, and his lean towards a Jewish style of discourse³ may have other generative roots, but his work consistently exposes the underbelly of Christianized psychology. This thread is extracted in an early chapter of *Interviews* entitled "A Running Engagement with Christianity," where Hillman reflects on the field's point of origin and states "that the repression which Freud placed at the basis of our relation with the unconscious is nothing more than the Christian myth at work in us each, cutting us off from our innate polytheistic imagination and renaming it, the unconscious."⁴

Giegerich's essay "God Must Not Die!" stands in complete opposition to this entire strain of Jungian perspective. Although he seems compelled to position himself within the tree of Jungian ideas, it's clearer than ever before that he's sawing off the already distant limb on which he's been sitting. In this most recent essay he doesn't offer a constructive critique or an alternate path of understanding Jung's religious perspective, and he doesn't just tweak, twist, or explore another angle. Rather, he argues that critical aspects of Jung's approach are marked by "archaic thinking"[5] and operate with "naïve kindergarten idea(s)."[6] He says Jung's view is "unprofessional,"[7] not even psychological,[8] and Jung is indulging in the very metaphysics and theology he carefully eschewed. In other words, Jung hasn't simply strayed in his perception of Christian one-sidedness; he's gone spectacularly off course. Then, pushing Jung's approach and conclusions to one side, Giegerich places a radically contrasting view before us: Within the inner logic of the Christian tradition we can find all we need, including an internal solution to the problem of evil—the lynch-pin of the tradition's shadow dynamics. Moreover, according to Giegerich, the inner logic of Christianity and that of psychology converge to form "the emergence of a new insight, of a new way to think, a new status of consciousness unheard of before."[9] After going to lengths to convey just how sidetracked by religious and mythological thinking Jung had become— referring at one point to "St. Jung" and his "new gospel"[10]—Giegerich proceeds to tell us that psychology must realize "in spirit and in truth"[11] the same absolute understanding of reality that an astute reading of Christianity already offers—namely his own. Along the way he suggests that the unconscious "has no place in a true psychology,"[12] refers to individuation as a "metaphysical process"[13] and calls Jung's notion of furthering the Christian myth a "family romance"[14] and "a utopia."[15]

Though he often appears to want his Jungian cake and eat it too, when placed alongside his writings over the past twenty years, particularly those that begin with *The Soul's Logical Life*, this essay reveals the degree to which Giegerich has departed from the underlying assumptions and lexicon of Jung's depth psychology. In many respects this isn't surprising. In 1998 he began his logical soul project with the claim that psychology "is at bottom pop psychology,"[16] telling us that "the time for indulging in myths and images of the Gods, the Self, the daimon etc. is past"[17] and proceeding to prescribe another form of psychology, one that "has to break with ordinary, customary and therefore comfortable 'logic' and rise above it and acquire a more complex, higher-level, more abstract, way of thinking."[18] For "now we live on a totally different, abstract level of reality."[19] In "God Must Not Die!" he has moved on to deride depth psychology to date as personalistic "psychologism,"[20] retaining the term "psychology" for his own perspective. Depth psychologists, according to Giegerich, have been doing ego psychology, while his *logos* psychology stands exclusively on the side of soul. This division of depth psychologists into those doing ego-level work and his soul-level work is underscored by the condescension he uses to describe the writings of others who have failed to catch onto his program.[21] The apparent rationale for this division and its absolutist rhetoric occurs early in *The Soul's Logical Life*, where he suggests one may only enter what he has now come to call "true psychology"[22] through confrontation with a "gatekeeper" who barks "no entry!" and "no admission!"[23] Such forceful rejection is supposed to keep all the pop psychologists out and initiate willing newcomers into the mode of logical negativity. This, apparently, is also the only way one can leave behind the psychology of "the child,"[24] who fails to comprehend the violent, negating nature of soul.

The central problem with Giegerich's argument in "God Must Not Die!" is to be found in the character of this division between the pre- and post- "logical life," its attendant gateway and what these formulations suggest. The problem is not buried in his argument, it's there from the start, pervading the very way he appraises and sets out his topic, the way he prepares his subject matter for entry into the terrain of logical negativity. A mind-trap is present from the beginning: One either steps up to the gates of logical negativity and takes up his argument on this basis, or one fails to recognize this division and its gates, with the implication that any counter-argument is deemed stuck at the semantic level and therefore dismissed.[25]

When sizing up his topic, Giegerich is only interested in that which is ready to be sacrificed on the altar of his special world and he interprets Jung accordingly. His reading of Jung is rendered to suit his purpose. Jung is turned into a suitable initiate, readied to lie prostrate at the gates of Giegerich's new psychological temple, guaranteeing in advance that understanding can be generated in terms of this threshold and entry into the special world of Hegelian dialectics, at what he claims to be the level of "syntax or logical constitution of consciousness."[26] To accomplish this task, Jung's perspective on Christian one-sidedness is presented as a shell of its former self, emptying its substance and replacing it with caricature—"Jung's own super-myth."[27]

When the distortion in this operation is recognized, two critical understandings cannot escape our attention. First, what Giegerich means by Christianity has little to do with the religious phenomenology that concerned Jung and continues to concern Jungians. Jung focused on the way Christian beliefs and symbols enter and shape lived experience, whereas Giegerich places Christianity "beyond people's psychology and their inner experience and individuation process."[28] Second, Giegerich's own peculiar Hegelian vision of soul, which "has no stake in images, nor in private experiences," only in "truths," "concrete universals" and "logical forms,"[29] bears no resemblance to that which Jung and Jungians of any ilk hold at the core of their work. The upshot of all this is clear: When neither the representation of Jung's ideas, nor the nature of the phenomenon being discussed, nor the sense of what constitutes the psyche or psychology bear any resemblance to existing streams of thought, the argument becomes, quite literally, beside the point. All of which leaves us with the glaringly obvious question: To what degree is dialogue or constructive critique even possible when a theorist draws such a sweeping division between existing perspectives and his own radical views? What follows in this essay attempts to place this question in sharp relief.

No "As If"

Let's consider another gateway, one already built into the kind of mythological thinking Jung engages in his approach to religious matters. For it is this gateway Giegerich deliberately puts aside in his description of Jung's "thesis"—a term that already grooms the topic for the sword of logical thinking. Between rational understanding and non-rational matters of the psyche, particularly matters of religion and myth, lies the realm of "as if"—arguably the most important term in depth psychology. For Jung there is no interpretation of psychic material, no apprehension of dream or image, no sound application of concepts that describe psychodynamics without passing through *this* gate, which serves to maintain the thoroughly metaphorical character of the psyche's expressions. Yet, when Giegerich says that "Jung sort-of writes the biography of God, the events in His life," that this is "substantiating thinking" not "psychological analysis or interpretation,"[30] that Jung "imagines in naturalistic terms . . . cultivates an archaic thinking,"[31] that he "posit(s) the transcendental object" and creates a "metaphysical hypostasis,"[32] he's not only describing something that deliberately circumvents the "as if" of depth psychological discourse, he's articulating a point of view no Jungian analyst, thinker, or scholar would recognize as a description of Jung's writings on Christianity. Giegerich writes:

> His (Jung's) is not psychological discourse, but a theosophic one. God is posited as existing outside *all* the different and separate stories from the Old Testament times onwards. Jung reads all these stories as records of the development of *God* 'in reality' from the creation onwards up to our time and beyond. The history of Biblical religious ideas or images is interpreted directly as a historical process of *God himself*.[33]

This description is a complete caricature of Jung's position. While forced to acknowledge Jung's continual effort to focus on psychic reality and avoid the metaphysical, Giegerich still manages to justify such descriptions by citing the way Jung sometimes leaves the door open to a "transcendental object" to which psychic images and processes may point.[34] He claims that Jung posits this object, and he then paints everything Jung says with this brush of dubious interpretation. Absented from view are the real *spirit* of Jung's stance and its actual locus of concern.

In the preface of *Answer to Job* Jung makes clear he doesn't distinguish between "transcendental" and unconscious processes. He goes on to state:

> If, for instance, we say 'God,' we give expression to an image or verbal concept which has undergone many changes in the course of time. We are, however, unable to say with any degree of certainty—unless it be by faith—whether these changes affect only the images and concepts, or the Unspeakable itself.[35]

Then, at the very end, he writes:

> It is only through the psyche that we can establish that God acts upon us, but we are unable to distinguish whether these actions emanate from God or from the unconscious. We cannot tell whether God and the unconscious are two different entities. Both are borderline concepts for transcendental contents.[36]

Jung no more posits or substantiates God than he does the unconscious; both are terms for the unknown. Thus, in the one work where he takes off the gloves to address divine action most directly, he couches the whole thing in terms of having no real knowledge of the relation between God-images and their referent—no knowledge of how the phenomenal and the noumenal are related or even if they are related. All he does is keep the door cracked open. But for Giegerich, this remains a problem, so the unconscious is also summarily dismissed as "a 'theological' term." In his essay, God, the unconscious and the self are *all* forms of "metaphysical noumen(a)."[37]

One can certainly cherry-pick Jung's writings to find places where the presence of a transcendental "object" seems vivid, or a sense of entity or "thingness" is more apparent. However, it is thoroughly disingenuous to relegate Jung's thinking to these categories. Giegerich understands full well that all three terms (God, the self, the unconscious) are most often (and more correctly) applied by Jung and by Jungians to refer to the *dynamic process quality* of events at the threshold of the known and unknown, not to static, rarified concepts. In this vein we find Jung's oft-quoted definition of God as "all things which cross my willful path,"[38] or the description of the self as a "greater personality" that emerges from the conscious-unconscious dialogue. And whereas we can note some of the traps involved in employing "the unconscious" as an abstract noun, the real point is maintaining awareness of a non-ego, autonomous realm that can act with something like intentionality.

"The unconscious" mitigates the chronically inflated modern ego and alerts the cocksure religionist that their beliefs are floating on a sea of fathomless mystery. It entered the world stage when the rational mind was at the very height of its absolutist claims on reality in both science and in religion, and it continues to serve as a placeholder for those aspects of psychic life that remain incompatible with, or simply devalued by the habitual state of consciousness. The concept itself reflects the psyche's inherent tendency to compensate one-sidedness. It designates the unrecognized role of history and tradition, as well as (in Jung) the teleological function of the psyche *as a whole*, which for most people remains submerged and unknown.

In terms of *these* understandings of "God" and "the unconscious," Jung's "thesis" of a one-sided Christian God-image is not a dedicated construct so much as an inevitable outgrowth of the overlap between the idea of psychic inclusivity and the religious instinct, which makes a transcendent, masculine, God of light and goodness one-sided *by definition*. Moreover, what Jung observed in the inner world of patients and in contemporary artistic expression was an active compensatory surge of chthonic, feminine, dark imagery. The one-sided God and its yet to incarnate aspect is, in essence, a personified image of that which is appearing on the threshold of the collective unconscious and calls to be recognized and hosted. It carries an awareness of the repressive apparatus that keeps the psyche split and compartmentalized as well as of those archetypal forms that are pushing for inclusion in present-day expressions of value and meaning. Considered along these lines, the ultimate significance and value of Jung's approach to the one-sided God is not in its details, nor even in the monotheistic frame in which it's expressed; it lies in the reorientation of consciousness towards a more encompassing and partly autonomous psychic sphere. It is, at bottom, an attempt to reconcile the present-day activity of the religious instinct with the traditional forms through which that instinct has expressed itself, inviting us to re-imagine the teleological function as it plays out on the cultural-historical stage.

The spirit of Jung's stance is to cultivate an attitude toward the unknown, one that emphasizes the psychic (phenomenal) foreground while locating the ultimate source of meaning and purpose beyond our complete grasp. This attitude precisely avoids the position Giegerich has now taken up in claiming that a psychological stance means the image "does not point to anything outside itself. It only points to itself."[39] For Jung it is vitally important, especially in matters of religion, to leave room for the numinous (the sense of radical otherness) on the one hand and prevent the mind from colonizing the sphere of understanding on the other. Giving in to the numinous would result in a mystical mess; giving in to the mind carries the danger of psychologism and intellectualism. Operating within the wake of the death of God (Nietzsche), Jung walks a line, acknowledging the hollowness of theological and metaphysical discourse while not succumbing to the excesses of nihilism and the abandonment of the past. Between these extremes he pursues a perspective that places the religious impulse in a modern context.

The door to metaphysical and theological implications in Jung's thought does not have to be welded shut for the gravity of his reflections on Christianity to remain with the expressions of the psyche, engaged with the "as if" eye of symbolic and metaphorical discourse. His general stance in this regard is described in his essay on the child archetype, where he writes: "Every interpretation *necessarily remains an 'as-if.'* The ultimate core of meaning may be circumscribed but not described."[40] He goes on: "If, then, we proceed in accordance with the above principle, *there is no longer any question* whether a myth refers to the sun or the moon, the father or the mother, sexuality or fire or water; all it does is to circumscribe and give an approximate description of an *unconscious core of meaning.*"[41] In *Revisioning Psychology*, Hillman underscores this general stance towards myth, religion, and other "fictions," tracing the gateway of "as if" from Vaihinger, through Jung and on into philosophers such as Paul Ricoeur. Along the way he notes, "the very fiction of the archetypes is that they posit themselves to be more than personal and human, because the psyche is both immanent in persons, and between persons, and also transcends persons."[42] For Jung, as for Hillman, as for the whole depth psychological turn to myth, the relation between images and transpersonal, "non-human" entities is understood to be part of the fictive mode of imaginal discourse.

When Jung writes, "God wanted to become man and he still wants to,"[43] he's saying it is *as if* God still wants to enter the world and if we imagine in this way something positions us to listen to the psyche's depth with a feeling of co-creative possibility. When he writes of the "service which man can render to God . . . that the Creator may become conscious of His creation . . ."[44] he's talking about the reflective instinct in a mythopoetic manner, describing the ultimate psychological value of holding a mirror up to the dark reaches of the cosmos and find meaning in the process—*as if* one were in dialogue with God. Far from being "his own yarn,"[45] the essence of Jung's envisioning of a contemporary religious life is already detectable in "the German mystical tradition of Meister Eckhart, John Tauler, and the *Theologia Germanica*," perhaps best summed by Angelus Silesius: "I know that God cannot live one instant without me;/Were I to become nothing, He must give up the ghost."[46] Far from being a personalistic program, this "myth" of Jung's is a very broad invitation to dialogue with the psyche, which opens ground for an individual's unique and particular connection to the larger movement of Western consciousness.

Giegerich refuses to hear these base notes. Instead, he magnifies and exploits the small crack in the doorway Jung leaves open to the metaphysical. His argument reflects neither the genuine realm of Jung's concern nor the spirit of "as if" understanding that actually characterizes Jung's approach to Christianity. When Jung offers another reading of the Christian story, intimating a new myth for modern times as it were, he's not "completely within the myth, enwrapped by it"[47] as Giegerich describes. And it cannot be neatly juxtaposed to the "demythologizing" dialectic. Jung's mythic sense has already passed through the stage of demythologizing. It is a reaching back through phenomenological and hermeneutic awareness to the language of the ancients, acknowledging the irreducible nature of the religious imagination, within which only the terms "God" or "gods" are adequate. Jung's sense of myth aligns with the following description:

> The moment you think you know what a myth *means* you have lost contact with the myth itself. Because a myth, whatever else it might do, does not *mean* in that way. If anything, it is a kind of predisposition toward meaning, a verbal *prima materia* where narrative and order, drama and metaphysics, the aboriginally linguistic and insuperably unspeakable all dance together in the moment before all other moments of human utterance. Myth is not *about*, it *is* that precarious energy exchange between self and other, language and silence, word and world . . .[48]

This passage on myth recalls another on religion, which kicks off Mark C. Taylor's treatise on the topic:

> Religion is about a certain about. What religion is about, however, remains obscure for it is never quite there—nor is it exactly not there. Religion is about what is always slipping away. . . . religion is, I believe, most interesting where it is least obvious.[49]

For Jung, myth is a natural extension of the symbolic life; it bridges the upper and lower regions of the psyche. Religion, in the stripped down form that he embraces, designates the quest for ultimate values— an apprehension of the meaning question. In "Psychology and Religion" Jung defines religious experience as "characterized by the highest appreciation, *no matter what the contents are*."[50] And earlier in the same work he writes: "Religion appears to me as a peculiar attitude . . . a careful consideration and observation of certain dynamic factors . . ."[51] These descriptions and the understanding to which they point already show a syntax of interiority rather than a syntax of archaic thought. And yet here is Giegerich trying to convince us that Jung simply took religion in its traditional form and recast it in the mold of the psychology of the unconscious.[52]

What Giegerich brings to his gate of logical negativity bears little resemblance to the form of *mythos* and idea of religion that Jung actually employs. Jung understands quite well that he's not talking about "the fate and development of God himself."[53] Even in *Answer to Job*, where he drops the guise of the empirical scientist and expresses his subjective reaction to the unjust and ignorant behavior of a supposedly just and omniscient God, he puts his affect-laden and poetic expressions in the container of "as if" psychological concepts and spends a good part of the aftermath reinforcing that container. Giegerich ignores these qualifications because he needs a caricature of Jung's position in order to divide it neatly and clearly from his own offerings. He needs to fit Jung's approach into his overarching theory of myths and images belonging to a past era, which he has laid out elsewhere, stating, for example, that "we and 'myth' do not live in the same world," that "our relation to myth is inevitably archeological." And further:

> As a narrative myth is (logically) dead. By being abstracted from
> its time (*like a medieval altarpiece in a modern museum*, removed
> from its original context in the living piety of its age), it has become
> universalized and forfeited its nature as living myth, and thus as
> myth in the first place.[54]

Myth is alive only in relation to "the mythological-ritualistic mode of being-in-the-world," when there is a "unity of (mythological) semantics and (mythological) syntax."[55] So, to show that Jung's mythologizing is hopelessly bound to the past, he tries to put Jung's thoughts on Christianity and God into this coffin of a by-gone worldview, making the semantic content of Jung's thought appear to be carried along by the syntax of old time religion and myth. Jung's thought just doesn't fit into this box.

No Between

Giegerich doesn't want to deal with the inherent ambiguity, affectivity, and imprecise nature of psychological discourse, which plays out in Jung's work as a round-table conversation between science, phenomenology, and the mythopoetic imagination, a conversation that can, on occasion, also invite an aura of mysticism. Giegerich's senex style of understanding can't abide the puer play in Jung's approach. His presentation of Jung must discredit the "as if" quality of discourse because "as if" keeps the door open to a perspective that is most at odds with the logos-centered view, namely soul as the *mediating realm* of all thought and all experience. That is, soul as something distinct from *mind* and requiring far more flexibility and inherent untidiness than an overwrought concern for *thought* allows. At the beginning of *Psychological Types*, in discussing the conflict between nominalism and realism, Jung writes the following:

> *Esse in intellectu* lacks tangible reality, *esse in re* lacks mind. Idea and thing come together, however, in the human psyche, which holds the balance between them. What would the idea amount to if the psyche did not provide its living value? What would the thing be worth if the psyche withheld from it the determining force of the sense-impression? What indeed is reality if it is not a reality in ourselves, an *esse in anima*?[56]

This quote describes Jung's basic stance towards the psyche as that reality existing *"in-between."* In the paragraph that follows it, he goes on to write: "The psyche creates reality every day. The only expression I can use for this activity is *fantasy*. Fantasy is as much feeling as thinking; as much intuition as sensation."[57] Here we have a quintessential statement about the nature of soul as that which belongs neither to the intellect nor to the material world, but exists as a mediating field between the two. The fantasy forms it produces cannot be fully grasped by the mind, nor fully reduced to matter. Soul must be apprehended on its own ground, a point Stephanie de Voogd punctuates after her examination of this passage by noting *"esse in anima* bespeaks an ontology all its own."[58] Elsewhere, after taking Jung to task for his failure to apply Kant in a fitting manner, she makes a point most relevant here: "Jung's archetypal psychology implies an epistemological stance which renders the noumena-phenomena distinction (Kant) wholly unnecessary." She adds, "to give the same point the much wider scope it deserves, the fact is that the Jungian world view *dissolved rather than developed* its Kantian counterpart."[59] Such an understanding would obviously make Giegerich's critique untenable. Even more importantly, it underscores the psyche's predilection for a form of logos that supports this middle ground.

Archetypal psychology has been particularly dedicated to substantiating this mediating terrain of the psyche. The fundamental role of fantasy is a key basis for its approach, joining imagination as one of two primary modes that bridge conscious and unconscious, thought and instinct to form the most immediate and irreducible expressions of soul. Anima, fantasy, imagination reflect soul's own archetypal ground as "in-between." Hillman expresses it this way:

> The soul itself stands amidst all sorts of opposites as the "third factor." It has always existed halfway between Heaven and Hell, spirit and flesh, inner and outer, individual and collective—or, these opposites have been held together within its unfathomed reaches.[60]

In *Revisioning Psychology*, his description of soul as "a perspective rather than a substance" emphasizes this characteristic: "This perspective is reflective; it mediates events and makes differences between ourselves and everything that happens. Between us and events, between the doer and the deed, there is a reflective moment—and soul-making means differentiating this middle ground."[61]

Whether in psychology, philosophy, or poetry, soul has always been described and apprehended as bridging major categories of experience. Even the "personal soul" (no doubt an oxymoron for Giegerich) is that which crosses and transcends life and death, the ultimate opposites of existence. Despite this enduring characteristic, which obtains further significance in a world perplexed by Cartesian dualisms, Giegerich insists on the extraordinarily abstract notion of soul as logical thought, where logos is not even homegrown but borrowed from Hegel's *Phenomenology of the Spirit*. By vivid contrast, a prior attempt to articulate *The Logos of Soul* by Evangelos Christou demonstrates how psyche's logos must be generated out of this middle ground rather than imported from philosophy, which deals with the *mind* and its *conceptions*. Of soul he writes: "On the one hand it is about life, about how people think, feel, behave, their problems and their ways . . . On the other hand it is also about spirit and the meaning of life to people and these meanings are not exhausted by a history or analysis of ideas."[62]

Giegerich begins *The Soul's Logical Life* indicating his intention to develop a psychology that stands on the side of "the daimon, the Self, the soul"[63] and speaks about the psyche from their vantage point. This is also what lies on the other side of his "gatekeeper," referred to at the start. It's an either/or situation—either you're in the realm of the ego or you're on this other side. However, from the point of view of soul as "between" and the "as if" mode of interpretive discourse, such a proposition is not just unworkable, its absurd. Only a purely spiritual perspective can leap into these transpersonal forms and look back at the ego world with such distain. In terms of both thought and experience, without one foot in the realm of everyday concern and immediate being, the quality of otherness and relativizing power that belongs to each of these transpersonal, non-ego notions evaporates. What daimon has ever been apprehended except as a visitor or intruder that *enters* the psychic home through the "as if" language of image, symbol, and myth?

In "God Must Not Die" this dismissal of soul as in-between is reflected most vividly in the dismissal of contemporary religious experience and in the definition of Christianity as something outside its actual symbolic and imaginal forms. Although Giegerich begins his argument with references to phenomenology, and claims that the logical character of Christianity has "unfolded over the course of time,"[64] he provides no historical illustrations that would demonstrate such unfolding. He writes of "Christian thinking," but dismisses "the thinking of popular believers" and offers no evidence of where we've seen what he has in mind short of his own description of it.[65] His discussion essentially draws a straight line between the appearance of Christ and his present thesis, which also stands alone, without amplifying parallels in theology, cultural studies, or the philosophy of religion. "The inner logic of the Christian idea," which is the essence of his topic, is even considered "incompatible" with Roman Catholicism, which he regards as "*syntactically* (as far as its logical form is concerned) still a pagan religion merely with Christian contents (a Christian semantics)."[66] So the quintessential phenomenal expression of the Christian tradition is deemed as having little to do with the actual essence of that tradition. Forget Protestantism; it wouldn't have a hope in hell.

This whole line of argument is a recapitulation of the idea of being able to stand on the side of the self and the daimon and look back at life from their vantage point. Here he wants to look back at the world from the very height of spiritual remove—the *kenôsis* and "Love as logical negativity."[67] The arena of personal religious experience as well as the symbolic and dogmatic expressions of tradition is simply leapt over. This failure to bridge worlds—past and present, personal and transpersonal, thinking and being—is a problem that extends beyond the world of depth psychology and its God question. It also raises questions about what passes as authentic understanding, period.

HERMENEUTICS AND LIFE

Depth psychology came to the fore in tandem with another approach to the expressions of soul, one that has much bearing on the topic at hand, namely the field of hermeneutics, which explores the very conditions and principles that make understanding and interpretation possible. Hermeneutics grew out of the challenge of reading biblical texts in light of historical, archeological, sociological, and literary modes of analysis. It countered theological and metaphysical readings by reconstructing the context of a text's creation while also accounting for the standpoint of interpretation. Early philologists like Ast and Wolf emphasized ideas such as connecting the spirit (*geist*) of a text with the *geist* of the times in which that text appears. Schleiermacher, often considered the father of modern hermeneutics, built on their work, emphasizing an awareness of interpretation as an "art" that uses the finite and definite to describe the infinite and indefinite. He also underscored the notion that "logic cannot fully account for the workings of understanding," which requires a circular movement that is part comparative, part intuition and divination—the famous *hermeneutic circle*.[68] Critically, Schleiermacher set down one principle of hermeneutics that would carry through Dilthey on into Heidegger and Gadamer: understanding comes "out of a relationship to life."[69] For Heidegger in particular, understanding is inseparable from being (*Dasein*), both necessitate an "an entering into an occurrence of transmission in which past and present are constantly being mediated."[70]

This short overview of some of the main principles of hermeneutics reveals at least three areas where Giegerich's approach is challenged: The inadequacy of logic in processes of understanding; the need for understanding to relate to life; and the importance mediating past and present. Gadamer actually points out the *impossibility* of interpretation that contains no relation to the present—the need for all understanding to account for the historical moment. In other words, interpretation must bridge the distance between the present historical horizon and that of the past. He writes, "In this 'between' is the true place of hermeneutics,"[71] and he amplifies the point with the following example:

> an ancient image of the gods . . . *now on show in a museum,* retains, even as it stands before us today, the world of religious experience from which it came; the important consequence is that its world still belongs to ours. What embraces both is the hermeneutic universe.[72]

Recall Giegerich's "medieval altarpiece" analogy for mythic thought, sitting in a museum without the possibility of understanding or interpretation that can bridge back to the context of its origin—mythic thought that can only be legitimately understood in terms of its ancient point of origin. In an almost word for word fashion, Giegerich's stance contradicts Gadamer's. Consider Gadamer's further reflection, "to speak of a work-in-itself, cut off from its ever renewed reality as it comes to stand *in experience,* is to take a very abstract view,"[73] and recall Giegerich's central point, that the Christian tradition has everything it needs for its own soulful unfolding. In other words, Christianity, far from being a dying tradition in need of reinterpreting via contemporary understandings of archetypal patterns and mythologies, needs only to have its intrinsic logic revealed, whereupon its significance as a "work-in-itself" can suddenly burst into our consciousness after a 2,000 year incubation. Here we see the way in which Giegerich's critiquing of mythic discourse and his cocooning of Christian truth both fall foul of hermeneutic principles.

Any understanding with hermeneutic integrity also contains the built-in sense that meaning is inexhaustible, backing onto an abyss of endless mystery. For Heidegger, understanding (and being) only occurs when we're in relation to "an oscillation between the erratic foreground and the mysterious background."[74] Christou echoes this understanding in psychological terms: "The fact is that the soul is both a mystery and a reality and that we cannot get very far unless we are prepared to accept it in both these aspects however paradoxical they appear to be."[75] If *both* understanding *and* soul require the interaction of the known and the mysterious, then an understanding *of* soul surely requires the same. This conclusion obviously underscores the critical role of symbolical and imaginal thinking. But Giegerich states emphatically: "The soul has no stake in images, nor in private experiences. The soul is about truths, it exists in concrete universals, in logical forms."[76] And when it comes to Christianity: "Everything was already there at the beginning," and only now can it become "explicit and explicated and thus fully conscious and fully real."[77] Mystery and unknowing have apparently little place in this picture, a view that is at total odds with prevailing psychological reflections on the religious question. For example, in his study of the overlapping perspectives of Heidegger and Hillman, Roberts Avens writes: "For it is precisely because 'the divine God' is hidden and concealed that it demands a multiplicity of forms (images) in which to reveal itself."[78]

One final point about hermeneutic integrity is that understanding must be generated in a way that adequately reflects the present day horizon. In other words it must contain a built-in answer to the question of where the author is coming from, and the "coming from" must in some manner already carry an undercurrent of meaning that fits the times. Hegel has obviously played a major role in the rise of modern philosophy and has inspired some and repelled others. However, the adoption of Hegelian dialectics as the basis of a depth psychological approach has no organic relationship to the evolving history of the field. Giegerich plucks Hegel out of history and places his philosophy at the very core of his work, rather than even following Hegelian philosophy through the history of ideas into its more fully digested and fruitful modern renderings, such as one finds—ironically enough—in the hermeneutics of Gadamer.[79] In paper after paper Giegerich places topics in the corner of a triangle between his own idiosyncratic view of depth psychology and Hegelian logic, neither of which reflect any current stream of thought in the field or beyond it. This is not to say there can be no breakthrough works of depth psychology. However, beneath the surface of any "new" perspective that suddenly shifts existing viewpoints lies a preparatory ground. Awareness of the philosophical background of Freud and Jung's depth psychologies reveals that the geyser of ideas they brought forth was sourced in a stream of thinking ready to break through the surface. Their ideas were timely because they tapped into a confluence of undercurrents that had gathered force in Romantic philosophy.[80] Hillman's *Revisioning Psychology*, arguably the last breakthrough text in depth psychology, is not only planted firmly in select areas of Jung's thought, but builds its perspective upon the ideas of modern theorists like Corbin and Bachelard, as well on a rich stream of Neoplatonic views. Giegerich's perspective is an intuitive leap without amplification or significant intellectual alliances. It fails the test of establishing itself on the horizon of contemporary knowledge forms. Most depth psychologists who encounter his work have no idea of where he's coming from.

These difficulties all come home when we consider the core theme of Giegerich's paper. His presentation of the soul logic of Christianity, which "finds itself only 'in spirit and in truth' (John 4:23),"[81] set apart from immediate human concerns, takes us beyond both the hermeneutic circle and the reality of the psyche. This preoccupation instantly removes us from the reflected, crafted quality of interpretation and understanding as well as from the multifaceted dimensionality of psychological life. As Hillman has said, "truth is revealed. It cannot ever be told. We cannot tell the truth. It has to appear, inside the telling or through the telling. That's why we listen to what's not said in psychoanalysis . . ."[82] Truth only shows through veils, between the lines. It doesn't matter how Giegerich gets to this truth or how he qualifies it in terms of negativity,[83] the pursuit itself renders his approach beyond the hermeneutic integrity of psychologically oriented discourse. In psychology the pursuit of truth corrupts and the pursuit of "absolute Truth"[84] corrupts absolutely.

INVERTING MIND AND SOUL

Only the mind can stand back and concede that we must accept the inevitable binding of history to the Christian project. The soul cannot. Its concerns refuse to be funneled into abstract ideas of truth, ethics and love. In siding with spirit as the basis of psyche, Giegerich inverts mind and soul. Instead of "remov(ing) discussion of ideas from the realm of thought to the realm of psyche,"[85] he reverses the process, taking everything psychic and putting it in the realm of thought. At the same time he takes the whole thrust of depth psychology and dissembles it on the basis of bad or poor thinking. Once this is understood, the gateway he presents to us as dividing the depth psychology of the past from his new logos-centered psychology reveals itself: Rather than a division *within* psychology it's *a division between psychology and philosophy*. Giegerich may be professing psychology but he's doing philosophy. His ideas have entered another field, a field where the mind can roam unfettered by the images and fantasies that actually shape human experience. The assumptions he starts with, the way he works ideas and the conclusions he reaches look, feel, sound, and smell like philosophical abstractions—like thought that has released its ties to the emotional and instinctual exigencies of life. He has anticipated and countered this criticism with the notion "that real thought is experience and labor, passive and active, unconscious and conscious, all inextricably (uroborically) in one . . . all experience, since it is human, conscious experience, *comes* as something already *produced* by the thinking mind . . ."[86] But psychological events of any significance are far more nuanced, shaded and indefinite than this idea allows. Moreover, when Giegerich actually presents "real thought," this supposed uroboric character seems strikingly absent.

The soul can't extract itself from the animal basis of being or the awareness of being embedded in the natural world. So depth psychology has always hosted what lies between the upper and lower reaches of existence, particularly between the world of thought and the world of instinctual impulses. Every patient walking into the therapy room straddles these realms; every form of psychopathology expresses their split. The turn to myth, symbol, and imagination are modes of perception that allow navigation between these realms, preserving the sensations and sensibility of a middle space. A psychology that is all *logos* and no *mythos* has abandoned these field-defining characteristics and removed itself from the fabric of existence. As such it is an approach that is unrecognizable as depth psychology.

By contrast, Jung's ideas about Christianity are a form of "healing fiction," resulting from his taking a therapeutic, analytical stance toward the tradition itself.[87] His work is on the imaginal field in which the symbols and teachings of Christianity are held. His notion of extending the myth is wholly about attempting to articulate a religious perspective that neither breaks with the ancestral background of the Western mind nor ignores the arising of a new cosmology befitting the character of our time. His focus is on the places where the tradition fails to nurse the modern psyche into a meaningful, soulful stance on critical aspects of lived experience. His work exemplifies what Greg Mogenson refers to as "crust-building"—working fragments of memory, dream, story, myth, and vision into a psychological container for the raw, undigested, traumatic events of life.[88]

Evidence for the psychic reality of the one-sided character of Christianity and the symptoms it produces is on the front page of each day's newspaper. Evidence for Christian "Love as logical negativity" and God's "self-sublation into Spirit" appears only in the mind of a German psychologist turned philosopher.[89] Even if we were to grant Giegerich's perspective the status of penetrating insight into the essential spirit of the Christian tradition, it stands at a cold distance from the phenomenology of today's Christian neurosis, which, like it or not, *is* the concern of our field. The irony of "God Must Not Die!" is that Giegerich's argument about the ultimate truth of Christianity and its significance has nothing incarnate about it. It tells us nothing of the desperate literalisms and black and white thinking that surround a disemboweled symbology, nothing of the denials and compensating excesses of the body, nothing of the spiritual quests buried in symptoms like anorexia, nothing of the anxiety and guilt that plague the Christianized psyche. We see the one-sided God in the divisive rhetoric of evangelical preachers, politicians, and moralizing talk-show hosts who tilt American society and fuel the devastation of foreign lands. It's in the election of Ratzinger to the increasingly rigid and soul destroying papacy. It's in the molestation of thousands at the hands of pious clergy. It's in every polluted river whose source is the idea of human dominion over nature. This is to say nothing of the horrors of history generated by the monstrous shadow of Christian idealism. We're swimming in it for Christ's sake! In the face of these actualities, how much sense does it make to hold the totally abstract notion that Christianity is simply what it is and we should accept its unerring and fateful path through history? One has to ask in the end, what is more utopian: stripping down to the religious instinct by passing through the spiritual void and entering a soul-based co-creative process (Jung), or situating ourselves beyond the cut and thrust of life by "negating one's natural impulses and naturalistic imaginal perspectives . . . placing oneself under supersensory ethical laws" in order to enter the logic of Love (Giegerich)?[90]

Jungian psychology touches the ground and enters into the field of immediate human concern. Every morning of his childhood Jung saw the one-sided nature of Christianity on the face of his father, which gave him the eyes to perceive it coursing through the Western psyche, fueling the twentieth century's darkest events. For Jung this was never a philosophical problem but a tangible psychological crisis. He went back into the tradition looking for a genesis and an antidote, which he found by diving into the Gnostic, alchemical, and pagan scrap heaps of history. Ever since, Jungian psychologists have moved in multiple directions to describe and cultivate the missing pieces, attending to the culture's blind spots rather than merely accepting the visionless march of progress. Giegerich's attempt to dismantle Jung's view of Christianity must be seen for what it is: a strategic move in furthering the logos psychology project and removing a pillar of the current Jungian worldview, clearing a path for his own idea of where the future of psychology lies. He may be trying to rewrite the rules of the game, but when it comes to critiquing Jung's religious perspective he's queered the pitch. Yet the game was over before it began because the teams are assembled on entirely different fields.

NOTES

1. Euripides, *The Bacchae*, 330-4.

2. C. G. Jung, *Memories, Dreams, Reflections* (New York: Pantheon Books, 1963), p. 378.

3. James Hillman, "How Jewish is Archetypal Psychology?" *Spring* 53, (1992), pp. 121-130.

4. James Hillman, *Interviews* (Woodstock, CT: Spring Publications, 1983), p. 82.

5. Wolfgang Giegerich, "God Must Not Die! C. G. Jung's Thesis of the One-Sidedness of Christianity," this volume, p. 31.

6. *Ibid.*, pp. 48-49.

7. *Ibid.*, p. 31.

8. *Ibid.*, p. 34.

9. *Ibid.*, p. 46.

10. *Ibid.*, pp. 50-51.

11. *Ibid.*, p. 31.

12. *Ibid,* p 39.

13. *Ibid.*, p. 52.

14. *Ibid.*, p. 33.

15. *Ibid.*, p. 52.

16. Wolfgang Giegerich, *The Soul's Logical Life* (Frankfurt am Main: Peter Lang, 1998), p. 14. In "God Must Not Die!" he refers to spirituality in the same manner: "one of our consumer goods; it is for people's subjective indulgence and gratification" (this volume, p. 32).

17. Giegerich, *Logical Life*, p. 23.

18. *Ibid.*, p. 26.

19. *Ibid.*, p. 27.

20. Giegerich, "God Must Not Die!," this volume, p. 61.

21. See, for example, "The Psychologist as Repentance Preacher and Revivalist: Robert Romanyshyn on the Melting of the Polar Ice," *Spring*, Vol. 82 (2009), pp. 193-221.

22. Giegerich, "God Must Not Die!," this volume, p. 39. Whereas he uses the term "*real* psychology" early in *The Soul's Logical Life* (p. 21), in the present paper he's moved on to the declaration of truth.

23. Giegerich, *Logical Life*, pp. 15ff.

24. Wolfgang Giegerich, *Soul-Violence: Collected English Papers Volume Three* (New Orleans: Spring Journal Books, 2008), pp. 49ff. In this book Giegerich refers to my own writing about soul and technology, describing it as "the way 'the child' imagines soul" (p. 10).

25. Even efforts to understand Giegerich's work, praised by him as such, are critiqued on the basis of failing to enter the special Hegelian world of sublated ideas and the syntactical level of understanding. For example, see Wolfgang Giegerich, "The Unassimilable Remnant— What is at Stake? A Dispute with Stanton Marlan," in Stanton Marlan, ed., *Archetypal Psychologies: Reflections in Honor of James Hillman* (New Orleans: Spring Journal Books, 2008), pp. 193ff.

26. Giegerich, "God Must Not Die!," this volume, p. 35.

27. *Ibid.*, p. 42.

28. *Ibid.*, p. 58.

29. *Ibid.*, p. 54.

30. *Ibid.*, p. 30.

31. *Ibid.*, p. 31.

32. *Ibid.*, p. 36.

33. *Ibid.*, pp. 16-17.

34. *Ibid.*, p. 34.

35. C. G. Jung, *CW* 11 § 555.

36. *Ibid.*, § 757.

37. Giegerich, "God Must Not Die!," this volume, p. 39.

38. Quoted in Edward F. Edinger, *The Creation of Consciousness: Jung's Myth for Modern Man* (Toronto: Inner City Books, 1984), p. 68.

39. Giegerich, "God Must Not Die!," this volume, p. 36. It is one thing to take an image and stay with it or "stick to it" as a discipline of engaging the imagination. However, it's quite another thing to decide the image "only points to itself." Such a stance may help the thinking mind, but it effectively closes down the imagination.

40. *CW* 9i § 265, italics added.

41. *CW* 9i § 266, italics added.

42. James Hillman, *Revisioning Psychology* (New York: Harper and Row, 1975), p. 151.

43. Quoted in Giegerich, "God Must Not Die!," this volume, p. 51.

44. *Ibid.*, p. 52.

45. *Ibid.*, p. 36.

46. Roberts Avens, *The New Gnosis* (Putnam, CT: Spring Publications, 1984), p. 111.

47. Giegerich, "God Must Not Die!," this volume, p. 37.

48. Frank McConnell, quoted in William G. Doty, *Mythography: The Study of Myths and Rituals* (Tuscaloosa: The University of Alabama Press, 1986), pp. 246-247.

49. Mark C. Taylor, *About Religion: Ecomonies of Faith in a Virtual Culture* (Chicago: The University of Chicago Press, 1999), p. 1.

50. C. G. Jung, *Psychology and Religion* (Yale: Yale University Press, 1938), p. 75.

51. *Ibid.*, p. 5.

52. Giegerich, "God Must Not Die!," p. 61.

53. *Ibid.*, p. 40.

54. Wolfgang Giegerich, David L. Miller, Greg Mogenson, *Dialectics and Analytical Psychology* (New Orleans: Spring Journal Books, 1975), p. 42, italics added.

55. *Ibid.*, pp. 42-43.

56. *CW* 6 § 77.

57. *Ibid.*, § 78.

58. Stephanie de Voogd, "Fantasy versus Fiction: Jung's Kantianism Appraised," in Renos K. Papadopoulos, ed., *Carl Gustav Jung: Critical Assessments* (London: Routledge, 1992), p. 47.

59. Stephanie de Voogd, "C. G. Jung: Psychologist of the Future; 'Philosopher' of the Past," *Spring*, 1977, pp. 180-181. Italics in original.

60. James Hillman, *Senex and Puer, Uniform Edition* Vol 3, G. Slater ed. (Putnam CT: Spring Publications, 2005), p. 40.

61. Hillman, *Revisioning*, p. xvi.

62. Evangelos Christou, *The Logos of Soul* (Dallas: Spring Publications, 1976), p. 30.

63. Giegerich, *Logical Life*, p. 18.

64. Giegerich, "God Must Not Die!," this volume, p. 12.

65. *Ibid.*, p. 31.

66. *Ibid.*, p. 14.

67. *Ibid.*, p. 47.

68. See Richard E. Palmer, *Hermeneutics* (Evanston, IL: Northwestern University Press, 1969), p. 87.

69. *Ibid.*, p. 96.

70. J. Kockelmans, *Martin Heidegger: A First Introduction to his Philosophy* (Pittsburgh: Duquesne University Press, 1965), p. 6.

71. Quoted in Palmer, *Hermeneutics*, p. 184.

72. Hans-Georg Gadamer, *Truth and Method*, second revised edition (New York: Continuum, 1994), p. xxxi, italics added.

73. Quoted in Palmer, *Hermeneutics*, p. 164, italics added.

74. Kockelmans, *Heidegger*, p. 17.

75. Christou, *Logos*, p. 46.

76. Giegerich, "God Must Not Die!," this volume, p. 54.

77. *Ibid.*, p. 12.

78. Avens, *Gnosis*, p. 126.

79. Gadamer, *Truth*.

80. Henri F. Ellenberger, *The Discovery of the Unconscious* (New York: Basic Books, 1970), pp. 534ff; pp. 727ff.

81. Giegerich, "God Must Not Die!," this volume, p. 14.

82. Hillman, *Interviews*, p. 6.

83. Giegerich, *Logical Life*, pp. 217ff.

84. *Ibid.*, p. 231.

85. Hillman, *Revisioning*, p. 121.

86. Wolfgang Giegerich, "Psychology as Anti-Philosophy," *Spring* 77 (2007), p. 48.

87. See Murray Stein, *Jung's Treatment of Christianity* (Wilmette, IL: Chiron Publications, 1985).

88. Greg Mogenson, *A Most Accursed Religion: When God Becomes a Trauma* (Putnam, CT: Spring Publications, 2005), pp. 111ff.

89. Giegerich, "God Must Not Die!," this volume, pp. 45-47.

90. *Ibid.*, p. 66.

JUNGIAN ANALYSIS *POST MORTEM DEI*

GREG MOGENSON

It is for your own good that I am going
Because unless I go
The Paraclete will not come to you;
But if I do go,
I will send him to you.

John 16:7

PART ONE

THE GOD QUESTION

I t has sometimes happened in the course of an analysis that a patient
has asked me if I believe in God. Recalling such occasions the rule
of these has been: they have always occurred in what would have
seemed the most unlikely of cases. That *this* patient would ask of me

Greg Mogenson is a Jungian psychoanalyst practicing in London, Ontario, Canada and the editor of The Studies in Archetypal Psychology Series of Spring Journal Books. The author of many articles in the field of analytical psychology, his books include *A Most Accursed Religion: When a Trauma becomes God, The Dove in the Consulting Room: Hysteria and the Anima in Bollas and Jung, Greeting the Angels: An Imaginal Approach to the Mourning Process, Northern Gnosis: Thor, Baldr, and the Volsungs in the Thought of Freud and Jung,* and (with Wolfgang Giegerich and David L. Miller) *Dialectics & Analytical Psychology: The El Capitan Seminar.* For more information, see the website: http://gregmogenson.com

that question, why, I would have never expected it. During the whole of our previous work together no indication of religious interests, let alone of any tendency to *think* in religious categories, had ever been communicated. On the contrary, session after session, week in and week out, talk about some private misery stubbornly held sway. The troubled marriage, the envied co-worker, the latest imposition or affront: no matter how thoroughly these topics were discussed, there was always more to say about them—transcendence be damned. Or so it seemed until one day the question was put to me: "Do you believe in God?"

Now it might be thought, given the well-known response of C.G. Jung to the same question, that an affirmative answer would come readily to the lips of any subsequent member of his guild. I allude here to the interview that the BBC conducted with Jung in 1959 for its television series "Face to Face." Asked if he believed in God, the 85-year-old psychologist balked at first at the word "belief." God for him was no matter of belief. As he famously stated at the time, "I *know*. I don't need to believe. I know."[1]

A precious statement, this. Preserved on film, it is a part of our spiritual heritage. And yet, if the interview were to be re-broadcast today some Grand Inquisitor of Correctness would require a disclaimer to be added: "The opinions expressed in this programme do not necessarily reflect the theory and practice of contemporary Jungian analysis."

The issue here is an ethical one. As analysts we are concerned about the deleterious effects of imposing our beliefs upon our patients. For what a doubtful enterprise analysis would be if our patients had to become like us, believing as we do, to become authenticated. But this said, there has also been a tradition within analytical psychology of valuing candor on the part of the analyst. In a lecture series that he gave at the Tavistock Clinic in 1935 Jung spoke of this to an audience largely made up of Freudian colleagues: "I put my patients in front of me and talk to them as one natural human being to another, and I expose myself completely and react with no restriction" (*CW* 18 § 319). Setting this technical recommendation alongside his other statement about knowing God, we may be prompted to ask: if it is not a matter of belief, but of knowledge, is a reply by the analyst to the God-question *de rigour* after all?

Jung, evidently, thought that it was. In yet another interview given in his old age, knowledge based upon religious experience was authoritatively declared by him to be the very touchstone of the analytic process:

> Without knowing it man is always concerned with God. What some people call instinct or intuition is nothing other than God. God is that voice inside us which tells us what to do and what not to do. In other words, our conscience. ... I make my patients understand that all the things which happen to them against their will are a superior force. They can call it God or devil, and that doesn't matter to me, as long as they realize that it is a superior force. God is nothing more than that superior force in our life. You can experience God every day.[2]

This statement, it is important to stress, was not intended as a theological assertion. It concerned, rather, Jung's psychological vision and analytic stance. When conveying his position as a psychologist with respect to the reality of the psyche, Jung drew upon divine epithets. Psychological reality, in his view, was a matter of what he called "immanent-transcendental" experience (*CW* 18 § 1505). Arising immanently out of inner subjective depths, it could be called transcendent at the same time inasmuch as our experiences happen to us.[3] And it was from this, let us call it the "objective" or even "divine" character of psychic reality, that Jung's use of "God" and "the unconscious" as synonymous terms stemmed. Just as the unconscious can be revelatory, so God, according to Jung, is "one of the most certain and immediate experiences," "as plain as a brick that falls on your head ..." (*MDR*, p. 62).

The great psychologist could not have been more adamant. And yet, to the careful reader such statements were by no means as unequivocal as they at first may have seemed. For even after repeated readings one could still wonder if the God that Jung spoke about in such tangible and concrete terms was of the same order of reality as the God that believer's relate to through their faith. And so, wanting to know where he really stood, many attempted to hold his feet to the fire on this question. But what had once been a fire to test heretics had waned in the meantime to the mere glow of a fading coal. Or was this coal, even as it faded, the ember of a new consciousness?

PSYCHOLOGIZING GOD

"I have been asked so often whether I believe in the existence of God," wrote Jung in *Answer to Job*, "that I am somewhat concerned lest I be taken for an adherent of 'psychologism.' What most people overlook or seem unable to understand is the fact that I regard the psyche as *real*. ... God is an obvious psychic and non-physical fact, i.e., a fact that can be established psychically but not physically" (*CW* 11 § 751).

The knowledge that Jung claimed with respect to God had to do with what could be known empirically about the soul by the psychologist. And if, as he put it, he did not need to believe because he knew, this knowing was based upon the empirical study of human ideas and human beliefs, that is, upon the phenomenology of religious experience both personal and communal.

As for his use of "God" and "the unconscious" as synonymous terms and his reference to "inner, transcendental experience" (*CW* 10 § 511), what Jung had in mind with these gestures and associations is evident from a passage from the 2nd century gnostic writer, Monoïmos, that he quoted in *Aion*:

> Seek him from out thyself, and learn who it is that taketh possession of everything in thee, saying: *my* god, *my* spirit, *my* understanding, *my* soul, *my* body; and learn whence is sorrow and joy, and love and hate, and waking though one would not, and sleeping though one would not, and getting angry though one would not, and falling in love though one would not. And if thou shouldst closely investigate these things, thou wilt find Him in thyself, the One and the Many, like to that little point ... for it is in thee that he hath his origin and his deliverance. (Cited in *CW* 9 ii § 347)

Just as the ancient author of this passage directs the seeker after God to the kinds of experiences which the modern psychoanalyst identifies with the unconscious, so Jung, many centuries later, advised his analysands to seek after the unconscious in the name of God.[4]

But what of the "how" and the "when," the "why" and the "wherefore" of using now one, now the other, of these interchangeable terms? In a discussion of this topic Jung explained that as a scientist and psychological theorist he "prefer[ed] the term 'the unconscious'" because it was "coined for scientific purposes" and was, thus, "better suited to dispassionate observation" than were its mythological equivalents. It was a different matter, however, when it came to his psychotherapeutic work. In that context his preference was to speak of "'mana,' 'daimon,' and 'God'" as he felt that these terms facilitated an altogether more vivid engagement with the psychic process.

> ... for certain purposes ... belief is far more useful and effective than a scientific concept. The great advantage of the concepts "daimon" and "God" lies in making possible a much better objectification of the *vis-à-vis*, namely, a *personification* of it. Their emotional quality confers life and effectuality upon them. Hate and love, fear and reverence, enter the scene of the confrontation and raise it to a drama. What has merely been "displayed" becomes "acted." The whole man is challenged and enters the fray with his total reality. Only then can he become whole and only then can "God be born," that is, enter into human reality and associate with man in the form of "man." By this act of incarnation man—that is, his ego—is inwardly replaced by "God," and God becomes outwardly man, in keeping with the saying of Jesus: "Who sees me, sees the Father." (*MDR*, p. 337)

Psychology, a Religion?

From the passages that I have quoted it is not surprising that Jung should have had to again and again respond to the question of whether analytical psychology is a religion. His answer, of course, was always to reject this admittedly understandable impression. Analytical psychology, he said, is not a religion, nor he a religious leader. His disclaimers, however, did little to settle the controversies that his playing so fast and loose with the God-concept stirred up.

In a 1922 letter to Freud, for example, an early defector from Jung's circle, the protestant minister and lay-analyst Oskar Pfister, declared himself "finished with the Jungian manner":

> Those high-falutin interpretations which proclaim every kind of muck to be spiritual jam of a high order and try to smuggle a minor Apollo or Christ into every corked-up little mind simply

will not do. It is Hegelianism transferred to psychology; everything that is must be reasonable. If only that theory were true![5]

And then, toward the end of his life and career, there was the rather bitter exchange between Jung and Martin Buber. Basing himself upon a thorough reading of Jung's texts, the great Jewish philosopher had charged Jung with bringing about an "eclipse of God" through his having substituted for the concept of an externally existing deity a false "religion of pure psychic immanence."[6] Jung, of course, defended himself manfully in his side of this public exchange. Not one to eat his words, he did find, however, that he had to chew over them more carefully in his subsequent response and in the many letters to correspondents that followed in the aftermath of this and the "Face to Face" interview which was broadcast some years later.

"What I have described is a psychic factor only," he wrote in his "Reply to Buber,"

> but one which exerts a considerable influence on the conscious mind. Thanks to its autonomy, it forms the counterposition to the subjective ego because it is a piece of the *objective psyche*. It can therefore be designated as a "Thou." For me its reality is amply attested by the truly diabolical deeds of our time: the six million murdered Jews, the uncounted victims of the slave labour camps in Russia, as well as the invention of the atom bomb, to name but a few examples of the darker side. But I have also seen the other side which can be expressed by the words beauty, goodness, wisdom, grace. These experiences of the depths and heights of human nature justify the metaphorical use of the term "daimon." (*CW* 18 § 1505)

We had just heard in the section above this one Jung's argument for the *therapeutic* advantages of using mythological terms and speaking the language of belief. Now, in defence of his frequent references to God *in his scientific writings*, he clarifies that what he refers to in this way "is a psychic factor only," but one that justifies "the metaphorical use" of the terms daimon and God. It might be wondered if Jung is drawing in his horns a little here. What has happened to the God that he did not believe in, but knew? While continuing to make reference to God, Jung now owns up to this as being a *façon de parler* that is useful in psychotherapy, "a psychic factor only," a metaphor.

Quite a come down, this rejoinder! Jung, evidently, had become aware of the vainglorious tenor of his claims with respect to God and seeking to redress this hastened to express himself in a more psychologically circumspect manner. Such, at any rate, is the impression that comes across from a reply that he penned to a correspondent who had written to him following the "Face to Face" interview:

> Mr Freeman [the BBC interviewer] in his characteristic manner fired the question you allude to at me in a somewhat surprising way, so that I was perplexed and had to say the next thing which came into my mind. As soon as the answer had left the "edge of my teeth" I knew I had said something controversial, puzzling, or even ambiguous. I was therefore just waiting for letters like yours. Mind you, I didn't say, "there is a God," I said: "I don't need to believe in God, I *know*." Which does not mean: I do know a certain God (Zeus, Yahweh, Allah, the Trinitarian God, etc.) but rather: I do know that I am obviously confronted with a factor unknown in itself and which I call "God" in *consensu omnium (quod semper, quod ubique, quod ab omnibus creditur).*
> (*Letters* 2, p. 525, to M. Leonard, 5 December 1959)

In this passage Jung demurs somewhat with respect to his controversial statement about knowing God. Perplexed by the abruptness of the interviewer's question, he had answered with the first thing that came into his mind. His answer, thus, had not been a well-considered one. It had had more the character of a reaction to one of the stimulus words that he used to detect complexes with in the word association experiments of his early days.[7] But while this was certainly true on this particular occasion, what are we to make of the other times when Jung said the same thing in a more considered manner?

An interview given in 1955 that Jung *was* able to read and approve prior to its publication in the *London Daily Mail* concluded with these words: "All that I have learned has led me step by step to an unshakable conviction of the existence of God. I only believe in what I know. And that eliminates believing. Therefore I do not take His existence on belief—I *know* that he exists."[8] Again, as in the "Face to Face" interview, Jung speaks most adamantly. On this occasion, however, he does not rest content with merely drawing his psychological distinction between believing and knowing, or confine himself to a psychic factor only; on top of this he affirms of the *existence* of God!

What is going on here? In Jung's usual phenomenological/empirical sense of knowing, knowing God means fathoming the meaning of any God-image, even if it were to be the image or idea of the death of God. But now he makes an ontological claim. He refers to the *existence* of God; he says, "I *know* that he exists."

It would seem that with these words Jung's position with respect to a really existing deity is stated in no uncertain terms and that theists everywhere can simply claim him as one of their own. This, however, is a mistaken impression arising, I believe, from the assumption that the meaning of his statement is the same as it would be if it were spoken from someone else's mouth. What Jung actually has in mind is a very different matter. And to get at this we must be able to square his statement about having been "led to an unshakable conviction of the existence of God" with the many others that fly in the face of it, such as the warning he issued on another occasion: "It would be a regrettable mistake if anybody should take my observations as a kind of proof of the existence of God. They prove only the existence of an archetypal God-image, which to my mind is the most we can assert about God psychologically" (*CW* 11 § 102; cf., *CW* 14 § 781).

No easy feat, the squaring of this circle. Reading now the one, now the other of Jung's statements, we may feel that we have come across an inconsistency or contradiction, even. But while this may be so, there is reason for the reader to persevere. Inconsistency and contradiction, after all, are not only the hallmarks of misconception and error; they can also herald the appearance of new truth. And this, arguably, was the case with Jung. Taken together, his inconsistent and contradicting statements were the avowal of a new God-term (though it is perhaps no longer appropriate to call it that): the *coincidentia oppositorum* of *Psychology itself* in the highest determination of Jung's conception of it.[9]

REVERSING THE RELATION

In the previous pages a small, but representative sample of the kinds of statements that Jung made when queried about his religious beliefs has been examined. And following upon this we have just now ventured the thesis that as a psychologist Jung had had to grapple with such questions, not because his analytical psychology was a religion, but because psychology in his sense is the successor to religion. Extending this a bit it could also be said that Jung was not first a psychologist who then transgressed the boundaries of his profession to take positions on theological questions; rather, it was the other way around: it was his tackling of the God question again and again that produced his sense of the psychological as its result.

Numerous texts come to mind in support of this contention. I will here mention only two, from "The Archetypes of the Collective Unconscious." In answer to the question— "Why is psychology the youngest of the empirical sciences? Why have we not long since discovered the unconscious and raised up its treasure-house of eternal images?"—Jung replies: "Simply because we [formerly had] had a religious formula for everything psychic—and one that is far more beautiful and comprehensive than immediate experience" (*CW* 9i § 11). Developing this point further in a later passage he then explains that an "unparalleled impoverishment of [religious] symbolism" was what opened the way for our "rediscovery of the gods as psychic factors, that is, as archetypes of the unconscious":

> Since the stars have fallen from heaven and our highest symbols have paled, a secret life holds sway in the unconscious. That is why we have a psychology today, and why we speak of the unconscious. All this would be quite superfluous in an age or culture that possessed symbols. Symbols are spirit from above, and under those conditions the spirit is above too. Therefore it would be a foolish and senseless undertaking for such people to wish to experience or investigate an unconscious that contains nothing but the silent, undisturbed sway of nature. Our unconscious, on the other hand, hides living water, spirit that has become nature, and that is why it is disturbed. (*CW* 9i § 50)

The provenance of psychology, according to these passages of Jung's, resides in the decline of the religions that preceded it. Having encountered one another in the various ways that modernity made possible, the World's religions contradicted or at least relativized one another. No longer could any one of them simply take the universality of its symbols for granted. Comparison and doubt had entered the picture. And, yet, the upshot of this mutually negating witness yielded an affirmative result. As what the various religions held in common became discernable, consciousness advanced to a higher level of complexity than it had had within the single faiths that it pushed off from in this way. This, at least, has been the case with Jung's psychology, which, by its own account, has given the truths of the religions a new form as what he called the archetypes of the collective unconscious.

But what about Christianity? While Jung was certainly interested in what could be learned about the psyche from the study of comparative religion, Christianity held a special significance for him as the most immediate precursor of modern psychology generally and of his analytical psychology in particular. Why, it could even be argued that his wider interest in comparative religion was redolent of a Christian story. Guided by Christ's star, the Magi from the East travelled from distant lands to Bethlehem to bestow their gifts upon the infant Jesus. Likewise, with his culture-transcending, religion-sublating concept of the collective unconscious, Jung followed a sunken version of that same star to the scene of that most ecumenical of all nativities, the nativity of psychology.[10]

Now my reference here is to a "sunken" star because in Jung's view it is "as the intensity of the Christian ideas begins to *fade*, [that] a recrudescence of individual symbol-formation may be expected" (*CW* 8 § 92, italics mine). No longer insulated from the actuality of our life's truth by the cultural mediation that the Christian faith had provided during the course of its flourishing, the individual is subject to a veritable onslaught of immediate experience, as the stigmata of his symptomatic suffering attests. Drawing upon Christian ideas, Jung regarded this experience, this suffering, to be constituted by a post-Christian outpouring of the Holy Spirit upon the many. Overflowing themselves, the symbols of Christianity became metaphors, symptoms, and psychological terms, even.

Examples abound. With regards to work with patients in the consulting room, Jung declared that, "Analysis should release an experience that grips us or falls upon us as from above, an experience that has substance and body such as those things which occurred to the ancients. If I were going to symbolize it I would choose the Annunciation."[11] Continuing the analogy he writes on other occasions of the incarnate Christ as a model of the human individuation process:

"The drama of the archetypal life of Christ describes in symbolic images the events in the conscious life—as well as in the life that transcends consciousness—of a man who has been transformed by his higher destiny" (*CW* 11 § 223).[12] Another important reference is to Pentecost. Consistent with his view that psychology is itself a kind of myth inasmuch as its theories are underpinned by the same archetypes that underpinned religion, Jung avers that the "further development of myth might well begin with the outpouring of the Holy Spirit upon the apostles [at Pentecost], by which they were made into sons of God ..." (*MDR*, p. 333). And, of course, in this connection we should also mention Jesus' reference to the Paraclete. Speaking to the disciples at the Last Supper, Jesus assured them that it was good that he was going to his death, for only with his going away could his spiritual form come to dwell within them and be known to them (John 16:7). Carrying this reference of Jesus' to the Paraclete ("Advocate" or "Comforter") forward into psychology, Jung identifies the action of this figure with the spontaneous manifestation of the unconscious in the modern individual, i.e., with the aforementioned "recrudescence of individual symbol-formation" that arises with the decline of religious symbolism:

> Despite the fact that he is potentially redeemed, the Christian [we may also read here, the patient or analysand—G.M.] is given over to moral suffering, and in his suffering he needs the Comforter, the Paraclete. He cannot overcome the conflict on his own resources; after all, he didn't invent it. He has to rely on divine comfort and mediation, that is to say on the spontaneous revelation of the spirit, which does not obey man's will but comes and goes as *it* wills. The spirit is an autonomous psychic happening, a hush that follows the storm, a reconciling light in the darknesses of man's mind, secretly bringing order into the chaos of his soul. (*CW* 11 § 260)

A SHEEPISH FEELING

In the above reflections we have been discussing the spirit of analytical psychology in relation to responses that Jung gave when questioned about his belief in God. While doing so, however, the situation that we began with in which *I* was the addressee of this question has not been forgotten. This, on the contrary, has been with me all along. But as on those occasions, so now in these pages: thoughts and associations have flashed to mind just as they did during the long seconds that ticked by as my patients' questions hung in the air between us.

Of course, I know that I do not have to answer, not then and not now. And I suspect, moreover, that my patients may have already known that as an analyst I very likely will not. But there is pressure all the same. A question has been asked and an answer is expected. Ordinary human etiquette, if not the rules of analysis, places an onus upon me.

And yet, as obliging as I would like to be, a certain wariness prevails. This I suspect may have partly to do with the strife-ridden history that has long been associated with matters of religion. More blood has been spilled over disputes about God than over any other cause. Would what I might say suffice for the inquisition writ small that this moment has become? And then, on the heels of this reflection, I am subject to a sheepish feeling. I think to myself about how halting and complicated my answer has probably become, though it be to a question for which my career as a Jungian analyst had once seemed to provide of itself such a hearty and affirmative answer. But faithful to my training, if to nothing else, I return the question unanswered to its sender. For what good is *my* belief to my patient? And by the same token, what good is *Jung's* to me? If there is a God to be found he only exists through each one's finding their own. "No one besides you has your God,"[13] writes Jung in his *Red Book*.

CAVEAT REDEMPTOR

But wait! Is this really enough? Batted back and forth like a shuttlecock or hot potato has not the question we began with been short-changed in the interaction I have just described? The problem here is not with the idea of finding one's own. That's true enough, each one must find into their own. The issue, rather, is with whether "one's own" must have the form of God. Reviewing what I have written, I notice that my final reflection shows a theistic bias. Effacing what the question—Do you believe in God?—actually asks, the thoughts through which I released myself from having to answer simply assume (to say it with the words of the oracle that Jung inscribed above his doorway in Küsnacht) that "summoned or not summoned, the God will be there." The other option, i.e., that there could be a non-theistic, atheistic, or post-theistic answer, is not even considered. Perhaps, then, in light of this, and in the interest of restoring the larger sense of the question, its addressee should no longer be the analyst or patient, *but psychology itself.* The challenge of this, let us now call it *"the soul's" own question,* would then become (given analytical psychology's rootedness in a religious sensibility) to consider whether Jungian analysis is conceivable *in absentia dei,* or to anticipate a bit what is to come in Part Two and Three below, whether it is conceivable *post mortem dei.*

Part Two

> *[We] should bend to the great task of reinterpreting all the Christian traditions ... [and since] it is a question of truths which are anchored deep in the soul ... the solution of this task must be possible. (CW 11 § 754)*
>
> C. G. Jung, Answer to Job

"God Must Not Die!"—Or Must He, Has He?

We now come to the essay of Giegerich's to which this volume of our journal is devoted. In formulating a response to it, my interest will be to show its critical importance with respect to the problematic that has been outlined above in Part One.

Jung, as we have been discussing, regarded God to be the touchstone of what he meant by soul even as the religions generally "express[ed] the whole range of the psychic problem in mighty images" (*CW* 10 § 367). And further to this, his psychology of individuation and self was predicated upon his interpretation of Christianity. By attending to dreams and other immanently transcendental psychic phenomena, the analytic process, in his view, was to *"dream the myth onwards* and give it a modern dress" (*CW* 9i § 271). Turning now to Giegerich's essay, the first thing to be noted is how aptly its title— "God Must Not Die!"—sums up the main thrust of this, let us call it Jung's theistic conception of psychology. Jung, as Giegerich has discussed elsewhere,[14] had wanted "a situation in which that thing [that had previously been mediated by Christian symbolism] becomes true once more ..." (*CW* 18 § 632). He had wanted, that is to say, that what he called "the symbolic life" should still be possible, even after the decline of collective symbolism. The realization of this want, however, was far from straightforward. Having become conscious of consciousness itself, modern man was divided by this awareness from what has been called the Age of Faith. Where formerly the existence of God had been an almost universal conviction, it had become possible, even fashionable in the 19th and 20th centuries to debate and question this. Jung, of course, knew where he stood on this matter. From childhood on he had regarded God to be one of the most certain of experiences (*MDR*, p. 62). As a mature psychologist and man of his times, however, he had also to reckon with the fact that consciousness had advanced to its current stage of development largely by negating God. And herein lay the tension in which his life's work was forged. Unable to go back as a believer to the symbolism of Christianity (since he "[knew] too much about it"), Jung sought instead to establish "a new form" to provide for the same needs (*CW* 18 § 632). This form, as we have already indicated, was the form of psychology, or to be more specific, of *the psychology of the unconscious.*

Simply put Jung's conception of the unconscious provided him with a counter-position to Nietzsche's atheism. The God whom Nietzsche had declared to be dead, and who had become less and less important in the conscious lives of Jung's contemporaries, was still a compelling reality according to Jung, along with a pantheon of other gods, in the realm of the unconscious.

Again, as we noted earlier, it was a case of falling stars, or as Fr. Victor White put it in his *God and the Unconscious*, of a "new disease of unconscious religion which becomes epidemic when man is filched of his gods."[15] Finding support in analytical psychology for his ministry to an increasingly secular age, White, a Dominican priest who published under ecclesiastical *imprimatur*, cited Jung: "...whenever the Spirit of God is excluded from human consideration, an unconscious substitute takes its place." "The Gods have become diseases; not Zeus but the solar plexus now rules Olympus." And again, "When God is not recognized, selfish desires develop, and out of this selfishness comes illness."[16]

But is there another selfishness (and with it, another illness)? A selfishness that does not deny God or fail to recognize him, but that stubbornly insists upon him? In the essay under discussion, Giegerich argues that there is and offers Jung up as the prime example. The touchstone of his analysis consists of references of Jung's to God along with certain features of the latter's interpretation of Christianity. Jung, as Giegerich shows, so insists upon a psychology *with God* that he is prepared to don the mantle of a myth-maker to provide one. Railing against such things as the apparent cruelty of Yahweh to Job, the sacrifice of Christ as the behest of a loving Father, and the divine and semi-divine status of Jesus and Mary which he regards as casting the incarnation into doubt, Jung, in something of the manner of today's narrative therapies, supplies what Giegerich calls a "super-myth" wherein the unconscious and ethically inferior Jewish-Christian God becomes conscious and redeemed in the wholeness that individuals may achieve as the result of their individuation processes.

As Jungians, of course, we all know this story. Not only is God unconscious (in the sense of being irresponsible with respect to his dark side), Christianity is one-sided. Hallowed as being without sin, the canonical Jesus lacks completeness. The remedy for this, according to Jung, lies in the compensatory potential of the counter-tradition, specifically, in the legends that cropped up concerning the Antichrist. Just as the puerile Peter Pan had had to have his shadow sewn to his heal, so the spotless Christ must integrate Satan. And then there is the problem of the Trinity. Regarded by Jung as being incomplete, it, too, must be transformed through the inclusion of evil, for only by becoming four-fold in this manner is the wholeness of God adequately presented. This, however, cannot be achieved by God alone. It requires human help. And this is where the human individuation process, characterized by Jung as "life in God,"[17] comes in. Subject to ethical dilemmas that are not of his own making, the individual is the vessel, as it were, of the divine opposites that are operative in the back of these, contributing to their synthesis through the choices that he makes. And "that," writes Jung with "the myth of the necessary incarnation of God" in mind, "is the meaning of divine service, of the service which man can render to God, that light may emerge from the darkness, that the Creator may become conscious of His creation, and man conscious of himself. (*MDR*, p. 338)

Now it is important to remember that in propounding these ideas Jung made no attempt to limit himself to a "carefully considered exegesis that tries to be fair to every detail ..." (*CW* 11 § 561). On the contrary, inspired by what he called "the shattering emotion which the unvarnished spectacle of divine savagery and ruthlessness produces in us," he wrote as one who has pulled out all the stops (*ibid.*). Little wonder, then, that his interpretation of Christianity sounded in mighty organ blasts! Upon closer examination, however, the astute reader may doubt that Jung's thoughts on these matters are truly *interpretative* in character. Interpretation, after all, is not an anthem of stormy affects.[18] Its aim and purpose is simply to bring out the truth of the matter at hand, not to dream it along by imagining what should have been or could be. But, of course, with respect to the psychology that bore his name, Jung enjoyed free rein. And if, as he once put it, he was glad that he was Jung and not a Jungian, this may have been in part because his interpretations had the distinction of being Jungian just by virtue of the fact that *he* had announced them. For us who follow, however, it is not so easy. We have to ask, with a rigor that Jung often spared himself, if the interpretations that have come down to us from him are truly psychological in the fullest sense that he rightly gave to that term.

This, to be sure, is no small challenge. Jung was a great man, a psychologist of enormous stature. Amongst the generations of his followers there have only been a very few who have possessed the wherewithal, let alone the temerity, to challenge his views. Giegerich, to his credit, has long been one of these. Writing in what might be called a "*with* Jung, *against* Jung, *beyond* Jung spirit" he has for upwards of forty years been turning Jung's thought around upon itself in an effort to advance it via immanent critique. In the present volume, as its sub-title indicates, it is Jung's interpretation of Christianity that is subjected to this treatment. Turning this around upon itself, Giegerich demonstrates, in the course of a thorough-going reflexive analysis, how on nearly every point it falls below the *niveau* of the psychological principles and interpretative standards that Jung had himself introduced into psychology and carefully applied when it was a question of other topics.

WEIGHED IN THE SCALES ...

It will not be necessary to précis here all the various short-comings and excesses that Giegerich exposes in Jung's reading of Christianity. The reader, I am sure, will have read these for himself before turning to my essay. For our purposes it is enough to simply recall several of the psychological principles and interpretative standards of Jung's which Giegerich shows him to have failed to apply when it came to Christianity.

The first of these has simply to do with a clear recognition of what psychology is *about*. In "Basic Postulates of Analytical Psychology" Jung argues for a "'psychology with soul,' that is, a psychology [*Seelenlehre*] based on the hypothesis of an autonomous mind [*Geist*]" (*CW* 8 § 661, W.G.'s modified transl.).[19] With this key statement he indicates that what might variously and interchangeably be referred to as consciousness, mindedness or the soul is not to be taken as secondary to something else which it can be reduced to, but must be seen as a reality in its own right that posits, expresses, and reflects *itself*. Concurring with Jung on this point, Giegerich in an earlier essay has given it the form of a shibboleth: "The psychological question is not, cannot be, what and how the soul is, but how the soul is reflected in its manifestations. ... psychology is the study of the reflection in some mirror and not the study of what the mirror is the reflection of."[20] Practically speaking, what this means is that in our work as psychologists we must not be taken in by the myriad versions of the seduction theory which psychic phenomena suggest through their sensuous, affective, and imagistic immediacy, but must form our interpretations by seeing through to what these phenomena, precisely by appearing as they do, say about the soul. Jung taught us, for example, that the incest motif does not mean incest in the literal sense, but indicates a symbolic reality or soul truth (*CW* 16 § 419). Likewise, in *The Visions Seminars*, he argues that his patient's dream of going to visit a doctor who lives by the sea should not to be taken as a reference to him, even though he is her doctor and lives by Lake Zurich. Stating this in the form a principle, he then concludes, "We should not judge dreams from realities because in the long run that leads nowhere."[21]

But what, it may be asked, can dreams and other soul texts mean if they are to be considered apart from any real referents? An important footnote in Giegerich's essay provides a "with Jung, against Jung, beyond Jung" answer to this question. In this note he works with a passage from *Answer to Job* in which Jung states the main tenet of his interpretation of Christianity. "Job," writes Jung, "... was an ordinary human being, and therefore the wrong done to him, and through him to mankind, can according to divine justice, only be repaired by an incarnation of God in an empirical human being. This act of expiation is performed by the Paraclete; for, just as man must suffer from God, so God must suffer from man. Otherwise there can be no reconciliation between the two" (*CW* 11 § 657). Now the problem with this passage, as Giegerich makes clear in the body of his essay, is that against his own rules Jung takes the figures he is dealing with for real. Though he knows well enough in other contexts that incest does not refer to actual incest and that dreams are not to be judged from realities, he here takes Job at face value as an ordinary human being and God quite literally and trans-textually as God. But this, as Giegerich rightly insists, will not do. Psychology is not about such realities as people and God (if God is indeed a reality) and not about their external relationships. Rather, it is about the soul *per se*, consciousness as such.[22] And in keeping with this its job is simply to ask, as Giegerich does with respect to the passage from Jung we have just cited, "What kind of consciousness is [it] that thinks about [such and such a topic and does so, moreover, in such and such a way]?"

Now, of course, Giegerich's actual sentence is more specific than this. For didactic purposes I removed for the moment the critical reference he makes in its latter half to the ideas he had quoted from Jung. In doing so my aim has been to produce the general form of what might be called *psychology's question*. Simply by examining what this question in its general form is driving at we can gain a keener grasp of what it means to say that psychology is about the soul. But here now, having obtained this keener grasp, let us add the redacted reference to Jung's text back in. On the heels of his having cited Jung's statement about the wrong that was done to Job by God and the expiation for this that would have to be performed by the Paraclete, Giegerich derisively inveighs:

> What kind of consciousness is it that thinks about human misfortunes and terrible suffering as a "*wrong* done to him" (by God/Fate/Life) and as obviously requiring the repairing of an injustice? Do we have a vested right to be well-treated by life and to fairness? A category mistake. Behind it all is the innocent childlike belief in and demand for an ideal world and a good and just God. (this volume, p. 66, note 1)[23]

As criticism goes this is a masterstroke. Simply by keeping the focus upon what psychology is about, Jung's failure to do so himself is exposed along with something of the mindset that led him astray. But this is not all. A sentence later another line from Jung is quoted: "[Modern man has] experienced things so unheard of and so staggering that the question of whether such things are in any way reconcilable with the idea of a good God has become burningly topical" (*CW* 11 § 736). And then, rounding upon this sentiment, Giegerich delivers the *coup de grace*. Far from being burningly topical, Jung's concerns as given in these statements amount to "The kindergarten idea of a good God"!!! (p. 66-67)[24]

As asked by Giegerich, psychology's question is simply devastating. A key part of Jung's interpretation of Christianity is shown to comprise a regressive sinking of psychology back into a wishful, low-grade version of the theological/theosophical style of thinking that preceded it. This is a shocking surprise. One would have thought that the great psychologist would have known his business—thought, that is to say, that he would have asked this question himself of his biblical sources. But having failed to do so, the question rebounds upon him instead— and this, moreover, in a manner that recalls that scene of priestly succession in the Grove of Diana at Nemi that Fraser discusses in *The Golden Bough*.[25] The *coup de grace*, indeed!

PSYCHOLOGY'S SELF-PRODUCTION VIA SAYING AGAIN AND SEEING THROUGH

At the end of Part One, after having shown Jung's investment in the God-image (and at times, even, in a really existing God), we asked if Jungian analysis is conceivable in *absentia dei*. Already, from our brief examination of only a footnote's worth of Giegerich's critique of Jung's reading of Christianity, the answer becomes apparent. Of course it is. Psychology is about the soul. And this means, among many other things, that when "God" is its topic the task is to see through to what the specific God-image or God-concept indicates with respect to consciousness, says about the soul.

But just here another question arises. As correct as the above statement may be (and I think that it is correct), has it not been rattled off a bit too glibly? Yes, psychology must see through. The trouble is, though, that for what Giegerich would call a truly psychological psychology to exist at all it must time and again produce itself anew through the very act of seeing through that it is supposed then to perform.

The problem I am pointing out is the problem of external reflection, or as this might also be called, of the positivity of psychology. Steering clear of these, it is of crucial importance that psychology not be thought of as a field of study existing independently over and against the phenomenon it studies, as for instance the "and" in the expression "psychology *and* religion" implies. Rather, it must produce itself—as true insight tends to—through the thoughtful process of interiorizing its subject matter, whatever that may be (a text, a dream, a life situation), into itself.[26]

Drawing upon a Hegelian vocabulary, Giegerich speaks in this connection of *absolute negative interiorization*. Absolute negative interiorization is a methodological stance that stresses the intrinsic interiority or self-character of any phenomenon that of its own accord has become the locus of our interest and attention. Sublated from the outset, having self-character to begin with, such phenomena are already the soul speaking about itself, already psychology, even, but of course only implicitly. They still need to be reflected into themselves, fathomed in the complexity of their mutually constituting moments, thought through to the end in order for their knowing to become explicit. And here it could be added that with these reflections Giegerich is only taking very seriously the interpretative principle that is contained in the statement of Jung's that he quotes in his essay: "What the dream, which is not manufactured by us, says is *just so*. Say it again as well as you can" (*Letters* 2 p. 591, to Herbert Read, 2 September 1960).

Interiorizing Christianity into Itself

We are now able to address the part of Giegerich's critique which is most pertinent to the question I have raised as to the tenure of God in analytical psychology.

In his aforementioned *Tavistock Lectures* Jung told his largely Freudian audience, "My problem is to wrestle with the big monster of the historical past, the great snake of the centuries, the burden of the human mind, the problem of Christianity" (*CW* 18 § 279). In Giegerich's view, Jung had the right instinct here. While other psychologies just start directly with what they are seduced into believing psychology to be about (introspective data, personal history, or what Jung called "the joys of the cradle or a bad upbringing" [*CW* 17 § 95]), a truly psychological psychology must first reflect itself, that is, the history of its subjectivity, the history of its consciousness, and in this venture, as Jung rightly indicates, there could hardly be a worthier prime matter than the religion whose waning has most immediately preceded the rise of modern psychology in the West, the religion of Christianity.

But what in this case does "reflecting itself" mean? Historical reflection in the ordinary sense of looking back behind psychology to its Christian pre-history is only one part of it. The more important part has to do with psychology's aforementioned self-production as an interpretive discipline via saying again and seeing through. We have learned from Giegerich that "psychology is the study of the reflection in some mirror and not the study of what the mirror is the reflection of." Clarifying this further he has advised that "since the soul cannot be approached directly, ... psychological investigation has to take the form of a commentary on given 'documents of the soul'."[27] Christianity, of course, is such a document, such a mirror, as is the interpretation or commentary that psychology subsequently and self-constitutively gives it. And from this the question arises as to whether the discourse of psychology is truly up to the documents it grapples with, or bringing this back to Jung, whether his interpretation does justice to the soul that is manifest in the Christianity that his psychology was developed to succeed, push off from, dream onward.[28]

We have already mentioned several of the interpretative principles of Jung's that Giegerich has drawn upon in forming his critique. There was the insistence upon a psychology with soul that is at the same time about the soul, the idea of psychology's producing itself by dwelling with the phenomenon and saying it again, and the cautionary remark about not explaining dreams (and other psychic phenomena) from realities. Two other statements of Jung's that Giegerich refers to throughout his work should be drawn into our discussion. The first of these has to do with what Giegerich, with the sealed retort of alchemy in mind, has called systematic closure: "Above all don't let anything from outside, that does not belong, get into it, for the fantasy-image has 'everything it needs' within itself" (*CW* 14 § 749, Giegerich's transl.).[29] The second has to do with what Giegerich conceives of as the tautological self-referentiality of soul texts: "In myths and fairytales, as in dreams, the soul speaks about itself, and the archetypes reveal themselves in their natural interplay, as 'formation, transformation / eternal Mind's eternal recreation'" (GW 9/1 § 400, Giegerich's transl.; cf., CW 9i § 400).[30] Taken together (and they do mutually define and complement each other) these interpretative principles, gleaned from Jung's writings, are like the bands that Odysseus had himself bound to the mast of his ship with so that he could listen to the singing of the Sirens without becoming entranced by them or bewitched. Such bands, of course, are essential to any kind of interpretative work, if the interpreter is not to be waylaid for too long, with some Circe or Calypso, through overvaluing one or another moment of the phenomenon that he or she holds particularly dear.

But the question arises: what happens to these constituting constraints of a truly psychological attitude when it comes to interpreting the Christian "dream" text? Again, we are surprised to be shown by Giegerich the extent to which Jung broke with key features of his own methodology. Though Jung well knew that Christianity and its history reflect the history of consciousness, writing from his emotions he treats it at the same time as if it were one of Rorschach's projective ink blots and weighs in, so to speak, with his own demand for personal meaning. The result of this, not surprisingly, is that the effort miscarries. Jung finds *his* "myth," but at the expense of the professional, "state of the art" level of psychology proper.

THE OPUS PARVUM/OPUS MAGNUM DISTINCTION

The problem I am pointing out has to do with a blurring of the distinction between what Giegerich has called the "little work" of an individual person's individuation process and the "great work" of mankind's individuation. In the Jungian literature there are a plethora of studies in which symbols and myths from diverse traditions have been wrenched from their historical, cultural, and communal contexts and drawn into the service of illustrating archetypal dimensions of the individual development and healing of contemporary men and women. Updating Jung's dictum that "the *tertium comparationis* of all … symbol[ism] is the libido" (CW 5 § 329) the impression comes across that "one's personal journey," as this has come to be called, is what the myths and symbols were about in the first place.

All this, of course, began with Jung and the inspiring account he gave of the life-enhancing importance of the individual's developing a position for himself with respect to the topics that from time immemorial have been of importance to the soul. Consider, for example, the paragraphs in *Memories* that preface the setting out of his views on a topic which has traditionally gone hand in hand with belief in God, life after death. Concerned about the injury that critical rationalism has dealt the full phenomenon of human life, Jung makes a compelling case for our imaginative reengagement with this erstwhile theme, for this as he sees it is "a healing and valid activity … [that] … gives existence a glamour which we would not like to do without."

> … A man should be able to say he has done his best to form
> a conception of life after death, or to create some image of
> it—even if he must confess his failure. Not to have done so is
> a vital loss. For the question that is posed to him is the age-
> old heritage of humanity: an archetype, rich in secret life,
> which seeks to add itself to our own individual life in order to
> make it whole. (*MDR*, p. 302)

Had Jung just left it at this we could perhaps let his views stand uncontradicted. For it is probably true that for many people life is more personally fulfilling if a sense of its mysteries is kept alive by their imaginatively participating in them. And if, as Jung also said, our speculations concerning a life after death are only a matter of one's telling a good ghost story by the fire as one smokes a pipe, well what is the harm in that?

But Jung goes much further than this. By the end of the chapter he advises that the most rigorous of his interpretative principles, such as those ones we discussed above as being constitutive of a true psychology, should be drawn upon in this effort:

> … it is all-important for a disciplined imagination to build up
> images of intangibles by logical principles and on the basis of
> empirical data, that is, on the evidence of dreams. The method
> employed is what I have called "the method of the necessary
> statement." It represents the principle of *amplification* in the
> interpretation of dreams … (*MDR*, p. 310)

The problem here, as I have already indicated, is not so much that the persons Jung has in mind will not benefit from such an approach.

Quite possibly they will (on an ego-security, if not ego-integrity level). The concern, rather, is about what happens to psychology (i.e., to the methodological stance of a true psychology) when the finger that applied this ointment is put back into the bottle.

We have already heard from Jung that "In myths and fairytales, as in dreams, the soul speaks about itself ..." With this remark Jung distinguishes the soul in its greater sense as consciousness *per se* or mindedness as such from the usual, personalistic sense of soul that derives from ego-determined wishes with respect to how we would like the soul to be during the various phases of the life-cycle from cradle to grave. This is a crucial distinction. Referred to by Giegerich as "the psychological difference," it is the difference between a psychology that is of the soul and about the soul and a psychology that is of and about persons, or again, between the psychic phenomena which animate a person or a people and the *truth* of those phenomena. As Giegerich has pointed out, when Jung was up to his soul-psychology/ego-psychology distinction he wrote in a manner that unfolded the psychology of the soulful phenomenon itself, be it the Trinity, the transformation symbolism of the Mass, the mythic features of U.F.O. accounts, or a schizophrenic's vision of a solar phallus.[31] Without reference to the interior of people, he worked out the logical life of those symbols that marked the horizon of the human. Just as often, however, he let the difference collapse, as when, for example, in the course of justifying his speculations concerning life after death he appealed to the fact that "for most people it means a great deal to assume that their lives will have an indefinite continuity beyond their present existence. They live more sensibly, feel better, and are more at peace" (*MDR*, p. 300).[32]

Here, it is important to realize, the consoling therapist in Jung got the better of the psychologist in him, so much so, in fact, that he even allowed his psychological method to be drawn into the service of providing comforting illusions! And this by no means is the only example of his working in such a pandering-to-the-ego manner. As Giegerich has reminded us in an earlier essay,[33] there is also Jung's story about the woman he met on his travels whose life he characterized as "... grotesquely banal, utterly poor, meaningless, with no point in it at all." Put in mind by her plight of the fulfilled dignity of the Pueblo Indians he had visited in New Mexico who believed that through their ritual they helped the Sun, their father, across the sky, Jung proposed a dose of the same medicine for her:

> If she is killed today, nothing has happened, nothing has vanished—because she was nothing! But if she could say, "I am the daughter of the Moon. Every night I must help the Moon, my Mother, over the horizon"—ah, that is something else! Then she lives, then her life makes sense, and makes sense in all continuity, and for the whole of humanity. That gives peace, when people feel that they are living the symbolic life, that they are actors in the divine drama. That gives the only meaning to human life; everything else is banal and you can dismiss it. A career, producing of children, are all *maya* compared with that one thing, that your life is meaningful. (*CW* 18 § 630)

Reading this passage one can only admire the prescience of Freud's warning to Jung, during the course of their very first meeting in 1907, about the danger of releasing, in the name of analysis, a "black tide of mud ... of occultism" (*MDR*, p. 150). For that is what this Daughter of the Moon therapy amounts to, a tide of consoling illusions which no doubt are quite comforting to the Beautiful Soul as it tightens up against that animus moment of the syzygy which, unrecognized as such by Jung, was vilified by him as the soul-less rationalism of the contemporary critical mind and modern world.

But the point I want to make has to do with the deleterious effect that this pandering to the ego and vilifying of the critical mind had upon Jung's principles of interpretation even after his consulting room was closed for the day and he was working over biblical texts in his study. In his preface to *Answer to Job* Jung makes a virtue of the fact that he was unable to write the book "in a coolly objective manner," but allowed his "emotional subjectivity to speak" (*CW* 11 § 559). Underscoring this point, he characterizes himself as having written out of a sense of provocation. Outraged by Yahweh's immoral treatment of Job, he drew inspiration from his own "equally ill-considered outburst of affect" and "smouldering resentment," "... express[ing] his affect fearlessly and ruthlessly ... and ... answer[ing] injustice with injustice" (*CW* 11 § 561). Quite rightly Giegerich asks, "Why does [Jung] write a book about a topic when he is still personally gripped by its 'numinosity'? Why did he not see it as his obligation as a psychologist to work off (to have long ago worked off for himself) this 'numinous' affect and overcome his feeling 'wounded' by it?" (this volume, p. 69, note 9)

Later in his Job book Jung again judges and re-writes the biblical text in terms of affects, desires, and subjective reactions as, for instance, when he takes the text-external "deep longing in the masses for an intercessor and mediatrix who would at last take her place alongside the Holy Trinity and be received as the 'Queen of Heaven and Bride at the heavenly court'" (*CW* 11 § 748) as an authenticating touchstone of his revisionist reading of Christianity. Just like the woman he had met with on his travels whose life, supposedly, would have been worthwhile if she could have said "I am the daughter of the Moon," so, thanks to the papal declaration of 1950, can the Catholic faithful find meaning in the Dogma of the Assumption of Mary and *Da Vinci Code* Jungians in the Sophia Jung imports from Proverbs and Ecclesiastes into his account of the Job story.[34]

Again, it is apparent from this that the therapist in Jung got the better of the depth psychologist in him. Rather than giving his heart and mind fully over to the task of dispassionately fathoming what the text's being as it is says about the soul, he imposes a subjectively conditioned politically correct make-over upon it that is designed to meet people's needs, e.g., for a good God, a metaphysical representation of the feminine, the resacralization of the secular, and whatnot. It is the exact opposite of Giegerich's insistence, in the spirit of alchemy, that as psychologists "our Christianity is not the people's Christianity." Jung's intent, by contrast, was to provide a psychology for the people. Even though he "strictly distinguished" between "the psychology of the religious person" and "the psychology of religion proper, i.e., of religious contents" and claimed that it was "chiefly [his] experiences in the latter field which [had] given [him] the courage to enter into the discussion of the religious question ..." (*CW* 11 §§ 751-752), he nevertheless got his wires crossed, such that his soul psychology was more personalistic than he realized. For, indeed, on his analysis, religion belonged not to the *intelligible* soul as its (now antiquated) mode of speaking about itself, but to people as their immediately felt, meaning-providing, self-validating experience.

THE BEAUTIFUL SOUL AND ITS TOO TERRIBLE TO BE TRUE OTHER

In passing above mention was made of the Beautiful Soul. The term itself comes from Hegel (amongst others) who used it to describe a determination of consciousness, typical of the Romantics but by no means exclusive to them, wherein the subject self-identically clings to innocence and purity by tightening up against the world or something bad within it that has been constituted as such out of all that offends its sense of soul. Closer to our own time, and with specific reference to Jung, this same problematic has been reformulated by Philip Rieff as what he calls "the triumph of the therapeutic."[35] In contrast to Freud, who had emphasized the disenchanting of neurosis via the analytic attitude, Jung is shown by Rieff to have sought a cure for his patients by means of "a meta-religion aiming at something beyond the criteria of true and false, or even good and evil …" and whose "… ideal character type … is neither mystic nor ascetic, but therapeutic—a person assessing even his own myth in terms of how much it contributes to his sense of personal well-being."[36]

In support of Rieff's contention any number of passages could be cited. The one that comes most immediately to my mind (next to the life after death and daughter of the Moon material discussed above) is from Jung's essay, "Psychology and Religion":

> Religious experience is absolute; it cannot be disputed. You can only say that you have never had such an experience, whereupon your opponent will reply: "Sorry, I have." And there your discussion will come to an end. No matter what the world thinks about religious experience, the one who has it possesses a great treasure, a thing that has become for him a source of life, meaning, and beauty, and that has given a new splendour to the world and to mankind. He has *pistis* and peace. Where is the criterion by which you could say that such a life is not legitimate, that such an experience is not valid, and that such *pistis* is mere illusion? Is there, as a matter of fact, any better truth about the ultimate things than the one that helps you to live? (*CW* 11 § 167)

The first sentences of this passage declare religious experience to be intrinsically authoritative, immediately self-validating and as such immune from criticism, unanswerable. In the conversation described by Jung, discussion is stopped short when the one party smugly asserts that he has had a religious experience—and that that's all there is to it. Evidently, for Jung, there is no need for any rational accounting with respect to a religious experience. No need for any "trying of the spirits" to see if it is true.[37] With the middle sentences we are taken a little further down the same path. Religious experience is set up as something to be treasured over and against what the world of others thinks. We may be reminded in this connection of Jung's insistence in *The Undiscovered Self* upon the individual's need of "the evidence of inner, transcendental experience which alone can protect him from the otherwise inevitable submersion in the [social, collective] mass." According to this view, "... an extramundane principle capable of relativizing the overpowering influence of external factors" is needed to safe-guard one's "spiritual and moral autonomy," for "the individual who is not anchored in God can offer no resistance on his own resources to the physical and moral blandishments of the world" (*CW* 10 § 511). God, as referred to in these lines, is not the immanent depth of one's total situation, not the inwardness and universality of the matter at hand, but one's own affects or affect images produced as wholly other to oneself and trumped up into a sort of Archimedean position-like anthropological constant and eternal verity.[38] As for the last sentences of the cited passage, with these the picture of the Beautiful Soul as it pertains to Jung's psychology is fully drawn. Clutching onto some affective experience as to a numinous talisman, the religiously-cathected analysand tinkers with the checks and balances of his personal well-being, there being, as Jung avers, "no better truth ... than the one that helps you to live."[39]

But is it really so that there is no better truth than this? Jung quoted with approval the adage that "the good is always the enemy of the better" (*CW* 17 § 320). Could this not be applied to Jung's religio-therapeutic pragmatism? Is what it offers not at best a good? And as this good is it not the enemy of that (sometimes terrible) better, truth itself?

A passage of Nietzsche's is helpful here in releasing Jung's psychology from the mandalated ethos of personal well-being in which it has come to be cocooned:

> How many people still make the inference: "one could not stand life if there were not God!" (or as they say in the circles of the Idealists: "one could not stand life if it lacked the ethical significance of its ground!")—consequently there *must* be a God

(or an ethical significance of existence)! … What presumption
to decree that all that is necessary for my preservation must also
really *be there*! As if my preservation were anything necessary![40]

There could hardly be a more chastening critique than this. Once
again the philosopher with a hammer percusses a treasured human value
and shows it to be hollow. But there is more to these lines of Nietzsche's
than even he saw. This becomes evident when we read them with
Giegerich's insights concerning the animus as negation and as the soul's
own other in mind. In *Dialectics & Analytical Psychology* and, again, in
Soul-Violence, Giegerich makes the crucial point that animus figures
such as Hades and Bluebeard are not external others with respect to
the anima figures they threaten, but rather, their very own internal
syzygial counterparts.[41] Read in this light the sentiment at the beginning
of Nietzsche's text—"one could not stand life if there were not God …
consequently there *must* be a God"—is the innocent *anima alba*
moment of the syzygy while the later remark about the presumption
of decreeing that what is necessary for my preservation must also really
be there is the negating (killing, raping, disillusioning) animus
moment. And from this it follows that what I am calling the animus-
aspect of Nietzsche's text (and we can expand this to include his
announcement of the death of God!) is not some kind of spoiling,
extraneous incursion of abstract atheism, but the moment of immanent
critique wherein the innocent initial position loses its innocence
through being as fully and seriously applied as was, if I may put it this
way, the feline curiosity that killed the proverbial cat. Prior to this, it
must be said, there was no animus. The animus, after all, is not a being
or thing. It has no separate existence, but only exists as the wounding
realization that what seemed to be the case no longer is so, if ever it
was.[42] Bringing this point back to our passage from Nietzsche, there
were in earlier times whole ages in which such a critical reflection would
have been just as preposterous as he rightly makes our clinging to God
seem today. Why? Because, like Thor appearing whenever there was a
giant to be grappled with or an ordeal to be surpassed, the Gods were
there! Nietzsche's text, by contrast, speaks from a time and into a time
in which all this has changed.

And what of this change? A passage from an essay of Giegerich's
titled "Rupture, Or: Psychology and Religion" is most pertinent in

this connection. Writing with reference to the soul's having gone through fundamental changes as a function of time,[43] Giegerich speaks of a "rupture [having] taken place." This, he explains (with especially the 18th and 19th centuries in mind), "… consist[s] in the fact that the world to which the known religions were answers has, as it were, *moved out from under them*," such that "… we are now confronted with a logically entirely new world, to which religion no longer corresponds."[44] Continuing some pages later he adds:

> I would … not ask what we can expect from religion and what concrete measures need to be taken to realize our expectations. I would not [suggest we] think about how to rescue our various religious traditions and bring them over into the changed world of today. For any such attempt would in my eyes only amount to an attempt to rescue the logical status or level of consciousness that we are subjectively living in and comfortably accustomed to and to freeze us psychologically in the past, while objectively we have for long been living in a reality characterized by a new logical status. The rupture in the objective world out there necessitates a corresponding rupture in us, and in us not as persons, but as the logic or psychology as which we live. It is not enough to try to adapt our religions to our new situation, it is not them that have to be adjusted. It is us. And this is why I think the answer to the problem of religion in our contemporary world is "psychology"—not psychology as a particular science, as this or that school of thought, but psychology as a move to be made, the move of turning the question of religion back onto ourselves, onto that which is closest to us: our status of consciousness; in other words, psychology as the realization of the unavoidable necessity of the death to be died by our frame of mind.[45]

THE RUPTURE IN THE SOUL

With his reference to "… a rupture [having] taken place…[wherein] … the world to which the known religions were answers has … *moved out from under them*," Giegerich soberly describes the situation Nietzsche spoke of when he issued his spectacular announcement regarding the death of God. Jung, of course, for his part also knew about this rupture. He knew, that is to say, that "we are living in what the Greeks called the καιρός—the right moment—for a 'metamorphosis of the gods,' of the fundamental principles and symbols" (*CW* 10 § 585). In a letter to Fr. White he even went so far as to declare that "we are actually living in the time of the splitting of the world and the invalidation of Christ" (*Letters* 2, p. 138, 24 November, 1953). But haunted by the diagnosis he had affixed to Nietzsche as its foremost casualty, he also resisted this development, as when, for example, a few sentences later in the same letter he reassures his Dominican friend that "Christ is still the valid symbol. Only God can 'invalidate' himself through the Paraclete." And then there is that line from "The Symbolic Life" that we mentioned earlier about his wanting "a situation in which that thing [that had previously been mediated by Christian symbolism] becomes true once more … [in] a new form" (*CW* 18 § 632). Reflecting upon these references we can again appreciate the aptness of Giegerich's characterization of Jung's position as "God Must Not Die!"

But why, it may be asked, did Jung insist that what had formerly been the form of truth—God and the religions—be true once more in the (not really so) "new form" of revisionist theosophizing? Why, to say it with that line from Hölderlin that David Miller discusses in his response (this volume, p. 73), could he not allow God's absence to help us into the opaque depths our new situation, so that we could meet its true character with open and active minds?

The answer to this question is a least two-fold. On the one hand, Jung upheld the validity of the Christ symbol, even at a time that he recognized to objectively involve its invalidation, due to his concerns about the unleashing of primitive, atavistic impulses:

> At a time when a large part of mankind is beginning to discard Christianity, it may be worth our while to try to understand why it was accepted in the first place. It was accepted as a means of escape from the brutality and unconsciousness of the ancient world. As soon as we discard it, the old brutality returns in force, as has been made overwhelmingly clear by contemporary events. … It is the same with individuals who lay aside one form of adaptation and have no new form to turn to: they infallibly regress along the old path and then find themselves at a great disadvantage, because the world around them has changed considerably in the meantime. (*CW* 5 § 341)

As for Jung's other reason for upholding the form of God and the validity of the Christ symbol (even at a time when the soul, in its animus moment, was turning against these forms of itself), this I submit is clearly expressed in a section of *Aion* that anticipates the interpretation that he later put forward in *Answer to Job*. Deeply concerned about "the splitting of our world" (by which he meant the divide between the conventional Christian God-image and the "sinister-realities" of the modern world that are not covered by that image and that lead to materialism, atheism, and other substitutes of the like), Jung issued an uncanny warning, sounded an ominous alarm:

> ... *the destruction of the God-image is followed by the annulment of the human personality.* (*CW* 9 ii § 170; Jung's italics)

No wonder Jung equivocated with regards to the invalidation of Christ that he himself had announced. No wonder he continued to insist upon the soul's having the form of God even after the death of God had been symbolically figured in the Christian "dream" text and upon his teaching that the demise of this form led straight away to inflation, brutality, or to an ism of some sort. Nietzsche may have mocked, as he did in the passage we quoted, but it truly would be too terrible—this seems to have been Jung's view—if there were no God. And to prove this point Jung never tired of holding up the insane Nietzsche as the prime exemplar of the annulment of the personality that follows the destruction of the God-image. This, however, was hardly credible. Nietzsche's insanity was not the result of his attacking Christianity, but of an organic disease process. Jung's use of him as "exhibit A" was, thus, just another variant of that trivial joke one sees from time to time scratched upon a desktop in a classroom or lecture hall, the one in which the statement, "'God is Dead'—Nietzsche," is contradicted by the statement, "'Nietzsche is Dead'—God." Never mind that for complex epistemological reasons Jung's Nietzsche-killing deity had to be an encapsulated in reservations and caveats Not-God-but-the-God-Image-in-me God. With this strange angel the Apostle of the God-image believed he had found his "new form."

FIGURES OF NEGATION

"The Rupture in the Soul," "The Split in the World," "The Invalidation of Christ," and "The Death of God": as various as these terms and topics may seem they are at the same time synonymous with one another as figures of negation. In a discussion of this concept, so key to his own contribution to psychology, Giegerich has pointed out that while the imagining mind apperceives it as some terrible incursion and violent action inflicted from outside, actually and in truth negation is merely the mind-internal, and yet world-embracing, recognition that the matter of interest, whatever that may be, "has all along *not* been what it had seemed ..."[46]

With this in mind let us look again at the anxiety-image that underpins Jung's interpretation of Christianity. Writing from feelings that would have taken the likes of an Edvard Munch to paint, the main thrust of Jung's psychology project has had to do with averting a catastrophe both psychic and spiritual, the aforementioned annulment of the human personality which he pictured as being consequent upon the destruction of the God-image. Reflecting upon this ominous prospect as upon the foil of his theory-making, we may be struck by the similarity of its fantasy-structure to that of persecutory pursuit-type dreams. Menaced by new truth, the figure of the dreamer in such dreams "conservatively adheres to the earlier attitude" (*CW* 4 § 350, modified), even as it frantically escapes to safety.[47] In Jung's case, the truth by which he was menaced was that of an increasingly godless present. Rather than exposing himself to this stark mystery and allowing its negating action to redefine what soul means at our present historical locus, he clung to the familiar, to the old religious definition of soul, with the aim of carrying this forward into our times. Ensconced in the safety of this effort (for what is the ire of a few theological critics compared to the godless void he feared?) the issue for him was all about keeping the tradition vital and the personality intact. And it was to this end that he advised his fellow "advocates of Christianity" not to "squander their energies in the mere preservation of what has come down to them," but to join him in the work of "building on to their house and making it roomier. [For] stagnation in these matters threatens in the long run with a lethal end" (*CW* 9ii § 170)

But the lethal end, if one wants to call it that, had already come. Indeed, it had been operative from the outset. As the bible puts it, on a cross in Jerusalem God had died. For the psychologist, however, this was an *image-internal* destruction of the God-image, its internal corruption and self-sublation. Its own doing, as Giegerich would say. Far from being the result of any stagnation, it was in itself fecund, as the vast cultural achievements that Christianity unfolded from this thought amply attest.

"Our passage," writes Giegerich (with Phil. 2:5-8 in mind), "tells of one powerful dynamic, one vigorous movement of going under":

> The incarnation is not only about Christ's being *born* as man ("Christmas") in the sense of a one-time event, as it appears to the merely imagining mind. It is continued beyond his birth and goes through his life on earth as a whole right into his death. The incarnation is a complete going under and is only fulfilled with his crucifixion. And not even with this crucifixion as such alone, but only with its culminating in his absolute loss of God ("My God, my God, why hast thou forsaken me?"), which is not mentioned in our passage. Only with this experience or insight had the *kenôsis* become absolute. Only then was the last trace of divinity truly emptied out. As long as there was trust in God Father and the faith or hope that he, Jesus Christ, was God's son, his child, did he indirectly still possess his divinity, even if he did not possess it immediately in himself (who had in fact already become nothing but human), but in his other, God, and in his faith in Him. The complete *kenôsis* includes the death of God, the loss of "having" a God altogether. Without the loss of God it would only be a partial or token "emptying." And only if he has lost his God has he really, unreservedly, become human, nothing but human, and emptied his cup fully. (this volume, p. 22)

Against Jung's restorative/revisionist reading of Christianity, which by his own lights was an attempt to make the Christian house roomier, Giegerich does not offer another interpretation, one of his own. Rather, with the likes of Hegel, Altizer, Jüngel, Žižek, Cupitt, and St. Paul before any of these, he "sticks to the image"—saves the phenomenon— of God's fully becoming man even as he dies as one.

The issue here, as I have been stressing throughout, is a methodological one. When St. Paul spoke to the Philippians of Christ's incarnation as his humbling himself, he did so for methodological reasons, that is, to teach the Christian ethic. The idea was that the Christian individual was to overcome his self-importance and petty jealousies, to empty himself of these even as Christ did on an even larger scale when he divested himself of his divinity and died on the cross as a man. And here it may be noted that far from annulling the human personality, the negation or destruction of the God-image that was figured in this text imparted to it its universality within the soul's new logic or successor notion, i.e., as the life "in Christ."

Now it is important to notice, further to this, that what Giegerich pointed out in his "Rupture: Or Psychology of Religion" essay with regards to our contemporary situation as a post-Enlightenment secular society was also true at that earlier rupture point at which the Christian aeon began. Then, too, a rupture in the objective world out there had necessitated a corresponding rupture in the people. "And Jesus cried out again with a loud voice and yielded up his spirit. And behold, the curtain of the temple was torn in two, from top to bottom. And the earth shook, and the rocks were split" (Matt. 27-50). But as Giegerich has stressed, such ruptures are not to be thought of as running through the people as persons (they are not their *fault!*); rather, they have to do with the objective character of the times, with the truth of the situation that was then prevailing. Or putting this distinction another way, we could say with Giegerich that it is not the psychology that the people *have* that is ruptured in the sense of some sort of intrapsychic dissociation; rather, rupture here refers to the liminal character of the logic or psychology which a person or a people *exists as*, or again, to be more specific, to the status of a reflecting consciousness which, being reflective, has broken with and emancipated itself from the immediacy of sense certainty, *participation mystique,* and what had formerly been its naïve relation to what it had been able to regard and propitiate as external to itself.

With these reflections we come to the crux of Giegerich's dispute with Jung. Frightened, as we have said, by what he variously called "the split in the world," "the invalidation of Christ," and "the annulment of the human personality," Jung propped up the form of God by divinizing human development and shoving it into that place where the reality of the world had been before it had "moved out from under" the religions which had become obsolete and redundant. I refer here, on the one hand, to the erstwhile psychologist's identification of the

Christian idea of incarnation with the personal individuation process
(e.g., "'incarnation' … on the human level appears as 'individuation'"
CW 11 § 233) and, on the other, to his experiences in active
imagination of self-deification and his interpretation of these as
imparting "immortal value to the individual."[48] In Jung's view, the
personal relationship to the soul as God was simply indispensable. And
even if now in the modern situation God needed the (graven!) images
of the human individuation process to shore him up, he still remained
a mighty enough reality to leave Jung wondering "… why the human
frame is not shattered by the incarnation … [since] man with all his
external characteristics seems little suited to representing a god" (*MDR*
p. 337, transl. modif.). So another fear cropped up. The remedy Jung
had proposed for what he saw as the problem of the annulment of the
personality—individuation—has an equally terrible side effect, the
shattering of the human frame! And here, in this contradiction, we see
the faultiness of the imaginal mode of thought, its tendency to literalize
negation and apperceive it as external, rather than letting itself be
emptied ("annulled," "shattered") and go under into the fluidity of a
thinking consciousness with the realization that the content of its
reflection has "… all along *not* been what it had seemed …"[49]

It could have been different. There could have been another way.
Instead of belatedly attempting to stave off the rupture in the soul by
collapsing the psychological difference and inserting a miniaturized
version of it into the inner of the individual person (as Jung did with
his emphasis upon individuation, personal growth, and an ego-
transcending Self that was nevertheless in us), the divine process of
incarnation, *kenôsis*, and death could have found its successor form in
the methodological stance of a truly psychological psychology.

I say "could have" here not to be wistful (though I do think that
our collective striving for a truly psychological method to be a more
important endeavor than our personal "Striving for Wholeness"). My
point, rather, is to highlight the fact that Giegerich's critique of Jung,
both in his "God Must Not Die!" essay and in many other works, is
rooted in essential impulses of Jung's concept of psychological reality
which Jung himself had been unable to house in his over-all theory
except as menacing spectres to be in flight from.

So the question arises: How is Jungian analysis to be awakened from
the persecutory-pursuit dream which it enacts in its theory? Or, to be

more specific, how is it to allow such menacing spectres as "the destruction of the God-image," "the annulment of the personality," "the shattering of the human frame" and, of course, the modern plight of meaninglessness to find their place within it?

In a discussion of persecutory-pursuit-type dreams Giegerich has insightfully argued that if what the dream has imaginatively presented as separate, externally-related dream-figures are grasped in their simultaneity as the refracted moments of a single, inclusive thought, the realization may dawn that what had at first been pictured and experienced as menace, on the one hand, and terrified flight, on the other, is not only ultimately compatible, but has all along been, even while it perused and escaped itself, the first immediacy of the *coniunctio*. For the real *coniunctio* is not some idealized representation of unity before which the subject stands unscathed, but rather has to do with the figure of the other having really rattled one's cage, gotten under one's skin, and cut into values which one had been attempting at all cost to preserve.[50]

Jung, of course, was well aware of this dynamic, at least insofar as it figured in the lives of his patients. He knew, for example, about how menacing it could be when at the turning points of life "the greater figure, which one always was but which remained invisible, appears to the lesser personality with the force of a revelation" (*CW* 9i § 217). The trouble, however, was with the application of his insights about this to psychological consciousness itself. When it was only a matter of a patient's neurosis or self-development, he could tough-mindedly interpret the challenge that the patient's encounter with his or her shadowy other was about, as for instance when he wrote, further to the line that we just quoted, that "he who is truly and hopelessly little will always drag the revelation of the greater down to the level of his littleness, and will never understand that the day of judgement for his littleness has dawned [while] ... the man who is inwardly great will know that the long expected friend of his soul, the immortal one, has now really come, 'to lead captivity captive,' that is, to seize hold of him by whom this immortal had always been confined and held prisoner, and to make his life flow into the greater life—a moment of deadliest peril!" (*ibid.*). But after reading Giegerich's contribution to this volume we have to realize that Jung fell foul of his own insight insofar as the constitution of his psychology was concerned. I refer here to those uncanny guests that his theory could not house. In the persecutory-dream to which his theory may be likened, Jung again and again dragged the revelation of the greater, which he met in such terrifying figures as "the destruction of the God image" and "the annulment of the human personally," down to the level of his littleness by taking flight from these into revisionist, restorative, theosophical counter-ideas such as the quaternity and the Self, Sophia and the Daughter of the Moon. Though, of course, this flight also indicates that he had to some extent also been reached by what he fled, he was nevertheless able to shield his overall conception of the soul from this by assigning the *coniunctio* to the individual as *his* task.[51]

Kenōsis as Method

In league with Giegerich, I have just characterized psychology's having foisted *its* individuation tasks off upon the individual as an example of psychology's "drag[ging] the revelation of the greater down to the level of [its] littleness, and ... [not] understand[ing[that the day of judgement for [its] littleness has dawned." Bringing these reflections to a close, let us briefly discuss the alternative to this wherein psychology recognizes, in the very shadows that menace it, "the long expected friend of [*its*] soul ... and make[s] [its] life flow into the greater life ..."

Jung, as we know, set up a miniaturized version of the psychological difference in the inner of the individual as his vis-à-vis with the God-image in the individuation process. The alterative to this happens on the theoretical plane or notional level. Referred to by Giegerich as "the soul's logical life," the individuation process of this, let us call it, the psychology we exist as, has to do with the self-constituting flow of psychology (in the sense of that "... most complex of psychic structures, a man's philosophy of life ..." *CW* 16 § 180) into the greatness of its concept which occurs when the psychological difference (and the negations that mediate it) is understood in its most radical sense as the difference between psychological consciousness, on the one hand, and people's psychologies, on the other, or again, between the methodological stance of a truly psychological psychology and the individuation process as it occurs in people.

But how, it may be asked, is this turn to be taken wherein the negations that Jung took so literally and sought to therapeutically stave off can be understood as mediating a more radical sense of the psychological difference, and along with this, an even greater conception of psychology and the soul?

In a line that can be read as the application of Jung's seminal insight about psychology's lack of an objective, extra-psychic vantage point to this question, Giegerich avers that "... psychology begins where any phenomenon (whether physical or mental, 'real' or fantasy image) is interiorized absolute-negatively into itself, and I find myself in its internal infinity. This is what it takes; psychology cannot be had for less."[52] Underscoring this point he declares in another passage that "what at first appears as a content [or object] of consciousness is in truth the seed of what wants to become a new form of consciousness at large."[53]

Apropos of these statements, and with the help of few more quotations from Giegerich, it is not difficult to show how the negating spectres which had so troubled Jung can be absolute negatively interiorized into themselves such that their character as the new form of consciousness and beginning point of a true psychology is disclosed. Take, for example, that terror of the soul that was propitiated by Jung as "the annulment of the human personality." When regarded as an internal other and absolute negatively interiorized into itself this menacing prospect is productive, not of the individuation process that Jung would have it spur on, but of an indispensable feature of a truly psychological stance: the negation of the ego. As Giegerich explains,

> [Psychological discourse] has to *be as* the negation of the ego,
> and the psychologist (of course only to the extent that he truly
> is a psychologist and speaks psychologically) has to speak as one
> who has long died as ego personality. The art of psychological
> discourse is to speak as someone already deceased.[54]

We can see from this passage that the personality is not annulled. On the contrary, having been superseded by Giegerich's insight that the psychologist must speak as someone who is already deceased, the prospect that it might be is shown to have been but the first immediacy of a *psychological consciousness* and *methodological stance* in which the ego-personality (which, as we know, is the principal subscriber of the

Beautiful Soul fallacy) has no place and "the notion of soul is logically released from its attachment to the notion of the human being."[55]

There was another worry mentioned by Jung. This had to do with dissociative pathology operative on the collective level, i.e., that neurosis of our times which he referred to as "the split in our world." Open to the inner infinity of the phenomena that this expression describes, Giegerich writes:

> ... neurosis is not at all the simple fact of a split. It is more complicated. The neurotic dissociation is a disunity plus its denial. ... In other words, the neurotic dissociation consists in the *denial* of *itself* (of the dissociation) and, therefore, in the insistence that each of the dissociated partial truths be the whole truth. Therefore the "cure" of neurosis cannot consist in ridding us of the disunity and making us "whole" again in this sense. To assume this would not only be naïve, *the one-sided insistence on harmony and unambiguous identity is also precisely what makes for neurosis.* Not the split, but the ideal of undialectical unity is what is behind neurosis.[56]

Though neurosis, disunity, dissociation, rupture, and splitting are usually regarded as mere contents of consciousness, Giegerich argues that in our time they have an over-arching, objective character. Indicative of that cut which consciousness inflicts upon itself through its being conscious of itself, they must even be given their dignity as the prevailing form of consciousness at large. As Giegerich explains:

> If psychology (as theory or consciousness) does not allow for division it itself, it inevitably has to project it out [such that it becomes merely the individual's task—G.M.]. No, the cure of neurosis consists in the cure of a consciousness fixated on continuity, unity, positivity, self-identity; it consists in allowing the split *to come home to* consciousness and to permeate the logical form of its constitution, in order for consciousness to become something that can give the disunity (in ourselves, in the world, in life) as well as the individual dissociated partial truths each their own legitimate place ...[57]

It only remains to bring "the destruction of the God-image" into the ambit of these reflections. Menaced by the prospect of such destruction, the cornerstone of Jung's therapeutics has had to do with revivifying the relation with the God-image by amplifying and interpreting all manner of images as God-Images. Unable to see the destruction of this image, which he accurately described, as the soul's own doing and to let the rupture that this expressed come home to consciousness, he even went so far as to declare, as he put it his *Red Book*, that "*God is an image, and those who worship him must worship him in the image of the supreme meaning.*"[58] But this line was written at a time when the death of God, which had already occurred at the inception of Christianity, had been raised to the power of two by Nietzsche among others such that consciousness at large had already long been emancipated from having to have the form of God. Jung, however, could not accept the empty sepulchre that his times had become. And so, countering this he resurrected and restored a plethora of decorative and therapeutic Gods.

The task of a true psychology would have been precisely the opposite of this. It would have been soulfully to *think* "the destruction of the God-image" without succumbing to either Jung's theosophizing or Nietzsche's nihilism, which is also to say, to allow the kenôtic movement of the death of God idea to permeate consciousness such that the soul, having released itself from the divine vestment that had been befitting for it in earlier times, can achieve a new definition of itself *extra ecclesiam, post mortem Dei*.

* * *

So, what are we left with? Having let so much of the positivity of Jung's psychology go under, what is it that remains? A new ability to be with that nothing that sees everything? A consciousness that can *think* rupture, rather than merely suturing it closed again with a syncretistic hodgepodge of images, myths, and meanings?

Writing with reference to an insight of Augustine's, Jung acknowledged the saint to have "apprehended a great truth, namely that every spiritual truth gradually turns into something material, becoming no more than a tool in the hand of man." Drawing the conclusion from this, he continues: "In consequence, man can hardly avoid seeing himself as a knower, yes even as a creator, with boundless possibilities at his command" (*CW* 13 § 302). Taking this insight further than the Jung who feared annulment would have been able to credit,[59] could it also be the case that that greatest of all spiritual truths, God, has become something material (or methodological), "a tool in the hand of man"?

A passage from Giegerich's "Rupture, Or: Psychology and Religion" essay well conveys the substance of this soul-*making* tool. Constituted by the very emptiness of the hands that hold it, it is the notionally-determined and negatively intensive methodological stance or analytic attitude of a truly psychological psychology. As Giegerich puts it:

> We have to learn to *suffer* our hands to be empty, in the fullest sense of the word suffer. No image. No symbols. No meaning. No Gods: No Religion.
>
> For is it not the empty hand, and the empty hand alone, that can be filled? As long as we cling to our religious traditions, we pretend to be in possession of something. We thereby prevent the advent of what can come, if at all, only as the free gift of the real world to him who is ready to receive because he has nothing whatsoever of his own accord, as the gift to him who no longer, with a modesty that is disguised arrogance, denounces our poverty as nihilism, but comprehends it as the presence of the unknown future.[60]

PART THREE

> I only know—and here I am expressing what countless other people know—that the present is a time of God's death and disappearance. The myth says he was not to be found where his body was laid. "Body" means the outward, visible form, the erstwhile but ephemeral setting for the highest value. The myth further says that the value rose again in a miraculous manner, transformed. It looks like a miracle, for, when a value disappears, it always seems to be lost irretrievably. So it is quite unexpected that it should come back. The three days' descent into hell during death describes the sinking of the vanished value into the unconscious, where, by conquering the power of darkness, it establishes a new order, and then rises up to heaven again, that is, attains supreme clarity of consciousness. The fact that only a few people see the Risen One means that no small difficulties stand in the way of finding and recognizing the transformed value. (*CW* 11 § 149)

C. G. Jung

The God-Question Again

For the sake of completeness we should probably take another look at the question we began with—"Do you believe in God?"—examining it in the light of the analytic attitude that Giegerich has distilled from Jung's psychology via the process of immanent critique.

The first step in this effort requires the setting aside of a bias of Jung's that led him to regard this question as being psychologically irrelevant. I refer here to Jung's privileging of an empirical approach over a speculative one. In default of his own recognition that the psyche is at once its own subject and object (a recognition that simply requires a speculative approach), Jung set himself up as an empiricist observing the facts of the psychic process. It was as if he had said, forget about the invisible, intangible, (and yet!) intelligible forest, forget about the invisible, intangible, and yet intelligible soul, just look at all the trees, or in Jung's case, all the God-images.

Consider for example his rejoinder to H. L. Philp. After reminding Jung of his statement in *Answer to Job*, "God is an obvious psychic and non-physical fact," Philp had added, "But I feel in the end you do not actually answer the question as to whether or not you believe in the existence of God other than as an archetype. Do you?" Answering at length Jung first discusses epistemological issues he was mindful of in formulating his archetype concept and then, speaking more directly to the question Philp had put, avers that:

> Speaking for myself, the question whether God exists or not is futile. I am sufficiently convinced of the effects man has always attributed to a divine being. If I should express a belief beyond that or should assert the existence of God, it would not only be superfluous and inefficient, it would show that I am not basing my opinion on facts. When people say they believe in the existence of God, it has never impressed me in the least. Either I know a thing and then I don't need to believe it; or I believe it because I am not sure that I know it. I am well satisfied with the fact that I know experiences which I cannot avoid calling numinous or divine. (*CW* 18 § 1589)

This is a tricky passage. On the surface of it, at least, the distinction between knowing and believing makes a lot of sense and we readily accept the image it suggests to us of Jung as a responsible and circumspect scientist. But this is only how it appears on the surface. Reading between the lines we find that they also comprise a diminutive version of the emphatic assertion that he would later make in his interview with the BBC, "I *know*. I don't need to believe. I know."[61] I say "diminutive version" here because in the BBC interview Jung claims to know God, while in the more considered passage that we are now examining it is "*experiences*" that he knows, "experiences which [he] cannot avoid calling numinous or divine." We may be reminded by this of yet another passage which we discussed earlier, the one in which Jung declared, "Religious experience is absolute; it cannot be disputed" (*CW* 11 § 167). Jung, I submit, is having much the same conversation with his theological critic Philp as he presented in that earlier text: "You can only say that you have never had such an experience, whereupon your opponent will reply: 'Sorry, I have.' And there your discussion will come to an end" (*CW* 11 § 167).

But are the soul and its highest value, God, something that we experience? Has not our consciousness of conscious (one corollary of which is Jung's psychology-constituting insight into the lack of an Archimedean point) negated and sublated our relation to what Jung continued to give out as immediate experience, numinous and divine?

In a recent interview Giegerich provides an important clarification with respect to this question. Asked by his interlocutor to provide an example from his own or someone else's experience of what he means by the soul's logical life, Giegerich replies:

> I am taken a little by surprise by your question. I have to think a bit. I wonder, is "soul" really something that we experience? I don't think so. It is accessible only on reflection and to our insight (after the fact), and this insight presupposes both some effort (study, so-called "analysis," "seeing through") and a particular eye for things psychological. Experiences are immediate and subjective. But "the soul" is, according to Jung [and here he is again citing Jung against Jung—G.M.], precisely non-ego, an objective psyche. He spoke of background processes, just as Hillman located the soul, metaphorically speaking, in the underworld. "Soul" is certainly not about us and what we feel or think. There is no direct access to it. If one wants to learn something about the soul and its logical life it is far better to turn away from us people and instead turn to myth, theology, archaic ritual (like the Roman Catholic Mass), great literature and art,

philosophy, or alchemy, on the one hand, and to the course of
real history, social changes, the development of technology and
the like, on the other.[62]

Contrary to Jung's view, the criterion Giegerich here lays out
identifies the "Do you believe in God?" question to be a worthy and
potentially soul-fathoming one. On the one hand, and weightily so, it
is a piece of theology; on the other, the issue at stake in it has long
figured in the course of actual history, real social changes and the like.
For, indeed, as we noted in Part One, more blood has been spilled over
this question than over any other. And this is to say nothing of the role
it has played in literature, art, philosophy, and the other genres of soul-
searching enquiry mentioned by Giegerich. Surely, then, we should
be able to learn something about the soul just by delving into what
this question's having arisen says about it. Our challenge, however,
further to Giegerich's comment that the soul is not reached
immediately, experientially, is to work with it speculatively, that is,
via study, analysis, and seeing through.

SPECULATIVE TREATMENT

Approached in this spirit, the main thing to be born in mind with
respect to the "Do you believe in God?" question is that it is *the
psychology of the question itself* that we are interested in and not the
psychology of the patient or analyst in a personalistic sense. This, of
course, is not to neglect the fact that there may be any number of
meanings, interests, and anxieties on the ego-level that figure in the
posing of the question. The patient, for example, may be wondering
if the help he is seeking will be compatible with his religious values.
Or, perhaps, the question is indicative of a transference, i.e., of the
patient's apperceiving the analyst on the model of an earlier figure
in his life to whose beliefs he was subject. There is also the possibility
that he is intimidated by the religious ambience that Jungian
psychology, at least in some quarters, gives off and wonders if he is
up to this. And in addition to these few possibilities there are
probably a whole host of others that might have to be dealt with as
part of the routine of analytic work. But for our purposes here it is
important to be clear that there is a difference—for Giegerich it is
an instance of what he calls "the psychological difference"—between

psychology in the sense of the interests, motives, feelings, and what not of the patient and/or analyst and the soul-bespeaking psychology of the question *per se*.

Jung, of course, also drew this distinction. He tended, however, to miniaturize it in the service of therapeutic ends, as we noted in Part Two. With respect to the present topic this shows in his contradictorily disdaining the God-question while at the same time amassing whatever experiential, "sorry, I have" evidence he could find to support a God-fearing and spirit-filled attitude on the part himself, his readers, and his patients. We have only to think of that famously precious statement of his from a letter he wrote in 1945, the one in which he declares that "... the main interest of my work is not concerned with the treatment of neuroses but rather with the approach to the numinous. But the fact is that the approach to the numinous is the real therapy and inasmuch as you attain to the numinous experiences you are released from the curse of pathology" (*Letters* 1, p. 377 to P.W. Martin, 20 August, 1945).

Now, my point here is not to dispute the possible significance of experiences that come of their own accord with that surplus of importance which Jung, with a nod to Rudolph Otto, called "numinous" (though these, too, may have become routine, the standard fare of a Jungian analysis). Rather, it is to point out that with his assumption that empirical knowledge of spiritual experiences simply trumps the God-question he performs a *petito principii* with respect to it while at the same time failing to consider what the question itself might involve as an utterance of the soul.

The issue here has to do with Jung's tendency not to sufficiently differentiate the event-character of experience from the interpretation-character of meaning. In Jungian circles one regularly finds that experiences are regarded as bearing soul meaning simply by virtue of their having a strong intensity. But here I would object that while it was enough for the doubter, Thomas, to put his hands into the wounds of the resurrected Christ (John 20:25-29), it is not enough for analysands to take their own pulse when dealing with an image. And this is so even when we are dealing with images and affects that have come together to form what has been called "self-validating experience." Having long been aware that all perception is apperception, the question of their interpretation, the question of their truth, is all the more urgent.

We mentioned in passing above in Part Two the line from 1 John 4:1 about trying the spirits whether they are of God. There is no getting around this version of the "Do you believe in God?" question. Images and experiences, as self-validating and numinous as they may be, are subject at the same time, in what might be called an animus moment of themselves, to that inquisitional court of the soul which has been irrevocably constituted for us by consciousness having become conscious of itself. And in this connection I am reminded of a statement that Jung made that is corrective of his usual claim that the psyche can be approached in the anima-only manner of the naturalistic observer and empirical scientist. "I see," he wrote to E. A. Bennet (*Letters 2*, p. 567, 11 June, 1960), "... that you understand by 'scientific evidence' something like a chemical or physical proof. But what about evidence in a Law Court? The concept of scientific proof is hardly applicable there, and yet the Court knows of evidence which suffices to cut a man's head off, which means a good deal more than the mere universality of a symbol. I think that there is such a thing as 'commensurability of evidence.'"[63]

This is a crucial point. Immediate psychology—Jung's empirical data of experience—must be reflected into itself via the hermeneutic circle as in a court proceeding or heresy trial even as in Dostoevsky's novel, *The Brothers Karamazov*, orthodox Christian piety (Alyosha), disavowal of belief in the existence of God and in the immortality of the soul (Ivan), and a murder trial (Dmitry) all figure together while at the same time a story is told wherein the return of the popular miracle-performing, experience-generating Christ is opposed by the Grand Inquisitor for having fallen below the *niveau* of the consciousness that the Church has achieved during the course of its many centuries.

THE RUPTURE IN THE QUESTION

There are, I am sure, many responses that the "Do you believe in God?" question might inspire, as many as there are analysts and patients. And this is so even if it is not *they* that are our focus, whether individually or as a dyad, but the God-question itself as the pressingly existent expression, when such it is, of what Giegerich has called (with psychology or "the soul" in mind) "the third of the two."[64] Citing with approval Jung's account of his work with Babette and the Solar Phallus Man, Giegerich has pointed out that Jung gave priority, not to the psychology of these patients in a personalistic sense, but to the content of their visions and delusions:

> The attitude of the psychologist is receptivity; the relation into which he is placed is the conversation through which he is addressed and experiences a challenge. That is, the phenomenon does the talking: the phenomenon and not, as one might think at first, the patient. ... What touched Jung ... was the content, the matter, that expressed itself and demanded his (as well as the patient's) attention. And we can probably say that Jung was in general of the opinion that a patient is then, and only then, taken seriously if the *message* that is contained in what he says and the *message* that comes to him through a dream, for example, is taken seriously in *what* it says, in its content and substance.[65]

Rising to the challenge of being receptive to what the God-question has to say about the soul perhaps the most important thing to be noted is that the question outstrips itself. I mean by this that as the question it is, it is more complex than either of the one-sided answers that persons operating on the ego-level might want to give to it. This, of course, is not evident at first. Reducing the greatness the question to the level of our own littleness, we may stand before it as before a mirror expecting to see our piety or atheism reflected therein. But as we have already learned from Giegerich, while psychology can be likened to the reflection in some mirror, its concern is with reflectedness *per se*, consciousness as such, and not with what the mirror is a reflection of. And the same can be said of our question. It is not its answer by you or by me that is revealing of the soul (in this regard Jung was right to be unimpressed by the claims people made concerning their beliefs in the existence of God); it is the fact that it can be asked at all.

This point may be more readily grasped when we realize that it was not always the case, as it seems to be now, that questions come first, their answers to follow. While this, certainly, is how things are for the modern ego, the history of consciousness tells another story. It tells of a time before the asking of questions. Writing with respect to this distinction, Giegerich has aptly described early man as simply starting out with those answers that he knew as his Gods.[66] It was only

much later, after much cultural development and at those rupture-
points at which the world, as it were, moved out from under the modes
of being in it that the Gods had provided for, that the capacity for
questioning arose. And so it is that the analyst might wonder: "Is this
why the God-question is being brought up in this session? Does its
being put to me now announce that my patient is at a similar rupture-
point in his own soul's life?"

Historically speaking it was especially with the Enlightenment that
the questioning of the existence of God became possible. We have only
to think of the constraints which Kant's critical philosophy placed upon
the knowing of truth and of how this, as Hegel put it (with the imagery
of Good Friday in mind), had brought the feeling "that God Himself
has died."[67] In the case of Kant and others of that time this feeling led
to charges of atheism, on the one hand, and as this was not to their
liking, to a flight into piety and faith, on the other. But answers either
way fell below the level of the consciousness that was brought by the
question. For, indeed, as Giegerich has pointed out in his Rupture essay,
"Both the believers or theologians and the critics of religion (such as
Voltaire, Marx, Nietzsche) experience religion, logically speaking, on
the same level. The only difference is that the ones say Yes to religion
and are for it, whereas the others say No to it and are against it. The
level of consciousness is the same."[68]

Recognizing in the God-question the implicit form of a
consciousness that transcends the alternatives it seems to propose, Hegel
hit upon the speculative approach wherein what was predicated of a
subject, most importantly of God, was not regarded as its attribute in
an external, empirical sense, but as reflecting its essence in such a
manner that even if it should be false and contradictory, it would
nevertheless lead the mind back, via that feedback process called
thinking, to reconsider and perhaps conceptually redefine the subject
itself (G = G and –G). It is the same point we made earlier when we
said that negation, far from being as untoward and violent as it may
seem to the imagining mind, carries within it the realization that what
we had believed to be the case is not truly as we had naively conceived
it to be. And it was along these lines that Hegel *thought* the crucifixion
drama. "Tarrying with the negative,"[69] even as Christ suffered upon
the cross, the feeling that God Himself has died is to be reflected into
itself in a God-redefining manner such that what Hegel called "the

speculative Good Friday" may earn its name again and again on successive levels of complexity in being shown to have been, even in its darkest hour, as when the veil of the temple was rent and the rocks were split, the first immediacy of what might reasonably be called a dialectical Easter Monday.

And here again the analyst might wonder: does the God-question as it comes up in this session now carry within it the Passion play of thinking that we have just described? Is the patient now at that rupture-point and juncture at which not he, but that greater subject, i.e., the psychology he exists as, is being led under and across? And the question mark at the end of the query he has put, is this to be read as the cross of a speculative Good Friday?

There is a story by Anatole France that Jung tells in *Symbols of Transformation*. Relevant in our context for the glimpse it affords of how the issues which are at stake in the "Do you believe in God?" question might have been represented within a consciousness that was still so entirely theistic that the prospect of not believing in God could not yet occur for it, the story concerns a pious priest by the name of Abbé Oegger who was vexed by the question of "whether [Judas] was really condemned to everlasting punishment, as the teaching of the Church declares, or whether God pardoned him after all" (*CW* 5 § 41). After much reflection and prayer, Oegger's concerns gave way to a heartening sense of the glory of God. Relieved and reconciled it had become evident to his faith that such was God's mercy that he had indeed pardoned Judas. This, however, was not the end of the story. A subsequent event in the action of Oegger's own life brought out into the open what his religious struggle had been more deeply about. "Not long afterwards," we are told by Jung, "[Oegger] left the Catholic Church and became a Swedenborgian." About this Jung comments: "Now we understand his Judas fantasy: *he was* the Judas who betrayed his Lord. Therefore he had first of all to assure himself of God's mercy in order to play the role of Judas undisturbed" (*CW* 5 § 43).

Doubtless, there is a certain validity to Jung's reading of Oegger's religious crisis. On the face of it, at least, it makes a lot of sense to say that "… the case of Abbé Oegger shows that his doubts and his hopes are only apparently concerned with the historical person of Judas, but in reality revolve round his own personality, which was seeking a way to freedom through the solution of the Judas problem" (*CW* 5 § 44).

But then again, upon a second reading, what a let down! Couched in personalistic, psychodynamic terms, Jung's interpretation amounts to the forfeiture of the kind of insight that his analytical psychology was intended to reach. Consider, by way of contrast, what a wiser Jung wrote in another context, "… we are obliged to reverse our rationalistic causal sequence, and instead of deriving these figures [Christ and Mercurius] from our psychic condition, must derive our psychic conditions from these figures" (*CW* 13 § 299). But here, with regards to the figure of Judas that featured in Oegger's religious struggle, Jung resorted to an utterly reductive approach. Oegger, we are told, is "only apparently" concerned with the fate of Judas, his real concerns being rather with "his own personality." From this it can be seen that it was not only Freud, as Jung charged, who "denies the great [and] blames the petty" (*CW* 10 § 367), but Jung as well. Forgetful of the psychological difference, Jung did not match the level of Oegger's engagement, which was an engagement with God, by holding to the soul-level, but explained Oegger's religious question it terms of Oegger's psychology. We may be reminded in this connection of Jung's regret that his religiously-conflicted father, a pastor in the Swiss Reformed Church, "… regarded his suffering as a personal affliction for which you might ask a doctor's advice; he did not see it as the suffering of the Christian in general" (*MDR*, p. 215).[70] Defaulting upon this position, Jung's approach to the Oegger story amounts to a doling out of the doctorly advice he so deplored in his father's case, witless it seems that Oegger could readily have served as a model for grappling with one's suffering as the suffering of the Christian in general.

HOMO ABSCONDITUS AND THE CALL TO TRUTH

So much for Oegger and the naive, precursor-form of the God-question. What about today?

I said above that the question outstrips itself. By this I meant that the consciousness that it expresses is more complex than the alternatives it seems to propose. Underscoring this point, it might even be argued that it is not really even a question any more, at least not a question for the soul. This is not to deny that there are believers aplenty. Nor that global-reach religious strife has everywhere become the cost of doing business. All this is true, and I should also not forget to mention the commodified "religious" content of New Age spirituality. But meanwhile and nevertheless, it has become readily apparent that for consciousness-at-large what once had had the form of God or gods has now the form of "the subject" and that with this development God is no longer the topic that "he" or "she" had once been.

Now, if this is so, and I think that it is, our question needs updating. This, however, is a somewhat complicated undertaking as it implies a negation. To be fully contemporized our question must be formulated as a "post-question." I am not suggesting here that we actually indulge in such post-speak. On the contrary, we may drop the term at once. All that is needed is a manner of hearing how the question, hopeful as it may be for an answer, cuts into its own innocence just by being able to be asked at all.

At the end of Part One I spoke of the sheepish feeling that crept over me when, prompted by the "Do you believe in God question?" having been put to me, I thought about "... how halting and complicated my answer has probably become, though it be to a question for which my career as a Jungian analyst had once seemed to provide of itself such a hearty and affirmative answer." But now I see that this feeling can come into its own as the updating of this question. The God-question is a question that wants to question big. And this, its bigness, is of the same kind as Hegel ascribed to philosophy when he defined it as being its own age comprehended in thought. Is this, then, what the God-question is immanently about?

Speculatively reformulated, our question becomes: living as we do in a time for which the death of God has already long become old hat, *what does it mean to be up to the challenge of what the God-question now asks through its no longer being asked at all?*

Two texts of Giegerich's bear upon this contemporary posing of our question. The first of these, from *The Soul's Logical Life*, is cited for the sake of the dialectical reversal that it performs with respect to the figure of the *deus absconditus* and the slogan "God is dead":

> In theology and philosophy (especially in this century), a lot has been said about the *deus absconditus*, the hidden God as opposed to the revealed God. The *ultimate* form of the *deus absconditus*, one might say, is the God of whom it has been said, "God is dead." But maybe the *deus absconditus* is more artefact than authentic experience. Maybe the idea of the *deus absconditus* is

no more than the mirror image of *homo absconditus*. Maybe this God image is the image in which modern man can know himself, can know his self-definition, the logical status in which he established himself, namely as having in the depths of his Being absconded from the world, even while *apparently* still living in this world. Could it be that "God is dead" is not speaking about God at all, but about man? About *man* being "dead" ... because he has forgone his humanness and instead defined himself as a "functionary" in the literal sense, as a functioning machine (even if a very complex one) and because he seems to see his highest purpose in assimilating himself more and more to the machines, robots, and automats that he surrounds himself with? And could it be that "God is dead" is thus not a theoretical insight or thesis, but an involuntary self-expression?[71]

Giegerich's point in this passage is not to overturn the "God is dead" idea. Nor is it part of a strategy to have a God again after all. Rather, it is to highlight the challenge-character of a situation in which "what used to be viewed as some numinous Other has *objectively* been seen through by the soul as a part of its own self-relation" such that "for the modern soul God has become impossible ..."[72] Now it is crucial to realize here—and this would amount to the resolution of the *homo absconditus* problem aptly emphasized by Giegerich—that far from indicating that we are bereft of truth, the *deus absconditus* and God is dead ideas reflect a radical form-change in its logic and constitution. Having integrated its former semantic content "God" into its syntax, consciousness is henceforth more explicitly generative with respect to truth. In an earlier and well-known essay, Giegerich has thematized this moment in the soul's logical life as "The End of Meaning and the Birth of Man." The reference is to man having been born out of his mythological mode of being in the world and to the soul's no longer presenting itself to him as divine other. For born man truth is no longer received through the immediacy of his immurement in nature and tradition. For his relation to all that is now a broken, reflected one. It has become historical. Nor is it empirically available to him though the supposedly raw, spontaneous experiences coming from *his* inner. For he knows that there is nothing "raw" and "spontaneous," that being only how things had seemed to a more naive consciousness that was not conscious of itself. No, truth now must be generated anew by our coming forward and showing presence even when this means exposing ourselves to the negations that assail us, time and again, at the abyss-edge of the split in the world.

The second text (and we shall be ending with this) speaks to the generative and explicitly soul-*making* character that consciousness, now as *knowing* consciousness, has with respect to the soul and its truths. Drawing upon Jung's statement in *Memories* (p. 325) that "I am *only* that" (a phrase that in Jung's context is used to indicate his awareness that it is only through the embracing and living of our fundamental finiteness that the relation to the infinite is opened up), Giegerich writes:

> When I am "*only* that," I am without higher orders, even without the mythical garment of an endowment (be it by Nature or by the Creator) with the "dignity of man" or "inalienable human rights," these inflated modern ideas. I cannot bask in the shine of an eternal truth, an absolute ideal, or higher values that would be in my possession. No such thing has revealed itself to me and claimed me. And yet, this does by no means mean that "anything goes."[73] I am not without truth, norms, values. But they, conversely, receive their authority and reality only from *my* being-so and *my* standing up for them. In this sense, they are fundamentally contingent, subjective: human, all-too-human; there is no essential difference to my liking this food or art or music and disliking that. What gives them their objectivity is the objective fact of my being-so. In the "Prologue" to *Memories, Dreams, Reflections* Jung wrote, "Whether or not the stories [that he was going to tell] are 'true' is not the problem. The only problem is whether what I tell is *my* fable, *my* truth." ... This is said in the spirit of truly being "*only* that."

Continuing, Giegerich adds,

> Certain things, views, possible behaviours, etc., happen to be incompatible with who and how I am. *This* is the only "proof" I have to offer for my truths. Here I stand, I cannot do otherwise. But here I *do* stand, and really *stand*.

And then there is this:

> In order to find *my* truth and my *truth*, I have to perceive, alchemically speaking, as the *homo totus* and observe, while focussing on the *logos* as the soul of my world, my wholehearted responses.[74]

Jungian analysis *post mortem dei*. The reason for my title is now fully disclosed. Prompted by Giegerich's essay to recall occasions when the God-question has been put to me (while being cognizant at the same time of Jung's characterization of the present as "a time of God's death and disappearance"), I have endeavored in these pages to work out *my* answer. Coming forward and showing presence after much study, analysis and seeing-through, I can state it now in a line or two: it is only by our *thinking the death of God,* here at the abyss-edge of the split in the world, that the birth of man, and along with this the challenge of *becoming self* (in contradistinction to *having a relationship to the Self* on the model of a relation to God) truly comes into its own. With Jung, against Jung, beyond Jung, and this in the spirit of being "*only* that": individuation after all.

NOTES

1. BBC Television, "Face to Face," broadcast October 22, 1959. In W. McGuire & R.F.C. Hull, eds., *C.G. Jung Speaking: Interviews and Encounters* (Princeton: Princeton University Press, 1977), p. 428.

2. McGuire & Hull, eds., *C.G. Jung Speaking,* pp. 249-250.

3. I allude here to the following passage of Jung's: "The ego stands to the self as the moved to the mover, or as object to subject, because the determining factors which radiate out from the self surround the ego on all sides and are therefore supraordinate to it. The self, like the unconscious, is an *a priori* existent out of which the ego evolves. ... *It is not I who create myself, rather I happen to myself.*" (*CW* 11 § 391, italics mine)

4. Justifying his identification of God and the unconscious Jung resorts to an epistemological style of argument: "It is only through the psyche that we can establish that God acts upon us, but we are unable to distinguish whether these actions emanate from God or from the unconscious. We cannot tell whether God and the unconscious are two different entities. Both are border-line concepts for transcendental contents. But empirically it can be established, with a sufficient degree of probability, that there is in the unconscious an archetype of wholeness which manifests itself spontaneously in dreams, etc., and a tendency, independent of the conscious will, to relate other archetypes to this centre. Consequently, it does not seem improbable that the

archetype of wholeness occupies as such a central position which approximates it to the God-image. ... These facts make possible a certain qualification of our above thesis concerning the indistinguishableness of God and the unconscious. Strictly speaking, the God-image does not coincide with the unconscious as such, but with a special content of it, namely the archetype of the self. It is this archetype from which we can no longer distinguish the God-image empirically." (*CW* 11 § 757)

5. Sigmund Freud & Oskar Pfister, *Psychoanalysis and Faith: The Letters of Sigmund Freud and Oskar Pfister* (London: Hogarth Press and the Institute of Psycho-Analysis, 1963), pp. 86-87.

6. Martin Buber, *Eclipse of God: Studies in the Relation between Religion and Philosophy* (New York: Harper & Row, 1952), p. 84.

7. Further to this point it is worth noting that Jung's whole concept of God seems to be redolent of his word association experiment research and his concept of the complex. In the lines immediately following those we are discussing here, he continues: "I remember Him, I evoke Him, whenever I use His name, overcome by anger or by fear, whenever I involuntarily say: 'Oh God.' That happens when I meet somebody or something stronger than myself. It is an apt name given to all overpowering emotions in my own psychic system, subduing my conscious will and usurping control over myself. This is the name by which I designate all things which cross my wilful path violently and recklessly, all things which upset my subjective views, plans, and intentions and change the course of my life for better or worse" (*Letters* 2, p. 525, to M. Leonard, 5 December 1959). Likewise in his 1906 article, "The Psychopathological Significance of the Association Experiment," Jung states that "The occurrences of everyday life are nothing but association experiments on a major scale; the things outside us are the stimulus-words to which we react ..." (*CW* 2 § 895). It could be argued from this basis that Jung's concept of God was overdetermined and undermined by his concept of the complex. While it may be possible to speak of a God-complex, it will hardly do to approach the notion or concept of God as if it were a complex. Although in this essay we are interested, not in the God-complex, but in the God-concept, Jung, doubtless, had such a complex. Aniela Jaffé writes of the ten-year-old Jung's overhearing his pastor father's pathetic prayers imploring God to help him to believe as constituting a childhood

trauma. His later distinction between believing and knowing may be a part of his answer to his father's plight. Aniela Jaffé, *Was C.G. Jung A Mystic? And Other Essays* (Einsiedeln: Daimon Verlag, 1989), p. 89.

8. McGuire & Hull, eds., *C. G. Jung Speaking*, p. 251.

9. Of course, it is true: many of Jung's inconsistencies can be explained by his having expressed himself in different ways to different audiences. This, however, does not relieve us of the challenge of reading his various statements in the light of one another. Jung needed a wide and disparate audience in order to say what he had to say. Each statement, then, may be considered to be a mediating, differentiating, individuating moment of a single position or concept.

10. For a fuller treatment of this topic see my *The Dove in the Consulting Room: Hysteria and the Anima in Bollas and Jung* (Hove & New York: Brunner-Routledge, 2003).

11. C. G. Jung, *Notes of the Seminar Given in 1925*, W. McGuire, ed. (Princeton: Princeton University Press, 1989), p. 111.

12. Cf.: "What happens in the life of Christ happens always and everywhere. In the Christian archetype all lives of this kind are prefigured." (*CW* 11 § 146)

13. C. G. Jung, *The Red Book: Liber Novus*, S. Shamdasani, ed. (New York & London, W.W. Norton & Company, 2009), p. 329.

14. Wolfgang Giegerich, "The End of Meaning and the Birth of Man: An Essay about the State Reached in the History of Consciousness and an Analysis of C. G. Jung's Psychology Project," *Journal of Jungian Theory and Practice*, Vol. 6, No. 1, 2004, p. 38.

15. Victor White, *God and the Unconscious: An Encounter between Psychology and Religion* (London & Glasgow: Fontana Books, 1960), p. 43.

16. These quotations from Jung are White's translations from the German. Their *Collected Works* equivalents are *CW* 8 § 359, *CW* 13 § 54, and *CW* 13 § 55 respectively.

17. "*Individuation is the life in God*, as mandala psychology clearly shows" (*CW* 18 § 1624).

18. In a letter to Henry Corbin Jung describes his coming to write *Answer to Job* as follows: "The book 'came to me' during the fever of an illness. It was as if accompanied by the great music of a Bach or a Handel .... I just had the feeling of listening to a great composition, or rather of being at a concert." 4 May, 1953, *Letters* 2, p. 116.

19. Cited by Giegerich in "What is 'Soul'?" unpublished manuscript, p. 2.

20. Wolfgang Giegerich, "Is the Soul 'Deep?' Entering and Following the Logical Movement of Heraclitus' 'Fragment 45'," *Histories-Spring 64* (1998), pp. 1-2. Compared to what I have called Giegerich's shibboleth, Jung's epistemologically-couched presentation of his psychological position with respect to God and god-images is rather lax: "An archetypal image is like the portrait of an unknown man in a gallery. His name, his biography, his existence in general are unknown, but we assume nevertheless that the picture portrays a once living subject, a man who was real. We find numberless images of God, but we cannot produce the original. There is no doubt in my mind that there is an original behind our images, but it is inaccessible. We could not even be aware of the original since its translation into psychic terms is necessary in order to make it perceptible at all" (*CW* 18 §1589). With his thinking in terms of "the original" that is "behind our images" and of "translation" Jung effectively undoes the point he is making about the reflectedness of the psyche, while showing at the same time (ironically enough, since his intention was to indicate the opposite) that not only as a man, but as a psychologist, he has a God. Tacking a few words onto another of his sentences we could put it this way: just as "…one [theologian] speaks of the paradoxical God of the Old Testament, another of the incarnate God of Love, a third of the God who has a heavenly bride" (*CW* 14 § 781), so Jung speaks of what could be called his 'Not God but the God-image God.'

21. C. G. Jung, *The Visions Seminars*, Book One (Zurich: Spring Publications, 1976), p. 8.

22. The following passage from Giegerich may help to make this clearer: "For a true psychology, only the soul, which is certainly undemonstrable, merely 'metaphorical' and for this reason a seeming nothing, can be the 'substrate' and subject of the phenomena. The human being is then their object; he or she is nothing but the place where soul shows itself, just like the world is the place where man shows himself and becomes active. We therefore must shift our standpoint away from 'the human person' to the 'soul.' (*N.B.*: I am talking of the shift of *our standpoint, perspective, or of the idea in terms of which* we study, just as before, the concrete experience of individuals or peoples.)" "The

Present as Dimension of the Soul: 'Actual Conflict' and Archetypal Psychology," in *The Neurosis of Psychology*, CEP, vol. 1, p. 115.

23. It is interesting to note that Edinger briefly considered the same criticism: "I know when I first read *Answer to Job* when it came out in translation in the fifties, what offended me was how seriously [Jung] took this Old Testament God-image, expecting something from Him. ... I thought, 'Grow up Jung, don't you realize you mustn't expect justice? The world isn't like that.'" Faithful to Jung, however, Edinger faulted himself for expressing a "rationalist position" with this objection. Edward F. Edinger, *Transformation of the God-mage: An Elucidation of Jung's Answer to Job* (Toronto, Inner City Books, 1992), p. 24.

24. To be fair to Jung it needs to be acknowledged that in his writings he emphasized the dark side of God. This, however, does not contradict Giegerich's point. It is the other side of the same kind of thinking in terms of our vested interests and our human lot.

25. I here follow Peter White in alluding to Sir James Frazer's account in *The Golden Bough* of the succession of priests at Nemi. His article "Thinking 'Murder': Following the Trail of Psychology's knowing of itself in *No Country for Old Men*." Forthcoming.

26. There is a crucial difference for Giegerich between interiorizing a soul-phenomenon or soul-text into itself and interiorizing it into us as a supposed anthropological constant which is to be realized during the course of the individuation process. In the former case, the adept forgets about himself and becomes, as it were, for the duration of his reflective effort a sublated moment of the phenomenon that thinks itself out through him. By means of this implicit/explicit dialectic, truth is created and opened up. The later approach of interiorizing the phenomenon into oneself takes us out of psychology into the boutique of the Beautiful Soul. See in this connection Jung's reference to "glamour" at the end of the "Life after Death" chapter of *MDR* and his later reference in the same chapter to the principle of necessary statement. While this principle appears to be synonymous with the interiorizing of phenomena into themselves, the pitch is queered because of identifications that result from not having forgotten oneself and fully gone over into the phenomenon.

27. Giegerich, "Is the Soul 'Deep?' Entering and Following the Logical Movement of Heraclitus' 'Fragment 45'," pp. 1-2.

28. "Psychology, in Jung's view ... *requires* otherness, difference—though not an utterly external other, something totally irrelevant, but its own internal other. Psychology must reflect itself in and base itself on a true (even if ultimately internal) other." Though Giegerich here is referring to Jung's work on alchemy it applies as well to his treatment of Christianity. As for what Giegerich means by "reflect itself and base itself on [its] true ... other," this comes across in the following question he poses: "... does psychological theory do justice to the spirit of its own internal other? Did what it discovered in the latter really come home to and permeate the constitution of the former? ... Is this other, [here Christianity], conceived, comprehended, and described by this theory in such a way that the "[Christian impulse]" (the inner motif power of [Christianity]) can really find fulfillment?" Wolfgang Giegerich, "Closure and Setting Free or The Bottled Spirit of Alchemy and Psychology," *Alchemy-Spring 74* (2006), pp. 32-33.

29. For a discussion of the application of systematic closure and of this principle quoted from Jung see Giegerich's essay, "Closure and Setting Free," *ibid.*, p. 57. The same quote from Jung is discussed by Giegerich under the heading "The presupposition of the 'self-sufficiency' of myths and fantasy images" in *The Soul's Logical Life*, p. 126.

30. For Giegerich's discussion of this passage from Jung see *The Soul's Logical Life*, p. 123. For his discussion of "The 'tautological' presupposition of myth interpretation" see pp. 119-122.

31. An example of Jung analyzing, not what people want in the way of life after death, but what the concept says about the soul can be found in his "Psychological Commentary on 'The Tibetan Book of the Dead'": "It is highly sensible of the *Bardo Thödol* to make clear to the dead man the primacy of the psyche, for that is the one thing which life does not make clear to us. We are so hemmed in by things which jostle and oppress that we never get a chance, in the midst of these 'given' things, to wonder by whom they are 'given.' It is from this world of 'given' things that the dead man liberates himself; and the purpose of the instruction is to help him towards this liberation" (*CW* 11 § 841).

32. Paul Kugler has drawn attention to Jung's tendency to interpret images of the dead on the objective level, noting that this

was in contravention to his own interpretive guidelines. See his "The Legacy of the Dead" in *Raids on the Unthinkable: Freudian and Jungian Psychoanalysis* (New Orleans: Spring Journal Books, 2005), pp. 120-124.

33. Giegerich, "The End of Meaning and the Birth of Man," pp. 29-30.

34. For a related critique of this topic see W. Giegerich, "The 'Patriachal Neglect of the Feminine Principle': A Psychological Fallacy in Jungian Theory," *Harvest: Journal for Jungian Studies* 45.1 (1999), pp. 7-30.

35. Philip Rieff, *The Triumph of the Therapeutic: Uses of Faith After Freud* (New York, Harper & Row, 1966).

36. Rieff, *The Triumph of the Therapeutic*, pp. 113-114.

37. 1 John 4:1. Cf. Giegerich's reference to "… 'trying the spirits,' whether they are in accordance with the developed constitution of psychology or not," *The Neurosis of Psychology*, *CEP*, vol. 1, p. 7.

38. With reference to my stating that "one's own affects or affect images … [are] *produced as* wholly other to oneself," the following passage from Jung is quite telling: "… all modern people feel alone in the world of the psyche because they assume that there is nothing there that they have not made up. … *But through a certain training* … something suddenly happens which one has not created, something objective, and then one is no longer alone. That is the object of [certain] initiations, *to train people to experience something which is not their intention*, something strange, something objective with which they cannot identify… This experience of the objective fact is all-important, because it denotes the presence of something which is not I, yet is still psychical. Such an experience can reach a climax where it becomes an experience of God." *The Visions Seminars*, Book One (Zürich: Spring Publications, 1976), p. 73, italics mine.

39. As for Jung's bluster-filled challenge — "Where is the criterion by which you could say that such a life is not legitimate, that such an experience is not valid, and that such *pistis* is mere illusion?"—it can readily be argued that the paragraph from which this is taken is itself the criterion by which Jung judged the life of the woman he met on his travels to be "… grotesquely banal, utterly poor, meaningless, with no point in it all."

40. Cited by Walter Kaufmann in *Nietzsche: Philosopher, Psychologist, Antichrist*, 3rd ed. (New York: Vintage Books, 1968), p. 356.

41. Wolfgang Giegerich, David L. Miller, Greg Mogenson, *Dialectics & Analytical Psychology: The El Capitan Canyon Seminar* (New Orleans, Spring Journal Books, 2005), pp. 108-112. Wolfgang Giegerich, "The Animus as Negation and as the Soul's Own Other," in *Soul Violence*, CEP, vol. 3, pp. 111-167.

42. Giegerich, "The Animus as Negation," *CEP*, vol. 3, pp. 112-13-13, 144-145, 147.

43. Time, in this context, needs to be understood, not as an external factor, but as the animus moment of the soul's syzygy. Critical of what he calls "anima-only" psychology, Giegerich has reacquainted Jungian and archetypal psychology with the animus of history.

44. Wolfgang Giegerich, "Rupture, Or: Psychology and Religion" in *The Neurosis of Psychology*, CEP, vol. 1 (New Orleans: Spring Journal Books), p. 227. Italics mine.

45. Giegerich, "Rupture, Or: Psychology and Religion," pp. 229-230.

46. Wolfgang Giegerich, "'The Unassimilable Remnant'—what is at Stake? A dispute with Stanton Marlan," in S. Marlan, ed., *Archetypal Psychologies: Reflections in Honor or James Hillman* (New Orleans: Spring Journal Books, 2008), p. 219.

47. Wolfgang Giegerich, "The Dream in Psychotherapy, Its Role and Significance," unpublished paper.

48. Jung, *Analytical Psychology: Notes of the Seminar Given in 1925*, pp. 96-97,

49. Giegerich, "'The Unassimilable Remnant'," in S. Marlan, ed., *Archetypal Psychologies*, up. 219.

50. Giegerich, "The Dream in Psychotherapy, Its Role and Significance," unpublished paper.

51. Commenting upon what he has called "the neurosis of psychology" Giegerich has alerted us to "The innocent tendency to focus on cases and on psychological material before consciousness [which] keeps psychology unconscious about the fact that the theory (or theories, in the plural) that guide its consciousness are always in on it, from the outset." Continuing he writes, "What should actually be the intrinsic *form of the constitution* of psychology is reduced to *empirical events* occurring in the course of the practice of psychology.

The empirical persons have to carry the load that psychology as theory or logical constitution of psychology does not want to shoulder." *The Neurosis of Psychology*, CEP, vol. 1, p. 9.

52. Giegerich, "Is the Soul 'Deep'?—Entering and Following the Logical Movement of Heraclitus' 'Fragment 45'," p. 31.

53. Giegerich, "Is the Soul 'Deep?'," p. 19.

54. Giegerich, *The Soul's Logical Life*, p. 24.

55. Giegerich, *The Soul's Logical Life*, quotation is from the back text.

56. Giegerich, *The Soul's Logical Life*, p. 25.

57. Giegerich, *The Soul's Logical Life*, p. 25.

58. Jung, *The Red Book: Liber Novus*, p. 229.

59. At the end of the same paragraph from which this line is taken Jung vilifies the light of man's intellect for bringing about a *Götterdämmerung*.

60. Giegerich, "Rupture, Or: Psychology and Religion," p. 231.

61. BBC Television, "Face to Face," broadcast October 22, 1959. In W. McGuire & R.F.C. Hull, eds., *C.G. Jung Speaking: Interviews and Encounters*, p. 428.

62. Wolfgang Giegerich interviewed in Robert & Janis Henderson, *Living With Jung. "Enterviews" with Jungian Analysts*, vol. 3 (New Orleans, LA: Spring Journal Books, 2010), p. 269.

63. C.G. Jung, *Letters*, vol. ii: 1951-1961, ed. G. Adler & A. Jaffé, trans. R. F. C. Hull (Princeton, NJ: Princeton University Press, 1975), pp. 565-566.

64. Wolfgang Giegerich, "On the Neurosis of Psychology or the Third of the Two," in *The Neurosis of Psychology*, CEP, vol. 1, pp. 41-67.

65. Wolfgang Giegerich, "The Provenance of C. G. Jung's Psychological Findings," in *CEP,* vol. 1, p. 137.

66. Giegerich, "The End of Meaning and the Birth of Man," p. 18.

67. Cited by Deland S. Anderson in *Hegel's Speculative Good Friday: The Death of God in Philosophical Perspective* (Atlanta, Georgia: Scholars Press, 1996), p. xvi.

68. Giegerich, "Rupture, Or: Psychology and Religion," *CEP*, vol. 1, p. 223.

69. G.W. F. Hegel, *Phenomenology of Spirit*, tr. A.V. Miller (Oxford: Oxford University Press, 1977), p. 19.

70. For Giegerich's discussion of this text see *The Soul's Logical Life*, p. 57.

71. Giegerich, *The Soul's Logical Life*, p. 227.

72. Giegerich interviewed in Robert & Janis Henderson, *Living With Jung*, p. 277.

73. In *The Brothers Karamazov*, Ivan had declared that if God is dead everything is permissible.

74. Giegerich, "The End of Meaning and the Birth of Man," p. 32.

Romanyshyn and Giegerich: Poles Apart

Rejoinders to Giegerich's Critique of Romanyshyn's "The Melting of the Polar Ice"

Spring published "The Melting of the Polar Ice: Revisting *Technology as Symptom and Dream*" by Robert Romanyshyn in Vol. 80 (Fall 2008). Wolfgang Giegerich wrote a critique of Romanyshyn's article called "The Psychologist as Repentence Preacher and Revivalist/ Robert Romanyshyn on the Melting Polar Ice" which Spring published in Vol. 82 (Fall 2009). Robert Romanyshyn, Susan Rowland, Joel Weishaus, and David Rosen have submitted rejoinders to Giegerich's critique, all of which are published in this section. The title for this section comes from the title of Susan Rowland's article and is used with her permission.

WHO IS WOLFGANG GIEGERICH?

ROBERT D. ROMANYSHYN

INTRODUCTION

The simplest and most direct answer to this question can be found in the biographical note about Giegerich that is on the first page of his article, "The Psychologist as Repentance Preacher and Revivalist/Robert Romanyshyn on the Melting Polar Ice."* Impressive—over 170 publications, in several languages, including fourteen books—and we are meant to be impressed. But the question lingers and I want to situate my response to his critique of my article, "The Melting of the Polar Ice: Revisiting Technology as Symptom and Dream,"** within it.

I do not think that it is the facts about global climate change that are in dispute between us. I assume that Giegerich accepts the overwhelming scientific evidence concerning the impact of our activities on nature. As Gretel Ehrlich notes,[1] the ice cores of Greenland and the eastern Antarctic offer a 450,000 year record of that impact, which

*Published in *Spring*, Vol 82 (fall 2009), pp. 193-221.
** Published in *Spring*, Vol. 80 (fall 2008), pp. 79-116.

Robert D. Romanyshyn is an Affiliate Member of the Inter-Regional Society of Jungian Analysts and a Senior Core Faculty Member in the Clinical Psychology program at Pacifica Graduate Institute. He has just finished a DVD, *Antarctica: Inner Journeys in the Outer World*, based upon his trip to that region. For information about this DVD, contact him at rdromanyshyn@gmail.com.

shows that the rise in greenhouse gases caused by human activity far exceeds that caused by natural fluctuations in the past.

What is in dispute between us is the difference about the meaning of the facts, how we understand and interpret them. It is a difference that has much to do with how each of us regards soul and nature, engages it, and is engaged by it.

So again, Who is Wolfgang Giegerich? For Giegerich it seems clear who I am. I am a repentance preacher, a revivalist, one who has committed a crime, a sinner, a spokesperson for "All the faddish slogans of the ecological variety of pop psychology," a moralist, an ego psychologist who has imposed a "false genealogy" on his reading of the cultural and historical emergence and development of linear perspective, one whose "quest for insight is drowned in emotionality, in a sinister mood," an anxious writer who is unable to take up "the ethical obligation of any writer striving for insight to first free himself of any emotion so as to become able to study his subject *sine ira et studio,*'" one in need of consolation and who he is "tempted to console by saying, requiescat in pace," and more.[2]

Given his images of me, I want to begin my remarks with one of the key themes in the work of Merleau-Ponty, the idea that man is a mirror for man, which was the theme that anchored my first book, *Psychological Life: From Science to Metaphor.*[3] A phenomenology of the mirror experience shows that the mirror is not a Xerox machine that reproduces a duplicate of oneself. The mirror reflection is a re-presentation of oneself through which one sees an image, a figure who refigures who one is. Through the mirror of the other one encounters that re-presentation of oneself. There is a circuit of reflection between self and other and within that circuit one experiences through the other an image of who he or she needs or desires to be. In this regard, the mirror is a complex affair that requires one to become as conscious as possible of the ways in which one transforms the other into his or her desire or need. In asking "Who is Wolfgang Giegerich?" I am saying that his representation of my work is by and large a misunderstanding or misrepresentation (deliberate?) of it. If the latter, then his presentation of me as repentance preacher and revivalist is rather excessive, and it raises the question if he wrote his critique *sine ira et studio*, as he advises I should have written my article. Are the repentance preacher and revivalist what he needs me to be in order to affirm his own position?

Of course to proceed in this way could easily lay me open to the charge that I am avoiding his criticisms. After all I must be desperate, since the charge has already been made that my work is criminal and the judgment rendered that I am a sinner. The trial has begun and the evidence has been marshaled, shaped, and presented. But who has shaped the evidence and to what ends? It is only by questioning the evidence in the context of the one who has shaped it that I can offer my response to the charges. I need to show how the evidence against me, especially with regard to the issue of emotions, my perspective on linear perspective, and my description of the negative gnosis of a metaphoric sensibility is a misunderstanding or misrepresentation (deliberate?) of my work.

WOLFGANG GIEGERICH AS THERAPIST:
THE ISSUE OF EMOTIONS

Giegerich opens his critique of my paper with the claim that it is "a well-argued and high-level example" of one kind of thinking, which he associates with eco-psychology. While he confesses that he does not know if I would label my work as eco-psychology, which I would not without explicit qualifications, he proceeds as if it "nicely exemplifies" that kind of thinking. Doing so, he says, allows him to demonstrate "one type of thinking based on certain premises and tenets, displaying certain attitudes, and leading to certain strategic moves that I find incompatible with what I would consider psychology proper, a 'psychology with soul' in the tradition of C.G. Jung."[4]

The kind of thinking of which I seem to be guilty and which disqualifies my work as a thinking without soul is one that begins, as he notes, with a feeling connection to the work, specifically with the mood of anxiety that opens my paper. The kind of thinking that is done with soul is one that acknowledges that "emotions in general inevitably make us unfree to the extent that we are under their spell." He adds, "They tend to make us blind." Giegerich then offers a well-chosen quote from Jung to support his view and claims that in quoting him he does not mean to "suggest that because Jung said this it must be right and everyone has to accept it." On the contrary, he adds that he has chosen this specific quote "because it hits the nail right on the head."[5]

Of course, a writer does this all the time, but in this context it strikes me as rather too convenient. The context I am pointing to is the assumption he makes, even when he is not sure, that my article is an example of eco-psychology. In this context Giegerich has already judged my work on grounds that he has adopted and according to an agenda that supports his own position in relation to the one he imagines belongs to me. This in fact is a key point in my response to his reply to my article. Throughout his piece his critique rests upon a misrepresentation (deliberate?) of what I have written. He does it here regarding emotions and he does it with respect to the issue of linear perspective, which is central to my reading of the melting polar ice.

Following his quote of Jung, Giegerich applies the difference between these two kinds of thinking to the context of being a therapist. And so, he writes that he ceases to be a therapist to his patient if and when he becomes anxious over a patient's "suppressed but powerful fury [that] uncannily fills the whole atmosphere of the consulting room." He continues, " In my fear of him or his threatening material I can no longer do justice to him, because I am no longer free...It is vital for the therapy that I struggle to overcome my anxiety and gain my freedom vis-à-vis what made me afraid." Then, shifting back to the issue in my article, Giegerich says, "In a very similar sense, how can I write on technology if I am under the spell of anxiety caused by the imminent prospect of a nuclear winter or the melting ice?" To do so he adds, "would be unprofessional."[6]

Who would not agree with Giegerich's position here? What therapist would argue against him? More than thirty years of practice within a depth orientation and especially a Jungian one, I know whereof he speaks. In addition what writer would disagree? The fact that my book on technology, which was seeded in my work with adolescents in the 1980s when the threat of nuclear war with the Soviet Union was extremely high and had deadening effects on their sense of any future, required ten years of thinking and research hardly illustrates a writer who was under the spell of anxiety. But Giegerich thinks that I am as a writer, and by implication as a therapist, guilty of such unprofessional behavior. He believes that I am guilty of that kind of thinking that is awash in emotion, a kind of thinking and writing that belongs to a psychology without soul. Here is what he says: "Strangely, very strangely, the possibility of overcoming one's anxiety seems to have no place in the first type of thinking." He continues, "The only way that Romanyshyn can imagine of dealing with this emotion, other than staying with it, is 'numb[ing] myself against this feeling,' 'going to sleep, benumbing myself,' entertaining a 'comfortable illusion.'"[7]

What I actually wrote, however, is that we have to stay with the anxiety, to linger with it, so that we do not slip into the temptation to go numb, and it is in this context that I quoted John Beebe's work about anxiety as the proper starting point for the discovery of integrity. I do not think I could have been clearer about my intention here. Indeed, I stated explicitly that as psychologists in service to soul we have an obligation to stay in touch with the experience of anxiety, examine it, and *not* benumb ourselves to it, particularly and specifically when the response of denial is so widespread in the cultural circumstances of our time. Anxiety and its denial over the melting polar ice in particular and climate changes in general is a pervasive cultural experience and as such a legitimate issue for psychology in general, and, I believe for depth psychology in particular. But Giegerich through the selective placement of his quotes from my article, especially where he places (misplaces) Beebe's words, cleverly distorts (deliberate?) my argument. This misrepresentation (deliberate?) occurs again when he cites the end of my article. Commenting on these passages, he writes, "Romanyshyn's paper ends with his confession that he is writing 'from this place of near despair.' 'The pull to go numb, to fall asleep…is strong.' One is tempted to console him by saying, *requiescat in pace*. The quest for insight is drowned in emotionality, in a sinister *mood*."[8] But what he leaves out in his clever formatting of his critique is the last sentence in my article where, regarding the melting polar ice as an inconvenient truth, I say, "Depth psychology has a special obligation to this truth."[9] For Giegerich that last sentence would be inconvenient, since for him I must remain the anxious writer in need of consolation in order to rest in peace.

But it is neither rest nor peace that I desire with respect to the melting polar ice. In the chapter on psychological writing in *The Wounded Researcher* I made a case for a style of writing that gives voice and body to one's words. Quoting a passage from Ortega Y Gasset, I noted that Hillman made use of those same words to open his landmark

Re-visioning Psychology: "Why write, if this too easy activity of pushing a pen across paper is not given a certain bull-fighting risk and we do not approach dangerous, agile, and two-horned topics?"[10] The melting polar ice is a dangerous topic and the anxiety that was present in engaging it was and is an index of that risk. Curiously, however, Giegerich cites the same passage but uses it to criticize my position. He writes, "One can hardly imagine a greater difference than that between the bull-fighting spirit vis-à-vis a dangerous topic and one's purposely rooting oneself as author in one's anxiety."[11]

As if I chose to do that purposely! The melting polar ice enters as a feeling, as anxiety. It stirs the depths before it reaches the surface of mind. My feeling of anxiety, then, about the melting polar ice is not a piece of "New Age kitsch," part of a chorus of "All the faddish slogans of the ecological variety of pop psychology..."[12], a call for some kind of new age activism. Standing within it, I place myself between that self-serving activism of much of eco-psychology, a psychology that often seems to lack a proper humility in the face of the *Anima Mundi*, and that icy mind, which Giegerich thinks "would be needed to do justice to the topic of polar ice."[13] His icy mind also seems short on humility both in this context and in the context of therapy. It lacks flesh and as such strikes me as rather detached and indifferent. Indeed, it strikes me as somewhat heroic and egoic.

A BRIEF PHENOMENOLOGY OF THE FLESH

Flesh is the term that the phenomenologist Merleau-Ponty adopts in his final work, *The Visible and the Invisible* to describe the lived body. For Alphonso Lingis, who translated that work, "The concept of flesh emerges as the ultimate notion of Merleau-Ponty's thought." Flesh is an elemental reality, like the elements of air, water, fire, earth, light, and to understand its elemental presence one finally has to surrender any positivist notion of the body as an empirical given, a corporeal piece of the visible world over against a mind, "the seer, which must be an incorporeal and non-sensorial knowing agency, an immaterial spirit, finally a pure clearing, a nothingness."[14] In the flesh Merleau-Ponty lays the foundation for a new ontology, for an embodied phenomenology of the relation between the flesh of body and that of the world. Through numerous examples in his work, Merleau-Ponty illustrates the basic aspect of this bond when, as he says, "Things have an internal equivalent in me; they arouse in me a carnal formula of their presence."[15] In that carnal formula the things of the world elicit from us a gesture that responds to their seductive appeals. One is drawn into the world of things, events, and others through the body, through a fleshy syntax of feelings and their expression.

Flesh is the locus of emotions that arise not within one but between one and the other. In the context of therapy, flesh unfolds itself as the transference field between the embodied presences of therapist and patient who infect, as it were, each other with the whole registry of feelings, complexes, desires, appeals, etc. Indeed, one of the most significant contributions that phenomenology makes to depth psychology is the way in which it re-visions transference as a gestural field, which is a theme I have pursued for many years in numerous publications from a discussion in *Technology as Symptom and Dream* of what the art historian Helen Gardner calls the pantomimic body that one finds in some of the paintings of Giotto in the 14th century, through its application to the bond between the embodied reader and the body of the text, a phenomenology of the gesture as a ground for dream work, the role and place of the flesh in research, to the most recent article which presents a detailed view of Merleau-Ponty's work and its application to psychotherapy.[16] As a phenomenology of the gesture shows, flesh is even the site of the ancestors. They dwell within one's carnal habits, a form of motor memory, and the dead as I described it in *The Soul in Grief: Love, Death and Transformation* [17] haunt the living through the flesh. Greg Mogenson makes the same point when he says, "twentieth century Oedipal man has forgotten his mythical forbears and is haunted by what he has failed to mourn."[18] The un-mourned, the forgotten, not only linger in our bones, they are the subtle texturing of our bones.

In light of those few remarks about the flesh I fail to see how Giegerich's remarks about "overcoming" one's anxiety, "of rising above it" square with his remarks to "let it be and expose myself to it" and "in full awareness allow Pandora's box to be opened."[19] This language of mastery, of overcoming, of rising above is the polar opposite of what the flesh of emotions demands, that psychological move of letting emotions be by sinking into the flesh to find the figure/image in the emotion. Indeed, even as I write this reply to Giegerich, he is here with me in my study, a companion of sorts—a bit irritating at times to be sure, but also amusing at times with the excess in his tone—whose felt presence is not to be denied. If I am to write my reply *sine ira et studio*, I must begin with where things are, with just as they are and stay with the fleshy entanglements in the field between us, just as a therapist must do in the transference field between himself or herself and the patient, and as I did with the carnal formula of the melting ice as the feeling of anxiety. I do not overcome that anxiety by "rising above it" as Giegerich advises. Rather, I must be with it, linger in it by sinking into it to encounter the images that live in the emotion, a move that was a central one for Jung in his development of active imagination. This is hard work, always, but it is also the necessary psychological move and an ethical move. In the same way, finding who lives within my anxiety is what makes my response to the melting polar ice a psychological one and not a political, or technical, or economic one.

WOLFGANG GIEGERICH AS PROFESSOR, POLICEMAN AND PURITAN PROPHET: THE ISSUE OF LINEAR PERSPECTIVE

When William Faulkner was asked why his novels so often dealt with the dead past, he was reported to have said, "The past isn't dead; it isn't even past." Although this is a creative novelist speaking, it is an accurate phenomenological description of the psychological experience of lived time. The past lingers in the present. It lingers there as possibility and as symptom.

TIME AS POSSIBILITY

With regard to possibility, the phenomenology of time indicates that what one wants to become informs what he/she remembers of what he/she has been, just as how one remembers what he/she has been informs how he/she imagines what he/she might be. The past remembered is the future imagined; the future imagined is the past remembered. Through memory and imagination time is the possibility of continuing creation, and because we are related to time as possibility, the world can become the vale of soul making. Because time is possibility we are able to stop, and turn and linger—to look back and take up once again what has been left by the side of the road. Both poet and psychologist bear witness to this possibility. Here is Rilke:

> Who's turned round like this, so that we always,
> do what we may, retain the attitude
> of someone who's departing? Just as he,
> on the last hill, that shows him all his valley,
> for the last time, will turn and stop and linger,
> we live our lives, for ever taking leave.

The question of "Who" matters deeply here. It emphasizes that this act of turning, this gestural incarnation of remembering, is a gift received and not something fashioned by us. It emphasizes that this work of remembering is a vocation. In this Eighth Elegy, "Who" calls us into this work of remembering remains unanswered, remains a mystery. But in the Ninth Elegy Rilke approaches a reply through more questions:

> ...Are we, perhaps, here just for saying: House,
> Bridge, Fountain, Gate, Jug, Olive tree, Window,—
> Possibly: Pillar, Tower?

Language too is a gift, a vocation. We are called into saying, addressed through things, through these simple things. A few lines down he wonders if this vocation "Is not the secret purpose of this sly earth..." and in the final stanza he asks again, "Earth, isn't this what you want: an invisible re-arising in us?" The man on the hill overlooking his valley for the last time—was he turned by the appeal of the world, by the appeal not to forget? Are language, memory, imagination all of a piece, different aspects of this gift of time? After Rilke asks if we are here just for saying things, he says, "but for saying, remember, / oh, for such saying as never the things themselves / hoped so intensely to be."[20] The things of the world appeal to us, as any phenomenologist knows. They inscribe, as we saw, their carnal formula in us and ask to be said and in that saying not passed by, not forgotten. To be said, perhaps, with a word in a poem or even just as a spontaneous ejaculation of joy and wonder in the moment when one says to a friend, "Look at that!" Or to be said with a note on a piano that echoes and resonates with the call of the bellbird in one's garden, or perhaps to be said with a splash of color on a canvas. We are here to hear and respond, and that obligation requires that we listen. And so, the poet after offering a catalogue of the things we are, perhaps, here for saying, inserts that one single word within his question: "Possibly."

The first logic of the world is this aesthetic bond between embodied flesh and the flesh of the world, and in that bond the soul's logical life rests within this aesthetic appeal. How can one rise above that first moment so rooted in one's flesh? What are the risks of doing so? Aesthetic means to perceive and in its roots it is related to perceiving as hearing, feeling, and obeying. What are the risks of keeping an eye upon the world while one is looking at it through a window that became a grid? The hermeneutic of linear perspective that I offered in *Technology as Symptom and Dream* began with this phenomenology of the window, the starting point of Albert's treatise on linear perspective.

Jung also offers examples of the lingering, even haunting presence of times past in the present, and he personifies that presence. He names it the ancestors, the dead who bequeath to us their unfinished business, who turn us back toward them to offer to us our inheritance.

> Our souls as well as our bodies are composed of individual elements which were already present in the ranks of our ancestors. The 'newness' in the individual psyche is an endlessly varied recombination of age-old components. Body and soul, therefore, have an intensely historical character and find no proper place in what is new...That is to say, our ancestral components are only part at home in such things.

Jung's words raise an important issue, which goes to the heart of my reading of history: how do we find our proper place in what is new, that is, in what is now? I will return to this point. First, however, I want to indicate how Jung responds to this question.

> We are very far from having finished completely with the Middle Ages, classical antiquity, and primitivity, as our modern psyches pretend. Nevertheless, we have plunged down a cataract of progress which sweeps us on into the future with ever wilder violence the farther it takes us from our roots. Once the past has been breached, it is usually annihilated, and there is no stopping the forward motion. But it is precisely the loss of connection with the past, our uprootedness, which has given rise to the 'discontents' of civilization...

Here Jung connects his question of how do we find our proper place in what is now with the concern that if we do not properly locate ourselves we will be swept away toward a future that has broken its ties to the past. How then do we find our proper place in the now and avoid being swept away? We have to attend to what is still not completely finished and as such still lingers in the now. We have to attend to the ancestors who carry that unfinished business, to the dead who wait for us to respond to their almost inaudible appeals.

> The less we understand of what our fathers and forefathers sought, the less we understand ourselves...In the Tower at Bollingen it is as if one lived in many centuries simultaneously. The place will outlive me, and in its location and style it points backwards to things of long ago.[21]

Like the past, the dead are not dead. Indeed, like the past, the dead are not even past yet!

How do we avoid being swept away by a future that has broken its ties to the past? We do so by lending an ear to the unfinished business of that past in the present. To make a place in the now for the unfinished business of the ancestors, to lend an ear to their appeals that they not be forgotten opens a pause in the drift of time. In that moment of pause we face in two directions, Janus-like, toward a past and a future and in remembering the former we simultaneously imagine the latter. Remembering is a creative act, a return to origins not in some straight, linear, logical line, but in a movement of mind that spirals back to those origins, re-collects them, and takes them forward into the present at another level of awareness.

This thinking that spirals back upon itself is one of the two traditions that have grounded not only my book on technology and my article on the melting polar ice, but also my style of psychological reflection throughout my writings on therapy, language, and other issues. In his reflections on the phenomenology of Merleau-Ponty, John Sallis emphasizes that this style of thinking *is* phenomenology when he titles his now classic text, *Phenomenology and the Return to Beginnings*.[22] Throughout that book Sallis shows how this kind of thinking happens when mind matters, when flesh is the ground of thought when the philosopher acknowledges his shadow, that is to say, the incarnate shadow of mind, as Merleau-Ponty eloquently describes in essays like *The Philosopher and his Shadow* and *Eye and Mind*.[23] Because my book on technology and the article on the ice, as well as my general approach to psychological issues over the years, has been to frame my inquiries in the place between phenomenology and depth psychology,[24] I should note as a quick aside that one of the things that Jung brings to phenomenology is the psychological depth of that shadow, its symbolic character and its complexity. In this regard, the incarnate philosopher's shadow is what is cast on his or her thinking by the ancestors of the tradition who carry its unfinished business, who linger with its enduing questions.

It is the questions that endure in those beginnings that summon us in the present into questioning, into a return to those beginnings, a return that is not in service to some kind of wooly-headed reductive thinking that returns to origins as cause that seems, for example, so prevalent today in depth psychology's fascination with neuroscience. Giegerich, however, accuses me of such regressive, reductive, causal thinking when I marshal the evidence that connects the melting polar ice to its origins in that shift in world view that arose with the creation and development of linear perspective. I have in his eyes constructed a "false geneology" between the melting polar ice and the invention of linear perspective "by viewing the latter as the starting point of the former, and the former as the end product of the latter." I have, he says, walked into Edgerton's trap, into the trap of a noted art historian whose evidence lent support to my position. Edgerton's work is "untenable," and so much so that he says of Edgerton and myself, "It is as if neither of them had looked at actual paintings that were inspired by the spirit inherent in and underlying the invention of linear perspective, and had not read Nicholas of Cusa, Ficino, Pico della Mirandola, Durer, Leonardo da Vinci, etc."[25] Is there a scent of arrogance in the air in the ambience of which I am expected to confess, *mea culpa, mea maxima culpa.*

Well, I wish not to be bullied into such a confession and in any case I have spent years wandering museums and looking at paintings. Indeed, the book on technology began in a museum, the circumstance of which I describe in the text, and from that circumstance to the publication of the book in 1989, I did ten years of research. I read not only Alberti's treatise on linear perspective, but also other tenable art historians like Helen Gardner, who says that linear perspective "made possible scale drawings, maps, charts, graphs, and diagrams—those means of exact representation without which modern science and technology would be impossible," and cultural historians like William

Ivins, who notes, "Many reasons are assigned for the mechanization of life and industry during the nineteenth century, but the mathematical development of perspective was absolutely prerequisite to it."[26]

In addition, I did read some of the sources Giegerich calls in support of his criticism of my position, especially Durer, and I find it puzzling to say the least that he ignores how for Durer the window as grid in linear perspective was a basis for his belief that "the ideal nude ought to be constructed by taking the face of one body, the breasts of another, the legs of a third, the shoulders of a fourth, the hands of a fifth—and so on."[27] I even presented one of his drawings —*Artist Drawing a Nude through a Gridded Screen*—to show how the window as grid was of a piece with the anatomical gaze as a foundation for some of the first studies of the body as a specimen for a spectator mind behind a window for whom the world was becoming a spectacle for measurement, observation, and calculative ways of knowing and being.

Giegerich, however, will have none of these sources because he is motivated to present and defend another starting point for our broken connection with nature. "The broken connection with nature has a fundamentally different origin…It in fact happened—in the depth of soul—around 1800 to 1830…"[28] I accept his perspective that such things happened in that period and even address some of them in the technology book. But his starting point, which he connects with the divine order absolutely crumbling away in the nineteenth century, is not only for me too late, but also begs the question of what made that collapse possible, what was a prerequisite for those moments.

Galileo, for example, practiced his belief that the book of nature is written in mathematical symbols while in church. Observing the swing of a lamp he timed its movements with his pulse. His genius is not the issue here. The point is that to do so he would have had to turn his attention elsewhere for a moment and away from the sacred proceedings of the mass. A radical change is at work here, a radical shift in the relation between the spaces of the sacred and the profane.

In addition, one of the key features of linear perspective is the eclipse of the Angel that follows upon the invention of linear perspective. At the horizon line there is no room for the Angel's halo and while Giegerich makes a good point regarding the entrance of the Angel into the human world at the vanishing point where the vertical dimension of the heavens meets the horizontal plane of earth, we cannot gainsay

the history of the Angel's demise long before the collapse of the divine
order in the nineteenth century. One has only to look at paintings more
or less on either side of the divide of the codification of linear perspective
in Alberti's treatise, *De Pictura* published in 1435, to appreciate this
change. The Angels who appear in Simone Martini's *Annunciation*
painted in 1333, Sassetta's *Mystical Marriage* painted in 1437, and as
late as da Vinci's *Annunciation* painted in 1472, show the other worldly
grandeur of the Angel. In these paintings we see that Angels belong to
another dimension. But at the vanishing point of linear perspective
the Angel will be brought into the human order and that Angel will
become an angel no longer worthy of its capital form. Again, while
Giegerich makes several fine points about the invention of linear
perspective, it is untenable for him to deny that one consequence of it
will be the domestication as it were, of the Angel. Look at some
paintings again! In 1632 Rubens' Angel has become Cupid in his
Garden of Love, and in 1763 the Angel in Joseph Vien's *The Merchant
of Love* are angels in a basket being offered for sale.

　　This evidence is not my judgment, my crime, my sin, my anxiety
working its way in me to find some rescue from the ways in which
we have taken up the many possibilities that this shift in human
existence offered. It is just the way things are and it "simply has to be
endured by us"[29] as Giegerich says in defense of his view and against
what he imagines I am doing. But what it means to endure means
something much different for me than it does for Giegerich. Giegerich's
endurance has a stoic quality to it. It comes through, for example, in
remarks like these:

> A mind that has some ice in it…does not need to get hysterical
> or depressed over the insight that melting polar ice may have
> terrible, disastrous effects. For millennia, people in most parts of
> the world have lived with the firm belief that there would be an
> end of the world…What is so special about a coming doom?
> *Media in vita in morte sumus.* We all know that we will have to
> die. Is this a reason to make, *in advance*, a huge fuss and bother
> about it? Let's keep both feet on the ground.[30]

　　This is sober, measured prose, and yes in the midst of life we are
in death and we all do know that we are going to die. While I admire

this stoic attitude, it seems for two reasons slightly out of place in the context of the melting polar ice.

First, the melting polar ice in particular and the global climate crisis in general are not just about us, about our death, and for Giegerich to speak this way strikes me as an example of the narcissistic indifference of an ego mind that is species centric. Second, as I showed in the technology book, the invention of linear perspective occurs in tandem with a radical shift in our attitude toward death and its place in life.

At the entrance to the anatomy theater in Padua, which was one of the first such theatres in Europe, and where Andreas Vesalius did his work and wrote his text on anatomy in 1543, *De humani corporis fabrica libri septem,* the inscription above the entrance, which predates the work of Vesalius, still holds death and life together. It reads: *Mors ubi Gaudet Succurrere Vitae*, which could be translated as "Where death rejoices to be of help to life." But as van den Berg points out in his reflections on a woodcut in Vesalius's text that shows him holding a dissected arm, "Death is absent here. It has been banished. It is in exile."[31] One of my claims about one of the consequences of the invention of linear perspective is that death is pushed away from life, and one of the other examples I give is the relocation of cemeteries outside the city, which begins near the end of the sixteenth century. Already in that period an olfactory dislike of the smell of cemeteries has emerged. Indeed, the stench of death has not only become intolerable, it has also become dangerous. As Ivan Illich has noted in his reflections on the work of Phillip Aries, "The miasma emanating from graves was declared dangerous to the living."[32] For the spectator mind it is no longer easy to say *Media in vita in morte sumus*. The spectator mind with its eye upon the world has placed death outside of life.

There are legitimate differences between Giegerich and myself about the issue of origins and about how each of us reads the events of history in light of them. Giegerich, however, adopts a moral tone that judges that difference in favor of his perspective. It is a curious move, given the fact that he claims that my view is "a pure moralism."[33] This charge, moreover, is tied for him to the claim that my reading of the fifteenth century origins of our broken connection with nature is an ego-based one while his, as noted in his quote above, is a deep matter of the soul. Convinced of his point and dismissive of any evidence that does not square with his agenda, Giegerich's moral rectitude—what else should I call it when it views me a sinner and criminal?—is a moralism of the soul, and as such an expression of the worst of Jungianism becoming a church whose dogmas and creeds are held for safekeeping in the hands of its high priests. Is there any wonder there are so many schisms in the analytic movement, so many accusations of heresy.

As I noted above Giegerich and I differ on how we endure history, how we suffer it, bear it. Nowhere in the text on technology or elsewhere in my writings do I argue or even claim that these developments were a crime, much less a sin. On the contrary, I acknowledge them as moments of transformation, as changes in human life and the world, which, as my mentor J.H. van den Berg would say, do not happen because of us but also do not happen without us. My thinking about origins is about how do we endure what does not happen without us even as we are not the authors of what has happened. It is a question of enduring our awareness of what we have done with that moment, a question of making as conscious as possible how we have made use of that inheritance, and a question of making ourselves ready to respond to the enduring questions that linger as the unfinished business in those origins.

This is not an endurance of the icy mind. It is an endurance of the engaged mind, of the mind that as flesh is inextricably bound to the world. It is an endurance borne by that style of thinking by way of return where, to do a riff on Merleau-Ponty, we would say that our fleshy entanglements with the world found our reflections about it, but only insofar as our reflections find themselves founded in that way. In this regard, the beginnings to which one is summoned to return are transformed by the very act of returning. The origins to which one returns, then, are different from the origins that sent one forth in the beginning. My return from the melting polar ice to the origins of linear perspective, then, does not, as Giegerich claims, establish the former as the effect of the latter. To think by way of return is to think in the space of the tension of that difference between origins as beginnings and origins as unfinished business. At the end of his book, Sallis names that tension strife and he says, "One of the names that the tradition has given to the power of persisting in that strife is imagination."[34] The imaginative logic of the soul takes up origins for the sake of a new beginning.

Earlier I used Rilke's image of the man on the hill to portray the backward glance, to depict that moment of being attuned to the call of the past, to those questions that endure as unfinished business, to the appeal of the ancestors. Rilke offers another image, which this time depicts the other side of the Janus face, the side that is turned toward the future that summons us through the past, through the past remembered as a future imagined.

> Sometimes a man stands up during supper
> and walks outdoors, and keeps on walking,
> because of a church that stands somewhere in the East.
>
> And his children say blessings on him as if he were dead.
>
> And another man, who remains inside his own house,
> stays there, inside the dishes and in the glasses,
> so that his children have to go far out into the world,
> toward that same church, which he forgot.[35]

The melting polar ice is a summons to stand up, to leave the comfortable surrounds of the supper table, and to die to the familiar dishes and the glasses, to let dissolve familiar ways of thinking. It is a summons to do all that, which, of course can be refused. Shut tight the door, close the window, stay inside the safe confines of your house, and indeed make it into a church for your ways of thinking and being so that you may forget the church that stands in the East. And forgetting, sink into the barely noticed compulsive repetition of the same routines. Stay in them, stuck in time. Put the invitation aside; leave the summons to those who follow as their inheritance, their obligation.

TIME AS SYMPTOM

This is the other possibility of time as a gift of the possibility of possibility. It is the moment when the question, "to be or not to be," is indeed the question, the question that in fact presents itself in every moment, but especially in those moments that carry an archetypal charge, like the moment of loss, for example, when grief and sorrow can pull one into preserving what was lost, fixing the past, staying with those dishes and the glasses. This is when and how the past becomes a symptom. This is when and how we begin to suffer from our reminiscences, which was one of the earliest insights of Freud's psychology. We get stuck in time, life becomes a sea of frozen forms, a life that has lost its horizons of any future and is weighed down by what has not been mourned.

In his book, *Greeting the Angels*, Greg Mogenson deepens the Freudian view of mourning within an imaginal perspective. Within this context he writes:

> The psyche is created, in large measure, by the mourning process itself. The more precisely we imagine our losses, the more psychological we become. We are the afterworld in which our loved ones dwell even as they are the cultural atmosphere in which we have our being. It is not simply that they live on in us; we live on in them.

In Mogenson's hands mourning as an imaginal process is the work of soul; it is the work of soul making. Moreover not only are we as individuals made within our losses, culture itself is made within them. "The meaning of life is something we find through the mourning of life lost," he writes, and then he adds, "Indeed, the mourning of losses and the making of culture are synonymous activities."[36]

My book on technology and my article on the melting polar ice were and are an imaginal approach to history, which takes up the past from the perspective of what has been forgotten, left behind, lost, but, un-mourned, still lingers. As such, in the context of my book on technology, I attended to the melting polar ice as a symptom, and in the article I described the symptom "as a vocation to remember something that is too vital to forget but which has been forgotten because it is too painful to remember."[37] In this context my argument rested upon two claims.

First, I claimed that as a symptom the melting polar ice carries a sense of loss individually for some and collectively for many whose grief lives with us and within culture as feelings of anxiety, dread, fear, despair, etc., which in turn feed much of our individual and cultural expressions of denial. My point here was that we have an obligation to attend to those experiences of loss—individually and collectively—, to stay with those feeling responses to them, and to make our forms of denial as conscious as possible so that we might make ourselves ready psychologically to re-imagine those origins as a new beginning in place of repeating them. This approach was and is the polar opposite of how Giegerich misinterprets (deliberate?) my remarks about anxiety in the face of the melting polar ice. He says, for example, "The only way that Romanyshyn can imagine of dealing with this emotion, other than staying with it, is 'numb[ing] myself against this feeling,' 'going to sleep, benumbing myself...'"[38] In passages like this one Giegerich makes it appear that I am counseling this kind of response, when in fact what I wrote challenges it:

> To stay with the anxiety of the moment is to be responsible, able-to-respond, because I am listening. The ecological problem which it expresses is a psychological problem, and the *bridge* that joins them is this movement of the soul against forgetting, against going to sleep, against benumbing myself, against the comfortable illusion that I am separate from the world, that the "inside" does not really matter in the calculus of this danger, and that the "outside" is, after all, "inanimate" and, as such, subject only to the limits of our technological reason.[39]

I italicize the word bridge in the quote above to underscore my original point and to recall my reply to Giegerich about Merleau-Ponty's notion of the flesh. Flesh is the locus of emotions that arise not within one but between one and the other. A feeling response to events is the first site where events become experiences. A feeling response is the first plank in the bridge between soul and world, the vale of soul making. e.e. cummings makes the same point poetically:

> since feeling is first
> who pays any attention
> to the syntax of things
> will never wholly kiss you;...[40]

Flesh keeps us in touch with the world, close enough to it to be kissed by it, awed by it, made anxious by it. Flesh is where the world matters, where the other matters, where the fiction of an inside psychological space and an outside material space is naturally dissolved. Flesh is the phenomenological locus of the *unio naturalis* of psyche and nature and not, as Giegerich would have you believe about my work, "a belief," or "An idea or illusion...of the oneness with nature."[41]

Phenomenology's mantra is "back to the things themselves." The return to things, the way back to the world, is through the flesh. Merleau-Ponty's field of flesh is the site where we are penetrated by the world, impregnated by it. The artist Paul Klee speaks to this point:

> In a forest, I have felt many times over that it was not I who looked at the forest. Some days I felt that the trees were looking at me, were speaking to me…I was there, listening…I think that the painter must be penetrated by the universe and not want to penetrate it…I expect to be inwardly submerged, buried. Perhaps I paint to break out.

Between the flesh and the skin of the world there is a con-spiracy, a breathing together, which Merleau-Ponty notes in his comments on this passage from Klee. "There really is inspiration and expiration of Being, action and passion so slightly discernible that it becomes impossible to distinguish between what sees and what is seen, what paints and what is painted."[42] With the window of linear perspective the kiss was lost. Flesh is the way back. Recovery of the flesh that has been forgotten, ignored, repressed with the rise of the scientific-technological world view, one of whose origins I traced back to linear perspective, is the work that inspired both phenomenology and depth psychology at the end of the nineteenth century.

Giegerich's argument it seems to me lacks flesh, or at least ignores it, which allows him to preach a moralism of soul, a version of his own preachiness whose tone reminded me at times of the eighteenth-century Puritan preacher Jonathan Edwards and his sermon, "Sinners in the Hands of an Angry God." Through this image of the puritan preacher I glimpsed how I could be for him what he needs me to be, the repentance preacher, an up-to-date nineteenth century version of the revivalist preacher, an image, perhaps, of the film character Elmer Gantry. But to champion flesh as the locus of emotions that does make feeling first does not make me Elmer Gantry, clever huckster, snake oil salesman, revivalist con artist, criminal.

Giegerich prefers to attend first to the syntax of things, the ordered arrangement of experience, the logical life of the soul in place of the aesthetics of the flesh, which allows him to say with respect to my views, "Regardless of what will factually happen…[and] Whether all the chances he sees will come true in real life or not makes no difference psychologically." For Giegerich that all matters only to the ego. Over against that position of ego, for "the salvation of the soul…it is perfectly sufficient that the eco-psychological ideology of those chances is being entertained and promoted." And for soul that matters only "if [it] happens to be so inclined."[43]

Like Rilke's Angel, Giegerich's Soul seems utterly indifferent to our cries. "Who, if I cried, would hear me among the angelic/orders?" is the opening line of the First Elegy of the *Duino Elegies*. An elegy is a song of lament and praise, and the lament that begins the work turns to praise for who we are in the face of the indifferent Angel, praise for how we, between Angel and "the wakefully-warm beast," learn in the Ninth Elegy that this between place is our blessing. "Tell the world to the Angel…Tell him things…" Tell the tale of the melting polar ice. Like Rilke's wanderer who "doesn't bring from the mountain slope/a handful of earth to the valley, untellable earth, but only/ some word he has won, a pure word, the yellow and blue/gentian," we can bring from the fields of polar ice some words we have won. '*Here* is the time for the Tellable, *here* is its home."[44]

The second claim in my argument is that the melting polar ice as a symptom is a lingering presence in the present of the origins of linear perspective, and in this context I identified one aspect of those origins—the spectator mind—as an especially significant expression of those forgotten origins. Both an imaginal and a symptomatic view of history emphasize that the past with its unfinished business and unanswered questions pervades the present, but not as a series of events. Rather, the past that lingers in the present does so as an atmosphere, a kind of quantum cloud of soul, as it were, whose forgotten possibilities await our engagement. Mogenson expresses a similar point when he quotes these lines from Auden's poem, "In Memory of Sigmund Freud": "to us he is no more a person/now but a whole climate of opinion."[45] Leon Battista Alberti through his codification of the mathematical laws of linear perspective has become a climate of opinion, and who, at times I imagine, wonders at what we have made of his gift. Perhaps he even waits with Filippo Brunelleschi near the Florentine Baptistery where Brunelleschi's earlier experiment with linear perspective drawing led to Alberti's text. Perhaps they linger there together waiting our re-collection of what they achieved.

To leave the lingering past unattended, to be deaf to its appeals is to remain outside of and apart from one of the key aspects of the post-modern mind. Reflecting on the meaning of "post" in the phrase post-modern, Lyotard argues that "post" is not to be understood "in the sense of a 'period which follows' but rather as a "dynamism" which allows us to go further than modernity in order to retrieve it in a kind of 'twist' or 'loop,'"[46] two images that are reminiscent of my earlier discussion of phenomenology as thinking by way of a return to and re-collection of origins that transforms them. In this twisting, looping return, the postmodern is, according to Richard Kearney, "a testament to the fact that the end of modernity is…a symptom as it were of its own unconscious infancy which needs to be retrieved and reworked if we are not to be condemned to an obsessional fixation upon, and compulsive repetition of, the sense of its ending."[47] This twisting, looping thinking by way of return is a work of imagination, the imagination in the practice of what Hillman has described as the work of "seeing through" and which I have described at different times as a work against forgetting, as a work of de-literalizing, and as a work of cultivating a metaphoric sensibility. But in the age of the image, in the age of *The Despotic Eye and its Shadow*[48] the power of imagination seems to wither. Kearney's book makes this point in its title, *The Wake of the Imagination.* He writes, "One of the greatest paradoxes of contemporary culture is that at a time when the image reigns supreme the very notion of imagination seems under mounting threat."[49] The threat to imagination was also the starting point of my book on technology, which, as the background of my article, also figures in it. Moreover, it was the concern of the poet Rilke long before the age of the image had fully taken hold. In the Ninth Elegy, between the line that tells us "Here is the time for the Tellable…" and the line that tells us "Praise the world to the Angel…", Rilke tells us why we are to "Speak and proclaim." He says, "More than ever/the things we can live with are falling away, and their place/being oustingly taken up by an imageless act," by things, which, he explains in a letter, are "empty, indifferent things, pseudo-things, Dummy-Life."[50]

Failing in this work of imagination is failing to understand that the task of the post-modern imagination is "to envision the end of modernity as a possibility of rebeginning."[51] In this context, Lyotard, sounding very much like Jung in the passages quoted earlier, says, "The modern is all too easily snapped up by the future, by all its values of pro-motion, pro-gram, pro-gress...dominated by a very strong emphasis on willful activism."[52]

Giegerich accuses me of such willful activism in depicting my work as a high level expression of an eco-psycholgy that is rooted in a program of salvation and redemption. But that accusation, as I have argued, either misunderstands what I have said or misrepresents (deliberate?) it. It summarily dismisses the phenomenological imperative of thinking as a return to beginnings, beginning with listening to the appeals of the past. He dismisses as "superstition or mystification" my claim that the melting polar ice is a way in which the un-attended origins of linear perspective are speaking to us today. Indeed, throughout his article he continuously misunderstands or misinterprets (deliberate?) this work of return as an attempt to go "back behind the radical loss of *mater natura*...", of return as a jump back behind origins, a jump back that is the function of a moralism "to uphold the dream of paradise not totally lost...", when in fact the phenomenological return, the Lyotardian "loop" or "twist," is a return to the origins.[53] My writings on technology and my article on the ice, as well as the metabletic phenomenology of my mentor J.H. van den Berg, are not nostalgic longings for some lost pre-lapsarian world. After all I did write, "I am not arguing here that the pre-linear perspective world was a better world,"[54] but Giegerich makes it seem that I am creating a straw man here, which is a fantasy of his own creation.

In contexts like these I am forced to wonder what Giegerich means by phenomenology, but whatever his program is, he applies his interpretation to my understanding of phenomenology, which I laid out in some detail above, to dismiss it as "illicit speculation and wishful thinking."[55] But on these grounds, he would also have to dismiss Lyotard's claim that the post-modern "implies, in its very movement...a capacity to listen openly to what is hidden within the happenings of today."[56]

But are my remarks fair? Does Giegerich listen? He says he does, but let's listen to how he listens. Passing judgment once more that my position is all ego, he says, "On all accounts it is the very opposite of the stance of psychology: psychology as the careful listening to the soul's speaking to *itself*, about *itself*, and only for *its own* sake (*not* to us and about us or about the world and for our sake, our better.)"[57] Giegerich is very clever here because the contrast as he draws it leaves the impression that my position is some form of eco-activism that keeps in place and serves our own narcissism. But a fair reading of my article and my other writings on technology, including *Technology as Symptom and Dream*, as well as my remarks in this reply do not and would not support his misinterpretation (deliberate?) of my position. Like a fairytale or a myth, as Giegerich notes, dreams and symptoms are the soul speaking to itself, about itself, and even for its own sake. But it strikes me as rather odd, to say the least, that for Giegerich the speech of soul is not to us or about us or about the world. What then is the point? Who is listening?

Giegerich must be listening because he knows somehow that the soul, in his opinion, is what he says it is, even though at another place in his article he asks in a tone that is meant to suggest humility, "Who are we to claim that we know what is right or wrong for the soul?,"[58] implying again that I do. So, we need to ask here "Who is listening when Giegerich listens?"

Depth psychology legitimized dreams and symptoms as the speech of soul and as therapists and patients we listen to them. While it is true that there has been the very strong move to harness the dream in service to the ego, Jung's contribution was to return to the dream at the origins of analysis and reverse that relation. In Jung's psychology the ego is in service to the dream. Furthermore, this thinking by way of return has in Hillman's psychology liberated the dream from the confines of the therapy room and in so doing has appreciated that the dreaming soul is in part the soul of nature dreaming itself through us. This is exactly the position I have taken in all my work on technology, including the article on ice. In this regard, technology is from the soul's perspective not something we do. It is soul working itself out through us, making us agents in service to soul while we eavesdrop on the way soul is making itself through the world that includes us and within history. Psychologists are eavesdroppers listening in on soul matters, on how soul matters.

From his own words it does not appear that Giegerich would see himself in this way because for him soul does not matter in this fashion. He says, "What is it to a psychologist—to the extent that he is really the representative of the standpoint of soul—whether the world is getting worse or better?" For Giegerich it would be un-natural for the psychologist to concern himself or herself about this issue, because if soul "were a piece of nature, there would be no soul at all."[59] If this is not a variant of the Spectator Mind, an icy variant of it, I would then cede to Giegerich his points that in my practice of psychology I have committed a crime and a sin. But if it is a variant, then it would be fair to wonder if my reflections on the "soul on ice" got too close to Giegerich's icy soul, his "soul on ice."

Regardless of how the court of public opinion might judge this case, I would rest my case by saying that Giegerich's position strikes me not only as odd, peculiar, and indifferent, but also as elitist, privileged, and deaf to how the world including us is the vale of soul making as, for example, poems of poets illustrate and as symptoms and dreams—individual and collective—also demonstrate. Odd, peculiar, indifferent, elitist, privileged, distant, and disconnected: Do we have here a catalogue of why depth psychology too often seems irrelevant today and perhaps even dangerous in its disregard of the world? As Hillman has noted, a depth psychology that "declares the mineral, vegetable, and animal world beyond the human person to be impersonal and inanimate is not only inadequate. It is delusional."[60]

The depth psychologist has to come back into the world with soul in mind, not to become a social worker, an activist, a do-gooder. He or she has to come back as a witness of soul, one who stands up in defense of its appeals. Back in the world, this psychologist will meet the phenomenologist who has been waiting there and together they can engage in the work of re-collecting the past that lingers in the present as the *prima materia* to imagine another beginning. Not just phenomenology, but also Jungian psychology is a work of returning to beginnings, a work of anamnesis, a work against forgetting.

Greg Mogenson makes this point when he notes, "the quality of the future we bequeath to our children depends, in large measure, upon the manner in which we have dealt with our ancestral ghosts." Here is the back and forth movement between past and future and the recognition that in attending to the ancestors we also are tending to our descendants, making a future that carries them forward. In several places in his article Giegerich characterizes my work as a work of redemption. If that be so, then so be it, because to return to the past to re-collect the ancestors serves them as well. Attending to the ancestors who carry the unanswered questions that still linger, we make a place for the redemptive rites of mourning. Mogenson makes this point when concerning the ancestral ghosts he notes, "We must continue to sense their influence upon our lives and to live in a manner that will have a redemptive influence on their souls as well."[61] But Mogenson's imperative here would be sinful, because as Giegerich says with regard to his claim that my work is one of redemption, "…only if there is sin—here the sin of the Spectator Mind's 'dream' of an ideal spirituality, of power, of control, and dominant mastery over the forces of the natural world, of leaving the earth, etc.—will there be need for redemption."[62]

Thinking by way of return is to return to re-member, re-collect, and redeem what has been left behind on the side of the road, unheard and forgotten. The Spectator Mind and Victor Frankenstein's creature await their proper burial rituals, which is the work of psychotherapy with soul in mind. The melting polar ice is their common gravesite, where they linger symptomatically. To perform these rites is to engage in a cultural therapeutics, which unfreezes our imaginations as it liberates them. In the performance of these rites phenomenology and Jung's psychology converge toward a radical eco-psychology, an eco-psychology that is founded not in the ego mind but in the flesh. Andy Fisher makes this point quite eloquently. For him a radical *eco*-psychology is not an *ego*-psychology because it undoes the attachment of much of eco-psychology to "those philosophical dualities (inner/outer, human/nature, subjective/objective) that eco-psychology must overcome," to which I would add that also keeps the imperialism of the ego in place. Fisher's radical eco-psychology is also a clear and emotionally honest confession of radical eco-psychology as one founded in loss and one that "…through the process of recollection [helps] us to find the strength and creativity to move forward."[63]

WOLFGANG GIEGERICH AS WARRIOR:
THE ISSUE OF A METAPHORIC SENSIBILITY

Near the very end of his article Giegerich critiques my argument regarding the negative gnosis of a metaphoric sensibility. It is important to reply to that critique because in spite of its placement in his article, it is a source of his claim that my reflections on the ice are ideological expressions of a dogmatic or cynical mind that are un-psychological. It is this move that allows Giegerich to claim that my work is not a psychology of soul, but an eco-psychology that in turn distorts my reading of the invention and historical unfolding of linear perspective. Imprisoned within this source—what a criminal deserves?—Giegerich's critique of my work already assumes that any psychological move that does not begin within his position regarding the soul's logical life as a work of negation is and has to be *ipso facto* at least a mistake, or in my case, a sin and a crime.

For Giegerich my claim that the negative gnosis of a metaphoric sensibility is "a linguistic alchemy, which always dissolves the certitude of 'is' in the possibilities of the 'is not' and thus holds the tension between the dogmatic arrogance of the fixed mind and the cynical despair of the postmodern mind" is a trick. My position, it seems, is for him a kind of recipe or formula whose ideal is to add "a little bit of this and a little bit of the opposite, of the 'is' and 'is not…'" It is the ruse of "switching back and forth between two disconnected rigid stances, playing the one against the other, and thereby creating the impression of flexibility and life." Giving only the impression of flexibility, the "undulating" movement of a metaphoric sensibility actually preserves the dogmatic character of an "I" that "does not make either position fully its own so as to be fatefully exposed to the negation coming from its own internal opposite." This "I" with its commitment to a metaphoric sensibility and its negative gnosis "stays aloof, uncommitted, [and] holds its place vis-à-vis the two positions as a separate third party, which is thus free to alternate at will between them, untouched." Not stiff enough as it were to stand up and take a stand, this "I only switches back and forth, [and] preserves the 'is' and the 'is not' in their initial form, locking them firmly in undialectical opposition, and preventing their possible clash and thus the resolution of their contradiction." Continuing, Giegerich says, "The dogmatism of the fixed mind here is just as much as the postmodern cynical mind over there, preserved intact—indeed, both are (alternatingly) being subscribed to by the ego, but they are also kept abstract, I-less: not real minds at all but abstract theoretical positions." Consequently, "Since the I does not take a stand, stake itself, and own up to its dogmatism (or, conversely, to its cynicism) as its own stance, it must not and cannot die as dogmatic I (or as cynical I, respectively) and thereby become a truly psychological I." And regarding this psychological I, Giegerich says it is an I that "is not dogmatic (it does, for example, not indulge in ideologies like that of the *unus mundus*) and it is not cynical (it does not switch between positions without committing itself).” On the contrary, this I “is committed, determined.” Committed, determined, this I, he concludes, 'knows that the position that it takes with determination to be '*only* that!': this one mortal I's personal view today.”[64]

Regarding the strange and questionable description of the *unus mundus* as an ideology, and regarding the description of the postmodern mind as cynical, which I do say in my article, I want to note about the former that such a description is completely dismissive of a key part of Jung's work, and note about the latter that that description is one perspective on the postmodern mind, as my earlier comments on Lyotard indicate. Furthermore, in anticipation of my reply to Giegerich's critique, I would suggest that Giegerich's comment might serve as an example of the determined stance that intends to establish a clash, and that my comment about perspective might serve as an example of that metaphoric sensibility that would value in each perspective the tension of “is” /“is not” and thereby dissolve the temptation in either position to close itself off from the other.

The is/is not tension of a metaphor is a trick. But that trick is not what Giegerich claims it is. On the contrary, its trick is to awaken one to the fact that one has forgotten that the metaphors one lives by individually and culturally are perspectives, which having been forgotten are lived out as unconscious projections. Its trick lies in the way it disturbs one's dogmatic slumber within which one lives one's perspectives as if they were fixed facts about the ways things are. Its trick is that it changes a mind that has a literal sensibility to one that has a metaphorical sensibility. Its trick is that it shifts one from the natural attitude to a psychological attitude.

In this context, awakening to one's projections is not a process of withdrawing them from the outside to the inside, which is a remnant of the Cartesian perspective that still lingers as a fact and idea in much of psychology whose consequence splits the fleshy bond of psyche and world. On the contrary, from the perspective of a metaphoric sensibility the withdrawal of projections is a transformation of mind. Within a metaphoric sensibility one's ideas, beliefs, attitudes, views, etc. are reflected back to one as perspectives, and in that reflection one is mirrored back to oneself as who that figure is who holds those views. The trick of metaphor, then, is that it forces one to take responsibility for the fact that the metaphors we live by say as much about us who live by them as they say about those who are the object and often the victim of our metaphors. Much of mainstream psychology would illustrate this point. Its DSM manual, for example, is not just a statement of objective clinical facts; it is also a perspective that carries unacknowledged assumptions and prejudices of a capitalistic culture. Cultivating a metaphoric sensibility is, then, an ethical move that recognizes that in the face of the other one might find an image of oneself. It is an ethics rooted in the necessity for and obligation to dialogue with the other. That transformation is the trick!

The other is "without" and "within," "without" as the existential other who is different from me and "within" as the complex other who shadows me. That there is always a chiasm between the other "within" and the other "without" is the ground for what Merleau-Ponty describes as "syncretic sociability," which in turn is the existential ground for the possibility of projection.[65] The other in both guises is lodged within the 'is not' pole of the metaphor as the one who questions, challenges, and might even negate one's perspective. Being responsive to being addressed by this challenge, a metaphoric sensibility invites one to be responsive to the differences between the other 'within' and the other 'without.'

That this work is difficult was clearly stated by Jung nearly 100 hundred years ago:

> The present day shows with appalling clarity how little able people are to let the other man's argument count, although this capacity is a fundamental and indispensable condition for any human community. Everyone who proposes to come to terms with himself must reckon with this basic problem. For, to the degree that he does not admit the validity of the other person, he denies the 'other' within himself the right to exist—and vice versa. The capacity for inner dialogue is the touchstone for outer objectivity.[66]

Those words appear in his essay, *The Transcendent Function*, where Jung describes the emergence of a third product that is influenced by both conscious and unconscious. That third is a symbol, which, Jung notes is to be taken seriously but not literally. Illustrating this process, Jung uses the example of transference in psychotherapy. The patient who projects onto the therapist his need for help and protection *is* the child who, however, *is not* the child. Jung calls this expression metaphorical, which is obviously the case, since the patient is not in fact a child and yet *behaves* in such a way that the analyst is not just an idea he has of the analyst as protector and helper.

A metaphorical sensibility lets the other person's argument count. In fact it insists on it. In doing so, it cultivates a psychological attitude that is necessary within that psychological landscape of the transcendent function where the image in the metaphor is a symbol to be taken seriously but not literally. Moreover, just as within that landscape the third product is influenced by both conscious and unconscious but is made neither by the one nor the other, the image in a metaphor is influenced by the one who makes the metaphor and the other framed by it, but is made neither by the one nor the other. The image in the metaphor is made in the dialogue between the two, as the poet and literary critic Howard Nemerov illustrates. He says, for example, he is made quite certain that the bird that he sees in his garden is a purple finch through the metaphor, "a purple finch is a sparrow dipped in raspberry juice!" This is not quite canny, he says, because he has never dipped a sparrow in raspberry juice, and yet, he adds, through the image in the metaphor he in his study and the bird in the garden are in agreement.[67]

The metaphor, Nemerov insists, is a third that is neither a thing nor a thought. It is way of seeing that, uncanny as it might seem to be, nevertheless opens up the world. Or to say this another way, the image in the metaphor is neither a fact to be empirically checked in the garden nor an idea in Nemerov's mind. Should he in some fit of empirical frenzy rush into his garden and grab the bird his hands would not drip with juice. And should he close his eyes before reading the metaphorical description in a field guide in an attempt to know what the bird is by plumbing the interior of his mind, he would not so readily succeed. The image in the metaphor is what draws him into the world and that is quite uncanny for a mind that is not so at home in the landscape of the transcendent function, with the reality of the symbol, in the environs of the image, in the precincts of soul.

In posing the question, "Who is Wolfgang Giegerich?," I have been attempting to move his critique and my reply to that third place where the images in my responses to the question—Wolfgang Giegerich, for example, as policeman, judge, puritan preacher, warrior—place my argument within a metaphoric frame. Given what I have been saying about a metaphoric sensibility, this way of framing my reply has had two intentions. One is to display my perspectives/complexes, and the other is to reframe his images of me—repentance preacher, revivalist, sinner, criminal—as his perspectives/complexes. Of course, as with all metaphors the test of their validity is the test over time of their engagement with the world. Are my perspectives of Giegerich canny? I would not, of course, *cum ira et studio* find handcuffs in his pockets, or a dagger under his cloak? Are his of me canny? The reply to these questions cannot be decided between us. The best each of us can hope for is that each lets the other's argument count. In the end, therefore, my article, his critique, and my reply are now in the court of public opinion where those who write, and think, and practice within a Jungian tradition will decide.

The neither/nor logic of metaphor is not an additive formula. A metaphoric sensibility is not a little bit of "is" added to a little bit of "is not" as Giegerich claims. Its logic is not one of both/and. On the contrary, the neither/nor logic of metaphor is the locus of its negative gnosis, the pivotal point where the alchemy of metaphor dissolves what has become fixed, coagulated, and thereby opens itself up to another turn in that alchemical tension of *solutio/coagulatio*.

But how does one take a stand in this place? How does one act from within a logic of neither/nor? How does one live a life of soul without losing a world?

Giegerich raises this question of how one takes a stand in his critique of a metaphoric sensibility. His critique, as noted above, is that it "preserves the 'is' and the 'is not' in their initial form, locking them firmly in undialectical opposition, and preventing their possible clash and thus the resolution of their contradiction." But the "'is/is not" logic of a metaphor is neither a contradiction nor an opposition. This logic is, as I tried to show above, an alchemical formula. It is a logic that simultaneously holds the tension between an affirmation and one that negates that affirmation. Giegerich's critique rests upon his perspective on metaphor that differs from mine. We are not, then, arguing over facts here. We are arguing about our perspectives on soul and from that place how each of us understands what it means to take a stand with soul in mind.

Giegerich's stand is one that is about a clash. It is a stand, he says, that a real mind takes. His language is tough minded, the stance perhaps of a warrior. It is heroic and perhaps rigid, inflexible and dogmatic, the very features he ascribes to the stance of a metaphoric sensibility. It is resolute and perhaps even revolutionary in its determination to overturn the old order—the Jungian world, perhaps like Luther did to the Catholic world order when he nailed his 95 theses to the door of All Saints' Church in Wittenburg? And it is a stance that expects a dying so that one can become a truly psychological I.

But who is that psychological I, and where does it hang out? Giegerich offers this description in one of his writings:

> Psychology, despite being committed to the soul of whatever is, is nevertheless, or precisely because of this, aware of having only modest assumptions and modest relevance and of on principle belonging only in an out-of-the-way corner of modern life as a whole.[68]

A metaphoric sensibility looks for another way, a stance that is guided by the image, a stance rooted in humility in the face of the third, a stance that by its very nature is and must be open to the embodied process of dialogue. It is a stance that is inclined toward a perspective, a stance that leans in with an ear open and receptive to what one has leaned away from. It is a stance that, for example, could feel at home with thirteen ways of looking at a blackbird to riff on the title of a poem by Wallace Stevens, a poem in which each stanza in the context of those that have preceded it and those that follow holds the tension of is/is not. It is a stance also at home "With the half colors of quarter-things," with those things that being and not being what they are "would never be quite expressed/ Where you yourself were not quite yourself/And did not want nor have to be," lines from another poem by Stevens, where he says,

> The motive for metaphor, shrinking from
> The weight of primary noon,
> The ABC of being,
>
> The ruddy temper, the hammer
> Of red and blue, the hard sound—
> Steel against intimation—the sharp flash,
> The vital, arrogant, fatal, dominant X[69]

The stance of a metaphoric sensibility is taken not on that X, the X that marks the spot, the spot where in Giegerich's language the psychological I would stake itself, would take its stand in anticipation of the clash. It is a stance in the world with others and not in some out-of-the-way corner cocooned in some abstract Hegelian dialectical process. It is a stance that invites life and encourages engagement with the world, knowing how imperfect that engagement will be and yet resolved to do so. It is a stance that in this instance takes its stand on the melting polar ice.

ANTARCTICA:
INNER JOURNEYS IN THE OUTER WORLD

The stance that I took on the melting polar ice in my article began more than thirty years ago with a dream that took me north to the Arctic, a dream that has found a sense of its vocation in a journey I took south to Antarctic in November, 2009. That landscape of ice is so much more than Giegerich's idea of ice as "cold, hard, crystal clear, sharp edged."[70] Those are facts and they are correct, but the experience, the felt experience, the fleshy experience is one of deep silence and slowness in that cold place, of strangeness and simplicity in its crystal clarity, of stillness and solitude in its hard nearly timeless forms, and of sorrow and serenity in those sharp-edged corners now being smoothed and softened in their melting. Something of us awakens in that place, in that crystal cathedral. In that place the straight lines of our linear lives dissolve, including those lines that separate us from nature. In that crystal cathedral there were moments when for a moment I did not know if I was dreaming or was a dream of the ice.

If I tell you that that journey has changed my life, it is not an exaggeration. *Antarctica:Inner Journeys in the Outer World* is a DVD that I have made in collaboration with a gifted composer, which in its own way of setting images to music is also my reply to Giegerich.[71] It is deliberately not a conceptual, logical work, but a work of images and music and words that flow from them. It is in this respect a work that is quite simple and quite deliberate in its intention to evoke the feeling function first, which as I have tried to argue in my reply, is the first condition for psychological change. As I wrote in the book on technology regarding the threat of nuclear war, "We need to mourn now, in the present, the loss of all that faces us, that is near to us, that matters to us. We need to develop the capacity to feel the sorrow of the trees, the lament of the oceans, the sadness of the stars, if we are to survive."[72] We need to do so because, as my research on the invention and subsequent unfolding of linear perspective indicated, that invention, which became a cultural convention, a habit of mind, espoused a new ideal of knowledge according to which the further we remove ourselves from the world the better we can know it. Giegerich's "out-of-the-way" corner as a place for a Jungian psychologist seems another variant of that ideal.

To end my reply I offer the final image from that DVD.

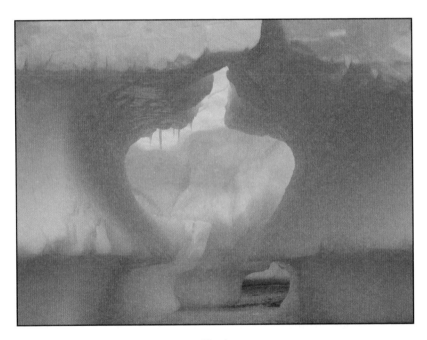

Fig. 1

NOTES

1. Gretel Ehrlich, *The Future of Ice* (New York: Pantheon, 2004).

2. Wolfgang Giegerich, "The Psychologist as Repentance Preacher and Revivalist: Robert Romanyshyn on the Melting of the Polar Ice," *Spring: A Journal of Archetype and Culture,* Vol. 82 (fall 2009), pp. 195, 197.

3. Robert Romanyshyn, *Psychological Life: From Science to Metaphor* (Austin: University of Texas Press, 1982). This book was reprinted with new material as *Mirror and Metaphor: Images and Stories of Psychological Life* (Pittsburgh: Trivium Publications, 2001).

4. Giegerich, "Psychologist as Repentance Preacher," p. 194.

5. *Ibid.*, pp. 194-95.

6. *Ibid.*, p. 195.

7. *Ibid.*, p. 195, his italics.

8. *Ibid.*, p. 197, his italics.

9. Robert Romanyshyn, "The Melting of the Polar Ice: Revisiting *Technology as Symptom and Dream,*" *Spring: A Journal of Archetype and Culture,* Vol.80 (Fall 2008), p. 113.

10. Robert Romanyshyn, *The Wounded Researcher: Research with Soul in Mind* (New Orleans: Spring Journal Books, 2007), p. 330.

11. Giegerich, "Psychologist as Repentance Preacher," p. 196.

12. *Ibid.*, p. 217.

13. *Ibid.*, p. 197.

14. Maurice Merleau-Ponty, *The Visible and the Invisible*, ed. Claude Lefort (Evanston: Northwestern University Press, 1968), pp. liv, lv.

15. "Eye and Mind," Maurice Merleau-Ponty, *The Primacy of Perception,* ed. James M. Edie (Evanston: Northwestern University Press, 1964), p. 164.

16. Robert Romanyshyn, *Technology as Symptom and Dream* (London, New York: Routledge, 1989); "Complex Knowing: Toward a Psychological Hermeneutics," *The Humanistic Psychologist,* 19 (1), Spring 1991, pp. 10-29; "Psychotherapy as Grief Work: Ghosts and the Gestures of Compassion," *Ways of the Heart: Essays toward an Imaginal Psychology* (Pittsburgh: Trivium Publications, 2002), pp. 50-62; *The Wounded Researcher*; "The Body in Psychotherapy: Contributions of Merleau-Ponty," *Body, Mind and Healing After Jung,* ed. Raya Jones (Routledge: London, 2010), pp. 41-61.

17. Robert Romanyshyn, *The Soul in Grief: Love, Death and Transformation* (Berkeley: North Atlantic Press, 1999).

18. Greg Mogenson, 'The Afterlife of the Image," *Spring: A Journal of Archetype and Culture*, Vol. 71, p. 110 n. 31.

19. Giegerich, "Psychologist as Repentance Preacher," p. 196, his italics.

20. Rainer Maria Rilke, *Duino Elegies*, trans. J.B. Leishman and Stephen Spender (New York: W. W. Norton, 1939), pp. 71, 75.

21. C.G. Jung, *Memories, Dreams, Reflections* (New York: Vintage Books, 1965), pp. 235-36, 236-37.

22. John Sallis, *Phenomenology and The Return to Beginnings* (Pittsburgh: Duquesne University Press, 1973).

23. Maurice Merleau-Ponty, "The Philosopher and his Shadow," trans. Richard C. McCleary, *Signs* (Evanston: Northwestern University Press, 1964), pp. 159-181; "Eye and Mind," pp. 159-190.

24. Robert Romanyshyn, "Thinking in the Space Between: Phenomenology and Archetypal Psychology," ed. Stanton Marlan *Archetypal Psychologies: Reflections in Honor of James Hillman* (New Orleans: Spring Journal Books, 2008).

25. Giegerich, "Psychologist as Repentance Preacher," p. 201.

26. As quoted in Romanyshyn, *Technology as Symptom and Dream*, p. 33.

27. *Ibid.*, pp. 117, 116.

28. Giegerich, "Psychologist as Repentance Preacher," p. 203.

29. *Ibid.*, p. 204.

30. *Ibid.*, p. 197, his italics.

31. As quoted in Romanyshyn, *Technology as Symptom and Dream*, p. 127.

32. *Ibid.*, p. 126.

33. Giegerich, "Psychologist as Repentance Preacher," p. 200.

34. Sallis, *Phenomenology*, p. 116.

35. Rainer Maria Rilke, *Selected Poems of Rainer Maria Rilke*, trans. Robert Bly (New York: Harper & Row, 1981), p. 49.

36. Greg Mogenson, *Greeting the Angels: An Imaginal View of the Mourning Process* (Amityville, New York: Baywood, 1992), pp. xi-xii, xv.

37. Romanyshyn, "The Melting of the Polar Ice," p. 84.

38. Giegerich, "Psychologist as Repentance Preacher," p. 195.

39. Romanyshyn, "The Melting of the Polar Ice," p. 80.

40. e.e.cummings, *100 Selected Poems* (New York: Grove Press, 1959), p. 35.

41. Giegerich, "Psychologist as Repentance Preacher," p. 219.

42. Merleau-Ponty, *The Primacy of Perception,* p. 167.

43. Giegerich, "Psychologist as Repentance Preacher," p. 219, his italics.

44. *Duino Elegies,* p. 21, 69, 75, his italics.

45. Mogenson, *Greeting the Angels,* p. xiii.

46. J.F. Lyotard, *Le Postmoderne* (Paris: Galilee, 1986), pp. 52-54.

47. Richard Kearney, *The Wake of Imagination* (Minneapolis: University of Minnesota Press, 1988), p. 27.

48. Robert Romanyshyn, "The Despotic Eye and Its Shadow," ed. David Michael Levin, *Modernity and the Hegemony of Vision* (Berkeley: University of California Press, 1993), pp. 339-360.

49. Kearney, *Wake of Imagination,* p. 3.

50. *Duino Elegies,* pp. 75, 129.

51. Kearney, *Wake of Imagination,* p. 27.

52. Lyotard, *Le Postmoderne.*

53. Giegerich, "Psychologist as Repentance Preacher," pp. 208, 209.

54. Romanyshyn, "The Melting of the Polar Ice," p. 93.

55.Giegerich, "Psychologist as Repentance Preacher," p. 209.

56. Lyotard, *Le Postmoderne.*

57. Giegerich, "Psychologist as Repentance Preacher," p. 212, his italics.

58. *Ibid.,* p. 205.

59. *Ibid.,* pp. 210, 208.

60. James Hillman, *Anima: Anatomy of a Personified Notion* (Dallas: Spring publications, 1985), p. 108.

61. Mogenson, *Greeting the Angels,* p. xv.

62. Giegerich, "Psychologist as Repentance Preacher," p. 209.

63. Andy Fisher, *Radical Ecopsychology: Psychology in the Service of Life* (Albany: State University of New York Press, 2002), p. xvi, 210, n. 78.

64. Giegerich, "Psychologist as Repentance Preacher," pp. 218-19, his italics.

65. Regarding this notion of syncretic sociability see Romanyshyn, *Mirror and Metaphor,* p. 78. For a discussion of projection in the context

of phenomenology see Romanyshyn, "Unconsciousness as a Lateral Depth: Perception and the Two Moments of Reflection," ed. Hugh J. Silverman, John Sallis, Thomas M. Seebohm *Continental Philosophy in America* (Pittsburgh: Duquesne University Press, 1983), pp. 227-244.

66. C. G. Jung, "The Transcendent Function," *The Structure and Dynamics of the Psyche, CW* 8 (Princeton: Princeton University Press, 1916/1960), § 187.

67. For a thorough discussion of this example see *Mirror and Metaphor,* pp. 173-74.

68. Wolfgang Giegerich, "'The Unassimilable Remnant'—What is at Stake? A Dispute with Stanton Marlan," *Archetypal Psychologies,* p. 220.

69. The lines about the blackbird are from "Thirteen Ways of Looking at a Blackbird," while the lines about the dominant X are from "The Motive for Metaphor." For a thorough discussion of both poems see Romanyshyn, *The Wounded Researcher,* pp. 337-39, and pp. 314-16.

70. Giegerich, "Psychologist as Repentance Preacher," p. 197.

71. This DVD, *Antarctica: Inner Journeys in the Outer World,* has 86 images set to music by Michael Mollura, who wrote the film score for *Climate Refugees*, a documentary that has been shown at the Sundance film festival, and at film festivals in Santa Barbara and Los Angeles. It also has a commentary about the power of the Psychoid Archetype to bring us into a healing relation with the natural world. The images taken of the Antarctic landscape restore the broken aesthetic connection between the flesh of the human body and the flesh of the world. As it reveals the awe-ful Antarctic beauty of stillness and silence, serenity, and solitude, it taps into the feeling function as our natal bond to the world. The making of the DVD, which began more than thirty years ago with a dream, also exemplifies that while we might forget our dreams they do not forget us. The DVD is now available for purchase. Contact rdromanyshyn@gmail.com.

72. *Technology as Symptom and Dream,* p. 232 n. 10, p. 38.

Robert Romanyshyn and Wolfgang Giegerich: Poles Apart

Susan Rowland

The Combatants

I n *Spring* 82 (2009), Wolfgang Giegerich writes a long criticism of Robert Romanyshyn's article, "The Melting of the Polar Ice: Revisiting *Technology as Symptom and Dream*," published in *Spring* 80 (2008).[1] In it he disputes Romanyshyn's foundational premises. Perhaps most striking in Giegerich's approach is his profound need to distance himself from Romanyshyn's project. Such a requirement is encapsulated in his title, "The Psychologist as Repentance Preacher and Revivalist: Robert Romanyshyn on the Melting of the Polar Ice."[2] As Giegerich repeats abundantly, he believes that Romanyshyn's writing has strayed outside "psychology proper" (used several times) and is floundering illegitimately in the wilder fringes of theology, unsupported by institutions or established epistemologies (Preacher and Revivalist).

Susan Rowland, Ph.D., a Professor of Literature and Jungian Studies, is author of several books on Jung, theory, gender, and the arts, including *C. G. Jung in the Humanities* (Spring Journal Books, 2010).

My Stance

I do not agree with Giegerich's taking to task of Romanyshyn on two levels. In the first place, while I recognize and honor Giegerich's fundamental attitude to knowledge, I do not consider it sufficient. Instead, I believe that Romanyshyn's equally historically and philosophically founded epistemology is more needed now, at least in part because it has been dangerously repressed in the past. Secondly, there are problems with the way that Giegerich has structured his criticism, which speak to my particular expertise as a literary scholar. Therefore I plan to sketch out some of the divide between these two psychologists before focusing more closely on what I can bring to the debate: the literary detective.

A Divide in Knowledge

Giegerich begins with divisions. Knowledge must be "properly" divided up and boundaries respected. In particular, he labels Romanyshyn's work "eco-psychology," while admitting that is not how Romanyshyn himself describes it in his polar ice article. Rather, Romanyshyn writes eloquently of his approach as phenomenology, research that he has substantiated and pioneered for many years. Unfortunately, to Giegerich, this work is a pollution problem. Ecopsychology is "incompatible with what I would consider psychology proper."[3]

There is a dualism in Giegerich's thinking that I have critiqued before for its pervasive monotheism.[4] There I pointed out that when Giegerich located the decisive evolution of consciousness in the male prehistoric hunter thrusting his spear, there was an-other form present.

> In the spear the male has his self (it was therefore not in himself!). Likewise the blood shed in the hunt was not merely the biological juice of life. Rather, the sacrificial animal's blood was collected by the women in a basket (in which they had their selves)...[5]

According to Giegerich's argument, the "women's basket" offers an-other structuring of consciousness that gets forgotten in the relentless logic inhabiting the modern soul. Similarly here, Giegerich starts his attack on Romanyshyn by evoking "two" kinds of thinking, while actually striving to prove that there is only "one" psychology, his own. Of course a rhetorical strategy of apparently ceding some ground to the opponent and then chipping away at it has a long history; Giegerich dignifies his methods under the term dialectics. What he does not address with any clarity is the question of the challenge to his own metaphysics.

It is easy to charge an-other with inaccuracies if the two approaches consist of incompatible worldviews. Dialectics is itself a form of idealism for it is more the product of a desire for a monotheistic culture than of rigorous logic. Deeply heir to the Newtonian perspective that believes in atomizing, dividing up knowledge as small as it can go in order to pursue it to its logical conclusion, Giegerich is profoundly asserting that "nature" has nothing to do with the soul.

> If it were not "un-natural," if it were itself a piece of nature, there would not be soul at all.[6]

Later on the passion for division reaches the polar ice itself. Melting ice is "empirical fact," which is not the same as "truth."[7] Romanyshyn's "error" is to bury the soul in a nature who is not the "divine Mother Nature of old, but the modern physical reality."[8] What has been achieved is merely "new age kitsch." Here is matter intrinsic to Giegerich's work, now in acid form: that the modern psyche has no access to past styles of consciousness. It is one of the many ways in which Giegerich's psychology parts from Jung's, as the latter believed that psyche and culture preserved forms of pastness that were important to present consciousness. Romanyshyn's work is heir to Jung's in this and much else.

To me there are real problems, not in Giegerich's modernism per se, but in his adherence to it as an exclusive reading of reality. For a start, it upholds boundaries of self and world, inside and outside, technology and science, as wholly rational modern enterprises. Such exclusive fidelity negates valuing other cultures that may have very different divisions. What Jung intuited, and so inscribed in his psyche as Eros and Logos qualities of consciousness, was that there are more significant modes of knowing than those espoused by Enlightenment reason. Romanyshyn's "anxiety" is first placed by Giegerich as "one kind of thinking," then dismissed. Yet emotion, particularly when it is more accurately described in Jung's terms as "feeling" or "valuing" can be a source of legitimate knowledge in Eros. Is this right because Jung says so?

No, Jung is not the only justification for treating "feeling" as a path to the real. Even from within our mainstream science we find that biology tells us that brain cells are not exclusively to be found in the skull, bringing an embodied and emotionally affected mode of "thinking." Nor does evolution claim a rational basis for our emotions in teaching us to make successful choices. There are a number of frameworks (some within rational division of knowledge themselves) beyond Jung and non-Western epistemologies that value emotion, affect, feeling, and connection as originating principles.

My basic quarrel with Giegerich's dualism is that it is really monotheism, so that it takes no account of its real "other," the animistic and connected mythical scheme of reading the real. What Jung more than intuited, so that it formed the bedrock of his archetypal schema, was that modernity inherited not a dialectic, but a dialogic between (patriarchal) monotheism, or the desire for one true path that only recognizes its other as "error," and an animistic legacy of great antiquity.

Jung's monotheistic "self," always in tension with the inherent multiplicity of archetypes, is one structure this ancient mythical dialogue takes in his work. The apparently neat duality between Eros and Logos is another. Here we might notice Logos as spirit and discrimination and separateness of ego and soul is entirely to be found vigorously re-worked in Giegerich's psychology of "soul" alone, severed from body, nature, emotion, and connection. Yet Jung added *and taught us to value* Eros as body, connectedness, feeling, and emotion. The path to "truth" cannot be restricted to one modern logic.

If Jung was serious about valuing a form of consciousness oriented to body and connectivity, then he, at least, re-joins the evolutionary sciences, which regard humans as an-other animal species. Thus Jung speculated that animals might possess archetypes similar to, or the same as, humans. Moreover, regarding the body as a nourishing basis for consciousness has to take account of the body as an eating, breathing creature. We have a consciousness that is eco-centered where we are knowing *because* we are part of nature. These structures of consciousness are multiple, multicultural, ecopsychological, and rooted in the psychoid mind/body union.

Here, most of all, are the liminal and the Gothic, those challenges to borders and categories that Giegerich admits are artificial. However, what the occluded animistic pole of modernity asserts is the necessity of the dialogical approach to texts of worlds as well as that of *the* world. Dialogics means that propositions are always constructed through dialogue with an-other in which no absolute conclusion can be reached. Knowledge has to be envisioned as a web rather than a purifying logic of truth. Put another way, a map of reality that consists of strict categories presupposes a chaos it replaces. That is the picture that Giegerich paints of his position. But suppose that chaos is rather *produced* by the rigid demarcations, and the "other" to modernity's rationality is a web of interconnectivity? From the point of view of Logos, Eros may look terrifyingly chaotic. That does not mean that we should only look out of "his" eyes. Such a gendered argument brings me to the literary detective.

SHERLOCK HOLMES & M. DUPIN AND RATIONAL, DISEMBODIED KNOWLEDGE

What bothers me in the method of Giegerich's criticism is its "animus" and its use of the metaphor of the literary detective. "Animus" is here an ambiguous term. In popular parlance, it signifies a motivated aggression, which I find in his piece, particularly in his remark I quoted earlier about "kitsch." It undermines Giegerich's own case because he has called for "icy" detachment when it comes to melting ice, and for pure, logical categories of argument. Yet "animus" is also a Jungian word used to signify the unconscious masculinity of women.

However, this ambiguity is trickier and more imaginatively fertile than it first seems. It is indeed the essence of my entire thesis here that categories that prove *not* firmly divided off from each other are also meaningful. Jung has too much animus in his animus! When he writes of a woman's animus, it is to indict a frightful propensity in women to "false logic:"

> The anima has an erotic, emotional character, the animus a rationalizing one. Hence most of what men say about feminine eroticism, and particularly about the emotional life of women, is derived from their own anima projections and distorted accordingly. On the other hand, the astonishing assumptions

and fantasies that women make about men come from the activity
of the animus, who produces an inexhaustible supply of illogical
arguments and false explanations.[9]

Of this quotation I have pointed out many times how Jung
undercuts himself in saying that men can never be objective about
women and then so comprehensively proving it! What is so delightfully
impossible here is to decide whether or not the author intended this
"slip" into animated language or not? Is Jung giving us his animus
against the animus as an example and warning, or has his ego truly
lost control? I suggest that our inability to logically deduce the status
of the animated sentence itself makes this piece of writing a valuable
source of knowledge. Not all epistemologies have to be based upon
strict division, especially when it comes to gender.

So I am speculating here that Giegerich's animus (aggression) is
not wholly divisible from "animus," an unconscious principle associated
with masculinity and Logos thinking. Which brings us to the detective.

Giegerich asserts a major historical break in consciousness in the
early nineteenth century, and notes the subsequent rise of related
cultural movements, the literary detective among them.[10] He then
accuses Romanyshyn of writing a sloppy detective story. Beginning with
the corpse in the melting ice, Romanyshyn slips into a "whodunit,"
yet fails to properly occupy the role of the rational mind of the true
detective. Rather, Romanyshyn falls into the character of the bumbling
policeman who arrests all the usual suspects rather than carefully
scrutinizing the clues that Giegerich himself, taking the detective role,
successfully secures. Hence, the true detective of the crimes against
modernity is Giegerich, not Romanyshyn.

This, in essence, is the structure of Giegerich's detective fiction
metaphor. One immediate consequence is to note that this is
supremely narrative. For an adherent of dividing off "empirical facts"
from "truth," Giegerich is suspiciously dependent upon a narrative
form—and moreover one dedicated to the conversion of facts into
truth as "clues." Secondly, I dispute Giegerich's portrayal of the true
detective as one who prioritizes logic and rationality above all other
forms of making knowledge.

No literary detective is such a being. And one can go back to
Giegerich's own "origin story" of consciousness to see this. But before
we do, let's remember that those supposed icons of rational self-

consciousness, Sherlock Holmes and M. Dupin, were no such thing. Fuelled by cocaine, Holmes is a Gothic detective who, in his famous *The Hound of the Baskervilles* (1902),[11] most resembles his quarry, a spectral dog and a trickster.[10] We may remember M. Dupin in his study advising the police chief in Edgar Allan Poe's "The Purloined Letter,"[12] but his successful "solution" depended upon a long mediated thirst for revenge.

Returning to the prehistoric hunter with a spear, the alternative *connected* way of viewing his ascent into modern man is to recall his embodied existence in a community with at least one other cultural form, the basket. In fact, as Lewis Hyde shows in *Trickster Makes This World* (2007), it is more likely to be the trickster myth that enables consciousness to develop from hunting.[13] Trickster can overleap and not eradicate boundaries and categories. "He" is multiple, embodied, sexual, amoral, both genders, animal, human, and divine.

Crucially, as a figure bound up with hunting he enabled consciousness to escape the dualistic either/or of being hunter or hunted. Trickster was both and neither. He is credited in various mythologies for inventing the net, the *web* method of engaging with the environment. He exists in culture today in many forms, particularly in the arts. Today, trickster's most intense incarnation is in the genre of the literary detective.

For I am not alleging that the literary detective is simply a trickster. He is quite capable of being, at least for a time, a Giegerich-like adherent of rational detachment. Rather, the literary detective *needs to be able* to be a trickster, in addition to one other related embodied role that is similarly enmeshed in nature: the shaman. Literary detectives are tricksters when Dupin makes sure he is paid before revealing the trick of his adversary, and when Holmes becomes a haunting figure personifying the Gothic horrors of the moor to that epitome of modernity, Dr Watson. Literary detectives are also shamans when they stick to their belief that truth is possible despite the messy, embodiment of the material world. Sometimes they combine the two in becoming false shamans in order to gain truth by leading witnesses astray.

Becoming trickster is so necessary because the essence of the detective literary genre is to revive the corpse, which Giegerich cannot do. The literary detective is more faithfully echoed by Romanyshyn than by Giegerich. Giegerich is quite correct to locate the genre at a key moment of modernity when nature has been "framed" as a dead body, yet what the literary detective is most deeply about—in various narrative disguises as trickster and shaman—is reviving the dead body of Mother Nature by hunting for what is meaningful.

> Trickster stories, even when they clearly have much more complicated cultural meanings, preserve a set of images, from the days when what mattered above all else was hunting.[14]

As a hunter, the trickster is not a hero. His stories are not about stupendous bravery in fighting a monster to the death. Rather he is the sponsor of a weak, slow animal (*Homo sapiens*) in developing a complex relationship to a world beset with dangers. Trickster, in fact, in the earliest myths, is the inventor of fishing nets. As Coyote in the Americas and Hermes in Ancient Greece, trickster's nets help thwart monsters who used to eat humans. Myth is both literal and metaphorical in giving us a trickster who responds to devouring forces in the world with a non-oppositional strategy.

When you cannot beat the game, you change the rules. Hence, when Sherlock Holmes is unable to protect a threatened client, in *The Hound of the Baskervilles*, by heroically asserting his ordering presence, he instead melts into Gothic mists and mysterious shadows.[15]

Hyde also makes an important point about the relation of the trickster and the shaman. While the trickster tends to parody a shaman, he suggests that this figure of fascinating unreliability is within the operative system of shamans, not outside as wholly other.[14] A "true" shaman surely welcomes the kind of alert consciousness that comes from learning from the trickster about "false" shamans. Finding tricksters and shamans together is to reveal something about the complexities of the recognition of truth. This subtle and insightful argument by Hyde is also illuminating, I suggest, for looking at the literary detective.

The detective hunts, but is not limited to the role of hunter, for that would be to put him into a dual, either/or relation to the criminal. He is also a shaman who by rituals and recognizing signs will ultimately uncover a "truth," even if, shaman-like, it provides no "doctrine" by which to expel chaos forever. Yet the detective is also a trickster, in exposing false strategies for truth, and is a shaman in revealing the criminal's false shamanism. As shaman and trickster, the detective trickily incorporates the embodied psyche of the reader in the world.

So trickster embodies two attitudes to the whole notion of reading reality for "truth." One is that there is a higher truth, only our access to it is complicated by this unreliable being. The second trickster-construing of prophecy is that no higher truth exists. Even more, the very idea of higher truth is a dangerous fantasy that imperils embodied life. Again, we see how trickster molds the literary detective as he tries to decide whether there is a stable, coherent truth "out there." Or perhaps the entire concept of detecting, based as it is upon a belief in signs pointing to truth, is merely an illusion drawing him into trouble. Detectives are haunted by the fear that their tricksterish "meddling" does more harm than good.

Of course, these figures of shaman and trickster entail, as Hyde demonstrates, a complex perspective on signs. Whereas the prophet and the shaman rely upon signs to be truthful, trickster has no compunction in using signs to deceive. Indeed, at a deeper level, trickster is the trickiness of signs, or is the tricky spirit inhabiting signs. Also by signs, we mean items, objects, symbols that are used to make meaning, to signify.

What the trickster shows, above all, is ingenuity in his embodied engagement with non-human nature. Emphatically, his stories do not portray a disembodied abstract mind. Trickster is a creature of appetites, very often pure and simple hunger. The myth animates the body. Yet the myth animates the body that works indivisibly from the psyche. In this, trickster again betrays his origins in Earth Mother consciousness. Hyde puts this very concretely. Trickster tells us that what modernity prizes about human beings, the development of the capacity to think, is derived from trickily securing meat. In other words, the trickster myth activates us as embodied, nature saturated, carnal creatures.

> These myths suggest that blending natural history and mental phenomena is not an unthinking conflation but on the contrary, an accurate description of the ways things are. To learn about intelligence from the meat-thief, Coyote, is to know that we are embodied thinkers. If the brain has cunning, it has it as a consequence of appetite; the blood that lights the mind gets its sugars from the gut.[16]

I propose that a major revival of the trickster myth occurred in the development of the literary detective. This revival is *not* that the detective is merely a trickster. It is the detective genre that most completely inherits the trickster myth. Here it is important not to confuse the genre with its defining protagonist. Rather, what we see in detective novels is akin to the trickster's primal scene: the negotiation between trickster and shaman, in the context of hunting.

Of course detective fiction is vitally concerned with social issues. Yet its trickster inheritance knows that just as mind cannot be considered apart from body, so too our social collective is entirely contained in the non-human environment. Detective fiction is a (relatively) modern attempt to realize this; to make it real for us.

To conclude, I suggest that the trickster and the literary detective refute Giegerich's claim that there can be *only* a psychology of soul separated from non-human nature. Rather it is the nature of consciousness, evolved by the trickster, to have an alternative to either/ or thinking, to be also embodied, erotic, tricky, and other. Moreover, such consciousness is embedded in the very trickiness of signs and the genres as they stick together in the making of culture. Giegerich's own text testifies to this aspect of connected embodied consciousness in its animus, which gains so much resonance from Jung's inability to categorize a concept (a woman's unconscious masculinity) securely apart from his feeling reaction.

Giegerich's divisive approach is that of the literary detective when that figure tries to turn the bloody mess of a corpse into clues, signs that can replace the body, and turn the crime into a ritual enactment in a court of law. Such structuring of consciousness is necessary and important to the modern psyche. Yet, what I believe Romanyshyn to have superbly demonstrated is the even more necessary, because so long repressed, work of the literary detective as a "revivalist" of the dead body, the body deadened by the effect of its too long exclusion in modernity!

Here Romanyshyn as detective is most intensely a trickster when enmeshed in the relations of bodies and meaning. So if trickster, as Hyde argues, preserves images from consciousness emerging through hunting for food, then appetite as filling the stomach becomes the appetite for meaning, a need to satisfy the mind. Trickster is Earth Goddess consciousness here because there is no fixed divorce in trickster, or detective, between body and mind.

Trickster and detective seek to redeem a body made empty of mind by murder. The detective tries to animate the corpse into meaning, tries to make discarded matter, dirt even, into signs as clues. By sticking with the matter-at-hand as potentially animate, potentially meaningful, the detective's trickster ambiguous relations re-animate the Earth Goddess in modernity.

Robert Romanyshyn's essay helps us to know who has been murdered, opening us to the full mystery of the solution.

NOTES

1. Robert D. Romanyshyn, "The Melting of the Polar Ice: Revisiting *Technology as Symptom and Dream*," published in *Spring: A Journal of Archetype and Culture* 80 (Fall 2008), pp. 79-116.

2. Wolfgang Giegerich, "The Psychologist as Repentance Preacher and Revivalist: Robert Romanyshyn on the Melting of the Polar Ice," *Spring: A Journal of Archetype and Culture* 82 (Fall 2009), pp. 193-221.

3. *Ibid.*, p. 194.

4. Susan Rowland, "Nature Writing: Jung's Eco-Logic in the Conjunctio of Comedy and Tragedy," *Spring: A Journal of Archetype and Culture* 75 (2006), pp. 275-298.

5. *Ibid.*

6. Wolfgang Giegerich, "Killings, *Spring: A Journal of Archetype and Culture* 54 (1993), pp. 5-18.

7. Wolfgang Giegerich, "The Psychologist as Repentance Preacher," p. 208.

8. *Ibid.*, p. 213.

9. C. G. Jung, *Collected Works* 17 § 338.

10. Wolfgang Giegerich, "The Psychologist as Repentance Preacher," p. 207.

11. Arthur Conan Doyle, *The Hound of the Baskervilles* (1902) (New York: Penguin Classics, 2010).

12. Edgar Allan Poe, "The Purloined Letter" (1844), *Stories and Poems of Edgar Allan Poe* (New York: Houghton Mifflin, 2000).

13. Lewis Hyde, *Trickster Makes This World: Mischief, Myth and Art* (1998).

14. *Ibid.*, p. 18.

15. *Ibid.*, pp. 295-305.

16. *Ibid.*, p. 57.

RESPONSE TO WOLFGANG GIEGERICH'S "THE PSYCHOLOGIST AS REPENTANCE PREACHER AND REVIVALIST: ROBERT ROMANYSHYN ON THE MELTING OF THE POLAR ICE"

JOEL WEISHAUS

I have admired Wolfgang Giegerich's work for many decades; and, although I didn't always agree with him—a sign of his fertile mind—his ideas always earned serious consideration...until now, with his cynical critique of Robert Romanyshyn's "The Melting of the Polar Ice," in which Dr. Giegerich displays an amazing lack of knowledge of what it is to be a creatively participating human being in the 21st Century.

Take, for instance, his statement that "it is the ethical obligation of any writer striving for insight to free himself of any emotion so as to become able to study his subject *sine ira et studio*, to become 'up to his task.'" (*Spring* vol. 82, p. 195). Perhaps Giegerich has in mind a ghost writer; surely not someone living in a post-Heisenbergian era. But he goes even further. "Distance," he says, "is the a priori condition of the

---

Joel Weishaus is an Independent Scholar, and a member of the International Association of Jungian Studies Executive Committee. He lives in Portland, Oregon.

human possibility of having a *world* and being in a 'world' instead of merely being, like animals, factually involved with, and an integral part of, the *environment*." (*Spring*, vol. 82, p. 202) How does this square with the man who, in 1993, wrote: "The birth of the Gods, piety, soul and consciousness, culture itself did not merely arise from the spirit of killing but from actual killing"? ("Killing: Psychology's Platonism and the Missing Link to Reality," *Spring* 54, p. 8) Although I do not agree with this theory in its sweeping approach, especially when it comes to the gestation of soul and consciousness, he *is* saying that they arose from being involved with the world. Now, he is bullying Robert Romanyshyn for doing just that!

Although I agree with Giegerich that "(t)he psychologist knows himself not to be the healer, the doer. He only accompanies and 'attends to' the real process" (*Spring*, vol. 82, p. 210), he should know that Robert Romanyshyn is writing as a Jungian psychologist who works within the frame of phenomenology, a task which begins, as Romanyshyn explains in his monumental book, *The Wounded Researcher*, "with our entanglement with the perceptual world, the world that makes sense as we sense it." (Spring Journal Books, 2007, p. 88)

What is least understandable of this long drawn-out essay that drips with sarcasm is what moved Giegerich to write it in the first place. For instead of expanding his, and our, knowledge, he seems to have snapped a few links with reality.

Response to Wolfgang Giegerich's "The Psychologist as Repentance Preacher and Revivalist: Robert Romanyshyn on the Melting of the Polar Ice"

David H. Rosen

The Grinch Who Stole Christmas

After reading this piece by Wolfgang Giegerich, I thought of him as the Grinch who stole Christmas. Robert Romanyshyn's article is a heartfelt and balanced feeling-based concern about the psyche and our planet. Giegerich's paper is a one-sided thinking-based treatise using rationality and sarcastic criticism, whereas Romanyshyn's imaginative and creative essay challenges us to feel and use intuition to grasp the problem of global warming. Romanyshyn's article also reflects a thoughtful and symbolic way to view the melting of the polar ice in both inner and

David H. Rosen, M.D., is the McMillan Professor of Analytical Psychology, Professor of Humanities in Medicine, and Professor of Psychiatry and Behavioral Science at Texas A&M University. He is the author of over one hundred articles and eight books, most recently, with Joel Weishaus, *The Healing Spirit of Haiku*. He is currently completing a memoir *Lost in Aotearoa: Finding My Way Home*.

outer ways. In addition he constructs bridges between ego and soul as well as integrates feminine eros with masculine logos. This is the path to wholeness and the basis of Jung's psychology. Giegerich's paper is cynical, nihilistic, and verges on hopelessness. I queried Nancy Cater as to why it was even published, especially in such a lengthy, vitriolic, and seemingly unedited form. As one who is fond of *Spring*, as an archetypal journal of Jungian scholarship, this kind of pessimistic and disparaging writing does a disservice to such a high quality publication. To be against eco-psychology, healing, and working in a soulful way to raise consciousness about the melting polar ice caps is to be against Mother Earth and possibly this points out one of Giegerich's blind spots.

> The Grinch who stole Christmas
> Lives in Berlin
> As an icy intellect

NEUROBIOLOGY IN THE CONSULTING ROOM: AN INTERVIEW WITH MARGARET WILKINSON

DANIELA SIEFF

Margaret Wilkinson is a Jungian analyst in private practice in North Derbyshire, England. She is also a professional member of the Society of Analytical Psychology, London and of the West Midlands Institute of Psychotherapy, and is on the editorial board of the *Journal of Analytical Psychology*. Wilkinson lectures widely on the application of insights from contemporary neuroscience, trauma theory, and attachment research to psychodynamic counselling and psychotherapy. Her second book, *Changing Minds in Therapy: Emotion, Attachment, Trauma & Neurobiology*, was published by W.W. Norton in March, 2010.

Daniela Sieff, D. Phil., has a Master's degree in psychology and anthropology and a D. Phil. in biological anthropology from the University of Oxford. Her academic research with the semi-nomadic cattle-herding Datoga of Tanzania explored human behavior through the lens of evolutionary theory. Since then she has produced television documentaries, written articles, and completed the leadership training program with the Marion Woodman Foundation. She is currently working on a book, *Connecting Conversations: The Art and Science of Healing Emotional Trauma*. It will be comprised of a series of interviews that explore the process of emotional wounding and healing from the perspectives of depth psychology, neurobiology, evolutionary anthropology, and psychology, and art.

Daniela Sieff [DS]: Your new book, *Changing Minds in Therapy*, has just been published. What is your aim for it?

Margaret Wilkinson [MW]: I want to show how clinical practice can be enriched by incorporating the latest scientific research on attachment dynamics, trauma, and the neurobiology of emotion. Research in these fields has taken off in the last 15 years; *Changing Minds in Therapy* is both my own exploration of the contribution that this research makes to clinical practice, and my attempt to make it more widely available.

DS: What seeded your interest in an interdisciplinary approach?

MW: In 2000, when I was teaching a psychoanalytic psychotherapy course at a university, I was responsible for the student's clinical case presentations. The students were working in very difficult settings, and analytic theory alone was not sufficient to help them with the early trauma of their patients. Explored alongside analytic theory, attachment theory—which I'd just come across—had much to offer. At the same time, I discovered the writings of Bessel van der Kolk and Russell Meares and I felt that they were using neurobiological findings on the effects of early trauma in a very creative way within their practices. I began to explore further, reading the work of Regina Pally and Allan Schore—and their work excited me. I began to see that the latest scientific research had a huge contribution to make to clinical practice.

One reason why I was open to these new scientific findings was that I had studied history at university, and having been particularly interested in the history of ideas, I knew there are no static truths and that all ideas develop. Neither Freud nor Jung possessed the Holy Grail —in fact, both of them knew that their theories were limited by the information available at the time. Thus, incorporating the latest scientific ideas into their path-breaking discoveries felt natural.

Another reason why I was open to the new scientific findings was that my Jungian training, somewhat unusually, had a strong emphasis on development. Not only was I was taught by Fordham, who introduced developmental thinking to Jung's ideas, but infant observation was also part of my training. Thus, when I discovered attachment theory I found I was referencing back to what I had learnt from Fordham and to the experience I had had observing an infant.

The pieces fell into place.

DS: What, for you, are key findings of neurobiology?

MW: First, and foremost, neurobiology has finally put an end to the Cartesian split. It has enabled us to understand man as a mind-brain-body being in the way that nothing else has.

Following Jung's second Tavistock Lecture, Bion asked Jung whether he considered mind and brain to be the same thing. Jung replied, "The psychic fact and the physiological fact come together in a peculiar way... we see them as two on account of the utter incapacity of the mind to think them together."[1] Neurobiology has not only proven Jung right, it has also enabled our mind to think about them together. Today, we know that the brain is made up of neurons that are either excited or passive, and that our current state of mind—our subjective experience—is the result of that neuronal activity.

Today we also know that the brain/mind cannot be separated from the body. Bion also asked Jung about the relationship between mind and body, and Jung commented, "It is due to our most lamentable mind that we cannot think of body and mind as one and the same thing; probably they are one thing, but we are unable to think it."[2] Again, modern neuroscience is enabling us to "think it."

The brain/mind and body come together on several levels. In terms of our moment-to-moment existence, hormones released by the brain in response to our subjective experience, affect our whole body. At the same time, our subjective experience emerges from the information that comes to us through our bodily senses. Antonio Damasio[3] conceptualizes emotion as adaptive changes that take place in the body as a result of some particular stimulus, whereas he sees feelings as the conscious mental representations of those emotional responses. Damasio observes, "emotions play out in the theater of the body. Feelings play out in the theater of the mind."[4]

The link between brain/mind and body doesn't just shape our moment-to-moment existence; it also has long-lasting effects. Recent large-scale studies of the effects of adverse childhood experiences on later health in the United States and the United Kingdom, identified a significantly increased risk of developing serious organic diseases, including cancer, heart disease, asthma, diabetes, and chronic obstructive pulmonary disease. In short, neurobiology is showing us that mind, brain, and body are inextricably linked; no one who works with any one of these can afford to ignore the other two.

The second scientific finding that enriches clinical work is that our brain has two hemispheres, and that each processes information in a different way. The right hemisphere has deeper links to the body. It is the seat of our emotions. Our moment-by-moment experience is unconsciously processed by the right hemisphere and given an emotional valance, depending on whether we deem the experience to be threatening or benign. The right hemisphere has a holistic world view, rather than a linear one. It can hold several possibilities simultaneously, but has little sense of time. Right-brain learning is primarily non-verbal, relational, and experiential. We reach the right hemisphere through embodied, affective empathy. At birth the right hemisphere is more mature and functional than the left hemisphere. In contrast, the left hemisphere's way of seeing the world is linear, cognitive, analytical, and verbal. It has a sense of past and future. It is essentially the thinking brain. Its currency is that of words and ideas. The left hemisphere comes "online" when we are about 2-3 years old.

Ultimately, it is the integrated activity of the right and left hemispheres that gives rise to the coherent sense of self which enables us to function in a healthy way. If the hemispheres do not work together we find ourselves in trouble. When the right hemisphere is dominant, emotions overwhelm us. A patient of mine, when catapulted back into her fears, felt that words were flitting past her, but that she couldn't catch the word that would describe what she was experiencing. In contrast, when we retreat into logical thinking and shut down our emotions, the left hemisphere is dominant.

Because most traditional psychotherapy relies on verbal interpretation it tends to ignore the less-verbal right hemisphere. Modern science, particularly the pioneering work of Allan Schore,[5&6] has shown us that we must also pay attention to the right-hemisphere in our consulting rooms. I now envision therapy to be rather like the double helix where left and right brain processes, one predominantly cognition and the other predominantly affect, intertwine.

A third important finding is one that has emerged from research on the neurobiology of attachment: the individual mind cannot be explored, or indeed changed, in isolation. The mind-brain-body develops in the context of our attachment relationships with our earliest care-givers; later in life, changing minds also depends on the interaction with a significant other. This research emphasizes the crucial importance of an attuned and empathetic relationship between patient and therapist within a clinical setting. For those who have experienced early relational trauma, only the dual approach of empathy and interpretation will facilitate healing.

DS: Can you talk more about how mind develops in the context of early attachment relationships?

MW: A baby's brain has more neuronal connections than are ultimately needed; which circuits are strengthened and which die depend on experience. In the emotional realm, it is the infant's attachment relationship with his or her primary care-giver that determines which neural circuits are strengthened and which are lost. The resulting patterns of neural connectivity encode the expectations that the infant forms about itself, relationships, and the world. Such early forming patterns, once created, stay with the infant as he or she develops. When new relationships are formed, children approach them with the expectations they formed during the attachment relationship. As Pally comments: "We learn from the past what to predict for the future and then live the future we expect. . . ."[7]

A physically and emotionally nurturing environment, consisting of an empathetic and attuned primary care-giver, is the key to creating the neural connections that allow for secure attachment, emotional well-being, healthy relationships, and the full realization of potential. In contrast, a poor early experience will lead to the fragile sense of self, the struggle to regulate emotions, and the impoverished social relations that brings many people into therapy.

I worked with a young man who, as a child, was looked after by *au pairs* that changed practically every year. This was a terrible situation; as soon as he formed an attachment to a care-giver, it was time to lose her. As an adult, when he found a woman he wanted to marry, he couldn't be faithful. Deep down, his unconscious expectation was that any woman that he attached to would abandon him, so he had an affair in order to line up another woman who would cushion him from the expected loss of his fiancée. Needless to say, when his fiancée found out about his affair, she left him. Thus he brought about what he most feared, replicating the early loss of the much loved *au pairs*. This pushed him further into the pattern of "womanizing" which was really a defense against the loss that he had learnt would be inevitable. Significantly it was when his first child, a son, was born that he realized he must address the problem rather than replicate the pattern of changing caregivers for his own son. Working with this young man, although I didn't talk about attachment theory with him, it was attachment theory that informed how I worked.

I now realize that for many patients arrival at a more secure attachment is the unconscious goal of therapy. It is coming to this place that will enable patients to live with a safe sense of separateness, curiosity, and confidence. What is more, I now think of the newly developed secure attachment as being "learned," because it is affective engagement in therapy that enables new emotional learning to occur, and such learning may bring about a profound change in the way the patient relates to others.

DS: To understand the profound effects of early relationships it is important to understand how human memory works. Can you speak to this?

MW: Memories are made when a group of neurons fire together and establish a particular neural pattern that remains after the stimulus has gone. Memories play a vital part in developing a sense of self. They also enable us to regulate our affect in the light of past experience and to build on earlier experience in a creative way.

Neuroscience has shown us that we have several kinds of memory. Short-term memory may last a few seconds, or a few minutes; something is held in mind for as long as that information is needed; then it is forgotten. An example might be remembering a phone number until it has been dialled.

In contrast long-term memory lasts for many years—even an entire life time. There are several forms of long-term memory and the one that is held in the left hemisphere of the brain is what we generally think of as memory. Experiences are recorded in an explicit, personal, and narrative form. The memory can be accessed consciously and spoken about as something that happened in the past, and in a particular setting. To form an explicit long-term memory a brain structure called the hippocampus has to be online, because it is the hippocampus that tags a time and a place (the "where" and the "when") to an experience.

The right hemisphere holds a form of long-term memory that is less well known. It records experiences in an implicit and embodied way. These memories cannot be consciously accessed, and they are not recorded as a linear narrative of something that has happened in the past. Instead, when something triggers the implicit memory, we respond in an embodied way, repeating the pattern of behavior that was learned at the time that the memory was laid down.

All of the experiences that are recorded during the first three of years of life are recorded implicitly for the simple reason that the left hemisphere is not yet online. It is implicit memory, formed in the context of our earliest social and emotional relationships, that establishes the ways we will relate to others throughout our life.

Similarly, in times of danger, the memories that are laid down are primarily implicit. Heightened activity of the right amygdala (the danger system), enhances the formation of implicit memory, but inhibits the consolidation of explicit memory as the hippocampus is deactivated. As a result, the memories can't be consciously remembered, and without such awareness, even low-intensity interpersonal stressors can activate the unmodulated emotional experiences that have been imprinted into right brain neural circuits.

A little girl of about 4 years old, whom I call Harriet, was part of a group of children in short-term fostering going to a *son et lumière* show in the local park. She chattered happily to her foster carer, enjoying the colored lights strung through the trees. Suddenly the park darkened and the first few notes of some rather scary music came out of the darkness. Then bright lights flashed at about the height of the child's face. Harriet became absolutely rigid; the change was noted instantly by the foster carer. The group walked away as quickly as possible, rapidly making their way to the well-lit area around the café in the park, and the foster carer managed to soothe Harriet. It turned out that Harriet had been abused in the illicit video industry, and her intense reaction to the sudden bright light and music was due to the way that they had awakened her implicitly held, right-brain memories of the abuse.

As Harriet's story poignantly illustrates, when implicitly stored emotional memories of trauma are triggered, the associated affect can't be regulated. With no time and place tagged to the memory, the past feels like the present and people respond in ways they don't understand.

Jung put it as well as anybody when he said, "The explosion of affect is a complete invasion of the individual. It pounces on him like an enemy or a wild animal."[8]

DS: Much of your book focuses on early relational trauma. What is "trauma" and how is it created?

MW: Trauma can be defined as difficult early experiences that remain buried within, unknown and unknowable, but which carry an instantly recognizable feeling tone that is a meld of helplessness, rage, terror, and dread. This feeling tone can be recreated in an instant by a triggering event or sensation, such as it was for Harriet. Such a feeling tone comes with a sense of *now*, not *then*. I call this the "old present." Many come to therapy because they struggle with intrusions of the old present.

The experiences that give rise to early relational trauma are varied, but in general they involve feeling fundamentally and profoundly threatened. For example, necessary but intrusive medical procedures and hospitalization early in life, carried out with the best intentions, can leave emotional scars. An infant's simultaneous experience of intrusion and abandonment may be overwhelming.

Alternatively, neglectful or abusive parenting may traumatize infants. Even an un-attuned primary care-giver is enough to leave a child traumatized. Infants are not easily able to modulate their emotions, so they rely on an external other—generally the mother— to help them. To do this the mother has to be attuned to her baby's emotions, and although this comes naturally to emotionally healthy mothers, some mothers struggle with this. A mother, who is depressed or ambivalent about having a child, will be muted in her response to her baby's emotions. At the other end of the continuum, a mother may be over-stimulating, intolerant, intrusive, or downright abusive. Either way, if the baby's emotional rhythms are not validated, then the baby can't learn to regulate his emotions, and he will be unable to develop a secure sense of self.

Bromberg explains that a person's core self is defined by whom the parents (or caregivers) perceive the child to be and, just as importantly, who they deny the child to be. When parents deny certain aspects of their child's self, those aspects become dissociated and unavailable to the child. Bromberg concludes that "disconfirmation, because it is relationally non-negotiable, is traumatic by definition..."[9]

DS: What happens neurobiologically, when we feel threatened?

MW: On sensing danger the amygdala—a key part of brain's fear circuit—will instantaneously activate the sympathetic nervous system, creating a state of hyperarousal and instigating a startle response. The person freezes to reduce the chance of being detected, and focuses their attention on the source of potential danger. If the danger abates, a state of relative relaxation returns. If the threat escalates, the person looks towards flight or fight as a means of dealing with the threat. For infants flight and fight are obviously impossible; they are also of little use for children who are being abused by their parents. So for infants, children, and indeed for adults when there is no possibility of escape, the parasympathetic nervous system comes in over the top of the sympathetic nervous system to create a hypoaroused and dissociated state. In such a state individuals are cut off from what is happening in both the outer and the inner world, collapse and play dead. Hypoarousal is accompanied by massive release of opiates that deadens pain. Playing dead originally evolved as a response to attacks by predators who do not like to eat already dead animals for fear that the flesh may be rotting and poisonous. Hypoarousal is the escape when there is no escape— the defense of last resort.

Every time an infant or child reverts to playing dead, the neural pathways that mediate dissociated hypoarousal are strengthened. In time, the pathways become so well established that dissociated hypoarousal becomes the defense of choice, irrespective of the degree of threat, and the other defensive options that are now available.

That said, not all dissociation is defensive or negative. Dissociation is most comprehensively defined as an active inhibitory process that screens internal and external stimuli from the field of consciousness, and the degree and circumstances in which we dissociate lie on a continuum from normal to pathological. Normal dissociation means unconsciously filtering out what might otherwise be distracting as our mind concentrates on one particular experience. For example, talking to you, my brain is screening out the sounds of the birds singing outside my window. However, as we become threatened, dissociation becomes progressively more defensive. An example of relatively benign defensive dissociation would be a child who escapes periods of loneliness by making up stories in which he is the hero. More serious dissociation would occur when the child's external environment is so intolerable that the child retreats into a world of fantasy and can no longer differentiate between fantasy and reality. At the extreme end of this dissociative continuum, where the parasympathetic nervous system has triggered a state of extreme hypoarousal, the child will fall into a hypoaroused, collapsed, zombie-like state.

It is important for clinicians to be aware that in the consulting room defensive dissociation may manifest itself in hidden, subtle ways: the averting of the gaze, the turning of the head, the momentary closing of the eyes, a glazed look manifest in an otherwise usually alert and engaged patient, the dulling of mind—and not only the patient's mind but also that of the therapist, caught in a transferential experience of the dissociated state. It is crucial that we, as therapists, pick this up because it tells us when difficult material has been touched and helps us focus our efforts.

DS: In addition to dissociative hypoarousal becoming the defence of choice, what are some other consequences of early trauma?

MW: There are several possible consequences that we need to look out for in the consulting room.

- The brain becomes hard-wired to cope in a hostile world. Fear of others becomes entrenched and relationships become a source of terror rather than support. In terms of the brain's biochemistry, the stress response is set to hyper-sensitive levels, making people more reactive to either real, imagined, or remembered threats. This affects the trauma victim's capacity to regulate their affects. Such patients may face the condemnation of "always overreacting" or "acting out," or being "far too sensitive for your own good," or "getting uptight far too easily."

- The development of empathy may be compromised. Empathy begins to arise in the second year of life, and depends on the mother mirroring the baby's affect in an empathetic and sensitive way. If the mother is not attuned, and the affects that she expresses are not congruent with those being experienced by the infant, the baby's capacity to develop appropriate labelling of internal states will be undermined and may lead to a deep confusion which impairs the development of empathy.

· The development of empathy may also be impaired because the young child simply can't allow himself to see what is in his parents' minds, when his parents have harmful intentions towards him. This is relevant to the clinical setting because if you can't let something into mind, you can't transform it, thus one of the things that therapists need to do is to help their patients to think what was once unthinkable.

· The child is likely to develop the fantasy that s/he is at fault. Helplessness is intolerable; it is psychologically easier for such children to see themselves as the cause of the abuse, rather than the victim. This results in a self defined by shame.

· The child's relationship to pain may be distorted. Pain's message is to stop whatever it is that is causing the pain, but because these children cannot escape, they unconsciously learn to over-ride the warnings of pain. Instead, they discover that the only way out of pain is to sit with it until their parasympathetic nervous system kicks in—instigating a state of hypoarousal and the concurrent release of pain-numbing endogenous opiates.

· Memory is commonly affected. If the degree of emotional arousal is moderate, then explicit memory formation is strengthened. However, in times of great stress the formation of explicit memory may be impaired whereas right-brain implicit memory is enhanced. Under such circumstances, the conscious mind has little or no memory of the experience, but the trauma is vividly remembered by the unconscious mind, albeit in a dissociated, split-off self-state. Splits develop between the part of the mind that knows what happened and the part that doesn't.

DS: Are the dissociated self-states which hold the implicit memory of the trauma another way of describing what Jung called complexes?

MW: If we understand Jungian complexes as spilt-off aspects of the psyche, then yes! In fact, in his early work, Jung himself emphasized the importance of dissociation, saying that with trauma, "the emotional significance of the experience remains hidden all along from the patient so that not reaching consciousness, the emotion never wears itself out, it is never used up."[10] Jung described traumatic complexes that bring about dissociation as being, "…not under the control of the will and for this reason it possesses the quality of psychic autonomy."[11]

That said, there is a continuum of dissociation: early in life the brain is un-associative rather than dissociative, and normal development brings ever-increasing connectivity. This, in turn, give rise to varied, but interlinked, self-states: we are one person with a friend, another at work, another with our lover, etc.—but at the same time we maintain a coherent core. When there has been early trauma this doesn't happen: unbearable painful experiences are split-off and so no coherent core can be formed. Then mind may become dissociative, leaving trauma to be expressed as it was experienced—in the body, and in the non-conscious parts of the brain. Taken to the extreme, this leads to dissociative identity disorder, where traumatic experience is encapsulated in multiple selves who do not know each other.

I generally work with people who are mid-way along this continuum. They don't feel coherently together and often find they are encountering very young, or angry, or frightened, or despairing parts of themselves. In fact, many people come to therapy when dissociative defenses start to break down—they can't cope with what is being experienced in their bodies—the overwhelming affect. They struggle to live with knowing and not-knowing.

We may imagine one such patient who I will call Jennifer. Jennifer came to me as an adult, because she'd had a terrible panic attack on the street. She told of being taken to hospital in an ambulance, whose siren had sounded weirdly terrifying as it echoed in the fog. Jennifer had lived her early childhood in a war zone, and she, with her immediate family, had escaped to England when she was seven years old. She had virtually no memory of any experiences before arriving in England. Only gradually, in the safety of the therapeutic relationship, could Jennifer begin to remember that as a child she was routinely sent out in the fog to fetch supplies—her parents thought that a child in the fog might go unnoticed. Her terror of being caught had been so overwhelming that Jennifer had had to burry it to survive. However, as an adult in England, the terror that had been so long denied had overwhelmed her and suddenly became manifest in a full-blown panic attack, when the trigger of the fog stimulated the old neuronal pathway, reviving the terrified child buried within.

DS: In your book you describe how the patterns that are laid down early in life come to the fore in the consulting room through transference. What does a clinician need to understand about this dynamic?

MW: Transference is the result of a patient transferring his or her past experience of relating onto the relationship with the therapist. Patients whose early experience was dominated by fear, anger, and abuse unconsciously expect their therapists to behave in a hostile manner. Such expectations, when activated, are typically described as "negative transference," but although the emotions are negative, it's important to understand that the emergence of negative transference offers a powerful means by which the therapeutic dyad can become conscious of the implicit patterning that was laid down during the patient's early childhood.

Also, if the therapist remains empathetically attuned to the patient despite the negative transference, the patient will eventually be able to forge different, and less negative, expectations of relationships. In fact, we now know that the creation of different expectations is a crucial part of therapy. Old neural pathways cannot be eradicated, but in the context of an empathetic relationship new ones can be formed. Such change depends on the right brain, and this explains why left-brain interpretational work alone is ineffective when confronted with the consequences of traumatic early experience. The solution lies in the relational approach: for the patient to remake his or her experience of relationships the unconscious affective exchanges between therapist and patient, patient and therapist are crucial.

Attention to affect-regulation is a key aspect of such therapy. Revisiting traumatic experience, whether stimulated by the negative transference, or by other reminders which trigger unconscious memories of painful earlier experience, may lead to a full blow re-experiencing of the old trauma. This process may be described as "psychological kindling" and once begun, it can escalate with the patient moving to extreme states of hyperarousal followed by hypoaroused disengagement. Such kindling, rather than helping the patient to form new neural networks, reinforces the old trauma-derived patterns.

Moreover, because hypoarousal is accompanied by the release of endogenous opioids which calm the patient, therapists and patients may mistakenly interpret the opioid calmness as recovery from kindling. In fact, those who have suffered chronic trauma may have become addicted to this opioid response, and care must be taken to avoid a situation where patients unconsciously seek retraumatisation in the consulting room in order to experience the endorphin "high" to which they have become accustomed in early and repetitive experiences of trauma.

Consequently, when negative transference begins to escalate into kindling, the therapist must help the patient return to a more regulated state. There are various tools that help an empathetic therapist to do this. Non-verbal signals are, generally, very effective. If the patient is beginning to disengage, the sensitive therapist may lean forward and engage the patient's eyes to bring him or her back. Similarly, if the patient becomes distressed, it will be reflected immediately in her breathing; he or she may become breathless, may hold the breath, or may breathe too rapidly, which, if unattended, could result in a panic attack. If the therapist breathes slowly and deliberately, the patient's breathing may soon follow—such are the powers of mirroring, resonance, and empathy. Some of our earliest affective experiences come to us through the musicality of our mother's voice: if the therapist uses calming, pastel tones, it may also help to prevent full-blown kindling. In contrast, interpretations and words are of limited use, because when feeling so severely threatened, the language centers of the brain are deactivated. That said, simple phrases, such as "It was then, not now" can help to pull the patient out of the old traumatic present and back into the now.

In short, if the therapist is attuned and empathetic this helps to prevent negative experience escalating into full blown kindling. Then the patient has a greater chance of remaining "in mind" whilst touching on the early patterns that are being acted out in the transference, and the door to change is opened.

DS: How do you understand countertransference within a neurobiological framework?

MW: I understand countertransference as deeply felt, embodied empathy. Through countertransference the therapist's unconscious mind and body picks up what happened to his or her patient and imagines what the experience felt like. Recent research suggests that there are two routes to empathy, (1) a left-brain, cognitive route—we think our way into what the other is experiencing, and (2) a right-brain affective route—we feel what the other is experiencing through the mind-brain-body's mirroring of what is happening in that other. It is affective and embodied empathy that underlies countertransference.

Sometimes we, as therapists, feel nothing in response to our patients. This supposed lack of empathic countertransference has generally been seen as an unconscious strategy on the part of the therapist to defend him or herself against unbearable states of mind evoked by the patient. However, feeling nothing may be a dissociative effect induced in the therapist by a patient for whom defensive dissociation has become habitual. I have often found it informative to ask myself "Why this state of mind with this patient at this moment?" Additionally, when I find myself switching off it can be helpful to say something along the lines of "I think there's something quite difficult around." My patient might then be able to get into touch with some new aspect of a previously unbearable and implicitly held early experience.

The importance of affective empathy is highlighted by a number of studies that conclude that it is the quality of the relationship between therapist and patient, rather than the theoretical orientation, that brings about a successful therapeutic outcome.

DS: What are the therapeutic benefits of enabling implicitly held traumatic memories to become conscious?

MW: Although creating new patterns of expectation occurs implicitly, we need consciousness to gain control over overwhelming affect. When the emotionally laden right-brain memories are made available to the left brain, the patient is able to put feelings into words and to think about them. Then the past can become the past, rather than forever being relived in the present.

In my concept of therapy as a double helix, right-brain and left-brain processes intertwine to make a whole. The right brain strand of the helix deals with implicit patterns and may become manifest through feelings, through bodily sensations, through visual images or through dreams. It is addressed through the affective encounter between therapist and patient. The left brain strand deals with explicit knowledge and is addressed through verbal interpretations of transference, dreams, images, and stories. Bringing these strands together creates the increased neuronal connectivity that constitutes change. Jung knew the truth of this, but not having the scientific knowledge to explain it this way, he put it differently: "What happens within oneself when one integrates previously unconscious contents with consciousness is something which can scarcely be described in words. It can only be experienced. It is a subjective affair quite beyond discussion… ."[12] Today, although the subjective experience is still hard to describe, science is illuminating the dynamics that he spoke about.

DS: You write about the role of metaphor and image in helping people become conscious of their implicitly held emotional patterns—why are metaphors so powerful?

MW: They are powerful because they give form and shape to the underlying emotional patterns that are typically lived at an implicit, and therefore unconscious, level. With metaphor, vivid images carry emotional truth from the world of the implicit right brain into the sphere of left-brain awareness. This heralds the development of a more coherent sense of self. Moreover, because more brain areas light up in response to metaphor than to any other form of human communication, it is one of our most powerful tools in forming new neural pathways and in establishing the integrated working of the two hemispheres after trauma.

For metaphor to emerge, and for it to be processed in a way that brings consciousness, the patient needs to feel safe, that is, the patient has to trust that regardless of what emerges, s/he will be held by an empathetic other. After all, what emerges through metaphor can reflect the trauma that is imprinted on the amygdala and that can be terrifying. One of my patients, who I call Clare, had been traumatized by her dominant, aggressive, and persecutory father during her childhood. He would regularly summon her to berate her for her shortcomings, often adding as a veiled threat, "And I don't even have to touch you to break you." Clare had worked with a male therapist before working with me, and when negative transference arose, Clare experienced her male therapist as a fearsome, black beast. She had imagined a tall, monstrous, black-cloaked figure who she felt would tear open her chest, almost like a surgeon pulling apart the two sides of a patient's ribcage, to remove her heart. Exploring this image, Clare felt that it symbolized the overwhelming anxiety that she had experienced as a child in the presence of her father, and which was imprinted on her neural circuits.

Trauma can also be expressed in a metaphorical way through somatization. Clare suffered with this. One of her worst memories was of the exercises that her father forced her to do for what seemed like hours every evening. Clare spoke of endless sessions when her father commandeered the blackboard, easel, and chalks that her aunt had bought her when she had noticed Clare's artistic ability. Instead of providing a chance to explore her creativity, the blackboard became associated with Clare's inadequacy when faced with trying to solve the long sums her father wrote on it. Years later Clare only had to touch chalk for her hands to break out in allergic eczema, a tendency that abated only after she and I worked on her trauma in therapy. In other words, Clare's eczema can be seen as an embodied metaphor that reflected the trauma that had been imprinted on her mind-brain-body.

DS: How do dreams function as metaphors?

MW: Dreams can be thought of as extended metaphors that enable material to move from unconscious implicit memory toward the explicit realm of knowledge and memory. As Jung wrote, "Dreams do not deceive, they do not lie, they do not distort or disguise, but naively announce what they are and what they mean... They are invariably seeking to express something that the ego does not know and does not understand."[13] Modern neurobiology shows that Jung was right. What is more, the encounter between conscious and unconscious that occurs when working with dreams helps to develop connections between and within hemispheres. Such integration then enables the models and beliefs that we hold to become more nuanced, complex, and adaptive.

That said, although dreams have traditionally been thought to arise within the confines of the dreamer's psyche, some Jungians are beginning to see dreams as emerging in the context of relationships, just as we now see the developing brain as emerging in the context of the relationship the infant has with its care-giver. It appears that if the patient has suffered from early relational trauma, it is the containing therapeutic relationship which makes it possible to dream the undreamable as a prelude to being able to think the unthinkable.

DS: In your book you recount how important art has been to some of your patients as they struggle to bring implicit emotional patterns into consciousness. Can you talk about this?

MW: Art, created in the context of therapy and characterized by novelty, is typically metaphorical. At first patients tend not to know what their pictures or sculptures symbolize; however, when the art is brought to therapy and the patient begins to talk about it, the metaphorical meaning begins to become apparent. This heralds a new capacity for symbolization which in turn enables patients to begin to link their affective experience (the domain of the right hemisphere) with their capacity to think about early experience (the task of the left). Once this happens trauma-created patterns can begin to move from the "here and now" to the "there and then."

This is best illustrated through the work that I did with a patient called Holly. Her images, often taken from her dreams, were transformational; they provided steppingstones by which she became able to put difficult feelings into words. One domain where this was particularly poignant was in relation to the aggressive and deeply hostile transference that was a result of her trauma. For a long time, I carried Holly's projection of her internalized hostile, destructive, persecutory mother. During a session she would suddenly change; her face would show fear and then would become hard as she closed off completely from me. A turning point came after one such session when Holly's dream contained a terrifyingly vivid image that she felt compelled to paint. It was of a fearsome black cat mauling a baby cat. Talking about it during her next session, Holly was haltingly able to discuss her uncertainty about whether I was the bad black cat mother attacking her, or whether she was the bad black cat tearing me to shreds. Through this image we became able to talk about how her experiences of past aggression were being experienced in her current relationships.

But working with images isn't enough in and of itself; how therapist and patient relate is crucial. The therapeutic relationship provides a "bridging function" that enables the patient to find a way to process the unconscious traumatic memories that are emerging in the images. The making, bringing, and discussing of Holly's pictures represented the symbolic and interpretative work that lies at the core of classic analysis, but for Holly, it was the relational style of therapy, with its capacity to address early trauma deep in the implicit memory store of the developing right hemisphere, that was crucial to the process of change.

DS: You stress that when the implicit emerges into consciousness, what is privileged is emotional truth rather than fine detail. What do you mean by that?

MW: Implicit memory, returning as it does in symbolic form, strongly represents the reality of the patient's internal emotional world. For example, in one session a patient vividly remembered her "Bunnikins" plate from which, in her earliest years, she ate every day. She remembered that Mrs. Rabbit was bathing her little rabbits in a tin bath by the fire. They looked up into her face, enjoying the moment. Another rabbit child was playing with a red and blue train. Above the window hung bunches of bright orange carrots and white turnips, presumably to be eaten at a later time. In the background was the dresser and on the shelves was a set of blue and white plates. After recounting this material in a session, the patient went home and looked again at the plate. The next day she commented that all was much as she had remembered, except for two significant differences: There were several rabbit children playing with toy horses, not one with a train, and the father rabbit was sitting close by reading his newspaper. The patient had a younger brother who loved to play with his toy train and would usually have been "in the picture." In contrast, her father was often absent and when present had found it difficult to accept his eldest child. In other words, the patient's memory had accurately represented her own inner world experience, rather than the actual picture. Emotional truth had been privileged over accurate physical detail.

In short, we've learnt that the kind of truth we can discover in the consulting room is the emotional gist of what happened to the child. Thus the crucial clinical questions are not about what actually happened, rather they are: (1) how early did the child experience relational trauma? (2) What did it do to the child? (3) What meaning did the child make of the event? (4) How has that affected the development of the child or adult who has come to us for help?

DS: You devote a chapter of your book to narrative and the making of meaning. What is the role of narrative in clinical practice?

MW: Narrative can be seen as the instrument of mind that constructs our version of reality and that gives meaning to our experience of life. Narrative is created when we pattern our memories to create meaning. Coherent narrative is characterized by a causal event structure, a lack of superfluous or tangential information, and a depiction of events that parallels the world of real experience. To achieve this, what is held in the right hemisphere's implicit memory has to be available to the left hemisphere. The narrative of patients who have suffered trauma may be confusing rather than coherent, it may miss things, and it may be intruded upon by flashbacks.

A secure therapeutic relationship enables the affect regulation that makes possible the cocreation of a coherent narrative for those who have not been able to build one during childhood. This in turn allows the patient's traumatically created "old present" to be placed firmly in the past. For example, the narrative of the young man that had been looked after by a string of *au pairs* was that the *au pairs* had left because he was unlovable. He unconsciously brought this trauma-derived narrative into his present and as a consequence was unable to believe that his fiancé would stay with him. However, having worked with me for some time, his narrative about his ever-changing *au pairs* changed. He realized that the *au pairs* had left not because he was unlovable, but because his mother had got rid of them; she hadn't wanted anybody else to become too emotionally important to him, even though she couldn't be there for him herself.

The coconstruction of a narrative (in therapy) also plays a vital part in mourning what was and what might have been. This then enables a greater capacity to leave the past in the past, and live life as it is now in the real world.

In terms of contemporary research, narrative neuroscience is a relatively new area of exploration; however, a striking finding is the degree of hemispheric integration required for story production. Thus, like metaphor, the creation of a coherent metaphor is an important tool in fostering integration within, and between, the hemispheres of our brain.

DS: What would your take home message be?

MW: Research findings suggest that although the predisposition to develop a sense of self is hard-wired from the beginning, the individual self that emerges is defined by the earliest experience of relationships. The neural patterns underlying these relationships are stored in the implicit memory system of the right brain. They determine our most fundamental ways of being.

Early relational trauma may leave the person with a store of painful implicit memories and expectations that make it difficult to function well in life. This often brings people into therapy. We now know that to work with early forming right-brain, affective, dissociative distress, a left-brain interpretive approach, traditionally privileged by analytic theory, is not enough. Instead, right-brain empathic relating is also essential. When our patients have suffered early relational trauma, our task is not merely that of making the unconscious conscious but rather of restructuring the unconscious itself. To do that requires the transformational power embedded in unconscious affective, human interactions.

That said, there is also a role for the left brain in changing minds; well-timed interpretations that involve putting implicitly experienced feelings into words encourage the integrated functioning of both hemispheres of the brain. This process also plays a crucial role in helping our patients gradually build a personal narrative that is not so unbearable that it has to be split off again. When what is remembered implicitly becomes explicit, it loses the "here-and-now" quality and frees the patient to live in the present.

In short, although there are many questions for science still to address, modern research is telling us that effective clinical work is not a case of *either/or* but *both–and*. Psychotherapy needs to take on board the importance of both the intrapersonal and the relational; both the explicit and the implicit; both the cognitive and the affective; both the interpretational and the experienced; both the left and the right hemispheres of the brain; both the mind and the body.

Similarly, as clinical practice moves forward, it needs to value both the insights from the fathers of psychoanalysis and new scientific discoveries. I strongly believe that such an interdisciplinary perspective should no longer be considered an optional "extra"—rather it behooves us as a profession to use the new knowledge available to us so that our discipline may truly come of age and prove even more beneficial to our patients.

NOTES

1. C. G. Jung, *The Collected Works of C.G. Jung* [hereinafter "*CW*"] trans. R. F. C. Hull, Bollinger Series XX (Princeton, NJ: Princeton University Press, 1935), Vol. 18 §§ 135-136.

2. C. G. Jung, *CW* 18 § 69.

3. A. R. Damasio, *Descartes' Error: Emotion, Reason, and the Human Brain* (New York: Putnam, 1994).

4. A. R. Damasio, *Looking for Spinoza: Joy, Sorrow, and the Feeling Brain* (London: Heinemann, 2003), p. 28.

5. A. N. Schore, *Affect Dysregulation and Disorders of the Self* (New York: Norton, 2003).

6. A. N. Schore, *Affect Regulation and the Repair of the Self* (New York: Norton, 2003).

7. R. Pally, "The predicting brain, unconscious repetition, conscious reflection and therapeutic change," *International Journal of Psychoanalysis 8* (2007), p. 863.

8. C. G. Jung, *CW* 16 § 267.

9. P. M. Bromberg, "MENTALIZE THIS! Dissociation, enactment, and clinical process," in E. L. Jurist, A. Slade & S. Burger, eds., *Mind to Mind: Infant Research, Neuroscience, and Psychoanalysis* (New York: Other Press, 2008), p. 424.

10. C. G. Jung, *CW* 4 § 224.

11. C. G. Jung, *CW* 16 § 266.

12. C. G. Jung, *Memories, Dreams, Reflections,* recorded and edited by A. Jaffé (New York: Pantheon and London: Collins and Routledge; and also Kegan Paul, paper back edition, London: Fontana, 1962), p. 318.

13. C. G. Jung, *CW* 17 § 189.

BOOK REVIEWS

Joseph Cambray. *Synchronicity: Nature and Psyche in an Interconnected Universe*. Carolyn and Ernest Fay Lecture Series in Analytical Psychology. College Station, Texas, Texas A & M Press, 2009.

REVIEWED BY F. DAVID PEAT

Joseph Cambray's new book is a welcome addition to the literature on synchronicity. In particular, because it stresses the role that the physicist Wolfgang Pauli played in encouraging Jung to refine his concept.

As Cambray explains, Pauli, who had already made important contributions with the discovery of the neutrino and his famous Exclusion Principle, was on the verge of a mental breakdown when he first consulted Jung. While Jung initially referred the physicist to a junior colleague, as time progressed the two men began to interact together and in Cambray's words "Pauli was somewhat unique amongst

David Peat was born in Liverpool where he obtained his Ph.D. After working for many years as a theoretical physicist with the National Research Council of Canada he turned to independent research. He has a particular interest in the ideas of Carl Jung and in promoting dialogue between Western Science and Indigenous knowledge systems. In 1996 he moved to the medieval village of Pari in Tuscany where he runs a cultural center. He is author of over twenty books. Peat is a Fellow of the World Academy of Art and Science.

Jung's correspondents with his ability to engage and challenge Jung in ways that truly altered his thinking." (p. 9)

In the first chapter Cambray therefore explores the implications of this relationship and the ways in which Pauli helped Jung to refine his concept of synchronicity. When Jung showed an interest in J.B. Rhine's work on parapsychology, for example, Pauli cautioned him that the phenomena in question did not contain an archetypal basis and were therefore totally different from synchronistic events. Pauli also stressed the significance of the psychoid and its relation to time in the simultaneity of a synchronistic "meaning-connection." Of course it was also Pauli who persuaded Jung to publish his essay "Synchronicity: An Acausal Connecting Principle" that appeared in "The Interpretation of Nature and the Psyche" alongside Pauli's "The Influence of Archetypal Ideas on the Scientific Theories of Kepler."

Cambray's book continues by exploring the nature of field theories in physics and their relationship to a sense of holism. He then enters into complexity theory with its important notion of emergence. While for Jung synchronicities were acausal and inexplicable, Cambray suggests that they become more understandable as emergence within systems that are at the boundary of order and chaos. Similarly he views the Self as an emergent property of the psyche. He also discusses the possible implications of the relatively recent discovery of "mirror neurons" in the brain which can fire when, for example, a person "mirrors" an aspect of our behavior. For Cambray this suggests a neurobiological basis for empathy. He also writes of mirror neurons as the "field resonators" which can allow for the emergence of the analytic "third."

The abstract symmetries of theoretical physics held a great fascination for Pauli, and in particular the important notion of symmetry breaking. Cambray likewise asserts that "the furthest reaches of Jung's psychology can only be accessed through breaking symmetry." (p. 59)

Of particular interest is Cambray's chapter on Cultural Synchronicities which he sees as applying not so much to individuals but to entire socio-political systems that can occur in *kairos,* that moment when "the time is right." As examples he explores the creation of democracy in fifth-century Greece and the reasons behind the success of Cortés in the conquest of Mexico, as well as the serendipity inherent in Fleming's discovery of penicillin.

It was a particular pleasure to read Cambray's afterword in which he writes that at times he felt a little like Jacob wrestling with the angel as he attempted to bring his scientific background into areas beyond his familiar clinical domain. In doing so he felt that both his scientific views and his analytical process had been transformed. Finally he turns to what he feels has been the leitmotif of the book, the image of the mirror which appears both as Jung's struggle with the concept of symmetry breaking and Pauli's own mirror complex, that appeared in his dreams. It is Cambray's belief that we may come to a deeper understanding of our interconnectedness to the world through the mirror of synchronicity. A particularly promising note on which to end this engaging book.

BOOK REVIEWS

Paul Bishop, *Analytical Psychology and German Classical Aesthetics: Goethe, Schiller, and Jung*, Vol. 1, *The Development of the Personality* (London and New York: Routledge, 2008) and Vol. 2, *The Constellation of the Self* (London and New York: Routledge, 2009)

REVIEWED BY DAVID TACEY

SLOUCHING TOWARDS BETHLEHEM OR REBORN IN ROME?
PAUL BISHOP AND THE CONTEXTS OF ANALYTICAL PSYCHOLOGY

One of the important contributions of non-clinical academic studies of Jungian psychology is the way in which such scholarship emphasizes the cultural contexts of Jung's thought. He is not seen as a "phenomenon" who emerges "out of the blue" without precedent or intellectual background. Some of Jung's early medical colleagues, not being sufficiently educated in the humanities, arts, or philosophy, tended to regard Jung as a lone genius, who, with almost supernatural skill, managed to bring soul and spirit into psychology and mental

David Tacey, Ph.D., is Associate Professor at La Trobe University, Melbourne, Australia, where he teaches literature and depth psychology. He is the author of 12 books and over a hundred articles on Jungian psychology, literary and cultural studies, and ecopsychology. His recent books include *Gods and Diseases* (Sydney: HarperCollins, 2011), *The Jung Reader* (London: Routledge, 2011), and *Edge of the Sacred: Jung, Psyche, Earth* (Einsiedeln, Switzerland: Daimon, 2009).

science. Moreover, many of Jung's detractors regarded him as the rebellious figure of the Freudian psychoanalytic fold, whose messianic ambition, overactive imagination and intractable pride encouraged him to rebel against Freud and invent his own brand of psychology. But works such as these by Paul Bishop encourage us to see Jung in a different light, as a product of a long line of cultural thought and philosophical speculation about the nature of reality and the psyche.[1]

Bishop shows Jung to be the heir of a strain of visionary thinking in German philosophical and literary high culture. He writes: "The cultural task of analytical psychology ... resides in its restatement—an urgent one for our age—of certain fundamental tenets of Weimar classicism."[2] Weimar classicism, also called in these volumes "German Classical Aesthetics," is a period of German cultural history, roughly 1788-1832, in which Johann Wolfgang von Goethe (1749-1832) and Friedrich von Schiller (1759-1805) established a new cultural aesthetics and philosophical attitude inspired by ancient Greek, Roman, and classical models. The central tenet of this movement in German culture was to promote a new-old philosophy of life in which organic wholeness and harmony were of central importance. The movement was to appeal to the whole of life, not merely to any part or bit of life, and to bring all parts into a satisfying spiritual and aesthetic arrangement. We can see the implications here for Jung's psychology, with its passion for wholeness, balance, reconciliation of opposites—and all of this regulated by the archetype of the Self and its handmaiden, the transcendent function. Bishop persuasively argues that the Weimar model is not merely a philosophical attitude but an aesthetics of being, in which certain classical precepts are embodied in aesthetic responses to the physical world, nature, beauty and the life of the body. The Weimar model is a way of being in the world, and not merely a few ideas held in the mind.

Jung drew constantly and significantly on the work of Goethe and Schiller. Jung was so obsessed with Goethe that he enjoyed promoting a family legend that he was the direct descendant of Goethe, and his grandfather had been an illegitimate child of the famous poet.[3] Bishop puts forward the plausible argument that Jung's "Number 2 personality," described in Jung's memoirs as an eighteenth-century gentleman riding in a carriage,[4] was based on the figure of Goethe, a view also supported by Henri F. Ellenberger.[5] There are references to Goethe in most of Jung's essays, and vital quotes from Goethe are found in all his writings. In particular, as he admits in his memoirs,[6] no single work seems to have impressed Jung more than Goethe's *Faust*. Goethe seemed to represent the ego ideal or philosophical mentor upon which Jung based his life. Jung's *Psychological Types* (1921) is heavily indebted to Schiller's ideas of the type problem, drawing on his *On the Aesthetic Education of Humankind* and *On Naïve and Sentimental Poetry* (1796). Bishop's primary objective in these two volumes is best summed up by the title of one of his articles: "The Birth of Analytical Psychology from the Spirit of Weimar Classicism." Bishop puts his case in plain language:

> The thesis of these two volumes is that [Weimar classicism] turned into analytical psychology. For Jung's work is shot through with concepts and vocabulary derived ... from Goethe. One might go so far as to say that analytical psychology represents a renaissance of classical precepts. In other words—this is the contention—it was from the spirit of Weimar classicism that analytical psychology was born. To read Jung with reference to Goethe and to Schiller is to return him to the cultural and intellectual tradition to which he belongs, as he himself partly recognized, and in the light of which, I believe, he may most fruitfully be read.[7]

The case is well argued, even if, one often feels, the case is slightly overstated, so that Jung's own intuitive insight and personal vision is eclipsed by the "influences" upon him. To proclaim that "analytical psychology was born from the spirit of Weimar classicism" is an overstatement, or at least, an academic poeticism. The problem with the academic tracing of influences is that it often seems that everything that an original thinker says or does is already determined by the heavy weight of cultural and literary influences bearing down on him. At times it feels that Jung is nothing more than a product of his influences, and we know that this can hardly be the case. As Harold Bloom argued in his classic work, *The Anxiety of Influence*,[8] an artist has to forge an original vision in order to guarantee his survival into posterity, and in this quest the influence of precursors inspires a sense of anxiety which can border on panic. Is the work merely derivative, a footnote on what has been better expressed in the past? Only a minority of strong artists, Bloom argues, manage to create original work in spite of the pressure of influence.

Nevertheless, Bishop's approach, in which most of Jung's theories, intuitions, and ideas are traced to historical sources, represents an antidote to a great deal of "Jungian" writing about Jung. I can recall when I was first introduced to Jung I was aware of the lack of historical contextualization of his psychology. He often seemed to be written up by early analysts and clinicians as a raw or pristine genius who fought his way into and out of Freudian analysis to arrive at his original, even eccentric, vision of psychology. This view tends to construct Jung as an isolated figure who manages to return psyche to "soul" and discovers a drive toward wholeness in the personality. Such attitudes lead either to the academic rejection of Jung as oddball and mystic, or to the cultic worship of Jung as prophet and seer. Neither view is conducive to a balanced or responsible reading of his psychology.

Bishop shows that Jung seized on and elaborated long-standing Germanic interests in the development of personality, symbol formation, aesthetic education, and philosophical discourse. He argues that this cultural heritage enabled Jung to become a modern interpreter of these sources and ideas—and Bishop concedes that Jung was the first to convert these literary-philosophical preoccupations into an explicit psychology for modern people. Jung's creativity, as Bishop sees it, was to convert high cultural sources into general theories that could be accessible to modern citizens who were not necessarily well versed in the history of former centuries. Jung was able to express and market a lot of ideas that would otherwise be buried under the sheer weight of specialist erudition and elite culture.

Bishop often hints that these ideas and theories were waiting to be discovered, or rather, retrieved, by someone willing and able to give them new life to a modern world starving for direction. This view does not make Jung any less of a genius, but it does make him less isolated, remote, and eccentric. It serves, if anything, to bolster his reputation as a popularizer of Germanic high culture, rather than to lower his reputation as a Freudian defector or a New Age guru. Thus Paul Bishop manages to rescue Jung from the Freudian marginalization of his work and from the widespread tendency to turn him into a counter-cultural wise man. Jung is wise, but Bishop argues that it is the wisdom of tradition that his work expresses, not the wisdom of bucking the system in an appeal to a pristine, anti-cultural source. If Jung seems eccentric and new to his interpreters it is because we have forgotten the cultural sources from which his work springs—or never knew them to begin with.

Bishop conducts a survey of recent work on Jung, noting that no major discussion of Goethe and Jung exists to date. He goes through most of the secondary literature, pointing to the glaring absence of a study of Jung in relation to Goethe and Schiller. The fact is, however, that few individuals have had the knowledge that he brings to this enterprise. As a German specialist in a British university, Bishop has an impressive command of German culture, literature, and philosophy. He has a mastery of the German language which seems unrivalled in Jungian circles in English-speaking countries. We have had no previous study of these correspondences because no one has been as qualified as Bishop to conduct this enquiry. His scholarship is detailed and meticulous, and he can work backwards or forwards in history, approaching Goethe and Schiller through the modern lens of Jung, or reading Jung as the product and heir of the cultural legacy of the past. This admirable double movement can only be conducted because he has such an impressive knowledge of Germanic literature, culture, philosophy, and depth psychology. Bishop is right to complain that "Goethe, Schiller, and Nietzsche are writers whom Jung frequently cited and yet who, because so few Jung scholars have read them, are rarely mentioned in the context of analytical psychology."[9] I felt genuinely humbled and enriched reading these volumes, because I was not formally educated in German literature, and yet I now feel I know something about it.

Jung and Goethe received conventional Protestant educations, and both were dissatisfied with their natal faiths. Bishop argues that Goethe found his inherited religion an "arid faith" governed by a distant, remote image of God. This God imposed a stifling morality on humanity and asked for dogmatic and unquestioning belief, neither of which proved stimulating to the budding geniuses of Goethe and Jung. But both remained deeply interested in religion, even though they rejected its conventional forms. Bishop says that Goethe and Jung "sought to establish a more direct contact with divinity."[10] As a 7-year-old, Goethe had built an altar to the God of Nature, "the God who is in direct contact with nature, who acknowledges and loves it as His work."[11] As a child of 4 or 5, Jung dreamt of an underground temple containing a giant ritual phallus which he called "a subterranean god not to be named," through which he felt he was "initiated into the secrets of the earth."[12] Jung and Goethe explored "occult" areas outside religion, sensing that spiritual possibilities could be found in fields designated as taboo or improper. At 18, Goethe discovered "various works on mysticism, alchemy, and theosophy." He "immersed himself in writings on Gnosticism, Hermetics, Kabbalah, and neo-Platonism." He also steeped himself in the ideas of Paracelsus, after which he declared himself "to have become a different person now." Goethe set up a small alchemical laboratory, and continued his investigations into what he called "my mystic-cabalistic chemistry."[13]

Does all this sound like Jung? As an example of the similitude of Weimar classicism and analytical psychology, Bishop quotes a passage stating that "Man cannot dwell for long in a conscious state, or in consciousness. He must again take refuge in the unconscious, for that is where his life is rooted." Bishop asks: Is this "a statement by Jung?" No, he answers, with an almost boyish sense of excitement, "it is, in fact, by Goethe."[14] Such parallels and affinities are astonishing at times, leading one to suspect that both are fashioned according to a particular "type" of scholar who is at once religious, philosophical, literary, and psychological. Schiller and Nietzsche, of course, are in the same mold. In recent times, the specialization of knowledge in our universities has made it almost impossible to recapture this wide-ranging and comprehensive field of enquiry. How can we explore the "wholeness" of life when our institutions force us into corners and departments of knowledge?

Bishop claims that Goethe and Jung created their own personal religions, based on what they could rescue from an ailing Christianity, and what they could add to it from their own intuitions and visions. Goethe believed that "in the last analysis every person has his or her own religion," and in *Poetry and Truth*, a text that Bishop explores in some detail, Goethe said:

> Since I could not be robbed of my affection for the Holy
> Scriptures or for Christianity's founder and its early believers, I
> made up a version of it for my own private use and tried to give

> this a foundation and structure by means of diligent historical studies and careful examination of those people who had been inclined to the same views as I.[15]

Jung recognized early that he would be forced to tread a similar pathway. He could not give up the Scriptures, which exerted a life-long fascination, but nor could he embrace the orthodox expressions of religion. Instead he would select from what was available and borrow parts of it in a bid to weave together his personal religious vision. Jung acknowledged his kinship with Goethe: "Goethe had no definite preconceived religious ideas. He too was *extra ecclesiam.*"[16] Jung often referred to himself as *extra ecclesiam,* "outside the Church," but close to it even in his state of exile.

Nevertheless, after the onslaught of Richard Noll, who notoriously accused Jung of inaugurating a charismatic religious cult,[17] it is not possible any more to say Jung invented a "personal religion" without offering some further explanation. As Bishop makes clear, Noll was following the lead of Philip Rieff, who had accused Jung in 1966 of inaugurating a "private religion."[18] Rieff attacked Jung for destroying the communal and traditional basis of religion, and replacing it with a narcissistic, self-indulgent "designer" religion for the "worried well" who could afford analysis and long-term therapy. But the attacks of Richard Noll and Philip Rieff miss the point: Jung is not collapsing the traditional faiths but reviving them from the inside, by activating the religious impulse in the psyche. He is adopting the time-honored mystical approach to religious experience. Jung's concern is to arrive at the primordial origins of faith, to show that it is part of our psychological makeup, and not merely an outside construct of Churches or dogmas. Jung seeks to reveal the difficult and esoteric dynamics of religious experience, and no more wants to destroy the religions than any mystical thinker who seeks to revive a tradition from within. But those who are traditionally religious, such as Philip Rieff (Jewish) and Richard Noll (Catholic), see Jung's work as destructive and repulsive. For them, he is relativizing and destabilizing the traditions by psychologizing their original impulses. They see him as casually destroying the faiths in the name of middle-class self-satisfaction. Nothing could be further from the truth, although this view is fashionable among religious circles, who seem to love to hate Jung's religious psychology.

Bishop tends to assume that the god or archetype at the heart of Goethe, Schiller, and Jung is not the Christian God, but the Greek figure of Dionysus. This is a theme he explored in his earlier work on Jung and Nietzsche, *The Dionysian Self: C. G. Jung's Reception of Friedrich Nietzsche*.[19] Dionysus appears to him to be the core archetypal principle at the heart of these thinkers, and with Dionysus in mind, much of what they write and assert makes sense. They are "natural" sons of Dionysus and the Greek spirit, who happened to be brought up in a social milieu governed by a version of Christianity that did not touch their core selves. As Bishop points out, Nietzsche was the first to recognize Dionysus at the heart of Goethe's vision:

> A spirit thus emancipated stands in the midst of the universe with a joyful and trusting fatalism, in the faith that only what is separate and individual may be rejected, that in the totality everything is redeemed and affirmed—he no longer *denies*....
> But such a faith is the highest of all possible faiths: I have baptised it with the name Dionysos.[20]

Nietzsche is only an "atheist" when it comes to Christianity, but when it comes to Dionysus he is a believer. And what Nietzsche *believes* in is the gospel of wholeness or totality: the unity of spirit and body, the totality of the personality, conscious and unconscious, and the reunification of mind and instinct, which he believes Christianity broke apart. There is little doubt that historical Christianity served to break up the primal wholeness of the Western soul, but whether Dionysus can be made to serve the symbolic function of bringing the parts back together remains a different concern. Bishop asserts that Jung's "psychoanalytic agenda is to transform Christ into Dionysos,"[21] but there is something larger going on in Jung's work that Bishop does not discern. Jung is not going Greek, Hellenistic, pantheistic, or polytheistic. Rather, he seeks to make Judeo-Christianity a more expansive and open religion, by incorporating Dionysian strains into its religious vision.

Jung is not a Greek Oedipus who seeks to destroy his father's religion, but is closer to the Egyptian Horus "who rises hawk-like above the father to redeem the father."[22] Jung's relation to his father's faith is prophetic and positive; he seeks, in James Hillman's words, to "redeem the father by surpassing him."[23] Most scholars who investigate Jung's view of religion get stuck in the Oedipal model. It is rare for us to see scholarship of Jung that correctly understands his relation to Christian tradition. Jung seeks, as he often said, not to destroy the Church but to "build on to it and make it roomier."[24] In his "Late Thoughts," the aging Jung turns again to serious reflections on Christianity and its critical condition:

> [Humanity] sickens from the lack of a myth commensurate with the situation. The Christian nations have come to a sorry pass; their Christianity slumbers and has neglected to develop its myth further in the course of the centuries. Those who gave expression to the dark stirrings of growth in mythic ideas were refused a hearing... People ... do not realise that a myth is dead if it no longer lives and grows. Our myth has become mute, and gives no answers. The fault lies not in it as it is set down in the Scriptures, but solely in us, who have not developed it further, who, rather, have suppressed any such attempts. The original version of the myth offers ample points of departure and possibilities of development.[25]

Bishop overlooks or ignores this important aspect of Jung's work. Even his contention that Jung's "psychoanalytic agenda is to transform Christ into Dionysos," is based on a slight misreading of Jung's letter to Freud. In this important letter, Jung said psychoanalysis had a great cultural task before it, and he wanted it "to revivify among intellectuals a feeling for symbol and myth, [and] ever so gently to transform Christ back into the soothsaying god of the vine, which he was."[26] Jung is not referring to Dionysus here, or to a transformation of Christianity into a Dionysian festival. Rather he is saying that Christ always *was* a soothsaying god of the vine, and Christianity has departed radically from this conception. His concern is not with Greek tragedy, Euripides, or *The Bacchae*, but with the Gospel of St. John: "I am the vine, you are the branches. Whoever remains in me, with me in him, bears fruit in plenty."[27] John's Jesus is the soothsaying god of the vine. There is no Greek monopoly on wine and vineyards; Jung is saying that this is in the original Christian vision, but it got lost, due to moralism and dogmatism. Jung's task is to renovate the Christian structures with a view to opening humanity to the life-giving sources which he feels are still at its core. In this regard, like Noll and Rieff, Bishop sees Jung as a destroyer of Christianity rather than its renovator. The only difference is that whereas Noll and Rieff rail against Jung for this apparent destructiveness, Bishop applauds it. His own interest, it would seem, is to see Christianity replaced by a cultural return to Greek and Roman classical sources.

Although Bishop explores the parallels in their lives in his chapter, "Affinities between Goethe and Jung," I felt he was trying to mold Jung into the image of Goethe, which he does not fit. Goethe's spiritual "rebirth" took place in Italy in 1786, and Bishop explores Goethe's "homecoming" to classical values and models that laid the foundations for the birth of the Weimar ideal. But Jung was not reborn in Rome like Goethe; in fact he resisted it, and felt it might disturb his precarious mental balance. Jung's spiritual rebirth took place in his dialogue with his natal faith, and his tireless attempt to revision Christianity in terms of the forces and figures of his unconscious. Although Goethe eventually stated that he was "definitely a non-Christian,"[28] Jung was in a far more complex situation. He could not get rid of the Hebrew God, but like Jacob at the ford of the river Jabbok, he wrestled constantly with him. And like Jesus or St. Paul, Jung tried to "dream onward" the Jewish God, and fit him into a new cultural milieu. Jung wanted this God to become relevant in a new historical epoch, and his task was about expanding his father's house. Jung sought to expand the Jewish-Christian God image to include the shadow, evil, the feminine, the future, and everything else that Jung saw as important to the soul. But he would never give up on Christianity. The idea of replacing it with Dionysus was never on Jung's mind. In fact, he roundly criticized this idea in his seminars on Nietzsche, and most memorably, in his paper "Wotan," where he describes the madness of Nazi Germany as a rampaging eruption of Wotan, whom he calls a Germanic "cousin" of Dionysus.[29] Jung was wary of Dionysus and of the unhinged madness that he can unleash in the psyche.

As Edward Edinger reminds us, Jung's concept of the new God image was more sober than Dionysus.[30] What he was after was a God image that could integrate the antithetical figures of Christ and Anti-Christ. Dionysus could enshrine and embody the Anti-Christ, but that would never be a satisfactory outcome for Jung. So in this regard, Jung was pointing to a religious and cultural future that was more complex than anything that Goethe or Nietzsche could imagine. Jung was not calling for the Christian thesis to be replaced by a non-Christian antithesis, but he was, in Hegelian fashion, looking for a synthesis that would incorporate and transcend Dionysus. Early in his career, Jung thought he saw such a model in the figure of Abraxas, the god who reconciles the forces of darkness and light.[31] He later abandoned his interest in Abraxas, but it was not replaced by an enduring interest in Dionysus. Although the figure of Christ is often said to be one-sided, Dionysus can represent one-sidedness of an opposite kind: frenzied indulgence in the body and instincts in the name of producing an intoxicating ecstasy.[32]

Dionysus, however, is a useful temporary measure, and an appropriate antidote to the moralistic vision of the Christian tradition, even if he is made to bear a burden he cannot carry. What Jung is tracking is an evolution of sorts within the Judeo-Christian image of God. At present this evolution looks as if it is turning toward Dionysus, but this may be an illusion. The "Dionysian" side of divinity is being drawn up, but this does not mean that the movement is backward in time, into the pre-Christian past. What is important for Jung is that this development is taking place *within* the Judeo-Christian tradition. It appears to be a backward step, but it is a spiralic journey, involving return and onward development. Bishop assumes that the Christian tradition has been overcome, but Jung would say it is being *changed*. There is a "changing of the gods" which does not mean that the tradition has been lost.

In Jung we discern a darkening of the Western religious vision, a sense that the human soul has become burdened by the shadows of a Christian religion that has too long emphasized the light. This is not something unique to Jung, but is found in the major poetic and visionary works of the modern period. In the vision of W. B. Yeats, an archetypal darkness, symbolized by the beast as Anti-Christ, "slouches towards Bethlehem to be born."[33] This darkness demands to be acknowledged as sacred and treated as part of the holy. It no longer wants to live a split off existence apart from the principle of light, but wants to be wedded to it. What we often fail to recognize is that this beast wants to be born in Bethlehem, not Athens or Rome. In other words, the birthplace of the Christian principle of light must now come to terms with the unlikely and somewhat repellent birth of sacred darkness. Jung felt this imperative during his entire life, from the time of 4 years old when God revealed himself to him as an underground phallus. It was this same demand that prompted him to write *Answer to Job*, and to scandalize the religious and theological world with his statements about the divine origin of darkness. It was this demand, too, that brought about the loss of his relationship to long-time friend and collaborator, the theologian Victor White.

The ethic of wholeness appears to have underpinned most of what Goethe and Schiller wrote. As Nietzsche said: "What Goethe aspired to was totality; he strove against the separation of reason, sensuality, feeling, will; he disciplined himself to a whole, he created himself."[34] According to Jack Herbert, "the *Bildungsideal* (cultural ideal)" of Weimar classicism envisaged "a harmonious individuality in which intellect and feeling were equally balanced and vehement passions firmly anchored, or in Schiller's terms reconciling the instincts and senses with reason's law."[35] Engagement with Goethe and Schiller urged Jung beyond his personal limits, because Goethe was, according to Jung, an "extraverted feeling type,"[36] and Schiller was profoundly engaged with questions of aesthetics, art, and beauty, which were not high on Jung's priorities. In my view, Jung was at his worst when writing about art and aesthetics; for instance, his essays on Picasso and Joyce are embarrassing from the point of view of art appreciation. It is apparent that the "sensation function," notoriously undeveloped in Jungians, is not a strong part of Jung's personality. Yet Schiller and Goethe's understanding of aesthetics, and their awareness that feeling, sensation, imagination, and memory must play a role in any *embodied* engagement with the concept of wholeness, seems to have had an educative effect on Jung. Jung considered himself an "introverted thinking type" and for him thinking about wholeness was an important way of approaching this topic. But Schiller and Goethe emphasized that if wholeness is to mean anything at all beyond a concept in the mind, it has to be grounded in the aesthetic appreciation and play of reality.

In this way, Jung's work represents a diminution of a vision more fully expounded by his forbears. His psychology pays little attention to aesthetic considerations, and in terms of his productions in the fields of painting, sculpture, and drawing, Jung tended to view "art" as a synonym for an inflated response to therapeutic expression. For Jung, everything was subordinate to the idea and concept, which were for him the primary carriers of cultural production. However, Weimar aesthetics gives body, form, and flesh to Jung's abstractions, which are sometimes abstruse in the extreme, especially when applied to alchemy and hermeticism. In Jungian terms, Goethe and Schiller add anima and soul to Jung's intellectual, animusy system. They develop what for Jung remains an "inferior function" and removed from the focus of conscious attention. We thus need to appreciate Goethe and Schiller not only as "raw materials" for psychology, but as more sophisticated and embodied versions of what Jung is seeking to portray. What Paul Bishop presents in these volumes is grist to the mill of James Hillman, the post-Jungian who frequently criticized Jung for privileging the concept above the image, abstraction above aesthetic appearance, and the idea above the embodiment of the idea.

There are some confusing features of these works. One is the loose ways in which the terms "romanticism" and "classicism" are used. I have always seen these as polarities of artistic expression and cultural history, but Bishop tends to blur the distinctions and to refuse to treat them as opposites. Both volumes argue that Jung is a direct descendant of "Weimar classicism," and yet on the first page we are told that he is characterized by "a Romantic yearning for 'intellectual intuition.'"[37] We are told that Jung can be read as a Romantic and "Jung's relationship with his mother stands out as a major source of his Romantic yearnings."[38] Quoting Richard Noll, Bishop refers to "Goethe and the German Romantics."[39] Are Jung and Goethe being constructed as classicists or romantics? If the terms are interchangeable, why use them at all, and what use are they as cultural descriptors? Bishop argues that "Jung is no friend of the Enlightenment," and yet on the next page we are told that "Weimar classicism belongs to the age of the Enlightenment."[40] These are puzzling statements for this reader, and I would have preferred detailed descriptions of classicism, romanticism, and further discussion on whether Jung is, or is not, an intellectual heir of the Enlightenment.

While admiring his scholarship and his facility with German and English languages, one of the elements of Bishop's work that concerns me is his attempt to camouflage his subjective involvement in the enterprise. Bishop tries to present his voice as objective and even neutral in its reporting of cultural and textual matters. One would have thought that Jungian psychology, perhaps more than other fields, calls for a personal engagement with the material and a feeling response to what is being discussed. It is difficult to write about Jung's thought, which is above all a science of subjectivity, without acknowledging that the enterprise has to be self-implicating. Why is Bishop drawn to these interests, even though, as he often states,[41] his Germanist academic colleagues give Jung and Jungians short shrift? Why has he sacrificed some of his academic purity to get involved in Jungian studies? How do these ideas of psychological development and wholeness impact on him? Has he had any experiences that would make him want to validate this field and its un-academic theories of archetypes and the collective unconscious? What is his investment in this exploration, and does he believe or not believe in the ideas he is explicating? I understand why he is adopting a neutral stance, but it is difficult to keep up this persona when one is faced with the often bizarre and outlandish ideas of Jung's psychology.

What I am pointing to may represent a difference in national styles. We in Australia have been strongly influenced by feminism and postmodernism, and it often seems to us that British universities have remained somewhat aloof and have not taken these influences to heart, especially postmodernism. Feminism taught academics that the personal is political, and thus the personal counts and has to be included in scholarship. Postmodernism has questioned the very notion of the objective stance, and whether this is desirable or even possible. No Australian literary scholar has attempted a stance of anonymity in any publication for the last 20 or 30 years, and thus I read these volumes with a degree of surprise. The problem is compounded by the content of the study. Bishop quotes with approval Nietzsche's idea of "a reduction of philosophical systems to the personal dossiers of the originators." Nietzsche wrote to Lou Salomé that a "philosophical system" might be refuted, "but the person behind it cannot be refuted, the person cannot ever be regarded as dead."[42] In *Beyond Good and Evil* (1886) Nietzsche wrote: "Every great philosophy so far has been ... the personal confession of its author and a kind of involuntary and unconscious memoir."[43] Jung made much of his observation, influenced by Nietzsche, that every psychological theory is an expression of the "personal equation" of its author. Jung is quoted as saying that psychology is "the only discipline which could grasp the subjective factor that underlay other sciences."[44] In view of these considerations, it is hard to see what support Bishop could find for his gesture of neutrality and self-erasure.

Bishop is constructing himself not as a Jungian scholar but as a scholar of Jung. He often inserts qualifications and phrases such as "it is claimed that," or "so this passage would have us believe," indicating that he assumes a high moral position and does not necessarily believe what he is outlining, nor does he support the particular view he is explicating. Bishop's hermeneutics of suspicion sits oddly beside Jung's psychology, which is a discourse of soul that calls for a hermeneutics of affirmation. Indeed it is this feature of Jung's psychology that makes things so problematical for academic scrutiny of Jung, because the academy does not know how to deal with a hermeneutics of affirmation, which it sees as intellectually soft, unrigorous. I am still not convinced that the academic exploration of Jung and his tradition is even possible, given this disjunction between Jung's soul-centered psychology and the highly rational and suspicious nature of academic thought. Many Jungian analysts assume that Jung is best kept outside the university system, because it cannot approach Jung in the right spirit. To engage Jung one has to respond as a whole person, not merely as a critical intellect feigning a superior position. Discussions of Jung cannot work if they do not involve, for instance, the functions of feeling and intuition, which are not encouraged in the academy. If an academic is too critical, he or she misses the whole point of Jung, which is to summon soul beyond the critical faculties. However, if a commentator is not critical enough, he or she ends up in hero-worship and dogmatic Jungianism.

A sensible discussion of Jung's psychology in the university system is not, to my mind, feasible at this stage. Things will have to get a lot worse before they get better. I mean, the bankruptcy of the purely rational approach will have to become more evident before we start to value, respect, and call on the non-rational functions of mind. Then we might begin to get somewhere in the academic study of Jung's work. But to date, academic studies—as distinct from studies conducted in the Jung training institutes—have tended either to feign a neutral position, thus avoiding the charge of Jungian cultism, or to adopt a fiercely critical attitude, in which case most of what Jung discusses is rendered nonsensical by an overly rational analysis. I am thinking in particular of the two "historical" studies of Jung by Harvard University researcher Richard Noll, already mentioned. Bishop seems to align himself with Noll, when he writes that Noll's "historicizing approach provides a much-needed corrective to the hagiographical ditch into which Jung scholarship had fallen."[45] But Noll's loathing of Jung is evident from the outset and it colors everything he writes. Noll's method may appear historical but his tone and value system is opposed to Jung and he interprets Jung's discourse about the gods in a non-symbolic and literal manner. He does this deliberately to make Jung look a fool and a cult-leader bent on destroying the Church. Academic neutrality is not something that Noll even approaches, and yet his works claim for themselves the status of academic writings.

What is behind Bishop's stance of academic neutrality? Unlike Noll, Bishop seems to delight in much of Jung's thought, although he holds himself back from showing this delight. Restraint is evident throughout, and his delight expresses itself indirectly as a wonderful sense of humor and a constant play with language. What comes across to the reader is Bishop's boundless love of culture, literature, and philosophy, his enquiring mind and enthusiasm for ideas that seek to track the invisible aspects of our existence. His "agenda," as we like to say, is twofold: he wants to wrench Jung free from Judeo-Christianity and place him firmly within the context of Greek, Greco-Roman, and Greco-German classicism. In addition, he seems to want to claim Jung for the humanities and philosophy, and to ignore Jung's right to be included in the history of science. Bishop refers to the "pseudo-scientificity of Jung's excursions into the time-space relationship"[46] and he is mostly scornful of the claim of Jungians to belong to a scientific profession. Bishop reverses the conventional notion that analytical psychology is primarily a clinical endeavor, and only secondarily a cultural or philosophical discourse. For him the cultural dimension is primary, and the use of these ideas in clinical situations is merely an "application" of a philosophy of life.

NOTES

1. See also Paul Bishop, ed., *Jung in Contexts: A Reader* (London and New York: Routledge, 1999).

2. Paul Bishop, *Analytical Psychology and German Classical Aesthetics: Goethe, Schiller, and Jung*, Vol. 2, *The Constellation of the Self* (London and New York: Routledge, 2009), p. 8.

3. C. G. Jung, *Memories, Dreams, Reflections*, ed. Aniela Jaffe (1963, London: Fontana Collins, 1995), pp. 52 and 261.

4. Jung, *Memories, Dreams, Reflections*, p. 50.

5. Henri F. Ellenberger, *The Discovery of the Unconscious: The History and Evolution of Dynamic Psychiatry* (New York: Basic Books, 1970), pp. 664 and 738.

6. Jung, *Memories, Dreams, Reflections*, p. 261.

7. Paul Bishop, *The Constellation of the Self*, p. 8.

8. Harold Bloom, *The Anxiety of Influence: A Theory of Poetry* (1973, New York: Oxford University Press, 1997).

9. Paul Bishop, *Analytical Psychology and German Classical Aesthetics: Goethe, Schiller, and Jung*, Volume 1, *The Development of the Personality* (London and New York: Routledge, 2008), p. 34.

10. Bishop, *The Development of the Personality*, p. 19.

11. Goethe, quoted in Bishop, *The Development of the Personality*, p. 19.

12. Jung, *Memories, Dreams, Reflections*, pp. 28 and 30.

13. Goethe, quoted in Bishop, *The Development of the Personality*, p. 21.

14. Bishop, *The Development of the Personality*, p. 9.

15. Johann Wolfgang von Goethe, *From My Life: Poetry and Truth: Parts One to Three*, in *Goethe's Collected Works*, ed. V. Lange, E. A. Blackall and C. Hamlin (New York: Suhrkamp/Insel, 1987), p. 466.

16. Jung, Letter to M. Zarine, 3 May 1939, in ed. Gerhard Adler *C. G. Jung Letters, Volume 1 1906-1950* (London: Routledge & Kegan Paul, 1973), p. 269.

17. Richard Noll, *The Jung Cult: Origins of a Charismatic Movement* (Princeton: Princeton University Press, 1994), and *The Aryan Christ: The Secret Life of Carl Jung* (New York: Random House, 1997).

18. Philip Rieff, "Jung's Language of Faith," in *The Triumph of the Therapeutic* (1966, Harmondsworth: Penguin, 1973), pp. 115 and 119-20.

19. Paul Bishop, *The Dionysian Self: C. G. Jung's Reception of Friedrich Nietzsche* (Berlin and New York: Walter de Gruyter, 1995).

20. Friedrich Nietzsche, *Twilight of the Idols / The Anti-Christ*, tr. R. J. Hollingdale (Harmondsworth: Penguin, 1968), pp. 103.

21. Paul Bishop, *The Development of the Personality*, p. 40.

22. James Hillman, "The Great Mother, Her Son, Her Hero, and the Puer" (1973), in ed. Patricia Berry, *Fathers and Mothers*, second edition (Dallas: Spring Publications, 1990), p. 167.

23. Hillman, *ibid.*

24. Jung, *Aion* (1951), *CW* Vol. 9i.

25. Jung, *Memories, Dreams, Reflections,* p. 364.

26. Jung, Letter to Freud, 1910, *The Freud/Jung Letters*, ed. William McGuire (London: Hogarth Press, 1974), p. 294.

27. *The Holy Bible*, John 15: 5.

28. Paul Bishop, *The Development of the Personality*, p. 31.

29. Jung, "Wotan" (1936), *CW* Vol. 10, § 386.

30. Edward Edinger, *The New God-Image* (Wilmette, IL: Chiron, 1996).

31. Jung, "Seven Sermons to the Dead" (1916), Appendix, in ed. Aniela Jaffe, *Memories, Dreams, Reflections* (1963, New York: Vintage, 1975).

32. See for instance, Walter Otto, *Dionysus: Myth and Cult* (Dallas: Spring Publications, 1981); and Karl Kerenyi, *Dionysus: Archetypal Image of Indestructible Life* (Princeton: Princeton University Press, 1976).

33. W. B. Yeats, "The Second Coming" (1920), in *W. B. Yeats: Selected Poetry*, ed. Timothy Webb (Harmondsworth: Penguin, 1991), p. 124, line 21.

34. Nietzsche, *Twilight of the Idols*, p. 102.

35. Jack Herbert, *The German Tradition: Uniting the Opposites: Goethe, Jung and Rilke* (London: Temenos Academy, 2001), p. 14.

36. Jung, *CW* Vol. 6, § 148.

37. Bishop, *The Development of the Personality*, p. 1. See also Paul Bishop, *Synchronicity and Intellectual Intuition in Kant, Swedenborg, and Jung* (Lewiston, N.Y.: Edwin Mellen Press, 2000).

38. Bishop, *The Development of the Personality*, p. 21.

39. Bishop, *The Development of the Personality*, p. 7.

40. Bishop, *The Development of the Personality*, pp. 1 and 2.

41. For instance, see Bishop, *The Development of the Personality*, p. 31.

42. Nietzsche to Lou Salomé, 16 September 1882, quoted in Paul Bishop, *The Development of Personality*, p. 3.

43. Nietzsche, *Beyond Good and Evil*, in *Basic Writings of Nietzsche*, ed. and tr. Walter Kaufmann (New York: Modern Library, 1968), p. 203.

44. Sonu Shamdasani, *Jung and the Making of Modern Psychology: The Dream of a Science* (Cambridge: Cambridge University Press, 2003), p. 11.

45. Bishop, *The Development of the Personality*, p. 6.

46. Bishop, *The Development of the Personality*, p. 1.

BOOK REVIEWS

Andreas Schweizer. Foreword by Erik Hornung. *The Sungod's Journey through the Netherworld: Reading the Ancient Egyptian Amduat.* Cornell University Press, 2010.

REVIEWED BY MURRAY STEIN

Job's ancient question, "But where shall wisdom be found?"[1] haunts modernity, since the Biblical answer given ("God understands the way to it, and he knows its place"[2]) falls on deaf ears and fails to satisfy the contemporary human longing for a cogent answer. Transposed in modern times into a clarion call for humanity to pursue deeper self-understanding, the same question has become a call for greater consciousness of dimensions of mind that lie beyond what is evident on the surface and available to simple introspection. For Jungians, the ancient answer to the question, "God understands the way to it," has been translated into: "The deep psyche, the collective unconscious, the self—this is the way to it." It is for us to probe these deep places and discover wisdom there.

Modern psychology, like other departments of learning in the social sciences and liberal arts, which descend from the faculty of philosophy

Murray Stein, Ph.D., is a training analyst at The International School of Analytical Psychology in Zurich, Switzerland, and since 2009 the President. He is the author of many articles and several books, including *Jung's Map of the Soul* and *The Principle of Individuation*, and the editor of the recently published *Jungian Psychoanalysis*.

in the West that once embraced all of these disciplines, proposes to
engage this question and does so (in all its variety and multitudes of
schools and branches) in basically two ways: through empirical
scientific studies (laboratory work, psychological tests, computer
modelling, statistical analysis of collected data) and through scholarly
inspection and interpretation of what the distinguished scholar, Harold
Bloom, Professor of Humanities at Yale University, calls "imaginative
literature" —myth, literature, religious texts, and so forth—and, I
would add, art.

As we know, C. G. Jung used both methods—the first most
obviously in his studies in Word Association (laboratory science,
statistical analysis), the second in his researches in alchemy, mythology
and world religions. His case studies, which form the backbone of several
important works in the over-all *oeuvre*, combine both methods—
empirical (as a study of clinical "facts") and hermeneutical (as
interpretation of dreams and active imagination).

When Bloom sets out to respond to Job's ancient question,[3] he turns
primarily to the great works of imaginative literature that are found in
the Western canon.[4] The magnificent works cited in his book, *Where
Shall Wisdom Be Found?*[5] belong to Bloom's list of the preeminent
shapers and sustainers of Western culture. They are largely familiar to
us as landmarks in religious, philosophical, and imaginative thought.
By brilliantly bringing these profound texts and figures into relation
with one another, Bloom creates a rich intellectual feast that, when
dished up by him in his inimitable style, promises to satisfy the most
discerning modern taste in the search for wisdom.

By contrast, when Jung and the Jungians following after him have
gone in search of wisdom (i.e., understanding of the self) in the world's
collections of imaginative literature, they have included and perhaps
even preferred works outside the limits of the Western canon, some of
them of distinctly inferior literary quality (e.g., Jung's frequently cited
She by Rider Haggard as a representation of the archetypal anima).
Jungians have traditionally reached out to a much broader range of the
world's literatures, arts, mythologies and religions, also to the world's
fairy tales, and above all to what appear to us today as marginal religious
movements such as gnosticism and alchemy in their search for insight
into the human psyche and knowledge of the self.

What Bloom and the Jungians share, in my view, is the conviction that it makes sense to look for wisdom in the treasures of the human imagination as these have been deposited throughout history in the various accounts of sacred and secular literature and in the arts such as painting, architecture, and sculpture. For Jungians, the idea is that to get to the most basic and telling features of the human mind one cannot do better than to study the great works of the human imagination, and these of course include the theologies of the world's spiritual traditions as well as more explicitly fictional narratives. Bloom's type of literary criticism and his reflections on imaginative literature are not so different from Jungians' studies of myth, religion, and fairytale, although the theoretical presuppositions are certainly not identical. The intended purpose of both is to find wisdom in the modern sense of self-knowledge.

In *The Sungod's Journey through the Netherworld: Reading the Ancient Egyptian Amduat*, the eminent Swiss Jungian psychoanalyst, Andreas Schweizer, offers us a psychological reading of a truly monumental work of the human imagination. The *Amduat* contains the account of the Sungod's daily experience of renewal during the twelve hours of the night as he passes through the Netherworld in his solar bargue from West to East. Working in the tradition of C. G. Jung, Erich Neumann, M.-L. von Franz and other Jungians who have undertaken similar studies in the interpretation of myth and the religious imagination, Schweizer engages in a hermeneutical effort to interpret in psychological terms the mythical narrative of the Sungod's night sea journey as offered in the *Amduat*. He casts it as a transformation process that reflects (and reveals) the dynamic movement of archetypal forces at work in the collective unconscious.

The basic argument is familiar: namely, that a psychological understanding of the narrative and images contained in this ancient mythological text can enlighten and inform us denizens of the modern world of what transpires in the deep unconscious levels of our souls as we make our own contemporary journeys through life. The individuation process, as it is understood in modern times, rests on psychic patterns that lie at perhaps a deeper level than we as moderns have access to, and these patterns are clearly revealed in such ancient imaginative texts as the *Amduat*. Since the premodern mythological imagination was less contrained by habits of mind that have been developed in the West since the Enlightenment, it had access to levels we no longer can plumb without considerable help. We have lost touch, for the most part, with religious (i.e., archetypal) imagination. Wisdom (i.e., knowledge of the self) can be discovered in these ancient texts that put forward an imagistic narrative account of psychic processes running their courses in the depths of the collective unconscious.

Knowledge of the self and therefore wisdom can be found in these texts, but of course only if we can decifer them. This is the argument. So what does Schweizer find in the *Amduat*?

The *Amduat* is "an illustrated vision of the hereafter...that ranks among the great achievements of humankind,"[6] writes the distinguished Swiss Egyptologist, Erik Hornung, in the book's Foreword. Dating from ca. 1500 BCE, it served as "the model for a whole literary genre, today known as the Books of the Afterlife or Books of the Netherworld."[7] The *Amduat* text was found in the tombs of the Pharaohs of the New Kingdom in the Valley of the Kings, with especially beautiful renditions in the burial chambers of Tuthmosis III and Amenophis II, according to Schweizer.[8] The hieroglyphic text and the painted figures, only recently deciphered, depict the process of renewal of the Sungod, Re, during his passage through the Netherworld following the setting of the sun in the West and before its reappearance the next morning in the East. As depicted in the *Amduat*, this journey of the Sungod during the nighttime hours is filled with dramatic tension, danger, and a broad range of emotions. In Schweizer's interpretation, this journey depicts an "encounter with figures and images emerging from the inner realm of the psyche," and it "leads slowly to the growth of a new consciousness."[9] So it is not only the renewal of a worn-out and tired conscious attitude that is being depicted here, but its transformation into an expanded and enlarged one. In short, the *Amduat* depicts the foundational features of the individuation process, the archetypal depth of this psychological dynamic.

The Egyptian mythological imagination divided this journey into twelve stages, matching the number of hours it took for the Sungod to pass through the Netherworld on his journey from West to East. These twelve stages can be seen, in turn, as moving in two large pulses, the first six hours being a descent to the extreme limits of darkness (midnight) and the second six an ascent to the dawn of a new day.

Schweizer comments on each of these hours in turn and in great and highly nuanced detail, using along the way in his hermeneutical efforts the scholarship of noted Egyptologists, such as the works of his friend from the University of Basel, Erik Hornung, as well as the resources of analytical psychology, with special reference to Jung himself and to the works of M. L. von Franz.

The brief version of Schweizer's account of the Twelve Hours, which corresponds to the books chapters, runs as follows.

The First Hour, titled "The Jubilation of the Baboons," begins the journey into night and features the Sungod's entry into the Netherworld riding on his barque and guarded by a host of deities who are prepared to fend off the threats and dangers that lie in wait. This is the twilight hour just after the sun sinks in the West (18:00h). Schweizer subtitles this Hour, "Getting in Touch with the Animal Soul," and he interprets it as an initial encounter with the unconscious —the first confrontation with the unknown and the shadow side of human consciousness. It is an opening to awareness of the instinctual level of human consciousness and also the beginning of a journey of transformation. The Baboons, who stand on the sides of the river and rejoice when they see the solar bargue approaching, welcome the Sungod into their domain. They greet the Sungod's entry into the Netherworld. Of this, Schweizer writes: "The celebration is intended to invoke divine mercy and benevolence and to induce the powers of heaven and earth to unite in a new and creative relationship."[10] It is a kind of evening prayer as the journey begins, perhaps also a celebration of the busy day's end.

The Second Hour, titled "The Fertile Region of Wernes," depicts the Sungod's entourage passing through a rich land of plenty. Schweizer names this: "First Encounter with the Psychic Totality: Creation and Destruction." Having passed through a gate called "He-who-devours-all," the Sungod and his companions enter into a paradisal land filled with all the good things available to the rich and prosperous in this life on earth. Perhaps this is an evening meal at the end of a long day of effort and work. Here, in the second Hour of the night (19:00h), which is still not consumed by darkness, the remembered "images and symbols openly proclaim the beauty of earthly existence."[11] These memories will fade as the Hours pass and darkness deepens, but here there is a respite before moving on to face the more troubled and difficult passage that lies ahead. Again, the elements of celebration and enjoyment are distinctively featured in this second Hour.

The Third Hour depicts a beautiful scene of love. Schweizer titles this Hour, "The Experience of Love through the World of Psychic Images." The evening progresses in a natural and harmonious fashion. Named by the Amduat, "Rowing on the Water of Osiris," the Lord of the Netherworld now makes his first appearance. The waters on which the solar barque floats "are filled with divine peace,"[12] and the quiet appreciation of life and the pleasures of a fruitful and loving intimate relationship are referenced in the figures of Osiris and Isis, whose child, Horus, represents the fruit of their union. "Whoever has to deal with the dark content of the unconscious," writes Schweizer, "or rather is forced to do so by fate, will stand a better chance of success if he or she has first experienced the good aspects of life as concretely as possible."[13] The second and third Hours appear to offer a physical and psychological preparation for the harsh trials ahead as the journey moves more deeply into the darkness of night. Celebration at the entry into evening, followed by abundant food and drink, and now the encouragement offered by images of love, constitute a three hour period of fortification for the grueling trials that begin in the fourth Hour.

Now that hour has come, darkness descends fully, it is 22:00h. In this Hour of the journey, titled "The Snake-Land of Sokar," the Sungod and his party abruptly encounter "the Dark Night of the Soul" (Schweizer's subtitle). The sun barque runs aground; there is no more lift and energy from the river's flowing waters to help the barque float ahead. This region is named "Rosetau," which means "act of towing,"[14] and here the boat must be pulled by hand. Pleasure and ease are now over, and the hard work of survival and endurance sets in. Rosetau is a dry and sandy landscape, a desert for the soul, where the darkness is "so intense that even the Sungod himself can no longer see."[15] The sun is utterly extinguished. This is when one wonders if there will ever be another day. Death anxiety prevails. Here nothing moves spontaneously and of its own accord. Schweizer speaks of depression. One suddenly feels that the process of renewal, previously presented as joyful and promising, has died, and there is no way back to the upper world. Stuck! At this low point, only patience is rewarded, anxious and prolonged waiting until some impulses from sources other than the ego and the will begin faintly to flicker to life. Inklings of such are shown in the pictographs accomanying this Hour, but they are mere hints and promises at this point and not real manifestations of the power needed to revive. Exhaustion has set in. While this is not the darkest Hour (that would be Hour Six), this may be the most ghastly and trying. It is significant, I think, that Schweizer, the psychotherapist, spends considerably more time in this Hour than in any other (25% more than in the nearest rivals for his attention, Hours 1 and 7). The soul-tending psychotherapist knows what it is to sit through such times with patients as they undergo the agony of utter despair, sometimes for months on end. It is a time when the temptation is great to visit the 21st Century pharmacy.

The Fifth Hour brings some slight relief. It is titled "The Mystery of the Cavern of Sokar," and Schweizer speaks in his subtitle of "the Regenerative Force of Depression." In this Hour (23:00h), the dieties who accompany the Sungod continue towing the solar barque stalwartly as darkness persists. The head of Isis dominates the pictogram in this Hour, however, and this provides some hope for a productive outcome for passing through this period of depression. The Cavern of Sokar is a protected space, the tomb where the Sungod lies buried. To survive and pass on through this troublesome Hour, there is only faith, but faith as a kind of gnosis or irrational conviction that this will be a meaningful experience and not the permanent grave of the soul. In this chapter, especially, Schweizer pays respect to the magical qualities of the unconscious.

The Sixth Hour, which is perhaps the most critical single period in the entire transformation process as depicted in this journey through the Netherworld, contains the decisive pivot on which the positive outcome of the entire process depends. "At the deepest point in the realm of the dead, the point where we reach the very edge of the primeval waters of Nun and their primordial darkness and where the domain of Apopis threatens creation with chaos and nonbeing, there lies a huge, ouroboric, multiheaded serpent with many faces, encircling the corpse of the Sungod...," writes Schweizer.[16] This appears at the midnight Hour, and all the "blessed dead participate in the mysterious transformation of the Sungod."[17] It is the moment when the Sungod's immortal *ba*-soul approaches his corpse and enters it, thereby engendering the New Being that will be born at dawn. At this moment, the mystery of the Sungod's rebirth is consummated. The new light will appear from out of the "densest night and the deepest blackness of matter (the corpse!)..."[18] when this union of transcendent soul and physical corpse is complete. In this Hour, we witness the mystery of a reversal - from death to new life, from an outworn and stale consciousness to a new emergence of the self. The intervention of the transcendent *ba*-soul is the critical element. This takes place as a spontaneous manifestion of the psyche.

Not that all danger is now past! On the contrary, the very success of this rebirth mystery calls forth the most dire threat of all. In the Seventh Hour, "Apopis, Enemy of the Sun" makes his frightening entry and shows his fierce dedication to banishing the first flickers of the new light. Now the most extreme forces of darkness and destruction, as classically portrayed in the figure of the montrous dragon Apopis, mobilize to extinguish the potential for rebirth. Schweizer wisely subtitles this critical Hour, "The Unstable Balance of the New," to indicate the fragility of this neonatal moment. When the descent has reached its depth and the first signals of a new light of consciousness begin to emerge, the threat of the destructive becomes most acute. In many mythologies, we find this crisis depicted as the threat posed to the infant hero. Transformation meets its arch-enemy in the most delicate moment of the whole process. Will this process lead to birth or will it end in miscarriage, abortion? The new must overcome resistance to its future and battle its way onward. In the pictograph for this Hour, there are sturdy defenses portrayed in powerful Goddesses, especially Isis, who are prepared to protect the fragile New Being from the force of "He-who-is-in-his-burning" (i.e., Apopis).

In the Eighth Hour, marvellously named "Provision with Clothes" in the *Amduat* ("Religious Renewal" by Schweizer), the figures in the solar barque can breath more freely. The changing of clothes signifies *solificatio* and attained illumination, Schweizer tells us. It is a sacred moment of respite in the struggle for new life. The worst is behind them; the "most difficult part of Re's journey is over."[19] The journey grows a bit lighter now as symmetry reappears in the pictograph and creation comes back into order. There is jubilation as the "blessed dead" celebrate the victorious Sungod and his emergence from the deepest darkness of the night. It is 2:00h and creativity beckons, but its power is not yet fully activated, only promised.

By the time the Ninth Hour ("The Sungod's Crew") is reached, the Sungod's helpers can take a break. They can be seen resting with their oars at the ready for the next segment of the journey, but for now there is peace, and reprovisioning is underway. When the crew begins rowing again, it is with vigor, and the sound of the splashing water along the river's banks resounds refreshingly and gives onlookers pleasure. There is a dynamic movment afoot now, precisely the contrary to what happened in the fourth Hour when the Sungod's bargue went aground and had to be towed. 3:00h is a good moment on the journey. Schweizer names this Hour "Manifestation of the New." From 2:00h to 4:00h, there is a space for much needed rest.

Still, dangers remain. The Sungod is still not in the clear, and the new day has not yet dawned. In the Tenth Hour (4:00h, sometimes in other contexts called "the hour of the wolf," a dire hour indeed), Apopis, "Horrible-of-Face," rears his head once more, and even though he was defeated in the Seventh Hour, the monster still retains the power to threaten the solar barque as it makes its way to the gate of dawn. "The Bodyguard of the Sungod" (*Amduat*), however, is "Ready to Fight for the New" (Schweizer). The fear of losing ground after all this effort, of being sucked back into the tomb, resurfaces and must be put to rest decisively. Apopis can still swallow them up in this critical hour, and in the Tenth Hour the final victory over the threatening Monster is accomplished, so that in the Eleventh Hour, "The Renewal of Time" (5:00h), the anticipation of the birth of the divine (solar) child can be properly attended to and the awaited new day of consciousness can now begin coming fully into manifestation. Here we are on the cusp of what promises to be a brand new day full of energy and potential. For the Egyptians, it seems, each new day was akin to the Christian Easter.

In the Twelfth Hour, we finally witness "The End of the Primeval Darkness" (*Amduat*) and "The Long-Awaited Birth" (Schweizer) of the renewed Sungod, as he rises gloriously on the Eastern horizon. It is 6:00h, the hour of dawn in Egypt. Poignantly, however, the reborn Sungod must take his leave of gentle Osiris in this Hour. Osiris is destined to remain forever in the Netherworld, there to await Re at the end of another day when once again he descends in the West and makes his journey through the darkness of night toward the light of yet another day, *Deo concidente.*

This is the Egyptian account of psychological transformation as a passage through the Netherworld. Schweizer has studied this difficult and rich text with amazing dedication and has drawn from it remarkable insights that can be applied to modern experiences of individuation. There are striking parallels, for instance, between what Schweizer writes about here and the account of transformation portrayed in Jung's recently published *Red Book,* where he depicts in a similar death-and-rebirth narrative his own personal transformation process at midlife. Jung had no knowledge of the *Amduat,* of course. The patterns are so similar that one stands in awe all over again at the magnetic power of the archetypal features operative in the depths of the human psyche. The psyche is without doubt as archaic today as it was 3,500 years ago. Schweizer's claim that "we must accept the wisdom of archaic psychology in order to understand the nature of the unconscious"[20] seems well-taken. Certainly the author has gleaned and learned much from the ancient *Amduat* that is relevant to modern persons who find themselves in the grips of powerful individuation dynamics originating at the archetypal level of the psyche.

If wisdom is self-knowledge, or knowledge of the self, then it does pay off to search for it in texts like the ancient *Amduat,* especially if one is equipped with tools like those displayed by Schweizer in this beautiful work, which includes several pages of gorgeous color plates.

NOTES

1. Job 28:12.

2. *Ibid.*, 28:23.

3. Harold Bloom, *Where Shall Wisdom be Found?* (New York: Riverhead Books, 2004).

4. Harold Bloom, *The Western Canon* (New York: Riverhead Books, 1995).

5. The major works included in Bloom's magnificent meditation are: The Bible, Plato and Homer, the Gospel of Thomas, Saint Augustine, Cervantes and Shakespeare, Montaigne and Francis Bacon, Samuel Johnson and Goethe, Emerson and Nietzsche, Freud and Proust

6. Erik Hornung, Foreword to *The Sungod's Journey through the Netherworld: Reading the Ancient Egyptian Amduat* (Ithaca, NY: Cornell Univ. Press, 2010), p. vii.

7. *Ibid.*

8. Schweizer, *Sungod's Journey*, p. 11.

9. *Ibid.*

10. *Ibid.*, p. 47.

11. *Ibid.*, p. 50.

12. *Ibid.*, p. 73.

13. *Ibid.*

14. *Ibid.*, p. 78.

15. *Ibid.*

16. *Ibid.*, p. 120.

17. *Ibid.*

18. *Ibid.*, p. 124.

19. *Ibid.*, p. 152.

20. *Ibid.*, p. 197.

BOOK REVIEWS

Craig E. Stephenson. *Possession: Jung's Comparative Anatomy of the Psyche*. London and New York: Routledge, 2009.

REVIEWED BY JEAN KIRSCH

I stepped from plank to plank
So slow and cautiously;
The stars about my head I felt,
About my feet the sea.

I knew not but the next
Would be my final inch, —
This gave me that precarious gait
Some call experience.

Emily Dickinson[1]

GENERAL

The subtitle of Craig Stephenson's book, "Jung's Comparative Anatomy of the Psyche," may perplex anyone who is not familiar with the importance of comparative anatomy in the fields of zoology and medicine in the 19th century, a centrality which prevailed well into

Jean Kirsch is a Jungian analyst practicing in Palo Alto, California. She received her medical degree from Stanford University School of Medicine and is a graduate of the C. G. Jung Institute of San Francisco, of which she served as president from 1996-98 and where she is an active member of the teaching faculty.

the 20ᵗʰ century, when pre-medical students typically studied embryology and comparative vertebrate anatomy, which traces the ontogeny of each individual organism along a developmental track that recapitulates the phylogenetic history of its species. Influenced by the scientific line of the era in which he was born, Jung approached his study of the psyche along a comparative track, searching for historical evidence to demonstrate that his observations about the psyche could be traced back in time and be found in nature and across cultures in fundamentally similar patterns, but in different forms of expression. However, the comparative method was not universally accepted because of its tendency toward essentialism and reductionism. William James, whom Jung deeply respected and whose work influenced him greatly, was skeptical of such comparisons and wrote, "There are great sources of error in the comparative method. The interpretation of the 'psychoses' of animals, savages, and infants is necessarily wild work, in which the personal equation of the investigator has things very much its own way.... the only thing then is to use as much sagacity as you possess and to be as candid as you can."[2] As Stephenson makes clear in Chapter 4, citing Jung's 1951 letter to Professor R. J. Werblowsky, Jung tried to avoid this pitfall when making his comparisons by writing equivocally about the psyche.

> The language I speak must be ambiguous, must have two meanings, in order to do justice to the dual aspect of our psychic nature. I strive quite consciously and deliberately for ambiguity of expression, because it is superior to unequivocalness and reflects the nature of life. My whole temperament inclines me to be very unequivocal indeed. That is not difficult, but it would be at the cost of truth. (p. 100)

In this way Jung, like Emily Dickinson, carefully made his way between opposites, so as to be true to his experience of the psyche.

Stephenson highlights the comparative dimension of Jung's thought, choosing as his focal point the psychological phenomenon of possession, which appears through all of Jung's writing from his earliest medical school dissertation in 1902 to his last published essay in 1961. He does so dialogically, the aim of which is diametric to essentialism, by offering a multivocal perspective, examining Jung's axial theme from many directions: historically, focusing upon the sensational events that occurred in the French town of Loudun in the early 16th C.; anthropologically, through several contemporary cultural studies of the phenomenon; medically, with a chapter on the significance of the inclusion of the term "possession" in the psychiatric nomenclature of *DSM IV*; linguistically, studying Jung's equivocal use of language in the light of the ideas of the early 18th C. rhetorician and philosopher Giambattista Vico; psychotherapeutically, comparing Jung's therapeutic methods with the equally synthetic, but interpersonal, methods developed by two European psychotherapists, Jean-Michel Oughourlian and Jacob L. Moreno; finally, aesthetically, analyzing the 1971 film directed by John Cassavetes, *Opening Night*. Therefore, Stephenson's text might more accurately be titled a dialogical anatomy of Jung's concept of possession. It is indeed a book of the 21st Century.

The meaning to be discovered in Stephenson's sequence of chapters is not obvious, until one teases out the implications of the sometimes tangential connections he makes for the reader. As one example, I puzzled over the significance of wedging a chapter on Jung's use of equivocal language between his chapter on the inclusion of the term possession into the *DSM IV* and his chapter on possession in the practice of psychotherapy, until I imagined trying to explain Jung's view of the phenomenon of possession and his methods of treatment to the average American psychiatrist or psychotherapist. Since the language of both fields tends to be unequivocal, the net of reflections cast by Jung in his efforts to bring multiple perspectives to bear on any psychological observation and his frequent reversals and use of paradox and mythopoetic language can be confusing to the average reader. What busy psychiatrist wants to hear that "Gleaming islands, indeed whole continents, can still add themselves to our modern consciousness"?[3] Even Jungian analysts are grateful to scholars like Stephenson and Rowland[4] for their clarification of Jung's writing style.

HISTORY

Several of the more fascinating events in the grim history of accusations of demonic possession in Western Christianity occurred in 1634 in Loudun, France. It is perhaps the most famous case of mass possession in past history, involving several Ursuline nuns who were allegedly visited and possessed by demons. The scapegoat in the public drama was Father Urbain Grandier, a 27-year-old worldly and ambitious priest, whose tactical errors led him to the stake as the accused sorcerer responsible for the demonic possession of the nuns.

The history of the battles of the Catholic Church for hegemony includes many accounts of demonic possession, of which the drama in Loudun is perhaps the best known and studied. In 1486 just three years after Martin Luther's birth, the Catholic Church published a tract to refute the reality of witchcraft called the *Malleus Maleficarum,* Latin for "The Hammer of the Witches." Perhaps the tract was innocently inspired by an ardent desire to fully Christianize the isolated settlements in the more rugged mountainous regions of Europe, where old pagan beliefs held the minds of the people and ancient rituals were still practiced; but sadly, the document was widely popularized and became the handbook for witch-hunters of subsequent generations, when the search for a scapegoat was institutionalized on a grand scale. The combination of unrelenting power at the top and popular fear below led to mass hysteria.[5]

In a later chapter on psychotherapy, hysteria is cited by Stephenson as described by Oughourlian as a refusal to acknowledge the reality of and annihilate desire for the Other (p. 133), making it the opposite mental state of possession by the Other. But it is a pair of opposites inseparably wedded, one to the other. What happened in Loudun, then, might be seen as a case of collective hysteria, fueled at each social level by loss or fear of loss—personal, political, or institutional—in which the aristocracy, clergy, and populace opposed and attempted to annihilate the psychic phenomenon of negation and loss, which had appeared to them in the imagined form of demons and was then projected upon a single human.

ANTHROPOLOGY

Stephenson locates Jung's source for his concept of possession not only in history, but in anthropology. Rather than attempting to provide a comprehensive overview of the anthropological view of possession, he gives us a small selection of recent studies not only to enrich our understanding of Jung's concept, but to contrast the cultural attitude and meaning the phenomenon holds in other cultures both to our contemporary bias, as well as to the beliefs and practices of 17th Century Europeans. He chides Jung for his cursory reading of and his over-reliance on the studies of only a few anthropologists to formulate a simplistic and primitivist view of possession and criticizes him for using Freud as a scapegoat, making him the recipient of a projection of his own misuse of anthropological data. Still, he credits Jung with trying to correct his own errors by finding new ways to view himself objectively, from a different perspective, and to give voice to the Other within.

The most interesting anthropological study he examines is that of Bruce Kapferer presenting his work among the Galle Sinhalese in Sri Lanka

> who differentiate between demons and deities who both create illusion but for different ends…[The] Sinhalese exorcists, as 'scientists of spirits,' light up the demon palace and thereby alter the sufferer's perceptions of their suffering, emphasizing not so much the exorcising of the tyrannical spirit as the placing of the demonic in context with the divine, illness in relationship to health, disorder with order. (p. 64)

The image of illuminating through ritual, dance, and drama the illusory world created by a possessing demon/complex is akin to Jung's methods of amplification and active imagination. This distant similarity, unconsciously perceived, is perhaps at the root of the longstanding antipathy of psychoanalysts and psychiatrists to Jung and his methods, for I have heard the typical Jungian personification of complexes and archetypes referred to as "demonization." It is probably safe to say that fear and suspicion of the unknown Other is a universal phenomenon, and to the extent that the unconscious psyche is still largely and widely unknown it remains Other, hence an object of fear. Psychologists, psychiatrists, and psychoanalysts are no exceptions to this "primitive" fear. One exception is the Kleinian/Bionian psychoanalyst, James Grotstein, who boldly urges a "return to pre-Enlightenment psychology in order to address the presence and clinical manifestation of what the term 'object' screened, i.e., demons, monsters, chimerae, ghosts, spirits, etc."[6] It would appear that anthropologists, who have done their best to distance their field from psychology, also distance themselves from the psychological fact that although the cultural attitudes and practices they study are, in a true sense, Other, the basic human experiences their beliefs and rituals strive to address are not. It is difficult to see a way between the extremes of essentialism and a plethora of detailed isolates in seeking truths about human cultures and/or the psyche, of recognizing commonalities, while respecting the individuality of cultural and psychological experience.

The most problematical area that Stephenson covers is that of psychiatry, particularly American psychiatry, specifically the American Psychiatric Association's bible, its *Diagnostic and Statistical Manual of Mental Disorders (DSM IV)*. Figure 3.2 on page 75 shows the cover page of the version that was in effect at the time his book went to press, *DSM-IV-TR*, published in 2000, alongside the cover page of the infamous 1486 diagnostic manual of demonological disorders, *Malleus Maleficarum*. Just as the 15th century diagnostic manual for the identification of witches was unequivocal in its language, so are the various versions of the *DSM*. In the early months of 2010 the proposed revisions for *DSM-V*, due to be published in 2012, were circulated for review. The term "possession" has been moved from its former place in the appendix, meant for items under consideration, to the first of five possible criteria for Dissociative Identity Disorder (code 300.14) which reads,

> [d]isruption of identity characterized by two or more distinct personality states or an experience of possession, as evidenced by discontinuities in sense of self, cognition, behavior, affect, perceptions, and/or memories. This disruption may be observed by others or reported by the patient.[7]

What a Jungian analyst might mean when he/she speaks of possession and what the average clinician making use of *DSM-V* might interpret the manual to mean may differ greatly. Jung had observed a tendency to personify the overt manifestations (affects and images) of the unconscious psyche, whether in dreams, delusions, waking fantasies, or projections. In his theory and clinical method he follows the psyche's inclination; his descriptions of complexes and archetypes give categorical names to the more common representations of the unconscious to consciousness—shadow, ego, anima/animus, wise old man/woman, negative father/mother, etc.. It is these unconscious structures that most commonly arise to co-opt the conscious mind in possession. Therefore, when a Jungian therapist speaks of possession, he is unlikely to be making reference to Dissociative Identity Disorder, which is a somewhat different form of possession, but rather to the common occupation of consciousness by an unconscious set of fixed perceptions, affects, and behavioral responses involving the individual in relationship to the Other—in other words, a complex.

While Stephenson is optimistic that Jungian psychology might shed light on the phenomenon of possession, I remain skeptical. The first problem is one of language. American psychiatry is not yet ready to perceive Jung's mythopoetic language in anything other than a suspicious light. Can the spirit of Jung's meaning and intent be conveyed by contemporary Jungian scholars and analysts in ways that will be useful, coherent, and acceptable to the average psychiatrist? It is not easy to set forth a clear and viable description of the subjective experience, with its potential for growth of the personality, and to make it possible for that hypothetical psychiatrist to discern the pathological elements from the potentially growth-inducing thrust of what is being witnessed and, hopefully, shared in the containment of an empathic human relationship. Fear and concern for the patient and those around him may be paramount under the circumstances. There may have been drastic personal loss and/or serious domestic conflict, perhaps with physical violence or threats of violence, precipitating the appearance of the phenomenon. The immediate impulse of the inexperienced psychiatrist might be to isolate and subdue the possessed individual, physically or psychopharmacologically, which would certainly aggravate his/her distress. Yet, to mistake the mental state of the patient as benign, or to become swept up in the colorful details of the patient's experience and identify with them, or to embellish them with even more colorful amplifications in the belief that one may thus further the patient's individuation may be an equally traumatizing error. Here is an instance in which the kind of equivocal language at which Jung was most adept will best serve the individual's psychological development. Can the contemporary psychiatrist, armed with the latest version of the *DSM*, an education that instills a belief in the accuracy of the diagnoses it sets forth, and an arsenal of psychopharmacological agents, along with a sense that he/she has an ethical obligation to uphold the current standards of psychiatric care, which urge their use, actually heed an equivocal explanation of what might be going on? Let us hope that it might be possible, that we actually might be capable, on average, of such an advanced level of civilization and human understanding.

However, with his strategic illustration Figure 3.1, Stephenson betrays skepticism that is akin to mine.

VICO

It may seem tangential to some readers to pay such close attention to Jung's use of language, but one of the more interesting developments in contemporary Jungian studies is a close examination of Jung's work from the perspective of many different disciplines. This only seems fair, since Jung himself employed the rhetorical device of intertextuality in his own writing style, as Susan Rowland so clearly demonstrates in her book *Jung as a Writer*[8] observing that Jung casts a net of reflections that "suggests what is now often referred to as 'intertextuality,' that all links on the net are made out of combinations of other texts, other forms of knowledge and disciplines." Jung drew heavily from the fields of philosophy, natural science, history, gnosticsm, the Kabbalah, and alchemy to illuminate his views of the psyche. Stephenson, following suit, reads Jung himself in the light of the work of the early 18th century philosopher, Giambatista Vico, who was critical of his contemporaries' avid study of the natural world in lieu of examining what was closest and most familiar: mankind itself. Vico thought that every civilization moves through three phases of development, first the mythical age of the gods, followed by an heroic age of aristocracy, and finally, a demotic age of the people. Each age develops its unique language to express its essence: the mytho-poetic; the heroic; and the vulgar, or vernacular. (p. 109) Once the final stage is reached the civilization evolves in one of two directions, either it spirals regressively into a repetition of its first mythical age, or it spirals progressively toward a more advanced mytho-poetic stage, recapitulating the cycle but at a higher level. (p. 106) It would appear that our own civilization entered the third phase with the Enlightenment, our language becoming more and more vernacular and driven by the impulse toward scientific objectivity, which devalues insight and self-knowledge. Consider, for example, the growing international reliance upon the English language and the cross-cultural neutrality of "Globish."[9] Jung expressed the belief that in many ways the Medieval mind was healthier than our own, for it could recognize and accept a transcendent, spiritual power, held by the Catholic church, alongside a worldly secular power, held by the aristocracy, while recognizing the discord between the two. "But once Mother Church and her motherly Eros fall into abeyance, the individual is at the mercy of any passing collectivism and the attendant mass psyche. He succumbs to social or national inflation, and the tragedy is that he does so with the same psychic attitude which had once bound him to a church."[10] In Jung's use of mytho-poetic language the image is just as, if not more, important than the concept; in this way, according to Vico's theory, he tries to move consciousness into a progressive spiral toward a higher stage of civilization with his enlarged use of mythopoetic language. But, the thread upon which humanity hangs, the psyche, is indeed thin and we are just as likely as the populace of 17th C. Loudun to tumble into the pit of possession by one unconscious dynamism or another with our vernacular language and our demotic civilization, despite our scientific and objective knowledge, as we confront the myriad difficulties of rapid globalization.

Psychotherapy

Stephenson's comparative perspective on the role of possession in psychotherapy hinges on the principle of mimesis, defined by the cultural critic and theorist Rene´ Girard as "the universal tendency of all human beings to imitate unwittingly the actions, attitudes and desires of others." (p. 31) Jung employed this tendency without designating it as such; he had rounded out his theory of complexes with his observation that unconscious aspects of the psyche tend to manifest in personified form and his psychotherapeutic method advocated an active engagement of the ego with the activated and personified complex as it appeared to the individual as a way of recognizing, accepting, and integrating the unconscious Otherness within. Stephenson stands Jung's approach alongside the work of two other psychotherapists, Jean-Michael Oughourlian, a disciple of Rene´ Girard and Jacob L. Moreno, the creator of psychodrama.

In contrast to Freud, who based psychoanalysis upon the dominant mechanism of repression, Jung based his analytical psychology on the inherent dissociablity of the psyche, which renders the individual ego susceptible to possession by unconscious complexes, when they are activated.[11] Rather than suppress or evacuate these powerful psychic contents or evade them through rationalization and sublimation, he encouraged his analysands to recognize and investigate them through active imagination, then to accept and integrate some aspects of them into the personality, on the assumption that the contents were not entirely undesirable, but offered images and affects that were essential for psychological equilibrium and wholeness. "Jung's therapeutic practice of personification or mimesis promotes not so much a mimetic identification with the Other as a differentiation from and relationship with the Other" (p. 165) Jung firmly believed that although it was necessary to be explicit in making a differentiation between the conscious mind and those unconscious contents which press to usurp its dominance, he knew that it was just as essential to use "equivocal" terms when speaking of psychological matters, since the fundamental bias of language is to deny both the power and the significance of the unconscious. (p. 115)

> The concept of possession addresses the ontological significance of Jung's practice and contrasts with a classical psychoanalytic practice which refers materialistically to what transpires in the [analytic] container as 'creative but illusory'. More to the point, Jung's concept of possession inscribes the fundamental problems of Western consciousness in terms not so much of how individual identity is analysed but of how selfhood is embodied. (p. 130)

Stephenson then examines the work of Jean-Michel Oughourlian, whose "intervidual psychology" is a psychosocial model based on the idea that selfhood arises through desire and is shaped in relationship to the Other. He "applied Girard's theory of mimetic desire to the psychology of possession, hysteria, and hypnosis, arguing that these phenomena are best understood as expressions of mimetic desire." (p. 131) Stephenson is critical of Oughourlian's oversimplification and misrepresentation of complex psychological and cultural phenomena. On the other hand, his perspective on hysteria as the opposite of possession in light of mimetic desire seems to offer intriguing theoretical and therapeutic possibilities.

Stephenson seems more comfortable with the theory and methods of Jacob Moreno, which is no surprise, since in addition to his Jungian education in Zurich, he is a graduate of the Institut für Psychodrama auf der Grundlage der Jungschen Psychologie, founded by the Swiss Jungian analyst, Helmut Barz, who had studied psychodrama with students of Moreno, Dean Elefthery, and Doreen Madden Elefthery. Stephenson sees the methods of Jung and Moreno as complementary in terms of the concepts of temenos, mimesis, and synthesis. (p. 121)

Moreno believed that selfhood arises not from within, but through our interactions with others and the roles we adopt in relationship. His notion of the "role conserve" is very similar to Jung's complex, in that the spontaneity and agency of the individual may be co-opted by partly or wholly unconscious adoption of a role. "Posssession enters Moreno's model in the sense that possessed individuals over-identify or fuse with a role and therefore suffer from a loss of self, and this fusion manifests as the inability to interact spontaneously and creatively."(p. 138) He developed a therapeutic triad of group psychotherapy, sociometry, and psychodrama in an effort to analyze these "role conserves" and support the individual's natural interactive spontaneity. In this sense his method is, like Jung's, inherently synthetic, rather than retrospectively analytic.

Summary

Stephenson casts a wide net to amplify the dynamic of possession, demonstrating the breadth of his personal interests and his capacity to write dialogically, more or less after the manner of Jung, bringing many perspectives to bear upon a single subject. With only one exception, "Reading Jung's Equivocal Language," all chapters are linked together by the common theme of possession. However, each chapter may be read and enjoyed independently of the others. The book seems to be aimed at the general academic reader rather than the clinician, Jungian or otherwise. In this light Stephenson's decision to eschew material drawn from his own practice of Jungian analysis, but instead to focus upon the 1977 film of John Cassavetes, *Opening Night*, makes good sense. However, this penultimate chapter seems the weakest knot in the fabric of the net Stephenson casts to catch the widespread and eternal phenomenon of possession. Although his focus is a comparative, not a clinical, study of his subject, during the weeks I have lived with his book in the process of writing this review, I have a wider perspective from which to receive my patients' experiences. Only yesterday, reflecting on the work he had done with me ten years ago, a man said about an extra-marital affair that had ended in disaster, "I watched myself doing it, I knew I was acting against my best interests, but I couldn't stop myself, I was powerless, it was as if I was possessed!" Thanks to a careful reading of Stephenson's book, I was able to hold in my mind both the typical Jungian apprehension of his experience (anima possession) and a psychiatric diagnosis: my patient had indeed suffered a traumatic episode of Dissociative Identity Disorder. A broad theoretical understanding and years of clinical experience, complemented by "deep reading,"[12] is the umbrella I use to shield me from the downpour of doubts that assail me in my daily encounter with the psyche, with the unknowable Other. My treatment of him, nonetheless, would have employed the same pedestrian formula: transference and dream analysis with the adjunctive use of sandplay. This is how we, too, step from plank to plank with a precarious gait.

NOTES

1. Emily Dickinson, "I stepped from plank to plank," *Poems by Emily Dickinson*, ed. M. Dickinson Bianchi and A. L. Hampson (Boston: Little, Brown and Company, 1957), p. 60.

2. Sonu Shamdasani, *Jung and the Making of Modern Psychology: The Dream of a Science* (Cambridge: Cambridge University Press, 2003), p. 34.

3. C. G. Jung, *Collected Works* 8 § 387.

4. Susan Rowland, *Jung as a Writer* (London: Routledge, 2005).

5. Teofilo F. Ruiz, "The Terror of History: Mystics, Heretics, and Witches in the Western Tradition, Lecture 20: The Witch Craze and Misogyny," CD disc (The Teaching Company, 2002).

6. James Grotstein, "'Internal objects' or 'chimerical monsters'?: the demonic 'third forms' of the internal world," *Journal of Analytical Psychology* 42:1 (1997) 47-80.

7. http://www.dsm5.org/ProposedRevisions/Pages/proposedrevision.aspx?rid=57.

8. Rowland, *Jung as a Writer*, p. 92.

9. http://en.wikipedia.org/wiki/Globish_(Nerriere)#cite_note-0.

10. Jung, *CW* 8 § 426.

11. George Hogenson, *Jung's Struggle With Freud* (South Bend, IN: Notre Dame University Press, 1983).

12. Harold Bloom, *How to Read and Why* (New York: Touchstone, 2001), pp. 25-29.

BOOK REVIEWS

Sally Porterfield, Keith Polette, and Tita French Baumlin, editors. *Perpetual Adolescence: Jungian Analyses of American Media, Literature, and Pop Culture*. Albany, New York: State University of New York Press, 2009.

REVIEWED BY BLAKE BURLESON

The fourteen essays in *Perpetual Adolescence* each stand on their own as important contributions to understanding the archetype of the Eternal Child in Western popular culture; taken together the volume represents the best work on the subject in the Jungian field since Marie-Louise von Franz's *Puer Aeternus* (1970), James Hillman's *Puer Papers* (1979) and *Senex and Puer* (2005), and Robert Bly's *The Sibling Society* (1996). Arguing that Western culture, and particularly America, is inhabited by adolescents who are unable to mature into adulthood, the essays provide scholars and analysts alike with poignant critiques of television, music, film, print, internet, education, and politics which arise from and amplify this enduring archetype. The authors, academics in the fields of literature, psychology, religious studies, film, and drama along with several practicing Jungian analysts and therapists, suggest

Blake Burleson, Ph.D., is Associate Dean for Undergraduate Studies in the College of Arts and Sciences and Senior Lecturer in Religion at Baylor University in Texas. He is the author of *Jung in Africa* (2005) and *Pathways to Integrity: Ethics and Psychological Type* (2000).

that the American *puer*-fixations are increasingly dangerous and if not remedied pose a threat to the survival of the planet.

In the "Introduction," George Jensen provides the disturbing reminder, quoting Jung, that "[e]ven the most highly developed individuals . . . c[an] not entirely rise above the mass-mindedness of the times." (p. 2) This is so, as Neumann writes, since archetypes represent "unitary reality." (p. 174) So what hope is there that America will evolve in an acceptable way? Or does Rome always have to fall? What chance is there that America will not destroy the planet? Or is apocalypse inevitable? Following Jung, Jensen suggests that our first priority is an examination of trauma at social and cultural levels. Until we can perceive that "archetypes had a role in terrorists flying airplanes into the World Trade towers and that archetypes had a role in the wars that followed" (8), we cannot rise beyond mass-mindedness.

The first essays in this volume examine the *puer* archetype from the perspective of psychotherapy. Anodea Judith in "Culture on the Couch" offers a clinical diagnosis of America as patient asking, "What if [America] were a client that came in for analysis?" Her initial observations, presenting problems, client history, and diagnosis are incisive (if not entertaining were it not for her prognosis of possible "suicide" with its cataclysmic consequences for the patient's relationships). What emerges is a portrait of white, male savior figure with severe delusions of grandeur combined with co-dependent tendencies; in short, she provides a caricature of George W. Bush—"paranoid and delusional, with an avoidant personality syndrome, evident in the denial of his environmental problems and his refusal to deal with increasing debt." (p. 22) Unfortunately, for the patient and for the world, America's passage into adulthood seems stuck and while Judith offers a prescribed treatment, one wonders if it is realistic. She does suggest, however, that the patient is "beginning to open to a realization of other races and cultures as viable voices within him." (p. 27) Certainly the election of an African-American as President provides evidence of this possibility. Judith's essay is a must read for practicing psychotherapists in America whose many patients are enveloped in a myth which if questioned leads them to feel un-American and unpatriotic. One popular TV program in the US and the UK which addresses the American myth is Buffy the Vampire Slayer. Susan Rowland's "Puer and Hellmouth" suggests that this program deconstructs the "Christian savior myth that bedevils America" and provides an alternative "positive ensouled mission", (p. 32) a new myth which heals the split between the *puer* and the *senex*. Rowland's typical incisive analysis makes the case that the program addresses the shadow elements of the myth of American heroic destiny, particularly its Christian embrace of the apocalypse, offering instead a "conversion of teleology into psychology." (p. 44) Rinda West's "Puer in Nature" examines two polarities of Western responses to the environment: the users or slackers who have a *senex* problem (as found in John Gardner's novel *Grendel*) and the dreamers or purists who have a *puer* problem (as found in Werner Herzog's documentary *Grizzly Man*). One of the best essays (and there are no weak ones) is Sally Porterfield's "The Puer as American Hero." In this piece, Porterfield explores the role of the media in contributing to the *puer* fixation in American culture. In harsh and biting analysis, Porterfield suggests that America's imagination has been denuded and replaced by the "synthetic TV universe, with its manufactured mana" dooming the culture to dependencies which tell us how to feel, think, and live. Evidence of this accelerating juvenility of the citizenry is the "Citizens United" decision of the U. S. Supreme Court holding that cooperate funding of independent political broadcasts cannot be limited under the First Amendment.

Other articles provide analysis of developmental issues which confront the individual stuck in the *puer* fixation. John A. Gosling's "Protracted Adolescence" suggests that American society is in a state of crisis citing the evidence that the "majority of Americans supported an administration that misled them about the reasons for engaging in a catastrophic war in Iraq, that seriously curtailed civil liberties in the name of national safety and security, and that sent the gross national debt spiraling to more than eight trillion dollars." (p. 137) Gosling poses that the American psyche is developmentally stuck in protracted adolescence which keeps it in a state of emotional immaturity. Of immediate and obvious relevance is his thesis that the American shadow is projected onto the "Other." Not only is Gosling's analysis incisive for understanding recent political events particularly during the Bush administration but it is timely given the dramatic reversal of political tides in America's 2010 midterm elections in which politicians artfully and diabolically used America's complexes (most notably Islamophobia) to their advantage. The retardation of America psychic growth was clearly evident in that election. Three articles focus on the developmental problems of cultural icons (two real, one fictional): Kurt Cobain's opposing urges to create and destroy (Dustin Eaton's "Grounding Icarus"), Sylvia Plath's desire to "excel and be loved but not to be known intimately" (Susan Swartz's "Little Lost Girl"), and Agent 007 James Bond's sexism, misogyny, racism, and voyeurism (Luke Hockley's "Shaken, Not Stirred"). Keith Polette analyzes educational development in "Senex and Puer in the Classroom," arguing that America's *senex*-oriented national testing in which students are told "*what* they need to know, *how much* they need to know, and *when* and *how* they need to know it" (p. 160) has had to disastrous consequences. While Darrell Dobson's personal analysis in "A Crown Must Be Earned Every Day" does not address the *puer*, per say, it does serves to compliment Polette's piece on education by arguing for the importance of the arts in developing masculine maturity. The Arts have, as is well known, been virtually removed from the American education system.

Finally, several essays focus on the influence of the *puer* archetype on broad cultural issues such as midlife passage (Marita Delaney's "Provincials in Time"), childhood trauma (Chaz Gormley's "The Marriage of the *Puer Aeternus* and Trickster Archetypes"), and obsession with quantitative research (Craig Chalquist's "Insanity by the Numbers, Knowings from the Ground"). Here, Jungian ideas are extended as these writers address the cure of the *puer* malaise—understood by Jung and von Franz to be personal engagement in "work." Delaney points out that given the destructive tendencies of Westerners' "work," not any work will do. "If we take up the ideal of being servants of the world, rather than creators, we may find a path toward self-knowledge and a middle way that serves all of humanity and the earth's inhabitants." (p. 221) Gormley suggests that the answer lies in marrying the *puer* with the trickster (p. 188), resulting in a combined archetype in which one's "work" is more humble, more earthy, less grandiose. Chalquist's essay challenges scientific "work" with its obsession with data, objectivity, quantity, and "facts."

Perpetual Adolescence is a timely, provocative, and sobering examination of the endemic suffering and pandemic consequences of mass-mindedness "driven by archetypes." (p. 10) Its authors invite us, following Jung, to be critical of unconscious forces which engender and embody our collective existence, particularly those traumatic events of our history which touch all of us.

BOOK REVIEWS

Helena Bassil-Morozow. *Tim Burton: The Monster and the Crowd: A Post-Jungian Perspective*. Routledge. 2010.

REVIEWED BY TERRIE WADDELL

A HOMAGE TO THE INNER LONER

I ve never been a pro-active champion of tapping into the auteur/ author, preferring to let the finished work speak for itself. Helena Bassil-Morozow provides a welcome other, dare I say, more cinephile perspective in acknowledging the porous relationship between creator and creation. For her it seems one must understand film-maker Tim Burton to more fully appreciate his imaginative depths. This need to plunge into the Burtonian mind is also baring itself out in wider public discourse. I suddenly find myself thrust up against "all things Burton." There's a very tangible cultural obligation in Melbourne, where I live, to mosey through ACMI's (The Australian Centre for the Moving

Dr. Terrie Waddell is a senior lecturer in Media and Cinema Studies at La Trobe University in Australia. She has taught and written widely on contemporary media, gender, and mythical approaches to screen texts. Previous publications include: *Wild/lives–Trickster, Place and Liminality on Screen* (Routledge, 2010); *Mis/takes–Archetype, Myth and Identity in Screen Fiction* (Routledge, 2006); *Lounge Critic–The Couch Theorist's Companion* (co-editor, ACMI, 2004); and *Cultural Expressions of Evil and Wickedness–Wrath, Sex, Crime* (editor, Rodopi, 2003).

Image) jam-packed Tim Burton exhibition and reverentially listen to the Australian interviews given by the *artiste of the moment* prior to its opening. To top that off I've been asked to assess a Ph.D. dissertation on his work, had students anxious to write Honors proposals on Burton the auteur, and of course I've been immersing myself in Bassil-Morozow's take on the man and his oeuvre. From an antipodean perspective anyway it's one of the most timely inclusions to Routledge Mental Health's "Jung and Film" sub-genre that I can think of. Perhaps the hunger for Burton's grotesque creativity (in the kindest possible sense) plays into a collective urge to return to childish things through adult eyes. Or maybe it says something about my immediate Burton inured Australian environment where (to rework the catch phrase of Garrison Keillor's Lake Wobegon monologues) ... all the women are tolerant, all the men are *puers*, and all the children are all imaginatively above average. Whatever the socio-cultural pull, seems like Bassil-Morozow is onto it.

Burton grew up in Burbank, California and as the brochure for ACMI's retrospective notes, "was fascinated with pop culture, taking inspiration from animation and cartoons, television, children's literature, Hammer horror films, Japanese monster movies and B-grade science fiction films." Launched during the July 2010 school holidays, the exhibition features a core "activity space" where children are able to discover their inner Burton. One of the walls displaying his early art tells us that the shape of each character was often based around an emotion. The descriptive note then encourages children to approach their drawings in a similar fashion. This aspect of his work, also noted by Bassil-Morozow when comparing it to Russian director Andrey Tarkovsky's technique (p. 18), struck me as quite a Jungian activity—an amplification of bubbling energies perhaps. And of course, as Bassil-Morozow tells us, Burton's output is riddled with "archetypal" mainstays which she has grouped under the chapter headings of The child, The monster, The superhero, The genius, The maniac, and The monstrous society. It is a neat way to contain Burton's beautifully messy output that, on a superficial level anyway, involves presenting personifications of only one or sometimes two archetypal motifs. That is, rather than combining multiple unconscious undercurrents in a reflection of human complexity, they emerge as more simply dimensioned echoes of fairytale characters.

The finished text though, with its intricate verbal and visual layers, fuses a variety of archetypal patterns. Whether it be *Pee Wee's Big Adventure* (1985), *Beetlejuice* (1988), *Batman* (1989), *Edward Scissorhands* (1990), *Ed Wood* (1994), *Sleepy Hollow* (1999), *Corpse Bride* (2005), or *Charlie and the Chocolate Factory* (2005), Burton's dark and psychologically encrusted pop/media adventures significantly contribute to the psycho-social discourses that govern our times. As Bassil-Morozow writes, they allow us to grasp a more emotionally geared perspective on modern and postmodern anxieties such as: "an excessively materialist and utilitarian view of the world and physical processes; efficiency and technology at the expense of humanity; the rationalisation and professionalization of private life; and even—ironically, given the general individualistic stance of Burton's *oeuvre*—loss of communal and familial ties." (p. 178)

While she argues that Burton's homage to the estranged individual is key to the appeal of his films, she reminds us that when he self-consciously moves beyond mythos to a more logos-toned approach something is lost. In trying to articulate the inner workings of his characters, their symbolism and tendency to act as a metaphors for social ills, the work lacks a certain credibility: "When he moves from the "personal element", the suffering hero, the emotional quality of his films subsides. In other words, for some reason, the brilliance of his perception dims when he "inflitartaes" the collective shadow from the inside, and attempts to understand its working principles." (p. 159) Once again she encourages us to understand the importance of Burton's intrinsically emotional, archetypal, unconscious, mythic world—a world that loses its power if the text itself errs on clumsy articulations of its underlying "messages."

By grouping the core themes of Burton's work under what can be seen as character-driven chapter descriptors, Bassil-Morozow exposes each film's play with alienation. Be it the *puer* who struggles with rites of passage, the misunderstood mastermind who longs for recognition, the shadow as monster who (like Gary Larson's drawings) *does* metaphorically inhabit children's closets, the crusader we feel we all can be, or the maniac we hope we're not, Burton understands the loner in us all—the misunderstood and sensitive individual who recognizes the stifling alienation of modernity and the potential shallowness of postmodernity. Bassil-Morozow's Jungian-based framework informed by academic film theory and various takes on auterism, is ideal for laying bare Burton's inconsistencies and revealing the power of the emotionally charged image to draw audiences into a unique relationship with his work—a relationship where one is both part of the fan-based crowd and an individual within it whose sense of struggle to fit in is heard, appreciated and treasured.

Given Burton's preoccupation with the multifaceted bigger picture issues of our times, and the simple, often intimate, echoes of childhood that rarely leave us, it is no wonder that he attracts a wide following. In so energetically dissecting these passions and exposing the Burtonian underbelly, Helena Bassil-Morozow is likely to draw in those from his sizable pool of devotees ... and beyond. *The Monster and the Crowd* should not just adorn academic library shelves, it is one for your own collection—one to return to after the first read—one to have in the back of your mind when Burton's next fantasy of alienation hits the screen.

THE 6TH JUNGIAN ODYSSEY

ANNUAL CONFERENCE & RETREAT

"In all chaos there is a cosmos, in all disorder a secret order." *CG Jung*

"It is on the edge between order and chaos that the subtle dance of life takes place." *I Ching*

ISAPZURICH

THE INTERNATIONAL SCHOOL OF ANALYTICAL PSYCHOLOGY ZURICH AGAP POSTGRADUATE JUNGIAN TRAINING

THE PLAYFUL PSYCHE

Entering Chaos, Coincidence, Creation

Monte Verità
Switzerland
May 28-June 4, 2011

Keynote Address
F. David Peat, PhD

Special Guests
Prof. Reinhard Nesper,
    Dr.sc.nat.ETH
Beverly Zabriskie, LCSW
Prof. Lisa Sokolov, MA, CMT
Joseph Cambray, PhD
with other guests and
faculty of ISAPZURICH

www.jungianodyssey.ch
info@jungianodyssey.ch

Imaginal
Objects

to see to touch
to make to buy

ANIMA figures

carved driftwood bark
from the Hudson River

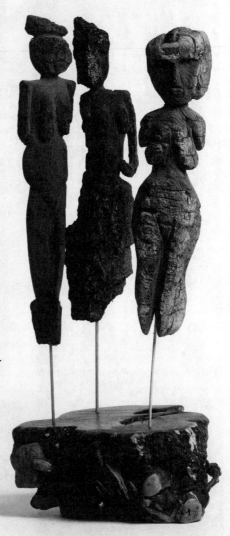

Daniel Mack
objects + workshops

danielmack.com
845.986.7293

Spring

A Journal of Archetype and Culture

Spring: A Journal of Archetype and Culture, founded in 1942, is the oldest Jungian psychology journal in the world. Published twice a year, each issue explores from the perspective of depth psychology a theme of contemporary relevance and contains articles as well as book and film reviews. Contributors include Jungian analysts, scholars from a wide variety of disciplines, and cultural commentators.

❖

Upcoming Issues of Spring Journal

On Home and the Wanderer
Volume 85 — Spring 2011

This issue will address: What does "home" really mean in our contemporary global society? What are the psychological consequences of loss of home, through war, through natural disaster, through divorce? What encourages us to leave home, to wander, to explore diverse cultures and places, and what does it mean to return home after exile?

Swiss Culture and Depth Psychology
Guest Editors: Stacy Wirth and Isabelle Meier, Jungian analysts, ISAPZURICH
Volume 86 — Fall 2011

Native American Culture and the Western Psyche:
A Bridge Between
Guest Editor: Jerome Bernstein, author of *Living in the Borderland*
Volume 87 — Spring 2012

❖

Subscribe to Spring Journal!

2 issues (1 year) *within United States* ($35.00)
2 issues (1 year) *foreign airmail* ($54.00)
4 issues (2 years) *within United States* ($60.00)
4 issues (2 years) *foreign airmail* ($100.00)

To order, please visit our online store at:
www.springjournalandbooks.com

Spring Journal, Inc.
627 Ursulines Street, #7 New Orleans, LA 70116 Tel: (504) 524-5117